Learning

Business Statistics

with

Microsoft® Excel

2000

Learning

Business Statistics

with

Microsoft® Excel

2000

John L. Neufeld

University of North Carolina at Greensboro

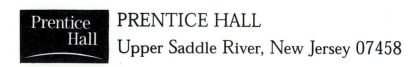

PRENTICE HALL
Upper Saddle River, New Jersey 07458

Library of Congress Cataloging-in-Publication Data

Neufeld, John L.
  Learning business statistics with Microsoft Excel 2000/John L. Neufeld.
    p. cm.
  Includes index.
  ISBN 0-13-030878-1
    1. Commercial statistics—Study and teaching 2.Commercial

statistics--Methodology--Computer programs 3. Microsoft Excel for Windows. I. Title.

HF1017 .N474 2000
519.5'0285'5369--dc21   00-058003

Executive Editor: Tom Tucker
Editorial Assistant: Roland Diaz
Assistant Editor: Jennifer Surich
Senior Marketing Manager: Debbie Clare
Managing Editor (Production): Cynthia Regan
Manufacturing Buyer/Supervisor: Arnold Vila
Design Manager: Patricia Smythe
Cover Design: Bruce Kenselaar

Microsoft and Windows are registered trademarks of the Microsoft Corporation in the U.S.A and other countries. Screen shots and icons reprinted with permission from Microsoft Corporation. This book is not sponsored or endorsed by or affiliated with the Microsoft Corporation.

10 9 8 7 6 5 4 3 2 1
ISBN 0-13-030878-1

To my parents Myra Gene and Jacob. You are always with me.

Brief Contents

Preface...xv

1   Introduction to Excel...1

2   Descriptive Statistics...39

3   Discrete Random Variables and Probability Distributions...86

4   The Binomial Distribution...107

5   The Normal Distribution...135

6   The Sampling Distribution of the Mean...170

7   Confidence Intervals on a Population Mean...206

8   Understanding Hypothesis Testing...224

9   Hypothesis Testing of a Population Mean...248

10   Inferences on a Population Proportion...273

11   Inferences on a Population Variance...291

12   Inferences on Two Population Means...308

13   Analysis of Variance...321

14   Simple Linear Regression...345

15   Multiple Regression...373

Appendix A—Obtaining the Data...409

Appendix B—Setting Up the Analysis Tools...410

Appendix C—Installing the Learning Business Statistics Add-In...411

Appendix D—Statistical Functions and Analysis Tools...412

Appendix E—Answers to Selected Exercises...430

Appendix F—Storing a Large File on a Diskette...440

Detailed Contents

PREFACE...xv
   What's Different about this Book?...xv
   Why Excel?...xviii
   What's New?...xix
   How Do I Get the Data?...xix
   Macintosh?...xix
   Acknowledgments...xx

1   INTRODUCTION TO EXCEL...1
   Using a Mouse...3
   Starting Excel...3
   The Title Bar...5
   The Menu Bar...5
   Using the Toolbars...7
   Getting Help—The Office Assistant...8
   Moving and Resizing a Window...9
   Getting Tips from the Office Assistant...10
   The Active Cell...11
   Selecting Cells...12
   Entering Data...13
   Numbers...13
   Editing a Cell...14
   Entering Text...15
   Changing the Width of a Column...16
   Made an Error? Undo!...17
   An Editing Shortcut—Text Highlighting...18
   Entering Formulas...20
   Order of Arithmetic Operations...20
   Using Cell Addresses in Formulas...22
   Scientific Notation...23
   Error Codes...24
   The Scroll Bars...26
   Worksheets and Worksheet Tabs...27
   Copying and Moving Cells...29
   Filling Cells...30
   Moving and Copying Regions of Cells...32
   Copying and Moving Formulas—Relative Cell Addresses...33
   Absolute versus Relative Cell Addresses...36

2   DESCRIPTIVE STATISTICS...39
        Using Graphics in Excel...39
        Changing the Chart Type...46
        Changing the Chart Colors...48
        Changing the Chart Title Font...50
        Adding Notes to a Chart...51
        Previewing a Printout...52
        Adding Headers and Footers to a Printout...53
        Numerical Summaries...55
        Using the Formula Palette...56
        Exploring the Difference Between the Mean and the Median...59
        Using the Sort Buttons...60
        Measures of Dispersion...61
        Copying a Range of Cells to a New Worksheet...65
        Using the Descriptive Statistics Tool...66
        Histograms...70
        Selecting a Range of Cells with the Keyboard...71
        Printing the Worksheet...74
        Sorting the Data...76
        Let Excel Choose the Intervals...78
        Embellishing the Histogram Charts...80
        Run Charts...81
        Exercises...84

3   DISCRETE RANDOM VARIABLES
        AND PROBABILITY DISTRIBUTIONS...86
        Probability Distributions...86
        Mean and Variance of a Probability Distribution...88
        Probability Distributions and Data...90
        Turning Off Automatic Calculation...100
        New Random Numbers...100
        Probability Distributions and Business Decisions...101
        Exercises...103

4   THE BINOMIAL DISTRIBUTION...107
        Simulating a Binomial Problem...108
        Counting the Number of Car Buyers...112
        Using the BINOMDIST Function...114
        The Binomial Mean and Standard Deviation ...115
        Exploring Other Binomial Distributions...117
        Using Excel to Solve Binomial Word Problems...120
        BINOMDIST and Cumulative Probabilities...121
        Converting between Cumulative
            and Noncumulative Probabilities...123
        Cumulative Probabilities and a Range of x Values...125

Practice Binomial Problems...126
The Wording of Binomial Word Problems...131
Exercises...131

5   THE NORMAL DISTRIBUTION...135
Graphing the Normal Density Function...137
Determining Probabilities from Intervals...146
Determining Probabilities for z Intervals...147
Determining Probabilities for Other Normal Distributions...150
Determining Intervals from Probabilities...153
Going from a Standard Normal
    Boundary to a General Normal Boundary...158
The Normal Distribution
    as an Approximation to the Binomial...161
Exercises...168

6   THE SAMPLING DISTRIBUTION OF THE MEAN...170
Sampling Techniques...171
Simulating the Sampling Distribution of the Mean...172
Drawing Samples with Excel...172
Setting Up a Uniform Population...174
Setting Up a Dynamic Histogram...175
Drawing the Samples...177
Calculate the Sample Means...177
The Theoretical Distribution of Sample Means...178
Examining the Distribution of Sample Means...181
The Normal Distribution and the Central Limit Theorem...182
Adding the Normal Expected Values to the Histogram...184
A Nonuniform Population...186
Skewed Population...189
The t Distribution...192
Looking at the t Distribution...194
Using Excel to Solve Distribution of Sample Means Problems...196
Exercises...203

7   CONFIDENCE INTERVALS ON A POPULATION MEAN...206
Using Excel to Determine Confidence Intervals...208
Using Excel to Determine Required Sample Size...210
Simulating the Accuracy of Confidence Intervals...212
Exercises...219

8   UNDERSTANDING HYPOTHESIS TESTING...224
The Population and the Null Hypothesis...225
Formulating the Null and Alternate Hypotheses...226
How Small a Difference Is Small?...227
An Unusual Sample or a Process Gone Bad?...229

Summary...230
Determining the p Value...231
From p Value to Conclusion...232
The Consequences of Error—Type I versus Type II...233
Simulating Type I Errors ...235
Significance Level and Type I Error...238
Simulating Type II Errors...239
Significance Level and Type II Errors...240
Hypothesis Testing—A Difficult Population...241
Significance Level and Type II Errors Revisited...242
Type II Errors and the Power of a Test...243
Failing to Reject versus Accepting a Null Hypothesis...245
Exercises...245

9 HYPOTHESIS TESTING OF A POPULATION MEAN...248
Classifying the Problem...248
Two-Tail Tests on a Population Mean, σ Known...250
The p Value Approach...252
The Critical Value Approach...254
One-Tail Tests on a Population Mean, σ Known...257
A Warning About One-Tail Tests...260
Hypothesis Tests on a Population Mean When σ Is Unknown...261
Using Sample Data to Test a Hypothesis...264
Using Data on a Diskette...267
Exercises...269

10 INFERENCES ON A POPULATION PROPORTION...273
Sampling Distribution of the Proportion...274
Confidence Intervals on a Population Proportion...274
Determining Sample Size for a Desired Sampling Error...277
Hypothesis Tests on a Population Proportion...280
Hypothesis Tests on π Using the Normal Approximation...280
Using the Binomial Distribution to Test Hypotheses on π...283
Which Approach Is Correct, Binomial or Normal?...285
Determining Other p Values from the Binomial Distribution...285
Exercises...288

11 INFERENCES ON A POPULATION VARIANCE...291
Confidence Intervals on a Population Variance...296
Hypothesis Tests on a Population Variance...299
Two-Tail Test on Population Standard Deviation
 (or Variance)...301
Test on a Population Variance Being Below a Given Value...302
Exercises...305

12   INFERENCES ON TWO POPULATION MEANS...308

Inferences from Paired Samples...309
Using the Analysis Tool for a Paired Samples Test...312
Tests of the Difference of Means for Independent Samples...313
Testing for a Difference in the Variance of Two Populations...317
Exercises...319

13   ANALYSIS OF VARIANCE...321

Single-Factor Analysis of Variance...321
Charting the Sample Values and the Means...325
Determining the Sum of Squares...328
Preparing the ANOVA Table...330
Analyzing Simulated Samples...332
Using the One-Factor ANOVA Tool...335
Two-Factor Analysis of Variance...336
Two-Factor Analysis without Replication...336
Two-Factor Analysis with Replication...339
Exercises...343

14   SIMPLE LINEAR REGRESSION...345

Linear Relationships...346
The Simple Linear Regression Model...349
Fitting a Line to Sample Data...350
Determining the Regression Line...353
Using Regression to Predict y Values...356
Goodness of Fit—Descriptive Approach...357
Goodness of Fit—Inferential Approach...361
Excel's Built-In Regression Capabilities...364
Using the Regression Tool for Simple Linear Regression...366
Exercises...371

15   MULTIPLE REGRESSION...373

Multiple Independent Variables...374
Nonlinear Relationships...378
Curved Relationships and Residuals Plots...380
Polynomial Regression...381
Estimating a Quadratic Regression...382
Partial Effects in Polynomial Regressions...384
When Should Polynomial Regression Be Used?...385
Dummy Variables and Categorical Data...385
Multilevel Categorical Data...389
Multicollinearity...394
Heteroscedasticity and Autocorrelation...397
Model Building...402
A Comprehensive Example...403
Exercises...406

APPENDIX A—OBTAINING THE DATA...409

APPENDIX B—SETTING UP THE ANALYSIS TOOLS...410
Installing the Data Analysis Tools...410

APPENDIX C—INSTALLING THE
LEARNING BUSINESS STATISTICS ADD-IN...411

APPENDIX D—STATISTICAL
FUNCTIONS AND ANALYSIS TOOLS...412
Statistical Functions...412
Data Analysis Tools...426

APPENDIX E—ANSWERS TO SELECTED EXERCISES...430

APPENDIX F—STORING A LARGE FILE ON A DISKETTE...440
File Compression...440
Compressing a Workbook—First Things First...441
Using Zip.exe to Compress a File...441
Using WinZip to Compress a File...442
Restoring a Workbook...443

Preface

▼ What's Different about this Book?

I wrote this book because I have been very dissatisfied with the way statistics is and has been taught to business students. The biggest impact on statistics is the advent of computers and the dramatic effect they have had on the practice of statistics. Incredibly, they have had practically no impact on the pedagogy of statistics. Although a number of textbooks now incorporate Excel, they treat it as simply a sophisticated calculator—a convenient way to get an answer. This is, of course, a valid use of computers; it is the way practitioners of statistics use computers all the time, and it is appropriate to teach students how to use computers as such a tool. But it is not, in my opinion, enough. Computer usage should be accompanied by important changes in the way in which statistics is taught. This has not been done. Let's consider a few examples of what I have in mind.

In the days before computers, an important tool for every statistical professional was a set of statistical tables. No longer. Statistical tables, such as the z table and the t table, have become something almost exclusively used by students who are required to learn how to use tables, which, if they become actual user of statistics, they will probably never see again. The impact of the use of tables in statistics is much more than simply a different way of obtaining information more conveniently available from a computer; tables have introduced compromises in the teaching of statistics, compromises which make the learning of statistics an even more complicated affair than it must be. We can see this in the inherent tendency of many of the most popular statistics texts to interpret problems as ones with which one can use the z distribution as an approximation for the theoretically appropriate distribution. This is almost universal, for example, in the treatment of hypothesis tests on a population proportion. The use of the normal distribution in such problems is based on the fact that the normal distribution, under certain circumstances, is a good approximation for the binomial. So why not use the binomial distribution directly? If one must depend on tables, the binomial distribution is problematic. With a computer, it is not. The use of the normal distribution in these cases suffers from two problems: It makes it more difficult for students to really understand the real basis of the hypothesis test, and it can give answers which are wrong.

Many textbooks repeat a rule which has gained authority solely in the repetition that the normal distribution can be used in hypothesis tests on a population proportion as long as $n\pi > 5$ and $n(1-\pi) > 5$. This is simply false; counterexamples can easily be found. Several are given in Chapter 10

Many textbooks continue to separate problems involving the distribution of sample means into "large sample" and "small sample" cases with the normal distribution used in the former and the t distribution in the latter. Although the complexity added by this practice is probably small, we should recognize it as an anachronism created because z tables were easier to use and had more information than t tables. With computers, this distinction should be only of historical interest, and the simpler approach of using the t distribution whenever the population variance is unknown is the simple, correct approach.

In one way computers may impede a student's understanding of statistics. A computer allows one to perform a complex statistical procedure, such as multiple regression analysis, without any knowledge of the procedure at all. Simply click an icon or enter a command, and the procedure is done. This may seem a strong reason not to use computers at all in a statistics course. Yet there are many ways in which computers could help support a student's understanding of statistics if they were incorporated in the pedagogy. Consider, for example, two topics at opposite ends of an introductory statistics course—the use of standard deviations to measure dispersion and the use of simple regression to measure the relationship between two random variables. I think it makes sense for students to have some experience doing both of these things by hand. Both, however, are computationally tedious, and an understanding of each procedure is complicated if one uses the methods that have been developed which are computationally easier but tend to obscure the relationships being actually computed. Introducing a computer which can perform the operation in complete "black-box" fashion and always get the correct answer does not encourage student understanding. This book takes a very different approach (see Chapters 2 and 14).

I try to take advantage of Excel's strong visual metaphor by having students use Excel's ability with arithmetic to introduce themselves to the computations involved both with standard deviation and with simple regressions (among others). This makes the structure of the computations as clear (or even more clear) than solving problems totally by hand. It also makes it possible for students to easily see how different data, with differences in the characteristic the procedure measures, result in different intermediate as well as final steps. Yet it frees the student from computational drudgery and likely error. After this experience, students are introduced to the facilities built into Excel to perform these computations automatically.

Computers (and Excel) also allow students to generate pseudorandom variables in ways which can reinforce their understanding of probability distributions and the concepts of expected value and the variance of a distribution. These are used in Chapters 3 and 4.

Others have used computer simulations to help students understand the Central Limit Theorem. The problem I have seen with these approaches is that if they are simply demonstrations without significant interaction, students who have difficulty understanding this foundation of inferential statistics will simply react as if they were viewing a foreign film in an unknown language without subtitles. By contrast, I try to have the student more actively involved with a demonstration of the theorem (in Chapter 6)

I am particularly proud of the way Excel is used in this book to help students strengthen their intuitional understanding of confidence intervals and hypothesis testing (Chapters 7 and 8). In my experience in teaching statistics, understanding hypothesis testing was often the most elusive goal of an introductory course in statistics. For me, this has changed since I began using Excel to perform 1,000 separate tests of a single Null Hypothesis on three different populations (Chapter 8). The great majority of my students now have a sophisticated understanding of such topics as the difference between Type I and Type II error and the role of the significance level in establishing the probability of each. The material in the chapter uses Excel to help students understand the power of a test and the relationship between sample size and the power of a test.

Many statistics texts now provide add-ins to Excel for use with their text. In my view, many are counterproductive. They add new "black boxes" to Excel, ones which students are unlikely to have access to once they leave their statistics class. Their purpose seems to me to change Excel to make it more suited to teaching with the traditional pedagogy. By contrast, I feel it is statistical pedagogy that should change to take advantage of the powerful new capabilities computers (and Excel) offer for the learning of statistics. I do provide an add-in to Excel, but it doesn't add new analysis tools, it provides pedagogical tools. For example, my add-in gives Excel the capability to draw multiple random samples from a population—a capability exploited when students explore the central limit theorem or perform multiple hypothesis tests on a population. These are capabilities centered on the learning of statistics. Students who understand statistics will not need these capabilities after they leave class.

This book provides more support than most to the student who is not "fluent" with Excel. Step-by-step instuctions are given as each new topic is introduced. As discussion of a topic progresses, students are given increasingly less detail in those instructions. Finally, problems are provided at the end of each chapter for students to do on their own, with answers given in Appendix E.

▼Why Excel?

Excel is certainly not the most capable statistical package available today—it is inferior in that respect to Minitab, not to mention real research tools like SAS or Stata. A student who really plans to concentrate in statistics will certainly need to become exposed to more capable statistical software. Nevertheless, Excel has some important characteristics which make it well suited for students in introductory statistics.

Excel is very visual. An Excel user faces a virtual field of numbers. Most statistical packages, reflecting their mainframe heritage, conceal this field of numbers. Consider the creation of a new variable in regression analysis. Most statistical packages have you do this by specifying an equation which is then applied to every observation in an unseen data set. Excel has you do this for one observation, except, instead of using variable names, you point to the variables with your mouse to include them in the formula. As soon as the formula is done, you see the numeric result for the first observation. You then copy that formula for all of the observations, and immediately all the values of the new variable are visible. For people who are novices in the use of computers to analyze data, Excel's approach is inherently more intuitive.

Excel has another advantage in that it is so widely used outside of statistics. Business students are likely to have had at least some Excel experience before they take introductory statistics, and they expect to have more exposure in accounting, finance, and other classes. They know they will benefit form learning Excel, and, in my experience, they are positive about the exposure they can gain in a statistics class.

It is far more likely that once a student graduates he or she will have access to Excel in the office than to any statistics package. For this reason, learning how to use Excel to do statistics is going to be more directly applicable to the data analysis graduates are likely to be doing than learning how to use any other software package.

▼ What's New?

As far as this book is concerned, there is very little about Excel 2000 which is different from Excel 97. I have used the opportunity this revision afforded me to strengthen its statistical pedagogy rather than to deal with changes in Excel's user interface. In fact, compared to the earlier editions, I have reduced the emphasis on Excel. I have moved away from the creation of spreadsheets which will automatically solve whole classes of statistical problems. I think I may have been overly affected by Excel's power and by how cool it was to use some of its capabilities. I now realize that it is best for students to learn how to construct the Excel formulas needed and be able to reenter them with each new problem.

I have made a number of changes to strengthen Chapters 6 through 8. This is the material of which I am the most proud, and which I feel constitutes the heart of this book's contribution to innovative pedagogy. These changes make the chapters easier for the student and also allow them to cover more material.

I have added additional problems to most of the chapters. A good statistics book can never have too many problems. No matter how clear the exposition, no reader of this book should think he or she understands statistics unless he or she can work the problems at the end of each chapter.

▼ How Do I Get the Data?

Much of the material in the book uses data files which I have prepared for that purpose. Rather than including the data with the book (which would have added to its cost), the data has been made freely available on the Internet. Please see Appendix A for detailed instructions.

▼ Macintosh?

Excel's original base of users was on the Macintosh, and it owes the Macintosh a lot. I hope Microsoft keeps that in mind as it continues to update its program. Microsoft has announced the intention to keep the Macintosh version current with the version for Windows machines. Excel 97 for Windows was followed by Excel 98 for the Mac, and the two were virtually identical. At the time this book was written, Excel 2000 existed only for Windows. I have tried to anticipate how the Mac version will be used once it is available. If you are using this book with a Mac, or if you plan to so use it, please check my web site (given in Appendix A), where I will try to add any Mac-specific information I gain once the Mac program is available. I would very much appreciate Mac users forwarding to me any information they have on problems they have encountered using this book or on Mac issues I have missed.

▼Acknowledgments

The number of people who have helped me on this or on previous versions is becoming quite long. I would like to particularly thank E. Philip Howrey of the University of Michigan, Erik Benrud of the University of Baltimore and Chris Higgins, U. of Western Ontario who generously shared specific advice for this version. I have previously benefited from the comments of Kent S. Borowick, Teresa Dalton, Paul J. Fields, Phillip C. Fry, Mehran Hojati, Steven Thorpe and David Tufte. I again owe special thanks to Joseph Zaremba at SUNY Geneseo whose valuable feedback has improved every new edition.

Many readers were kind enough to send me e-mail pointing out errors and offering suggestions. I cannot list them all, but many made major contributions, and I am grateful to all of them.

Thanks also to Tom Tucker, the Decision Sciences Editor at Prentice Hall, his able staff, and all the others at Prentice Hall who contributed.

My greatest thanks go to the hundreds of students who have shared classrooms with me and from whom I have learned more than I have ever taught.

There are doubtless errors, and the fault is entirely mine. As I learn of them, I will post errata on the web site given below. Please get a copy and please send me e-mail if you discover an error not covered there.

If you have any comments, suggestions, or criticisms you would like to share with me, I will welcome them. I'm only a mouse click away.

John L. Neufeld
Department of Economics
University of North Carolina at Greensboro
Greensboro, NC 27412

email: **john_neufeld@uncg.edu**

web: **http://www.uncg.edu/bus_stat/**

Learning

Business Statistics

with

Microsoft® Excel

2000

Chapter 1

Introduction to Excel

Microsoft Excel® has become the best-known and most-used *spreadsheet* program used on desktop computers. Other well-known spreadsheet programs include Quattro Pro® and Lotus 1-2-3®. Spreadsheets are extremely versatile tools for manipulating and analyzing numeric data. Spreadsheets are used by accountants, salespeople, managers, and nearly everyone working in business today. The ability to use a spreadsheet is a skill you will find useful in many different careers.

Spreadsheets traditionally have not been used for statistical analysis. Computers have long been used for statistical analysis, and computer programs to do that analysis existed long before the first spreadsheet program. As the use of computers became more widespread, statistics programs continued to develop even as the popularity of spreadsheets became firmly established for other types of quantitative analysis. Many excellent statistics packages, such as Minitab®, SPSS®, and SAS®, are in wide use today. Spreadsheet programs also continued to develop, including the capability of doing statistical analysis. The current spreadsheet programs have considerable statistical capabilities—all you will need for the typical introductory college business statistics course.

Why use a spreadsheet program for statistics? There are two excellent reasons. First, spreadsheets are easier to learn and use than are traditional statistics programs. Although most statistics programs are constantly being improved, they continue to show their mainframe heritage in the way they often require users to use cryptic commands much like a programming language. By contrast, spreadsheets use a newer interface, which, for most people, is more intuitive than the command language approach. In addition, the market for spreadsheet programs is huge, and the companies developing for that market can afford to devote enormous resources to develop any competitive advantage. Ease of use is one of the most important competitive advantages, and producers of spreadsheet programs are constantly working to improve their programs' ease of use. The much smaller market for statistical programs makes it difficult for ease of use to receive as much attention.

Most statistical programs are tools written for those who already understand statistics. Many statistical procedures require extensive arithmetic, and statistical packages are designed to free users from the drudgery and potential errors of doing statistics. For the expert user, it is convenient to have a computer program that turns a statistical procedure into an automatic routine which crunches data without exposing any of the intermediate steps. For the *student*, however, such procedures make it even harder to learn how a statistical procedure works. Although Excel can be used this way, the intuitive interface of spreadsheets makes it possible to look at the structure of statistical procedures while still avoiding manual arithmetic. Spreadsheets can be superior to standard statistical programs for *learning*, as opposed to *using*, statistical procedures. To take advantage of this, you have to have instructional materials (such as this book) which use this approach with spreadsheets and the learning of statistics.

Another big advantage of using a spreadsheet for statistics is that, unless you become a professional statistician, you are far more likely to be using a spreadsheet in your career than a statistical package. For most business people, the need to do statistical analysis will be occasional. If you use a spreadsheet program for other purposes, statistical analysis will be easier (and will more likely be done) if you can use that same software.

Specialized statistical programs do have important advantages over spreadsheets. Most statistical programs provide a far greater variety of statistical procedures than does Excel. Even for those procedures which Excel does provide, statistical programs often provide additional or optional information not available with Excel. If your study of statistics goes much beyond the first course, you will need to learn to use a statistical program. If your career requires frequent statistical analysis or analysis near the "cutting edge" of statistical sophistication, you will need to learn and use a specialized statistical package. There is, however, every expectation that the statistical capabilities of spreadsheet programs like Excel will improve as new versions are released, and the role of spreadsheet programs in statistical analysis is likely to grow.

This chapter is designed to introduce you to Excel's basic features and operations. If you are familiar with any Windows® or Macintosh® program, some of the material here will be familiar to you, and you may be able to skim it. Some of the material is unique to Excel, and, unless you are already familiar with Excel, you should go over it more carefully.

▼Using a Mouse

Although it is possible to use Excel without a mouse, it is not recommended. It takes most people a little practice to get used to using a mouse, so don't worry if you initially have difficulty controlling the mouse pointer. If you are using an IBM-compatible PC, your mouse will have two buttons. Some PCs have a mouse with three buttons, but the middle button is not used with Excel. Many of the newest mice for IBM-compatibles have wheel in the middle for easier scrolling. If you are using a Macintosh, your mouse will have only a single button. Many actions require that you position the mouse pointer at a particular location on the screen and click the mouse button. On a PC, most actions involve clicking the left button, but a few require clicking the right button. In this book, "clicking" a particular location on the screen will mean placing the mouse pointer on that location and then quickly pressing and releasing the *left* mouse button. If the right button is to be used, it will be clearly stated. Sometimes an action will require "double clicking." This means you position the mouse pointer and push the button quickly twice in a row. On a PC, double clicking is always done with the *left* mouse button. New users often find double clicking tricky at first, but it too will come with time.

▼Starting Excel

- If you are using Windows, click the Start button on the lower left of your screen. A menu will open. Click "Programs." On the new menu, look for the Excel icon (shown on the left) and click it. If you don't find the Excel icon, look for an icon titled "Microsoft Office" in the shape of a folder and click it. The Excel icon will be in the window that opens.

- If you are using a Macintosh, look for the icon in Finder and double click it.

When Excel starts, it will be in a *window*. That window may fill your machine's screen, or it may fill only a portion of the screen.

- If the window fills only a portion of your screen, make it fill the entire screen by clicking a special place on the upper right-hand corner of the window. In Windows, this is called the "Maximize button" and looks like ☐. On a Macintosh, it is called a "Zoom Box."

- Once the Excel window fills the screen, it should look approximately like the picture on the next page. Don't worry if your window isn't ex-

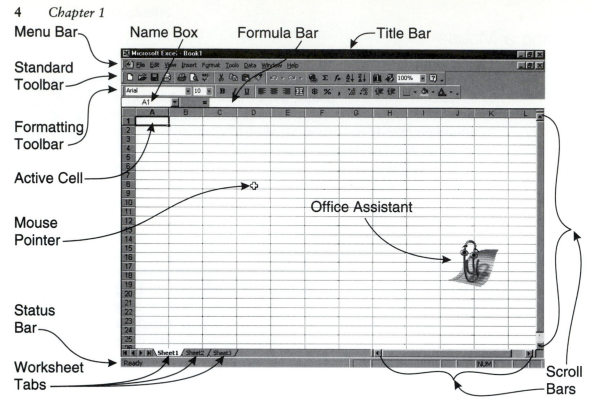

Menu Bar | Name Box | Formula Bar | Title Bar
Standard Toolbar
Formatting Toolbar
Active Cell
Mouse Pointer
Office Assistant
Status Bar
Worksheet Tabs
Scroll Bars

actly like that shown. Excel allows a user to change some aspects of its appearance. This may have been done with your Excel.

Pay attention to the names shown for various parts of the screen. You likely will want to refer back to this picture as those names are used later in this book.

- Practice moving the mouse pointer by moving your mouse. It's important that you be able to accurately place the mouse pointer on part of the screen. Notice that the shape of the mouse pointer changes as you move to various parts of the screen. The shape of the mouse pointer changes to indicate the kind of operation you can do with the mouse in that portion of the screen.

As long as you have the mouse pointer in the central part of the screen (the *cells*), it has the shape of a white plus sign: ✛. This shape indicates that you can use the mouse pointer to *select cells* (which will be discussed later). Move the mouse pointer into the Formula Bar and it changes to this "I-beam" shape: I. When the mouse pointer has this shape, Excel will allow you to *enter numbers or letters* from the keyboard. Move the mouse pointer to the button bars, the Menu Bar, or the Title Bar, and the mouse pointer will have the shape of an arrow pointing to the upper left: ↖.

As you use Excel, you will discover that there are other shapes the mouse pointer can take. These shapes indicate the operation Excel expects you to perform. Sometimes, when you are having difficulty getting Excel to do what you want, the shape of the mouse pointer will clue you in to what Excel thinks you should be doing.

Let's take a quick tour of the main Excel screen from top to bottom. The features mentioned here will be discussed in more detail later.

▼The Title Bar

The *Title Bar* on top tells us what is in this window. As you use Excel, you will find that some operations open windows *within* the main Excel window. These "subwindows" will generally also have a Title Bar indicating the operation that window performs. For the main Excel window, this includes the name of the application (Microsoft Excel) and the name of the *workbook* (Book1). When you use Excel, you create a workbook that can be saved in a file. Another common name for what Excel calls a workbook is a *spreadsheet*.

Find the Close button (✕) on the right side of the Title Bar. Most windows will have this button. Clicking it will generally close the window, and clicking the Close button in the main Excel window will end the Excel session.

- Click the Close button. A window may open with a question about whether or not you wish to "save the changes in 'Book1'?" If you see this window (and you may not), place the mouse pointer directly on the word "No" and click the (left) mouse button. Your Excel session will end.

Many windows will have special buttons or menu items that will close them, but using the Close button or Control Menu button will work with virtually any window.

- Start Excel again by clicking or double clicking the Excel icon.

▼The Menu Bar

Below the Title Bar is the Menu Bar.

- Place the mouse pointer over the word View. The outlines of a "button" will appear around the word. Click the left mouse button to "press" the button. If you are using a Macintosh, push and hold the mouse button. This menu opens in two stages. At the bottom of the menu which opens you will see two downward pointing carets (❤). Either click the bar containing the carets or just wait. The full View menu will open as shown on the left.

- Notice the checkmarks beside "Formula Bar" and "Status Bar." These two features can be either *on* or *off*. The checkmarks indicate that both are currently *on*.

- Place the mouse pointer over the words "Formula Bar" and click the (left) mouse button (on a PC), or release the mouse button (on a Mac). The Formula Bar will disappear from your screen. (I bet you've forgotten where the Formula Bar should be. Look back at the picture on page 4.)

- Again open the View menu. Notice that the checkmark beside "Formula Bar" is now gone (the feature is *off*). Choose "Formula Bar" as you did above (click on a PC, release button on a Mac).

The Formula Bar will reappear. If you lose the Formula Bar (or the Status Bar), this is the way you get them back. Be sure that they are showing whenever you use this book.

Some of the menu choices are followed by an ellipsis (…). This indicates that if you make that choice, there will be further choices to make. When you choose an item with an ellipsis, a *dialog window* will open. A dialog window will give you the opportunity to make further choices.

The "Toolbars" choice on the View menu has a small arrowhead pointing to the right: ▶. This indicates that this choice has further choices made in a *submenu*.

- Open the View menu and place the mouse pointer over "Toolbars."

A submenu (like that shown on the top of the next page) will open, showing the names of all of Excel's toolbars (except the Menu Bar, which cannot be closed). When Excel is first started, the toolbars that are visible are the Standard and Formatting toolbars. These are the ones shown on the screen picture on page 4. (The Standard toolbar is on top in that picture, but may not be on your screen.) In the submenu shown, there are checkmarks in the boxes beside "Standard" and "Formatting."

- Even though it is already open, click "Toolbars" on the View menu. This will keep the Toolbars submenu open even if your mouse pointer moves off it.

A submenu will open whenever the mouse pointer rests on the main menu option referring to it so that you can see the choices in the

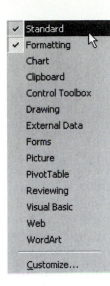

submenu. Once you are sure you want to use the submenu, it is a good idea to click its name on the main menu.

- Place the mouse pointer on the word "Standard" and click the (left) mouse button. The menus will close and the Standard toolbar will also close (disappear). Reopen the menus and notice that there is now no checkmark beside "Standard."

- Using the View menu, also make the Formatting menu disappear.

Both toolbars will be gone from your screen.

- Open the View menu again, and select "Toolbars" again. When the window opens, select "Standard." The Standard toolbar should reappear.

- Use the View menu to make the Formatting toolbar reappear.

Your Excel screen should now have the same toolbars as the screen pictured on page 4. Whenever you are using this book, you should be sure that you start Excel with the Standard and Formatting toolbars showing (and no others). Use the procedures you have just practiced to make sure these toolbars are showing when you start an Excel session.

▼Using the Toolbars

Each toolbar consists of a group of icons (little pictures) or "buttons" (also called "speed buttons"). When you place the mouse pointer over an icon, the outline of a button will appear as it did when you opened the View menu. You "press" a button by clicking (and then releasing) the (left) mouse button. When you do this, the button will appear to be pressed; it will seem recessed. When you move the mouse pointer away from a button, the color of the button will lighten, making it easier to tell which buttons are pressed. Most of the buttons perform operations that could also be performed by using the menus. The buttons are a convenience because they are faster to use than the menus, and they are always visible. The menus are designed to be organized logically by operation, while the buttons are meant to provide an easy way of accessing the most frequently used operations. Excel provides extensive facilities for the user to control what buttons are shown and even to define new buttons. If you are interested, consult a manual or the Help system (which is discussed below).

- Place the mouse pointer over one of the buttons, but don't click a mouse button.

Notice that the name of the button will appear directly below the button. Macintosh users can activate a similar feature by selecting "Show Balloons" from the Help icon menu near the right end of the Menu Bar. This useful feature can help you remember which button is which.

▼Getting Help—The Office Assistant

A distinctive feature of Excel (and other Microsoft Office applications) is the Office Assistant, which is Microsoft's interface to the Help system. This feature has proven to be somewhat controversial. Although it is cute, the use of computers inevitably involves some moments of frustration. Combine cuteness with frustration and, for many users, the result is annoyance. The programming effort which went into implementing the Office Assistant was doubtless significant. You will likely have moments in which you wish that effort was used to improve Excel in some other way. It is possible to hide, or even completely banish, the Office Assistant, which you may always do.

Although there are several Office Assistants available for you to choose, the one Excel initially starts with (on a PC) is "Clippit," shown to the left. Clippit will be the one depicted in this book.

- If the Office Assistant does not appear on your screen, open the Help menu on the Menu Bar and click "Show the Office Assistant."

You will notice as you work that Clippit is constantly in motion, rolling his eyes, taking notes, and changing shapes. If you enjoy watching him perform, he will gladly do so on command.

- Place the mouse pointer on Clippit and click the right mouse pointer. A menu will open. One of the menu choices is "Animate!" Place the mouse pointer on that choice and click the (left) mouse pointer.

Clippit has a repertory of motions. The next time you ask him to perform, he will do something different.

If you have a question about Excel, ask the Assistant. For example, let's suppose that you are working through this book, but have to leave the computer and want to save your workbook on a diskette. You can't remember how to do it. Here's how to ask the Assistant:

- Place the mouse pointer on the Assistant and click the (left) button.

A cartoon speech "balloon" will open in which Clippit asks, "What would you like to do?" You may or may not see a list of possible actions. At the bottom will be a white field into which you can enter your own question.

- Enter "Save my workbook," as shown in the picture on the left. Click the Search button.

Clippit will search for the topics in its database that seem closest to your request. Clippit's "balloon" will close and reopen. When it reopens, it will show a new list of tasks. Your next step is to click the text closest to what you want. Sometimes (as in this case) not all of the tasks appear in the first list.

- Place the mouse pointer on "See more…" at the bottom of the list and notice how the blue dot to the left lights up. Click the (left) mouse button.

- Put the mouse pointer over "Save a new, unnamed workbook" and click. A Help window will open giving step-by-step instructions.

You will notice that the Help window contains "hyperlinks" (like a web page). An example is the phrase "use long descriptive file names." Clicking that phrase would give you additional information about that phrase. Clicking an underlined hyperlink will take you to a new page in the Help system. At the top of the help page there is a small toolbar which includes arrow buttons: ⇦ ⇨. These arrows will allow you to navigate backwards and forwards through the Help pages you have seen.

▼ Moving and Resizing a Window

One problem with Help windows is that they cover up your work. This can be a problem with any type of window. One way of dealing with the problem is to move the window or make it smaller. Not all windows can be resized, but most, including Help windows, can.

- To resize the Help window, carefully place the mouse pointer directly over the border on the left side of the Help window. When you have it in the right place, the pointer's shape will become a two-headed arrow (◄━━►). Once it has this shape, press and hold the (left) mouse button and move the border left and right. Release the mouse button and the border will keep the new position. This method of moving an object on the screen while you press and hold the mouse button is called *dragging*. The same technique will be used to move other objects in Excel.

- To make the window taller or shorter, simply place the mouse pointer over the top or bottom border. The directions pointed by the two arrows show the directions in which that border can be dragged. If you place the mouse pointer over a corner, you can change the height and width of the window at the same time.

Moving a window without resizing it is also easy. Almost all windows have Title Bars, and you can always move a window with a Title Bar by following the instructions below.

• The title on the Help window's Title Bar is "Microsoft Excel Help." Place the mouse pointer directly on the Title Bar. Press and hold the (left) mouse button and *drag* the window to a new location.

• Click the close button on the Help window.

Clippit has no Title Bar. You can *drag* Clippit by first placing the mouse pointer anywhere on Clippit and then clicking and holding the (left) mouse button as you move the mouse pointer.

• Use the method described above to move Clippit's window around on your screen.

Other moveable screen objects without Title Bars can be moved in the same way.

▼Getting Tips from the Office Assistant

Sometimes the Office Assistant will offer you help before you have even had a chance to ask for it. The Office Assistant pays attention to the steps you are doing with Excel, and if he thinks there is another, better way to accomplish what you are doing, he offers to give you a tip.

Generally, the Office Assistant only offers you a particular tip once. That way, every time he offers a tip, that tip is new, and you don't have to have him keep giving you the same tip over and over again if you have decided not to use it. Just to be sure the example below works, let's have the Assistant "forget" that he has given any tips.

• Click the Office Assistant. When its balloon opens, click the Options button.

• When the Office Assistant window opens, click the Options tab. Next click the Reset my tips button. The Office Assistant should respond by warning that you might see tips you have seen before. Click the OK button.

One of Excel's clever features is its ability to automatically fill cells with a series of words or numbers once you have started the series. Excel, for example, knows the days of the week, and if you want to enter a series of days of the week, you can enter just the name of the first day and have Excel finish. We will explore this in more detail later. Here we will pretend we don't know about this so that Clippit will give us a tip.

- Place the mouse pointer in cell D1, in the top row of cells just below the letter "D," and click the (left) mouse button. That cell will have a dark border around it, becoming the active cell.

- Type the letters "Mon" (without the quotation marks) and press the Enter or Return key. This three-letter abbreviation for "Monday" will appear in the cell and the cell below it will become the active cell.

- Type the letters "Tue" (again, without quotes) and press the Enter or Return key.

Mon
Tue
Wed

- Type the letters "Wed" (no quotes) and again press the Enter or Return key. The three cells should look like the illustration on the left.

- Look at the Office Assistant. A light bulb should appear on the right side of the window. Place the mouse pointer directly on this bulb and click the (left) mouse button.

A balloon should appear with Clippit's tip. Don't worry if you can't understand Clippit's explanation because this will be carefully explained below. Once you are really using Excel, pay attention when the Office Assistant offers a tip. Often (not always) it will be useful and will help you become a better Excel user.

- Click the OK button in the tip balloon.

If you feel Clippit is more of an annoyance than a help, open the Help menu on the Menu Bar and click "Hide the Office Assistant." You can always get Clippit back from the same menu or simply by clicking Excel's Help button (🔣).

▼The Active Cell

The heart of an Excel workbook is the *cells* in the central part of the window. Each of the cells has an address determined by the row and column in which the cell is located. At the top of each column is a *Column Heading* with a letter, and to the left of each row is a *Row Heading* with a number. A cell's address is the letter of its column followed by the number of its row. In the section of the worksheet shown below, the active cell is in column A and row 1. Its address is therefore A1. Notice that this address is shown in the Name Box. The Name Box shows the address of the active cell.

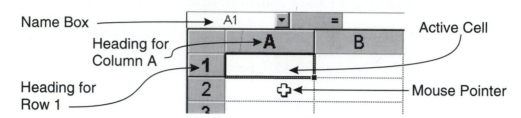

The active cell is the cell in which you can enter data. You can tell which cell is the active cell because it is surrounded by a special border, the active cell border: ⬜. In addition, the letter for the column heading (A) and the number for the row heading (1) will be darker than those of the other columns and rows and will appear slightly raised.

A cell is made active by placing the mouse pointer in the cell and clicking the (left) mouse button.

- Make cell C2 active.

If you have done this correctly, the Name Box will contain the address "C2." Notice the appearance of the headings of the "C" column and the "2" row. They should appear raised above the other row and column headings, helping you locate the active cell.

▼ Selecting Cells

The active cell is always a single cell. Some operations in Excel involve more than a single cell and require that you *select* a *range* of cells. A selection of cells is usually a rectangular block of cells. Since it is rectangular, it can be referred to by the cell addresses of its corners. Excel requires that these addresses be separated by a colon. For example, suppose we wanted to select the rectangular array of cells consisting of cells A1, B1, A2, B2, A3, and B3. The four corners of this array are A1, B1, B3, and A3. This book will use the convention of referring to the array by the addresses of the upper left cell (A1 in this case), and the lower-right cell (B3). This range would be referred to as A1:B3. Select this range of cells by doing the following:

- Place the mouse pointer on cell A1 and press and hold the (left) mouse button.

You will see cell A1 immediately become the active cell.

- While continuing to press the mouse button, drag the mouse pointer to cell B3 and release the mouse button (as illustrated below).

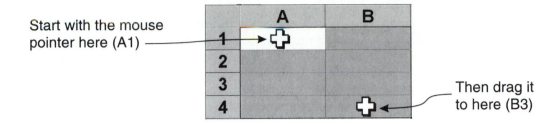

Start with the mouse pointer here (A1)

Then drag it to here (B3)

The selected region of cells will include the active cell (A1 in this case). When the active cell is in a selected region, it will be white while the other cells in the selected region are black.

- Press the Tab key repeatedly and notice how the active cell changes within the selected region. Press the Enter key repeatedly and notice the active cell also changes but in a different pattern.

When you select a region of cells, the headings for the rows and columns of all the cells in the region appear raised and their numbers or letters become darker.

▼Entering Data

Data are entered into the active cell from the keyboard. There are three types of data that can be entered:

1. Numbers. When you use Excel for statistical or other quantitative analysis, numbers are the starting point of the analysis.

2. Text. Text should be used liberally in an Excel workbook to document the numbers and calculations to make it easy to remember what the numbers mean. Excel is capable of producing beautiful tables, which can be used in reports. Every table should have text defining the rows and columns.

3. Formulas. Much of the work done by Excel will be in formulas you enter, which tell Excel the calculations you want done.

▼Numbers

To enter a number in the active cell, simply type the number on your keyboard. To complete the entry of a number, press the Enter key.

As you enter the number specified below, notice the following:

1. As you enter a number, the characters you type appear in the cell and in the Formula Bar.

2. As you enter a number, a vertical line called the *insertion point* shows where the next character you type will appear. As long as the insertion point is visible, you can correct typing errors with the Backspace key. Once you press the Enter key, the insertion point will disappear.

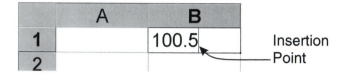

- Click cell B1 (make it the active cell). This should also remove the black selected region.

- Enter the number "100.5" (don't enter the quotation marks). Observe the Formula Bar as you enter the number. Press the Enter key when you are finished.

▼Editing a Cell

It is easy to edit a cell that already has an entry by placing the mouse pointer in the cell and double clicking. This will cause both that cell to become the active cell and the insertion point to appear within the cell. When you first were entering the number, the insertion point was always to the right of the last character you typed. When you edit a cell, you can move the insertion point by using the left or right cursor (arrow) keys or by positioning the mouse pointer exactly where you want the insertion point and clicking. This lets you add a character in the middle without retyping the rest of the number. You can erase the character to the right of the insertion point by pressing the Delete key. The Backspace key deletes the character to the left of the insertion point.

- Double click cell B1. You should see the insertion point in the cell.

- Place the mouse pointer between the decimal point and the "5," and click the mouse button.

Notice that when a cell has been double clicked and is ready for editing, the mouse pointer changes shape when it is in that cell. The new shape (the "I-beam") makes it easier to point precisely where you want the insertion point to be. Clicking between the decimal point and the "5" will cause the insertion point to appear at that location.

- Type the character "4" (without the quotation marks) and press the Enter key.

The contents of cell B1 should now be 100.45.

It is also possible to edit the contents of a cell in the Formula Bar.

- Make cell B1 the active cell, but don't double click the cell.

- Move the mouse pointer to the Formula Bar. Place the mouse pointer to the right of the "5" and click.

An insertion point will appear at the end of the number.

- Type a "6" (without the quotation marks). Press the Enter key.

The number in cell B1 should now be 100.456.

▼Entering Text

Entering text is as simple as entering numbers.

- Double click cell A1.

- Type the following text (without the quotation marks): "The First Number."

Notice that before you press the Enter key, the text that you enter goes beyond the right border of cell A1 and causes the contents of cell B1 to disappear.

	A	B
1	The First Number	
2		

After the Enter key is pressed, the contents of B1 reappear, but part of the text is covered as shown below.

	A	B
1	The First N	100.456
2		

- Click cell A1 to again make it the active cell, but don't double click.

Notice the Formula Bar. The full text appears there. Even though cell A1 on the worksheet is not wide enough to show the entire text, *it is there*.

Excel stores the entire text correctly. It displays what it can given the available space.

Excel behaves similarly with numbers. It keeps track of all decimal places even if the cell is too narrow to display them all and even though the value displayed in the cell may be rounded. The full number is stored and can be seen in the Formula Bar when the cell containing the number is made active.

- Click cell A2.

- Enter the following text (without the quotation marks): "The Second Number." As soon as you type the letter "T," Excel will immediately enter the last text you entered in a cell which started with "T" ("The First Number" in this case). Simply ignore this and continue typing "The Second Number."

- Press the Enter key. The cells should look like this:

	A	B
1	The First N	100.456
2	The Second Number	
3		

Notice this time that the full text appears even after the Enter key is pressed. This is because cell B2 is empty. If something is later entered into that cell, part of the text in A2 would disappear just as you saw in the first row.

▼Changing the Width of a Column

If you increase the width of column A, the full text of cell A1 can be viewed in the cell.

Carefully place the mouse pointer on the border between the heading for column A and the heading for column B. (Row and column headings are shown on page 12.) When you have it correct, the pointer will change to a new shape: ✛. This is the *column-width* mouse pointer.

The column headings and mouse pointer should look like the following picture:

- Once you see the column-width mouse pointer, press and hold the (left) mouse button, and *drag* the headings boundary to the right.

Move it to the right about half an inch (no need to be precise). Release the mouse button.

The width of column A will increase and shift the columns to the right further to the right.

- Again position the mouse pointer on the boundary between the heading for column A and that for column B. This time, *drag* the boundary to the left until it is just to the right of the word "First" in cell A1. Release the mouse button. This enables you to reduce the width of a column.

Although this method gives you complete control over column width, it is hard to know exactly how wide to make the column to display its contents without wasting space. Fortunately, there is a shortcut for when you want simply to make a column wide enough to display the cell contents.

- Again position the mouse pointer on the boundary between the headings of columns A and B. Instead of dragging, double click without moving the mouse.

The width of column A will immediately adjust to display the text in the cells in that column. The cells should look like the picture below.

	A	B
1	The First Number	100.456
2	The Second Number	
3		

▼Made an Error? Undo!

Excel remembers all the changes you make to the cells of a spreadsheet and allows you to "undo" any or all of them. This is a fantastic time saver if you discover you have made a mistake. (If you are the kind of person who never makes mistakes, you should be writing—instead of reading—this book.)

- Look for the Undo button on the Standard Toolbar: ⟳▾. Place the mouse pointer on the curved arrow and click the mouse button. Immediately you should see column A's width narrow until the right border is just to the right of the word "First" in A2. This is exactly where it was before you double clicked on the column boundary.

- Click the arrow on the Undo button again. Now you should see the column width become wide. This is the result of the first column width change you made.

- Click the Undo button again. Now column A has returned to its original width.

- Click the Undo button once again. The contents of cell A2 should have disappeared.

- Continue clicking the Undo button until the only thing remaining on an otherwise blank worksheet is "Mon" in cell D1. Click the Undo button one more time, and the worksheet should be completely blank.

Not only can you undo an operation, but you can also undo the undo (Excel calls this "redo").

- Click the Redo button on the Standard Toolbar: ▣▾. The "Mon" should reappear in cell D2.

- Repeatedly click the Redo button. Each time you should see one of your earlier operations being replayed. Continue clicking the button until it no longer works. When this happens, the button will be "grayed." You'll be able to see the shape of the Redo button, but it will have lost its color.

- Click the small arrow on the right side of the Undo button. A list will open showing all of the actions you have made that can be undone. By using the list, you can undo several changes in a single click. This, however, is usually not a good idea.

▼An Editing Shortcut—Text Highlighting

Suppose that we wanted to change the word "First" in cell A1 to "1st," and the word "Second" to "2nd." One way of doing this would be to first erase the word "First" and then enter "1st." There will be many times when you will want to replace one thing with another, and there is a useful shortcut for this operation.

- Double click cell A1 so that you can edit it.

- Move the mouse pointer so that it is immediately to the left of the "F" in "First."

- Press and hold the (left) mouse button.

- Move the mouse pointer to the right (across the word "First") while continuing to press the mouse button.

As the mouse pointer moves across the letters, notice that the colors switch from black letters on a white background to white letters on a black background. This is called *highlighting* the letters.

- Continue moving the mouse until you have highlighted the word "First" and only the word "First." Release the mouse button.

Your screen should look like the picture below:

	A	B
1	The **First** Number	100.456
2	The Second Number	

- On your keyboard type "1st" (without the quotation marks).

As soon as you begin typing, the highlighted text ("First") is deleted and new text appears in its place. Your screen should look like the picture below:

	A	B
1	The 1st Number	100.456
2	The Second Number	

- Press the Enter key to complete the cell editing.

This "text highlighting" can be used anywhere in Excel (including dialog windows) when you want to edit text. "Text" in this sense means anything you could enter from the keyboard, including numbers and formulas.

- Practice the technique by changing the word "Second" in cell A2 to "2nd." Be sure to press the Enter key.

- Use the method described on page 17 to have Excel automatically adjust the width of column A to fit the data in the column. Although this was used above to expand the column's width, the same method can also reduce a column's width.

Your screen should look like the picture below.

	A	B
1	The 1st Number	100.456
2	The 2nd Number	

▼Entering Formulas

- Make cell C1 the active cell.

- Enter (without the quotation marks) "=3+2" and press the Enter key.

- Again make cell C1 the active cell.

You indicate to Excel that you are entering a formula when you first enter an equal sign. Notice that cell C1 appears to have a "5" but that the Formula Bar shows the formula you entered (as shown below).

C1	▼	=	=3+2

	A	B	C
1	The 1st Number	100.456	5
2	The 2nd Number		

This formula, of course, directs Excel to add 3 and 2.

- Edit cell C1 and change the plus sign to a minus sign (-). Press Enter. Cell C1 should have a "1."

- Change the minus sign to a forward slash (/). This is the symbol for division, and the formula now directs Excel to divide 3 by 2. Press Enter and cell C1 should have "1.5."

- Change the forward slash to an asterisk (*). There is no real multiplication sign on a computer keyboard, and Excel uses the asterisk for that purpose. Press Enter, and cell C1 will have a "6," the product of 3 and 2.

- Change the asterisk to a carat (^). This is Excel's symbol for exponentiation, raising a number to a power. Press Enter, and cell C1 will have the value of 3^2, or 9.

▼Order of Arithmetic Operations

When a long formula with several operations is entered, Excel uses the standard "order of precedence" to determine which operations to do first. This means that first exponentiation will be done. Multiplication and division will be done next. Addition and subtraction will be done last. You can control the order in which operations are done by using parentheses.

- Enter "=(3+2)*6" (without quotation marks) in cell C1 and press Enter.

The value will be 30. Excel first does the operation inside the parentheses by adding 3 and 2. The result of that operation, 5, is then multiplied by 6.

• Enter "=3+(2*6)" in cell C1 and press the Enter key.

This time the value is 15. Excel first multiplies 2 times 6 and then adds the result (12) to 3.

• Enter "=3+2*6" in C1 with no parentheses. Press the Enter key.

Again, the answer is 15 because the order of precedence causes Excel to do the multiplication before the addition. It's a good idea to freely use parentheses in any formula with more than one operation so that you will be sure that the calculations will be done in the order you want. Remember that you always have to explicitly use the asterisk to indicate multiplication, even if you use parentheses. In mathematics, notation like (2)(3) is often understood to mean that the two values should be multiplied. With Excel, however, the multiplication must always be explicitly shown by an asterisk.

In addition to the basic arithmetic operations, Excel has a large number of mathematical functions. These functions can be entered directly in a formula. For example, suppose we wanted to calculate the square root of 9.

• In cell C1 enter "=sqrt(9)" and press the Enter key.

Cell C1 should now show a "3." The square root function has the name "sqrt" in Excel. Notice that the "9" is in parentheses and immediately follows the "sqrt." The "9" is called an *argument* of the function; it's the value we want the function to work on. Some functions have more than one argument. A few functions have no arguments. Regardless of the number of arguments, they all appear within a single set of parentheses. If there is more than one argument, they are separated by commas. If there are no arguments, the function name is followed by empty parentheses: "()."

• Make C1 the active cell. Notice the Formula Bar.

Excel converts the function name to uppercase. You can enter a function name either in uppercase or lowercase, but it will always appear in the Formula Bar as uppercase.

As you will learn later, Excel has a very clever feature that makes its built-in functions much easier to use. This feature is called the Formula Palette, and much use will be made of it in this book.

▼Using Cell Addresses in Formulas

A particularly useful and powerful facility in Excel is the ability to create formulas that refer to a cell whose contents are used in the calculation.

- Enter the following formula in cell C2 (without the quotes): "=b1+10." Press the Enter key.

The value displayed in cell C2 should be 110.456, which is the number in cell B1 plus the number 10.

Use the up-arrow cursor key to make C2 the active cell again. Notice that in the Formula Bar, the contents of the cell are displayed as =B1+10. Just as in the case of the SQRT function, Excel changes a cell address to uppercase letters even if you enter it in lowercase.

- Click cell B1 to make it the active cell (but don't double click). Enter the number "50" (without the quotation marks). Press the Enter key.

Notice that entering something new in an active cell that already has something in it simply erases the old contents and replaces it with the new. What does cell C2 now show? It should have the value 60, the contents of cell B1 (now 50) plus 10.

- Change the value of cell B1 to −20. Press the Enter key.

No matter what value you enter in cell B1, the displayed value of cell C2 will be 10 more. In this case, 10 more than −20 is −10.

It is also possible to enter a cell address by pointing to it with the mouse pointer.

- Make cell C3 the active cell. Begin a formula by entering an equal sign (=). Move the mouse pointer over cell B1 and click the (left) mouse button once.

A "B1" should be entered into the formula in cell C3 immediately after the equal sign.

- Enter a plus sign (+). Move the mouse pointer directly over cell C1 and click the (left) mouse button once.

The formula in cell C3 should now be "=B1+C1."

- Press the Enter key.

The value of cell C3 should display as −17, assuming that B1 has the value −20 and C1 has the value 3. Remember that C1 contains a formula ("=sqrt(9)"), not a number. As long as a cell *displays* a number, its address can be used within a formula even though that number is the result of a formula.

- Change cell C1's value to 50. What now is the value of cell C3?

Cell C3 should now display 30. Whenever the value of a cell changes, the displayed value of any cell containing a formula that references that cell will also change. This very important feature makes it possible to set up a workbook to analyze a particular *type* of problem and easily use it to handle different data by simply changing the numbers in cells referenced by equations in other cells that do the real analysis.

▼Scientific Notation

Sometimes the result of a calculation will be an extremely large or an extremely small number. When this happens, Excel uses a format that is similar to what is called *scientific notation*.

- Make C1 active and enter the formula "=55^13." Press the Enter key.

This formula directs Excel to calculate 55^{13}, which is a very large number. Cell C1 will have the value 4.2142E+22. (Your display might show other numbers between the "1" and the "E.") In scientific notation, this number would be:

$$4.2142 \times 10^{22}$$

where 10^{22} is twenty-two 10s all multiplied together. This number is a 1 followed by 22 zeros. The "E" in this notation is short for "exponent." In the scientific notation shown above, the "22" is called the *exponent* of 10. To represent this number in the notation we are most familiar with, the decimal place would have to be shifted 22 (the amount of the exponent) places to the right of where it is in 4.21. So this number is a bit larger than 4 followed by 22 zeros.

If you are not used to scientific notation, you probably don't feel comfortable with it. Excel can convert the number to the more familiar notation for you.

- Make cell C1 the active cell. Find the Comma Style button on the Formatting Toolbar: ▪. Click it.

Excel automatically adjusts the column width to show the number in its new format. It may be easier for you to make sense of now, but it takes up a lot of space.

Very small numbers in this notation have negative exponents.

- Make cell D1 active and enter "=1/(55^13)." Press the Enter key.

This directs Excel to calculate 1 divided by the same huge number it just calculated. This, of course, will be very small. Excel will show it as 2.37293E-23. Notice that the exponent is *negative* (−23). To see this number in standard notation, we would have to shift the decimal place 23 positions to the *left* of where it is in 2.37293.

To get Excel to show you the number in more familiar notation, do the following.

- Make cell D1 active and click the Comma Style speed button.

You may be surprised that cell D1 appears to contain zero. This is because the Comma Style button sets the cell to display only two decimal places. Another speed button will increase the number of displayed decimal places.

- Click the Increase Decimal speed button: ⬚. You will have to click it many times before you see enough decimal places to display a nonzero digit.

Here again, although this format is probably easier for you to read than Excel's scientific format, it takes up much more space. Numbers like this will occasionally be produced by some statistical procedures, and it is best (but not essential) to get used to Excel's standard representation of them.

▼Error Codes

Some calculations cannot be done and result in an error. In these cases, Excel displays an *error value* in the cell. Let's see what they look like. The examples discussed below are going to involve making pretty obvious errors, ones you might be very unlikely to make. As your use of Excel becomes more sophisticated, however, errors become much more subtle and less obvious than these examples.

- In cell D1 enter the formula "=10/0" (without quotes). Press the Enter key.

This formula instructs Excel to divide the number 10 by zero, although division by zero is not defined. Instead of a value, cell D1 contains the error value "#DIV/0!" All Excel error values begin with "#." It's not hard to see that this error value warns of division by zero.

- Does Clippit want to give you a tip? Click his light bulb to read it.

- Make D1 the active cell. Look at the Formula Bar.

As in the case of a valid calculation, the Formula Bar shows us that Excel continues to store the formula in the cell and simply displays the answer as an error value.

- Edit the formula, changing the "0" to a "5." Press the Enter key.

A nonerror value (2) now appears in cell D1. Excel continues to display many digits to the right of the decimal point.

- Make cell D1 active and click the Comma Style button again. The display returns to showing only two values to the right of the decimal.

You are likely to encounter other error values as you work with Excel. The meaning of some of them may not be so obvious. Whenever Excel does something unexpected, a good first place to turn is the on-line help.

Suppose you wanted to use Excel to take the absolute value of a number and were unsure of the name Excel uses for the absolute value function. One reasonable approach to this problem is to guess.

- Enter in cell D1 the formula "=absval(-10)" without the quotation marks. Press the Enter key.

At this point you can probably guess what the error value, "#NAME?," means. Suppose, however, that you needed an explanation of the error message. This is an excellent opportunity to experiment with Excel's extensive on-line help system.

- Clippit is trying to show you a tip. Click the light bulb, and you should get a message explaining that the error message means Excel doesn't recognize a name that was used. Suppose we need more help.

- Click on Clippit so you can ask him a question. Simply enter the error code "#NAME?" (without quotes) and click the Search button.

- The second topic in Clippit's list should be, "What does the error #NAME? mean?" Click on the dot just to the right of this topic and a large Help window will open explaining possible causes of the error.

You will notice in the left side of the Help window that there are several possible causes for the error listed, including "Misspelling the name." This is likely confirmation that we have misspelled the name of Excel's function to take the absolute value. How can we determine what the correct spelling is?

- Use Excel's Help system to search for the name of the Excel formula that determines the absolute value. Do this by asking for help for "absolute value."

- Which do you think is a more likely name for the absolute value function, IMABS or ABS? Click your choice and read the definition to see if you were correct. If you are unsure after reading the Help window, close it, click Clippit again, click "Search," and click the other choice. Decide which one seems more likely to be correct.

- Close the Help window.

- Edit the formula in cell D1 to change "absval" to "abs." Press the Enter key. The error value should be replaced by 10—the absolute value of −10

▼The Scroll Bars

Excel displays only a portion of a worksheet on your computer screen. It frequently will be necessary to view the other cells. Think of your screen as a small window on a very large worksheet. To view portions of the worksheet that are not currently visible, you need to move your screen's window on the worksheet until it is over the cells you want to see. One way of doing this is to use the Scroll Bars.

There are two Scroll Bars. The horizontal Scroll Bar moves the screen window horizontally, while the vertical bar moves the window vertically. The parts of the Scroll Bar are shown in the picture below. Note that the Scroll Bars on your screen will be longer than those shown, and your screen should include worksheet tabs.

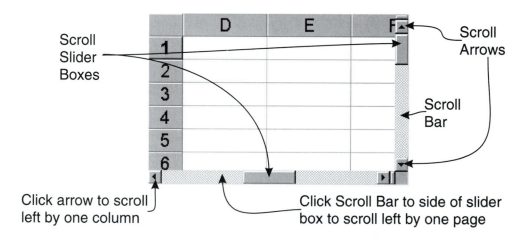

Each Scroll Bar has a scroll slider box and two scroll arrows. The position of the scroll box within the Scroll Bar shows the relative position of the screen window on the worksheet. For example, in the picture the scroll box is at the top of the vertical Scroll Bar, indicating that the screen window is at the top of the worksheet.

The scroll box in the horizontal Scroll Bar, on the other hand, is more or less in the middle of the Scroll Bar. The visible portion of the worksheet is to the right of the first column (column A). To move the screen window over the worksheet, you move the scroll box within its Scroll Bar.

- On your worksheet, place the mouse pointer on the bottom scroll arrow of the vertical Scroll Bar on the right of your screen. Click the (left) mouse button once.

The screen window will move down one row. The top row visible on your screen should be row 2 and the bottom row should be one row below that which was originally visible.

- Click the top scroll arrow so that row 1 is again the top row visible on your screen.

- Place the mouse pointer on the vertical Scroll Bar so that it is below the scroll box and above the scroll arrow. Click the (left) mouse button once.

The screen window will scroll down by a "page" (the total number of rows displayed). All of the rows now visible are below what was the bottom row. Anytime you click the mouse pointer on any part of the Scroll Bar below the scroll box but above the scroll arrow, the screen window will move down a page. If you click the Scroll Bar above the scroll box, the screen window will move up a page.

- Place the mouse pointer directly on the scroll slider box. Press and hold the (left) mouse button. While holding the mouse button, slowly move the scroll box up. Notice the Name Box. Position the slider box so that the Name Box contains "Row: 10." Release the mouse button.

Row 10 should now be the top row on your screen.

- Experiment with the horizontal Scroll Bar by clicking the scroll arrows, Scroll Bars, and moving the scroll box.

▼Worksheets and Worksheet Tabs

An Excel worksheet, as you have seen, contains far more cells than can be seen on your screen at one time. In addition, an Excel *workbook* contains many *worksheets*. Tabs for some of these worksheets can be found at the bottom of the Excel window to the left of the horizontal Scroll Bar. The current worksheet is "Sheet1," and you will notice that the tab for that worksheet appears on top and is lighter than the other worksheet tabs.

- Click the "Sheet2" tab.

Notice that a blank worksheet appears with all the columns set to their original width. Notice also that the "Sheet2" tab now appears to be on top and is the lightest tab.

- Click the "Sheet1" tab.

The previous worksheet reappears.

Worksheets give you a way to help you organize the information in a workbook. In addition, some operations in Excel create new worksheets. As you will see, some worksheets will contain a graphic chart rather than cells.

Initially, Excel starts with three worksheets. It is easy to add more.

- Click "Insert" on the Menu Bar to open the Insert menu. Click "Worksheet" on that menu.

A new worksheet, "Sheet4," will be created. It will not necessarily be placed after Sheet3. It is easy, however, to drag it to that location.

- Place the mouse pointer directly on the "Sheet4" tab. Click and hold the (left) mouse button. The mouse pointer will change shape to a white arrow with a sheet of paper under it: ▯. Move the mouse pointer to the right and notice the small dark pointer that moves between sheet tabs. This indicator shows the position to which the worksheet will be moved once the mouse button is released.

- Move the mouse pointer until the marker is to the right of the "Sheet3" tab and release it. The worksheets should now be in order.

- Create enough new worksheets (six or more) so that not all the worksheet tabs will be visible at the same time on your screen.

When there are many worksheets, the tabs that are visible can be scrolled using the special scroll arrows immediately to the left of the worksheet tabs. The functions of those arrows are described in the picture on the next page.

- Click each of the worksheet tab scroll arrows and observe its operation.

In addition to entering data in cells, you can also put values in cells by filling, copying, and moving cells. "Filling" refers to the ability of Excel to automatically extend a sequence of values.

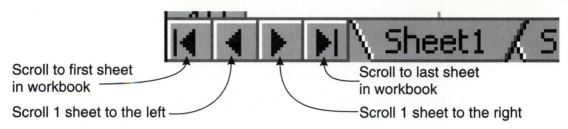

Scroll to first sheet in workbook

Scroll 1 sheet to the left

Scroll to last sheet in workbook

Scroll 1 sheet to the right

▼Copying and Moving Cells

- Click the "Sheet2" worksheet tab so that you can work with a clean worksheet.

Excel provides a number of different methods to copy or move cells. It is common to want to copy the contents of a single cell to several adjacent cells, either in the same row or the same column. As will be discussed below, this is a particularly useful operation when the cell to be copied contains a formula, but the procedure will work when the cell contains text or numbers.

- Enter the number "1" (without quotes) in cell A1. Press the Enter key.

- Click cell A1 to again make it the active cell, but don't double click since you don't want to edit the cell.

Look carefully at the border around the active cell. In the lower-right corner there is a small square called the *fill handle*. Carefully position the mouse pointer over the fill handle. When you have it correctly positioned, the pointer will change from a thick white cross to a thin black cross as shown in the picture below.

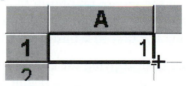

- Click and hold the (left) mouse button while it is in the shape of a black cross. Drag the mouse pointer down column A until the selection frame includes cell A10. Release the mouse button. Cell A1 will be white, and cells A2 through A10 will be black.

- Release the mouse button.

The "1" originally in cell A1 has been copied to all the cells in the range.

- Press the Delete or Del key on your keyboard. This will erase the contents of the selected range. (The Del key on the numeric keypad will only work if NumLock is *off*.)

- Click cell A1 and enter the word "Total" (without quotes). Press the Enter key. Reselect cell A1.

- Position the mouse pointer over the lower-right corner so that it changes into a black cross.

- Hold the mouse button and drag to the *right* until the selection boundary includes the cell at the top of row E. Release the mouse button.

The word "Total" will have been copied to all of the cells within the selected region A1 through E1.

- Erase the contents of cells A1 through E1 using the Delete key.

▼Filling Cells

- Enter the number "1" in cell A1 and the number "2" in cell B1.

- Select the cell range A1:B1.

- Place the mouse pointer over the square in the lower-right corner of the selection boundary until it becomes a black cross, as shown in the picture below.

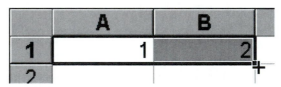

- With the mouse pointer in the shape of a black cross, click and hold the (left) mouse button and drag the selection outline to the right along the first row until it includes cell G1. Release the mouse button.

Rather than copying the contents of cells A1 and B1 to the other cells, Excel continues the series begun in those cells, with cells A1 through G1 containing the numbers 1 through 7. A small indicator follows your mouse pointer and tells the value that will go in the last cell.

- Erase the contents of the cells in the first row.

- Put the number "5" (no quotes) in cell A1 and the number "10" in cell A2.

- Create a selected region containing cells A1 and A2 by placing the mouse pointer in the center of cell A1, pressing and holding the (left) mouse button, dragging the mouse pointer to the center of cell A2, and releasing the mouse pointer in cell A2.

- Place the mouse pointer over the small square in the lower right-hand corner, press the (left) mouse button, and drag the selection outline down to cell A10. Release the mouse button.

Since cells A1 and A2 had values that differed by 5, Excel extended the series by adding 5 to each number. Try repeating the process after putting "2" in A1 and "4" in A2. Try again with "1920" in A1 and "1930" in A2. Excel's ability to fill a range of cells is an excellent demonstration of intelligence in a computer program.

Excel's ability to fill with certain text values is even more remarkable.

- Follow the steps on page 30 to copy the word "Total" from cell A1 to E1, except use the word "Monday" instead of "Total" (without quotation marks).

Instead of copying, Excel fills the cells with the other names of the days of the week!

- Excel can also fill (and copy) several series at once. To see this, enter the values shown below in the first row of the worksheet (enter "2/25/2000" in A1). Excel recognizes the value in cell A1 as a date, but it, and all the others, should be entered in the same way as you enter text.

	A	B	C	D	E	F	G
1	2/25/00	Mon	Jan	january	Week 1	1st	1st Quarter

- Select the region from A1 to G1. Do this by placing the mouse pointer on A1, holding down the (left) mouse button, and dragging the selection boundary to the right until it includes G1. Your screen should look like the picture below:

	A	B	C	D	E	F	G
1	2/25/00	Mon	Jan	january	Week 1	1st	1st Quarter

- Notice that the selected region has a small square in the lower-right corner, the same as that which you used earlier to copy and fill. Place the mouse pointer over that square until it becomes a black cross.

- When the mouse pointer is a black cross, press the (left) mouse button and drag the mouse pointer downward until the selection boundary includes row 15. Notice the small tag by the mouse pointer indicates what Excel will place in the last cell of the first column. Release the mouse button.

Excel has filled each column in the selected region. If you look carefully at each series, you will notice some remarkable examples of Excel's built-in intelligence.

Look at the dates in the first column. Notice that the date after 2/29/00 is 3/1/00. Not only does Excel know how many days are in each month, it also knows that 2000 is a leap year.

If a name begins with a lowercase letter (like "January" in cell D1), Excel will fill the series with names all beginning with lowercase letters.

Compare the series in columns F and G. Excel knows that there are only four "Quarters," and begins renumbering after the fourth.

▼Moving and Copying Regions of Cells

Excel provides a method for moving and copying cells using the mouse. Let's use this method to move the information in columns E, F, and G one column to the right so that column E is cleared.

- Select the region of cells from E1 to G15. Do this by dragging the mouse pointer (with the mouse button pressed) from cell E1 to cell G15.
- Position the mouse pointer on a boundary (any of the four boundaries will work) of the selected region. When it is correctly positioned, its shape will change from a white cross to a white arrow: .
- While the mouse pointer is in the shape of an arrow, press and hold the (left) mouse button.
- With the mouse button pressed, move the mouse pointer to the right. After you have moved at least one column, an outline of the selected region will appear which moves with the mouse pointer. A small marker will show the address the outline is currently on.
- Position the outline so that it is in columns F, G, and H, in the first 15 rows (F1:H15). Your worksheet should look like the picture on the next page. When the outline is correctly positioned, release the mouse button.

The selected region will move to the new area and column E will be empty. This method of moving a region of cells is called the *drag and drop* method. You drag a region of cells (holding the mouse button down) and drop it where you want it.

	A	B	C	D	E	F	G	H
1	2/25/00	Mon	Jan	january	Week 1	1st	1st Quarter	
2	2/26/00	Tue	Feb	february	Week 2	2nd	2nd Quarter	
3	2/27/00	Wed	Mar	march	Week 3	3rd	3rd Quarter	
4	2/28/00	Thu	Apr	april	Week 4	4th	4th Quarter	
5	2/29/00	Fri	May	may	Week 5	5th	1st Quarter	
6	3/1/00	Sat	Jun	june	Week 6	6th	2nd Quarter	
7	3/2/00	Sun	Jul	july	Week 7	7th	3rd Quarter	
8	3/3/00	Mon	Aug	august	Week 8	8th	4th Quarter	
9	3/4/00	Tue	Sep	september	Week 9	9th	1st Quarter	
10	3/5/00	Wed	Oct	october	Week 10	10th	2nd Quarter	
11	3/6/00	Thu	Nov	november	Week 11	11th	3rd Quarter	
12	3/7/00	Fri	Dec	december	Week 12	12th	4th Quarter	
13	3/8/00	Sat	Jan	january	Week 13	13th	1st Quarter	
14	3/9/00	Sun	Feb	february	Week 14	14th	2nd Quarter	
15	3/10/00	Mon	Mar	march	Week 15	15th	3rd Quarter	
16								F1:H15

There is also a drag and drop method of copying a region of cells. Let's use it to copy the days of the week in column B to the now empty column E.

- Select the region of cells from B1 to B15.

- Place the mouse pointer over the border of the selected region so that its shape changes to a white arrow.

- With the mouse pointer in the shape of an arrow, press and hold the Ctrl key (PC) or OPTION key (Mac) on your keyboard. A small plus sign will appear beside the arrow.

- Continue to press the Ctrl or OPTION key and also press and hold the (left) mouse button. Drag the selected region outline until it is over column E (E1:E15).

- Release the mouse button first and then release the keyboard key.

The days of the week will be copied to column E and will also still be in column B.

▼Copying and Moving Formulas—Relative Cell Addresses

Special attention has to be paid when formulas containing cell addresses are moved or copied. Let's examine the way Excel handles these situations.

- Click an unused sheet tab so that this exercise may be done on a blank worksheet.

- Enter the letters and numbers in cells A1 through B3 and C1 as shown below:

	A	B	C
1	1st Value	2nd Value	Sum
2	1	10	
3	2	20	

Use Excel's fill capability to extend the series in columns A and B through row 10.

- Select the region A2:B3, then drag the small rectangle in the lower-right corner down until the selection boundary includes row 10.

Column A should show the series of numbers from 1 through 9, while column B should show 10, 20, 30, up to 90.

- Enter this formula in cell C2 (without quotation marks): "=a2+b2."

The value displayed in cell C2 should, of course, be 11.

- Move cell C2 to C3. A single cell can be moved exactly like a larger selected region. Click C2 to make it the active cell, place the mouse pointer on a boundary of the cell until the pointer turns into a white arrow, then hold the (left) mouse button and drag the cell boundary until it is in cell C3. Release the mouse button.

Moving the formula from C2 to C3 shouldn't change it. It still should display "11." The Formula Bar should show "=A2+B2" when C3 is active. *Moving* a cell with a formula doesn't change it. This may not surprise you since moving a number or text also doesn't change the value entered in a cell. *Copying* a formula, however, *may* change it in a way that can be quite useful.

- Move the formula from C3 back to C2.

- Now *copy* the formula from C2 to C3. Use the drag and drop method.

Instead of "11," cell C3 should display "22."

- Click on cell C3 to make it the active cell.

- Drag the rectangle in the lower right-hand corner down until the selection boundary includes cell C10.

- The displayed value of each cell will differ. Cell C4 shows "33," while cell C5 shows "44," and so on.

- Click on cell C6 to make it the active cell and observe the cell's contents in the Formula Bar.

Instead of "=A2+B2," the contents of C6 are "=A6+B6." When the formula was copied, the cell addresses were changed.

- Click on each of the cells in column C from C2 to C9 and observe the formula in each cell in the Formula Bar.

Each cell contains a formula adding the values in the two cells immediately to the left. Thus cell C2 adds the numbers in columns A and B, which are in the same row (2) as cell C2. The formula in cell C4 does the same, only since C4 is in row 4, the two cells whose values are added are also in row 4.

When you put the formula "=A2+B2" in cell C2, Excel interpreted the addresses "A2" and "B2" as *relative* cell addresses. Excel determined where those cells were *relative* to the cell containing the formula. Thus cell A2 is two cells to the left of cell C2, and B2 is one cell to the left of cell C2. When the formula in C2 is copied to another cell, those addresses are changed to the addresses of the cells that are in the same position *relative* to the copied formula's position. For example, the formula in cell C4 adds the value of the cell two cells to the left of C4 (which is A4) and the value of the cell that is one cell to the left of C4 (which is B4).

This ability of Excel to change cell addresses in this way is very useful. Many spreadsheet problems will require performing the same calculations on several rows or several columns of numbers. With relative cell addressing, you need only specify the calculation in a formula for one of the rows or columns, and then copy that formula to the other rows or columns.

Let's take a look at the use of relative cell addresses on operations involving columns. Suppose that we want the cells in row 11 to display the sum of the numbers in the column above. Thus cell A11 would show the sum of A2 through A10, B11 would show the sum of B2 through B10, and C11 would show the sum of C2 through C10.

Let's start by entering the formula in A11 to add the numbers in A2 through A10.

- Click cell A11 to make it the active cell.

Summing a row or column is such a common operation on a spreadsheet that Excel provides a speed button specifically for that operation.

- Find the AutoSum button on the Standard Toolbar, Σ, and click it.

Excel will insert the formula in cell A11 that it *thinks* you want. You should see the following in that cell: =SUM(A2:A10). The most likely error

Excel might make is to guess the wrong cell addresses you want added. To help you correct the cell addresses, Excel has already highlighted them in the formula. In this case, however, Excel has guessed correctly.

- Press the Enter key and the sum of the column, 45, will display in cell A11.

- Copy cell A11 to B11 and C11. B11 should display 450 and C11 should display 495.

▼ Absolute versus Relative Cell Addresses

Suppose that we would like column D to contain the percentage each value in column C is of the total for column C. The sum of the values in column C is 495, so we would like cell D2 to indicate what percentage of 495 is 11 (the value in C2). Cell D3 should indicate what percentage of 495 is 22, and so on.

- In cell D1 enter the text label "Percent" (without quotation marks).

- In cell D2, enter the following formula (without quotation marks): "=c2/c11." Press the Enter key.

The value 0.022222 should be displayed in D2. Note that this is a proportion rather than a percentage. To convert a proportion to a percentage, we must multiply by 100. Excel, however, has a special formatting that allows a proportion to *display* as a percentage.

- Make D2 the active cell. Click the Percent Style speed button, %, on the Formatting Toolbar.

The value 2% will be displayed.

- Click the Increase Decimal speed button, .00, on the Formatting Toolbar twice.

The value 2.22% should now be displayed. The Percent Style button formats the cell but doesn't change its value. If C2 were used in a mathematical formula, the value that would be used would be 0.022222, not 2.22.

- Copy the formula in D2 to D3.

Although our objective is for D3 to calculate C3 as a percentage of the total, this clearly did not happen. Instead, D3 shows an error (#DIV/0!). This error indicates an attempt to divide a number by 0.

- Make D3 the active cell and observe the formula in the Formula Bar.

The formula in D3 is =C3/C12. But this is not correct. C12 is blank. What we want is for the value in C3 to be divided by the value in C11, not C12. The problem is that when the formula in D2 (=C2/C11) was copied, the C2 was changed to C3 and the C11 was changed to C12. What we wanted, however, was for just the C2 to be changed. The way to do this is to make the C12 in the formula in D2 an *absolute* address, which won't change when it is copied.

- Double click cell D2 so that you can edit it. When you edit a formula with cell addresses, Excel uses color coding to show you the location of the cells in the formula.

- Highlight the "C11" in the formula so that you can edit that portion of the formula.

- With the "C11" appearing as white against a black background, press the F4 function key. The "C11" should change to "$C$11."

The dollar signs make the address absolute. Without the dollar signs, the address is relative. An absolute address will not change if it is copied to another cell, while a relative address will change. You can also make an address absolute by manually entering the "$" rather than using the function key.

- Press the Enter key to indicate that you have finished editing the cell.

- Copy cell D2 to cells D3 through D10.

Each of the cells should now display a correct value. Examine the formulas in several of the cells. Notice that in each of them the numerator is the cell address of the cell immediately to the left, while the divisor is always "$C$11."

Notice also that Excel has copied the formatting to the cells. Thus each cell appears as a percentage with two decimal points.

- Copy the formula in cell C11 (which sums column C) to cell D11 so that D11 will have the sum of the numbers in column D.

Are you surprised that the value is 1 instead of 100? Although the percentages add up to 100%, remember that the numbers in the cells in column D are *proportions*, not percentages. The Percent Style button causes them to be displayed as percentages, but the numbers that are added are all between 0 and 1. Of course, we could use the Percent Style button on D11 to make it also display as a percentage.

Congratulations! You have now learned enough Excel to begin to use it to explore data and perform statistical analysis. You will be introduced to new features but this will always be done in the context of using Excel to explore statistics. Don't be surprised if you need to refer back to this chapter. As time goes on, you'll remember more and more about Excel, and you will find the discussions in this book will deal increasingly with statistics and decreasingly with Excel.

Chapter 2

Descriptive Statistics

Chances are that what you think of today as *statistics* is more precisely called *descriptive statistics*. There are many times when a business person will need to understand information provided by a collection of numbers—such as sales figures, labor turnover, expenditure records, and many more. We mortals do not have the ability to look at more than a handful of numbers and immediately have a sense of the information those numbers contain. To get a sense of the information contained in a huge collection of numbers, we have to summarize, or we have to convert the numbers into a chart or graph.

Vision is our keenest sense. You take advantage of that sense when you use graphics to represent the information in numbers. Before computers, graphical representations of data were difficult and time-consuming to do well. Computers, and programs like Excel, make it easy to prepare graphics, although it still takes some skill to know how to use graphics effectively.

Data summaries, or descriptive statistics, are also important. Most of your study of statistics will not be of descriptive statistics. It will be of *inferential statistics*. Inferential statistics provides us with a way to investigate the characteristics of a *population* when we only have data from a *sample*. A common example is a poll that provides information on the attitudes of an entire electorate by questioning only a tiny proportion of all the people in that electorate. The techniques of inferential statistics require calculating numerical summaries of the sample data and using them to develop information about the population.

▼Using Graphics in Excel

Let's explore Excel's graphics capability through the use of an example using data on the size of the civilian workforce in the United States, classified by gender.

Start Excel (if you have not already done so).

The data for this example are available in the Excel worksheet named "labor.xls." To read that worksheet into Excel, do the following:

- If the data files are on a diskette, insert the data diskette in the A drive on your computer. If the files are on a hard drive or a network drive, skip this step. (See Appendix A to obtain the data diskette.)

- Click the Open (📂) speed button on the Standard Toolbar. The Open dialog window will open.

At the top of the dialog window (shown below) you will see a field labeled "Look in:." In the picture below, that field refers to the folder "My Documents." To read from a diskette, you need to have that field refer to the diskette drive.

Click here

- Click the small downward-pointing arrowhead just to the right of the "Look in:" field as shown in the picture. A list of locations will open (as shown below).

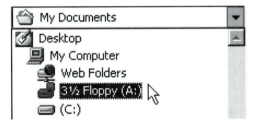

- Click the mouse pointer on "(C:)" if the data is on your hard disk or "3½ Floppy (A:)" if it is on a diskette. If your data is on a network drive, you will need to know which drive it is on and choose that drive.

- If the data is on a hard disk or network drive, it is probably in a folder. Look for the icon of the correct folder (might be "BusStats," and double click it.

- The dialog window should look like the picture on the next page.

The data for each chapter is in a separate folder on the diskette (not all chapters have data).

- Since this is Chapter 2, place the mouse pointer on the icon labeled "Chap_2" and double click. The "Look in:" field will now have "Chap_2."

- Two file names should appear in the large field, "Chapter 2 Data.xls" and "Civilian Labor Force.xls." Place the mouse pointer on "Civilian Labor Force.xls" and double click.

The Open dialog window will close and Excel will load the workbook shown below.

	A	B	C
1	**Civilian Labor Force (1,000)**		
2	**Year**	**Males**	**Females**
3	1948	40,619	14,974
4	1949	40,803	15,580
5	1950	41,129	16,285
6	1951	40,831	17,000
7	1952	40,712	17,593
8	1953	41,334	17,957
9	1954	41,496	17,492
10	1955	41,749	18,266
11	1956	42,645	19,456

These data show the size of the civilian labor force (20 years old and older) by gender for several recent years. The numbers shown come from the U.S. Bureau of Labor Statistics and provide the seasonally adjusted January figures for each year. At the end of the worksheet are links which, if clicked, will take you to the U.S. government web site from which the data came.

These data provide information on how the total labor force size has changed and how the proportion of the labor force consisting of women has changed. This information would be much easier to understand, however, if it were shown in a chart. Let's use Excel to create such a chart.

You have the option in Excel to place a chart on the same worksheet as the data or to place it on a worksheet by itself. For this exercise, you will do the latter.

The first step is to select the data which will be graphed. For this exercise we will create a bar chart which will provide an excellent graphical depiction of the way the labor force has changed over time and the way the proportion of males and females has changed.

The first step is to decide exactly what data is to be charted. Clearly the number of people employed is to be charted. What about the years? With a bar chart, the height of the bars should be determined by the number of people employed. The year should label the bars, but is not actually part of the data to be charted.

- Select the data in columns B and C starting with row 2. An easy way to do this is: Select cell B1. Press and hold both a Shift key and a Ctrl key. While both those keys are being pressed, press and release the right arrow key. This should cause the selection area to extend from A1 to C1. While continuing to press the Shift and Ctrl keys, press and release the down-arrow key. This should extend the selected area to row 54.

When Excel sees a column of data, it frequently will interpret the cells in the first row as labels rather than data. By starting with row 2, we have taken advantage of this behavior.

- Click the Chart Wizard button (📊) on the Standard Toolbar.

Excel will start the Chart Wizard, which provides a sequence of dialog windows for you to specify details about the type of chart you want. In the first step you tell Excel what type of chart you want. We'll create what Excels calls a *stacked column chart*. A column chart is a bar chart in which the bars are vertical. A stacked column chart divides each bar into two parts so that each bar graphically shows two numbers rather than one.

- In the left field ("Chart type") select "Column." Notice that the sample pictures in the right field change as the selected chart type changes.

- In the right field ("Chart sub-type"), select the stacked-column chart. This is the second choice in the top row. Notice that beneath the sample pictures is an explanation of the chart subtype you have chosen. The dialog window should look like the picture on the next page.

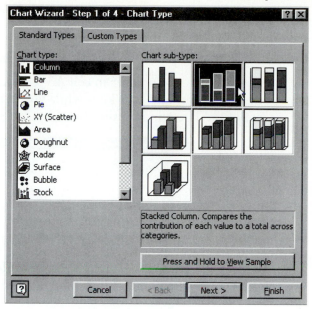

- Click the Next> button.

In the next dialog window (which has "Chart Source" in the Title Bar) we can tell Excel exactly which data we want charted. Excel makes a guess, and the small chart shown in the dialog window depicts the chart that would display if Excel's guess were accepted. Although Excel's guesses are pretty good, this guess is wrong.

The type of chart we want is one in which there is a separate bar for each year, and each bar is subdivided into two parts: one representing the number of males and the other representing the number of females in the civilian labor force.

The chart is almost exactly what we want, but there are a few points which need fine-tuning. The most important one is that we want the numbers along the horizontal axis at the bottom of the chart to show years. Currently those numbers simply label the bars with the sequential row number. Thus 1948 is "1." Most of the numbers are omitted to improve the (tiny) sample chart's readability.

Click here

- There are two tabs at the top of the window. You are probably viewing "Data Range." Click the "Series" tab.

At the bottom of the window is a field labeled "Category (X) axis labels." In this field we will place the cell addresses which contain the years. These cells could contain words rather than numbers, and Excel would use those words to label the axis. In this case, we need to be sure not to include cell A2 (which contains the word "Year") because Excel would simply use that word to label the first bar rather than "1948," the first year.

- Click the mouse pointer in the "Category (X) axis labels" field.

- Place the mouse pointer in cell A3 (containing "1948"). Press and hold the Shift and Ctrl keys while you press and release the down-arrow key. The window should look like the below.

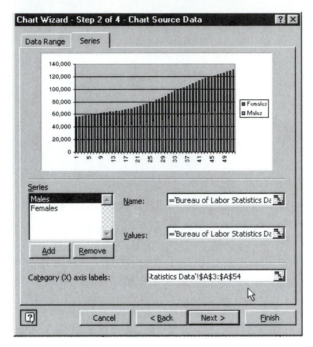

- Click the mouse pointer either in the "Name" or "Values" field. This tells Excel you are finished with the "Category" field, and the preview chart will immediately show years on the horizontal axis.

- Click the Next> button. The "Step 3 (Chart Options)" dialog window will open.

This dialog window presents you with a number of options for how your chart will look. The file tabs at the top of the window give you access to the window's various features. It is easy to "try on" different options because they will immediately be shown in the small chart in the window.

- Click the "Titles" file tab. In the "Chart title" field enter "Civilian Labor Force." In the "Category (X) axis" field enter "Year." In the "Value (Y) axis field" enter "1,000's."

- Click the "Legend" file tab. Under "Placement" click the "Bottom" radio button. The window should look like the picture on the next page.

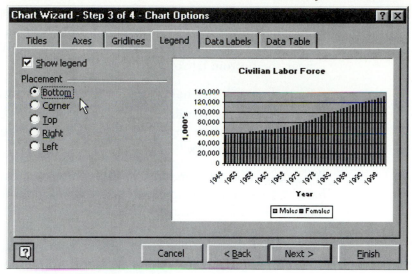

Click the Next> button.

The last step lets you determine whether you want the chart on a new worksheet by itself or whether you want it to share a worksheet, perhaps so the chart and its data will be together. This decision will affect the way the chart will appear on your screen, and it also will affect the way it will appear if it is printed. With each choice there is a field in which you can enter a worksheet name. If you choose to put the chart on a separate worksheet, you can give that worksheet a name here (or Excel will give it the name already in the field, "Chart1"). If you choose to put the chart in an existing worksheet, and you have more than one worksheet, you can put the name of the existing worksheet here. Since there is only one worksheet in this workbook ("Civilian Labor Force"), Excel puts that name in the field.

• Have Excel put the chart on its own worksheet named "CLF Chart." The dialog window should look like the picture below.

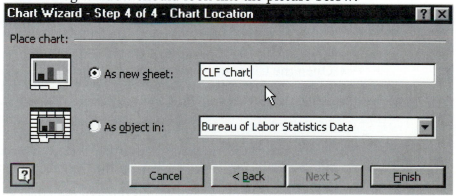

- Click the Finish Button. The Chart Wizard will close the last dialog window and you will see the completed chart on its own worksheet. Notice the name of the worksheet by looking at the worksheet tabs near the bottom left of your screen

- Save the work you have done up to this point by clicking the Save button (▣) on the Standard Toolbar. Get in the habit of frequently clicking the button to ensure that a computer problem will not result in losing your work.

What does this chart show? The eye will tend to connect the tops of the bars and also the place on each bar which divides it into males and females (with males making up the lower part). This makes it easy to compare the growth in the total civilian labor force with the growth in the male labor force. The chart makes clear that the total labor force has been growing faster than the male labor force—women have been making up an increasing proportion of the labor force.

Let's examine some ways in which this chart might be changed. Suppose we wanted to make the following changes:

1. Convert the chart to a type of side-by-side bar chart with a three-dimensional look to the bars.

2. Change the title to "Civilian Labor Force by Gender."

3. Change the bars from colors to gray-scale patterns that will show on a black-and-white printer.

4. Print the chart.

Many other changes are possible, but these will demonstrate how you can change an existing chart. As these changes are made, think about how they influence the chart's basic message.

▼Changing the Chart Type

- Open the Chart menu on the Menu Bar. Select "Chart Type." The "Chart Type" dialog window will open. You should recognize this as the same dialog window first used by the Chart Wizard (and shown on page 43).

- At the top of the window are two folder tabs. The current one is labeled "Standard Types." Click on the "Custom Types" tab.

- Click several of the choices and observe the effect on the small chart in the window. Because of the relatively large amount of data in this chart, many of the choices look rather cluttered. Select, finally, "Columns with Depth" (as shown below). Click the OK button.

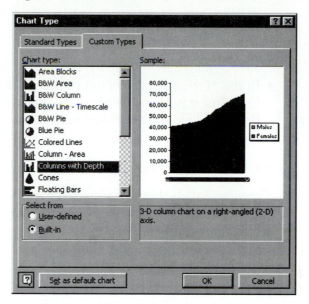

The display will return to the worksheet with the chart. As you see, the bars now appear three dimensional, and the data for males and females are represented by bars that are side by side.

Unfortunately, changing the chart type also changed a number of other things that we did not want changed. The legend, which was at the bottom of the chart, is now on the right side. The titles and the labels on both axes are now gone. The "Years" labels on the horizontal axis overlap in a way which makes them unreadable. These things can all be easily corrected.

Let's first correct the problem with the years on the horizontal axis. In the previous chart, only every second year's value was shown, and the numbers were tilted so they could fit closer together.

- Place the mouse pointer directly on the years below the horizontal axis. After a second or two, the words "Category Axis" will appear in a small box (as shown on the left).

- Click the (left) mouse button once. Open the Format menu on the Menu Bar and click "Selected Axis." A dialog window will open with several tabs at the top. Click the "Scale" tab.

The first field is labeled "Number of categories between tick-mark labels." The value in this field determines how many bars will appear between each label. We will make a change resulting in every second bar being labeled.

- Change the "1" in the "Number of categories between tick-mark labels" field to a "2." Click the "Alignment" tab.

The "Alignment" tab determines the angle at which the labels are written. We will change the current horizontal alignment to a 45° alignment from the lower left to the upper right.

- In the "Orientation" region of the window is the word "Text" with a line after it pointing to a red dot. Place the mouse pointer on the red dot and click and drag the pointer upward until the dot halfway to the top becomes red (see the picture at the left).

- Click the OK button at the bottom of the window.

The years labels should now appear as they did in the previous chart. We will make the other changes using the same dialog windows used to create the previous chart.

- Open the Chart menu on the Menu Bar. Select "Chart Options...."

This is the same dialog window used by Step 3 of the Chart Wizard when you were first creating the chart (page 45).

- Using the Chart Options dialog window, move the chart legend to the bottom, give the chart the title "Civilian Labor Force by Gender," label the X axis "Year," and label the Z axis "1,000's."

The next step is to change the colors used in the bars to gray-scale patterns, which print better on black-and-white printers.

▼Changing the Chart Colors

You can change the color of every element in the chart. There are several ways of doing this, but each way starts the same: you have to select the element you want to change. Color can effectively add interest to a chart. Sometimes when we want to print a chart, however, we have to use a black-and-white printer. We will change the colors of the data series, that is, the bars, so that they will be black and white. In doing this you will learn how to make any color change and even how to add interesting patterns to any element of a chart.

- Place the mouse pointer directly over one of the bars in front representing a data value for females. Let it sit in one spot for a second. A small window will open identifying exactly which data series the pointer is on. If the window does not say "Series 'Females,'" move the pointer slightly to the right or left and wait a second until the window reappears. Do this until the window verifies that it is on a "Female" bar.

- Click the (left) mouse button once. Small squares should appear at corners of several (but not all) of the bars representing data on females. If these squares do not appear or appear only on one bar, place the mouse pointer off the chart, click, and retry this step.

- To the right of the Fill Color button (⬛) on the Formatting Toolbar is a small downward pointing arrow. Click the arrow. A dialog window offering a choice of colors will open below the toolbar.

- Place the mouse pointer on one of the colored squares. After a second you will see a small window with that color's name. Place the mouse pointer on the white-colored square and click the mouse button once.

The Fill Color dialog window will close and the bars representing females will all be white. Let's add a pattern. Excel will let you use very elaborate patterns (and even pictures) to color a chart element. These should be done carefully, however, lest a complex pattern detract from the information the chart is meant to convey.

- Make sure the bars representing females are still selected. If so, once again click the small arrow beside the Fill Color button. Once the dialog window appears, click the Fill Effects... button at the bottom of the window.

- The Fill Effects dialog window has several folder tabs at the top, labeled "Gradient," "Pattern," "Texture," and "Picture." Look at each of them except "Picture," try different selections, and observe the effect each has in the "Sample" area in the bottom-right portion of the dialog window. You can choose only one fill effect. You cannot, for example, combine a pattern and a gradient; you have to choose between them.

- Switch to "Pattern," and choose the pattern that looks like this : ▤. Click the OK button. The window will close and all the bars representing females in the work force will have a horizontal lines pattern.

- Using the method just described, select the bars representing males and change their color to white with no pattern.

How does this chart compare to the stacked-bar chart? From an esthetic point, it is becoming a little busy, owing to the large amount of data presented on the chart. Adding depth to the bars increased the amount of visual clutter—Excel makes these enhancements so easy that there is a tendency to overuse them. It is necessary to devote a full worksheet to this chart. A simpler chart—such as a line chart—could convey the same information in a smaller space

Having the bars side by side obscures the overall growth of the labor force, but makes even clearer that the female component of the labor force has grown faster than the male. A glance at 1948 shows that in that year the number of women in the labor force was less than half the number of men. By 1999, the number of women in the labor force was almost as large as the number of men.

We will continue to modify this chart to explore Excel's abilities.

▼Changing the Chart Title Font

It is easy to make changes to the chart title or to either of the axis titles. These changes include moving the titles, changing the fonts, adding colors, and more. In this example you will increase the font size of the title so that it appears larger.

- Place the mouse button on the chart title ("Civilian Labor Force by Gender") and click the mouse button once. A border will appear around the title indicating that the title is "active": ▱.

- Find the Font Size button on the Formatting Toolbar (12 ▾). Click the arrow on the right side. A drop-down list of numbers will appear. Click the number "20."

The title will become larger. Once a title is active, you also can change its font with the Font button (Arial ▾).

- Note the font currently shown by the Font button ("Arial" in the illustration above.) If it is not Arial, write its name in the margin to the left. Click the arrow on the right side. A drop-down list of fonts available on your computer will open. Experiment with different fonts by clicking another font name and observe the change in the title. Try this for several different fonts and keep the title with the font you think looks best.

Some of the fonts on your computer may be symbol fonts, which do not include the letters of the alphabet. Selecting one of these fonts will make your title unreadable. As will be explained later, you can change the font of a single letter. The symbol fonts have special characters not available in the ordinary alphabetic characters, and by changing the font of a single letter you can include one of these special characters in your text.

- Change the title to a readable alphabetic font.

- With the title still active, place the mouse pointer directly on the title. Notice that the pointer changes to the "I-beam" shape. This lets you directly edit a title by entering and deleting and by highlighting portions of the text. If you highlight one or more letters in the title, the buttons on the Formatting Toolbar will affect only the highlighted letters.

- Use the Italic button (*I*) to change the word "Gender" to italics.

This method of direct editing can be used to change any text not based on worksheet values. This includes all labels and notes.

▼Adding Notes to a Chart

Excel makes it easy to add text to a chart. Such notes are often added to provide information about the source of the data depicted on the chart, or to warn about any problems with the data which might not be immediately obvious to the viewer.

- Click the mouse pointer in the Formula Bar. (Forgot where the Formula Bar is? See page 4.)

- Enter the following text in the Formula Bar (without quotation marks): "Source: Bureau of Labor Statistics." Press the Enter or Return key on your keyboard.

The text you entered in the Formula Bar will appear in a Text Box in the center of your chart. It will be surrounded by a special "active object" border made up of dots: ⬚. It may be a little hard to see clearly because of the bars behind it.

- Place the mouse pointer directly on the border around the Text Box. When it is correctly positioned, it will change to a white arrow with four small black arrows pointing in different directions: ⬩.

- Press and hold the (left) mouse pointer. Drag the text window to a position below the labels on the horizontal axis so that the left side on the "S" in "Source" lines up with the left side of the chart border (as shown below). Move the mouse pointer to a position off the chart and click the mouse pointer to deselect the Text Box.

With the Text Box selected, you can change the font or font size as you did with the chart title, and you can edit the text by placing the mouse pointer on the text and clicking once so that it changes to the "I-beam" shape.

The connection between a chart in an Excel workbook and the data from which that chart is made is dynamic. That is, if the data change, those changes will be immediately reflected in the chart. To see this, do the following:

- Click the worksheet tab titled "Bureau of Labor Statistics Data."

- Change the word in cell B2 from "Males" to "Men," and change the word in cell C2 from "Females" to "Women."

- Return to the chart by clicking the "Chart1" worksheet tab. Notice how the chart legend has changed.

In this example, a change of labels in the data changed the legend in the chart. If, however, the numbers in any of the cells containing data were changed, the height of the bars in the chart would also change.

▼Previewing a Printout

Although there is a Print button, you can often save time and paper by previewing a printout before it is actually printed.

- With the chart displayed on your screen, click the Print Preview button on the Standard Toolbar: 🔍.

The Print Preview screen opens. The Print Preview screen gives you the best representation of how the chart will look when it is printed.

- Place the mouse pointer on the part of the screen showing the chart. Notice the pointer is shaped like a small magnifying glass: 🔍.

- Place the mouse pointer over the chart legend. Click the (left) mouse button. An enlarged view of the area around the mouse pointer will enable you to examine details more closely.

- Notice the mouse pointer has returned to being an arrow. Click the mouse button again, and the view will return to its original magnification.

The print preview screen also allows you to change some of the characteristics of the printout. You can, for example, add text to the very top of the page (in the "header") and the very bottom of the page (the "footer"). You also can control exactly how large the chart is on the printed page, whether it is centered, the width of the margins, and other things. For this chart, it is best to leave these things alone, but there will be times when you will want to make these changes. Let's modify the printout by adding your name to the right side of the header.

- The upper part of the screen has a row of buttons. Click the [Setup...] button. This will open the Page Setup dialog window, which will have several file folder tabs at the top. Each allows you to control different aspects of how the printout will appear.

▼Adding Headers and Footers to a Printout

- Click the "Header/Footer" tab. The dialog window should look like that shown below.

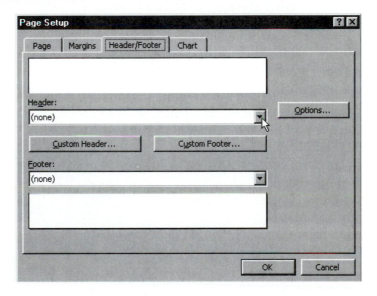

There are two ways of changing the headers and the footers that appear on the printed page. Excel has a number of preset headers and footers, which show such things as today's date and the name of the owner of the Excel software (which was entered when the program was installed). In addition, you can enter a "custom" header or footer, which will allow you to use anything for a header or footer. If, for example, you were submitting a printout from Excel in response to a homework assignment, you might want to have the course name and your name appear in the header.

You can use a preset header by clicking the small arrow to the left of the "Header:" field in the dialog window. (The illustration above shows the mouse pointer on this arrow.)

- Click the arrow allowing you to use a preset header. Scroll down through the list that opens. Click one of the preset headers. Then click the OK button at the bottom of the dialog window.

You should see your choice at the top of the page. The preset headers give you an easy way of selecting one of several useful headers, but sometimes you don't want that restriction. Let's make a header that has only your name on the right side.

- Click the Setup button and return to the "Header/Footer" part of the Setup dialog window.

- Click the [Custom Header...] button on the dialog window. The Header dialog window will open. The window has three fields for you to enter headers for the left, center, and right-hand portions of the header. One or more of these fields will contain text from the preset header you tried above.

- Erase the contents of all non blank fields by clicking the mouse pointer in each field, highlighting all the text in the field, and then pressing the Delete key.

- Click the mouse pointer in the window for the right section and enter your name. The window should look like the picture below (except with your name, of course).

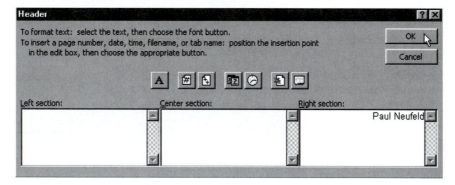

- Click the OK button to return to the Page Setup dialog window. Check the two preview windows to be certain the header is correct. If it is, click the OK button. This will return you to the Print Preview screen, with the new header displayed.

- Click the [Print...] button. One or more dialog windows will open concerning the print. If Windows has been properly set up, just click OK in each of these dialog windows, and your chart will be printed.

- Be sure to save the worksheet in its final form by clicking the Save button.

▼Numerical Summaries

We will look further at graphical data presentations, but first let's consider the issues of numerical summaries, the core of descriptive statistics. There are a couple of approaches to descriptive statistics, the mean-variance approach and the quantile approach. Both approaches are frequently used, but the former is much more important in inferential statistics. One method starts with the *mean,* the other with the *median.*

When a set of numbers is reduced to a single descriptive statistic, that statistic should give the maximum information about the set of numbers. The mean (or arithmetic mean) is commonly known as the *average*, by far the most widely used descriptive statistic. The other commonly used measure of central location is the *median,* which, in a sense, lies in the middle of a set of numbers. Let's use Excel to examine the differences between these two measures. We can use Excel's built-in *functions,* which saves us from having to specify exactly how the statistic is calculated.

- Click the New button on the Standard Toolbar: ▯. A new workbook will open.

- Double click the worksheet tab "Sheet1." The name "Sheet1" will be highlighted, and you will be able to change that name. Change it to "Num Smry."

- Drop the File menu again and click "Save As…." A window will open similar in appearance to the Open File dialog window discussed earlier (page 5). Pay attention to the location where you want the file saved!

Look opposite the words "Save in:." If you have closed Excel since last opening the "Civilian Labor Force" workbook, you probably see ▢ My Documents ▾. Excel will save the workbook in the folder named "My Documents" on the hard drive of the computer you are working on. If you are using your own computer, that's probably a pretty good place. If you are using a lab computer, or any computer you don't necessarily expect to use with this book next time, it would be better to store the file on a diskette.

- Click the arrow on the right side of the field and look for "3½ Floppy (A:)." Select that and be sure you have a diskette in the A drive. If you plan to save the workbook on the same diskette that has the data for this book, save it in the "Chap_2" folder by double clicking on that folder's icon in the large field in the dialog window. After doing that, the field should contain the names of the other workbooks in that folder ("Chapter 2 Data.xls" and "Labor.xls").

- Enter the name "Chapter 2.xls" in the "File Name:" field which is second from the bottom in the dialog window. The name you enter should replace a name like "Book2.xls." Press the Enter or Return key or click the Save button.

- In the first column (cells A1:A5), enter the numbers 10, 20, 30, 40, 50.

- In cell A7, enter the label "Mean" (without quotes).

- In cell A8, enter the label "Median" (without quotes).

- Click on cell B7 to make it active.

▼Using the Formula Palette

In the previous chapter you learned how to directly enter an Excel formula into a worksheet cell. When you need to enter a formula containing one or more functions, Excel's Formula Palette makes the task much easier.

- With cell B7 active, click the Edit Formula button (■) located on the left side of the Formula Bar (page 4). This will open the Formula Palette (shown below).

Function Box— showing most recently used function.

On the left side of the Formula Palette you will see the Function Box with the name of the most recently used function on it ("SQRT" in the picture). If you want to use that function, simply click the button. To use another function, click the small arrow to the right of that name.

- Click the small arrow to the right of the name of the most recently used function. A list will drop down. This list contains the names of other functions of other recently used functions.

- Click the last choice on the list ("More Functions..."). The Paste Function dialog window will open.

The Paste Function dialog window gives you access to all of Excel's built-in functions. The window contains two lists. The one on the left is labeled "Function Category" and the one on the right is labeled "Function Name." Both lists have Scroll Bars that can be used to see choices not immediately visible. When you highlight a function, a description of that function appears in the window. This is very useful when you know what you want done but don't know the name of the Excel function that will do it.

- From the "Function Category" list, choose "Statistical" by placing the mouse pointer on that word and clicking the mouse button once. The word will then appear in white letters with a black background, and the choices in the "Function Name" list will change.

- In the "Function Name" list, choose "AVERAGE." The dialog window should look like the picture below. Notice the brief description of the function whose name has been chosen.

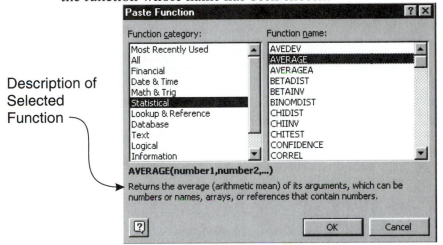

- Click the OK button. The Formula Palette will expand to include a dialog window for the AVERAGE function. Although different functions will have different dialog windows, all have certain features in common, as shown in the picture below.

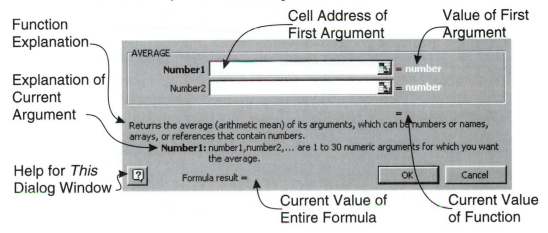

A function will have an *argument* or *arguments* from which it will derive a *result*. (Arguments are also often called *parameters*.) In the case of the AVERAGE function, the numbers to be averaged are the arguments and the value of the average is the result.

The dialog window provides quite a bit of information to help you use the function. Two fields are provided for you to tell Excel the cell addresses (or values) of the arguments. The first one is labeled **Number1** (in bold). The bold indicates that Excel requires you to provide information in this field. The second field, Number2, is not bold. You may use this field, but you don't have to. Usually it won't be used.

The dialog window explains what the function does and also explains the arguments. The argument with the insertion point is the *current* argument; that is the one explained. If you click the mouse pointer in another argument field, the explanation changes to that argument. In the case of AVERAGE, however, both arguments are the same.

Once you have entered values or cell addresses in an argument field, the values Excel will use in the calculations (usually the cell contents) appear to the right of the field. Excel also provides the function result and the formula result. When a formula consists solely of a single function (as in this case), the two will always be the same.

- The cell addresses that we want Excel to average are A1:A5. Unfortunately, the dialog window completely covers them. Move the dialog window by placing the mouse pointer anywhere in the window except a button or argument field, press the (left) mouse button, and drag the window down and to the right so that you can see columns A and B.

- Place the mouse pointer in the "Number1" field and click. An insertion point will become visible in the field.

- Although you could enter the cell addresses directly with the keyboard, use your mouse to perform the operation to "select" cells A1 through A5. When you finish, these cells will have a moving border surrounding them.

- Immediately to the right of the field where you have entered the addresses is a field in which Excel shows the *values* in those cells (10, 20, 30, 40, and 50). Checking this field helps you be sure you have given Excel the correct cell addresses.

- Look at the Function Result. You should see the value 30, which is the average of 10 through 50. Since the formula in cell B7 only has the AVERAGE function, you should also see "30" displayed as the Formula Result.

- Click the OK button at the bottom of the dialog window.

The dialog window will close and cell B7 should show "30." Look at the Formula Bar. It should contain "=AVERAGE(A1:A5)." This is what the Formula Palette has entered into the cell. You could achieve the same result by entering this yourself, but it is usually wise to use the Formula Palette unless you are very familiar with a particular Excel function.

- Use the Formula Palette to have Excel calculate the median of the numbers in cells A1:A5 and place the result in cell B8. The median function is in the same category as the mean function ("Statistical") and has the name MEDIAN. Be sure to check the Formula Bar that an Excel function has been entered. When you finish, your worksheet should look like the picture below:

	A	B
1	10	
2	20	
3	30	
4	40	
5	50	
6		
7	Mean	30
8	Median	30

▼ Exploring the Difference Between the Mean and the Median

For the data originally entered, the mean and median are the same, 30. To understand the differences and the advantages and disadvantages of each of these measures, let's experiment with the types of changes that can cause these two statistics to differ.

- Change the value of the number in cell A5 from 50 to 523. The value of the mean changes to 124.6, but the value of the median does not change.

In a list of five numbers sorted in order, the median will always be the third number. The median divides the list into two equal-sized groups: those that are smaller than the third number (the first two numbers) and those that are greater (the fourth and fifth).

- Change the value of the number in cell A1 from 10 to -100. The mean will fall to 102.6, but the median remains unchanged. The list of numbers is still in order, and 30 is still the third number. There are still two numbers in the list greater than 30 and two numbers smaller than 30.

- Change the value of the number in cell A1 from -100 to 55. In addition to the mean changing, the median also changes—to 40. 30 is still the third number in the list, why has the median changed to 40? With 55 as the first number, the list is no longer in order. Let's resort the list.

▼Using the Sort Buttons

- Select the cell region A1:A5.

- Click the Sort Ascending button: 🔲. The list is put in order, and 40 is now the third number.

If the number of numbers in the list is odd (like five), and the list is put in order, the median will always be the middle number. What if the number of numbers in the list is even?

- Double click cell B7. Change the "A5" in the formula "=AVERAGE(A1:A5)" to "A6."

- Change the "A5" in the formula in cell B8 to "A6."

- Enter the number 610 in cell A6.

The mean showing in cell B7 should now be 213, and the median showing in cell B8 should now be 47.5. The number of numbers in the list is now six. There is no single middle number. Instead, the numbers in positions 3 and 4 are in the middle. In a sense, we can think of the middle as lying halfway between position 3 and position 4. There is, of course, no number, between the 40 in position 3 and the 55 in position 4. Instead, the median is defined as the number *halfway between* the two values 40 and 55. This is the same as the average of 40 and 55:

$$\frac{40+55}{2} = \frac{95}{2} = 47.5$$

- Change the number in cell A6 from 610 to 40. What is the median now?

Remember that the median will be halfway between the number in position 3 and the number in position 4 only if the list is sorted. Putting the value 40 at the end of the list makes the list out of order.

- Resort cells A1:A6 using the method described above (be sure to include A6 in the selected region). Is the median now halfway between the number in position 3 and the number in position 4? If you have done this correctly, both A3 and A4 should have the value 40.

- Change the number in position 4 (cell A4) from 40 to 42. The median is now **41**, the number halfway between 40 and 42.

- Change the number in cell A6 from 523 to 521. The median should still be 41, and the mean should change to 118.

These examples only looked at sets of five and six numbers, but the definition of the median can be applied to any size set. If the set of numbers is ordered from highest to lowest, the median will either be the value of the middle number (if the set has an odd number of numbers) or halfway between the values of the two middle numbers (if the set has an even number of numbers).

▼Measures of Dispersion

If the first and most important descriptive statistic is a measure of location, what is the second most important? For the mean-variance approach, it is the *variance* or *standard deviation* of the data. These are both closely related measures of dispersion—they indicate how far the individual data items are likely to be from the mean. Although Excel has built-in functions to calculate the variance and standard deviation, we will first use Excel to calculate these "by hand" to better see exactly what they measure.

The formulas for the sample variance and standard deviation are:

$$\text{variance} = s^2 = \frac{\sum (x - \bar{x})^2}{n - 1}$$

$$\text{standard deviation} = s = \sqrt{s^2}$$

The instructions below will direct you in the construction of a worksheet to calculate these formulas. Here is the way we will proceed: Column A will contain the x values whose variance and standard deviation we want to determine. Column C will contain the mean of the x's ($\bar{x}$), with the identical value in each cell (column B will be skipped). Each row of column D will contain the difference between the values in the corresponding rows of rows A and B. Thus each cell of column D will contain a value of $x - \bar{x}$. Each row of column E will contain the square of the corresponding row of column D. Thus each cell of E will contain a value of $(x - \bar{x})^2$. The sum of the cells in column E will give $\sum (x - \bar{x})^2$, the numerator of the variance. Dividing this by $n - 1$ will give the variance, and the square root of the result will give the standard deviation.

- Place the mouse pointer on the heading for row 1 and click the mouse button to select the entire first row. (See page 12 for the location of the row heading.)

- Open the Insert menu on the Menu Bar and choose "Rows." This will insert a new row above the numbers on the worksheet, moving down the rows already there. We will put labels in this row to indicate the calculation for each cell's column.

- In cell A1 enter the label "x" (without the quotes).

- Skip cell B1 and enter in cell C1 the label "x bar."

- Enter in cell D1 the label "x-x bar."

- Enter in cell E1 the label "(x-x bar)2."

- Select C2 to make it the active cell and begin entering a formula by typing an equal sign ("=").

- Place the mouse pointer on cell B8 (where the mean is now displayed) and press the mouse button. Look at the Formula Bar. You should see "=B8."

- Before pressing the Enter key, press the F4 (on a PC) or the COMMAND and T key (on a Mac) to make the address absolute. The Formula Bar should show "=$B$8."

- Press the Enter key, and the mean, 118, should be displayed in cell C2. (Note: It is important to follow the instructions in entering a *formula* and not just the *number* result.)

- Copy the formula in cell C2 to cells C3 through C7. The absolute address in cell C2 should copy unchanged, and all the cells in column C should display the same value (118).

Column D will be used to calculate the difference between each of the *x* values in column A and the mean of all of the *x*'s in column C. Enter the formula in cell D2 to calculate the difference between the value of *x* in row 2 (the number in cell A2, which is 20) and the mean of the *x*'s in cell C2.

- Make D2 the active cell, and enter "=" to start a formula. Place the mouse pointer on cell A2 and click the mouse button. Enter a minus sign "-." Place the mouse pointer on cell C2 and click the mouse button. The formula in the cell and on the Formula Bar should be "=A2-C2." Notice that relative addresses are used in this formula.

- Press the Enter key, and cell D2 should show "-98."

- Copy the formula in cell D2 to cells D3 through D7.

Since relative addressing was used in D2, the address will change as it is copied to each cell. In each case, the number will be the difference between the value of x (column A) for that row and the mean of all of the x's (118), which appears in column C of each row. Cell D7, for example, should display 403.

Column E will be used to square the difference between each x value and the mean of the x's.

- Click cell E2. Enter an equal sign to begin a formula. Click cell D2. Enter Excel's symbol to square a value ("^2"). The formula in E2 should be "=D2^2." Press the Enter key and the value 9604 should be displayed.

- Copy the formula in cell E2 to cells E3 through E7.

- Have you remembered to save this worksheet as you work on it? If not, do it now and do it periodically as you continue to change it.

Because relative addressing was used in E2, the displayed values in E3 through E7 should differ, each being the square of the value displayed in the corresponding cell of column D. Cell E7 should display "162409."

The next step is to sum the values in column E. Although not required by the calculations, the values in column D will also be summed.

- In cell C8 enter the label "Sum."

- In cell D9 enter the label "Variance," and in cell D10 enter the label "Standard Deviation," and adjust column D's width.

- Make D8 the active cell. Use the AutoSum button, Σ, to put the sum of cells D2 through D7 in D8. You must press the Enter key for the result to be displayed. The displayed value in D8 should be 0.

- Make E8 the active cell and use the AutoSum button to put there the sum of cells E2 through E7. The displayed value should be "195586."

Cell E8 evaluates $\sum (x - \bar{x})^2$, the numerator of the formula for the variance (page 61). The next step is to divide this by the denominator, $n - 1$. The number of data values (n) in this table is 6, and $n - 1$ therefore is 5.

- Enter the formula in cell E9 that will divide the value in cell E8 by 5. The value displayed in E9 should be "39117.2."

- Enter the formula in cell E10 that will calculate the square root of the value in cell E9. This requires using the built-in square root function. One way of doing this is to use the Formula Palette. The Function

Category is "Math & Trig," and the Function Name is "SQRT." The value displayed in cell E10 should be "197.7807."

Check the appearance of your worksheet with the illustration below. If you spot a difference, do not simply change cells in your worksheet so they contain the numbers displayed by the corresponding cells in the illustration. The x values in the A column are going to be changed. Many of the cells contain formulas, and if you do not enter the correct formulas, the effects of changing the x values will not be correctly calculated.

	A	B	C	D	E
1	x		x bar	x - x bar	(x-x bar)2
2	20		118	-98	9604
3	30		118	-88	7744
4	42		118	-76	5776
5	40		118	-78	6084
6	55		118	-63	3969
7	521		118	403	162409
8	Mean	118	Sum	0	195586
9	Median	41		Variance	39117.2
10				Standard Deviation	197.7807

Notice that the sum of the x-x bar (D) column is 0. Some of the numbers in the column are negative and one is positive. Could this be a coincidence of the particular x values used in this example?

The numbers in column E2:E7 are the squares of those in D2:D7. Squaring a number always produces a positive result, and the numbers in E2:E7 are all positive. As long as any of the numbers in D2:D7 are nonzero, the sum in cell E8 must be a positive number.

If most of the numbers in a set of numbers are close to the mean, the differences between each number and the mean will be relatively small, the square of those differences will also be relatively small, and the variance and standard deviation will also be relatively small. Two different sets of numbers could have the same mean and yet differ in how far the individual numbers tended to be from that mean. Let's consider some examples.

- Enter the following numbers in cells A2:A7:
      80, 85, 90, 100, 110, 135.
  As you enter each number, notice that the worksheet immediately changes the calculated values, including the mean shown in column C. Once all six numbers have been entered, the displayed mean should be "100" and the displayed standard deviation should be "20.24846." Observe the values in column D, which show the difference between each x value and the overall mean.

- Copy the contents of cells A2:E10 to A12:E20. If you have forgotten how to copy a set of cells, review the method given on page 33. You now have two tables to calculate variances and standard deviations. (The formulas in C12:C17 will still equal B8 instead of B18 since the copied references were absolute. As long as B8 equals B18, this will not cause a problem.)

- Now enter the following set of numbers in A2:A7:
  20, 40, 60, 80, 195, 205.
  These numbers have the same mean, 100, but a higher standard deviation, 80.06248. Again observe the values in column D.

- Compare the two sets of numbers in column A in the two tables on your worksheet. Compare the differences in column D between the numbers in each set and the mean.

Both sets of numbers have the same mean, but the top set has greater *dispersion*. All of the numbers in column D in the top set are greater in absolute value than the corresponding numbers in the bottom set. The individual values in the top set tend to be further from the mean than those in the bottom set, and this difference between the two sets is dispersion. The measures of dispersion—variance and standard deviation— are thus larger for the top set than the bottom set.

- Save the worksheet.

▼Copying a Range of Cells to a New Worksheet

In the previous chapter you learned a method for using the mouse to copy or move a range of cells. Although convenient, this method is difficult to use if the range is very large or if there is a need for the move or copy to occur between worksheets. Another procedure is preferable for these situations. This procedure involves use of the *Windows clipboard*, a kind of holding area. You *copy* a selected range of cells to the clipboard and then *paste* the range from the clipboard to a new location. Let's do this in preparation for the use of the Descriptive Statistics Analysis Tool:

- Select cells A1:A7.

- Click the Copy speed button: ⧉. This will copy the contents of the selected cell to the clipboard. Notice that a moving border appears around the selected range.

- Click the worksheet tab "Sheet2."

- Select cell A1 to make it the active cell.

- Click the Paste button: 📋. Cells A1:A7 on this worksheet will now be a copy of those on worksheet "Num Smry."

The procedure to move a range of cells is much the same. Instead of clicking the Copy button after the range of cells is selected, the Cut button, ✂️, would be clicked. Like the Copy button, the Cut button copies the selected range to the clipboard. The Cut button also erases the selected range of cells after the Paste button is clicked.

- Rename "Sheet2" to "Desc Stats Tool" (page 55).

▼Using the Descriptive Statistics Tool

In addition to the built-in functions, Excel contains a very useful set of analysis tools, which includes tools for statistical analyses. The analysis tools generally perform more complex calculations than does any single function. The results provided by an analysis tool are written to more than a single cell. For some of the procedures, the results will fill many cells.

An important difference between the Data Analysis Tools and the built-in functions is that there is no link between the cells containing the input and the output of an Analysis Tool as there is between the cells containing the arguments of a function and the displayed value of the cell with the equation containing the function. If you change the value of the argument cells in a function, the value of the function immediately changes. The output of an Analysis Tool is numbers; these numbers will not change when the values of the analyzed cells change unless the analysis tool is rerun and the new results overwrite the old.

The Analysis Tools are provided by Excel's Analysis ToolPak. Although the Analysis ToolPak is a standard part of Excel, it must be specifically installed. Excel is often set up without the Analysis ToolPak; fortunately, it is easy to add after installation (see Appendix B).

- Open the Tools menu on the Menu Bar. The Menu Bar will partially open. If "Data Analysis…" is not visible, click the two downward pointing carets at the bottom: ⌄. The full menu will open and should appear similar to the picture at the left. If "Data Analysis…" is still not on your Tools menu, follow the instructions given in Appendix B.

- Click "Data Analysis…." The Data Analysis dialog window will open.

- Choose "Descriptive Statistics" by double clicking it or by clicking it once and then clicking the OK button. The Descriptive Statistics dialog window will open.

- The first field in the dialog window is labeled "Input Range," and the window opens with an insertion point in it. Use the mouse to select the cell range A1:A7. A moving border will appear around that range of cells, and the address "$A$1:$A$7" will appear in the field. As an alternative to using the mouse, the cell address A1:A7 could be entered directly into the field.

- Click the mouse pointer in the box beside "Labels in First Row." A checkmark should appear in the box.

This box needs to be clicked because the cell in the first row (A1) contains a label rather than data. If the first field were given the cell range A2:A7, then the box beside "Labels in First Row" should *not* be checked because the first row (cell A2 in this case) contains data, *not* a label. When an Analysis Tool is "told" the first row contains a label, that label will be used in the Tool's output.

At the bottom of the dialog window is a section called "Output Options." Three radio buttons enable you to specify where you want the output placed. "Output Range" results in the output being placed on this worksheet. "New Worksheet Ply" causes Excel to create a new worksheet with the results, and "New Workbook" creates a new workbook with the results.

- Click the Output Range radio button.

- Immediately to the right of the words "Output Range" is an input field. Click the mouse pointer in this field so an insertion point will appear.

- Click cell B1. The address "$B$1" will appear in the "Output Range" field. This establishes the upper left-hand corner of the section of the worksheet where the Tool will place the results.

The four options below the radio buttons let you specify the output you want the tool to produce. At least one of these options must be chosen.

- Click the box beside "Summary statistics" at the bottom of the dialog window. This option will cause the tool to produce what we generally think of as descriptive statistics.

When you have finished with the dialog window, it should look like the illustration below.

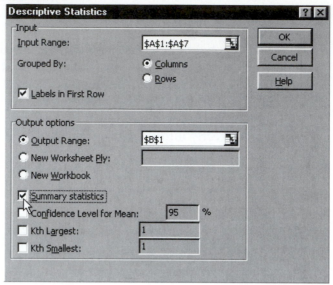

- Click the OK button.

The results of the Descriptive Statistics Tool will be in columns B and C and in rows 1 through 15.

When an Excel Analysis Tool finishes, the region where the results are placed will be selected. The Analysis Tool does not adjust the width of the columns so that you can see all of the labels.

- Make sure the region containing the output is still selected.

- Open the Format menu on the Menu Bar.

- On the drop-down menu, click "Column." A cascading menu will appear.

- Click "AutoFit Selection" as shown in the picture below. The widths of columns B and C will automatically adjust.

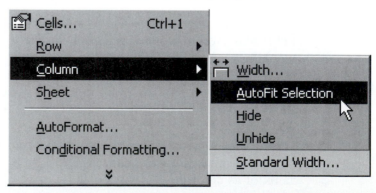

An alternative to using "AutoFit Selection" on the Menu Bar would be to double click the border between columns B and C in the column headers. Adjusting the columns is always needed after using an Analysis Tool, and sometimes more than one column will need to be adjusted. In those cases, using "AutoFit Selection" will adjust all the columns at once.

- Click any visible cell on the worksheet to deselect the region with the results.

As you can see, the Descriptive Analysis Tool automatically provides a number of descriptive statistics.

- Compare the mean, variance (called "Sample Variance"), and standard deviation with those on the "Num Smry" worksheet. Do they agree? (They should.)

- Click the "Desc Stats Tool" worksheet tab to make that the active worksheet.

- Change the "205" in cell A7 to "305." Do any of the descriptive statistics provided by the Analysis Tool change?

As discussed earlier, no link is maintained between the input of an Analysis Tool and its output. Thus when one of the data items changes, the Analysis Tool output is not automatically updated. To update the output of the Analysis Tool, it would have to be rerun.

Let's try the Descriptive Statistics Tool on another set of data.

- Open the workbook "Chapter 2 Data.xls," which is located on the data diskette in the "Chap_2" folder.

This workbook contains several worksheets. The first provides data by state on the median value of owner-occupied houses. [Data are from U.S. Bureau of the Census, *Statistical Abstract of the United States: 1994* (114th edition.), p. 736.]

- Select the "Housing" worksheet.

- Use the Descriptive Statistics Tool to summarize the data on the median value of owner-occupied homes (in column B). Have Excel put the results in the region beginning with cell C1. Don't forget to use "Format...Column...AutoFit Selection" to adjust the column widths.

- If you have done this correctly, the mean should be 84209.80392, while the median is 68900.

Why is the median so much less than the mean in this case? The average value for the state medians is over $84,000, but only half the values exceed $68,900. Consider what must be true about the set of numbers for such a difference to exist. Answering this question requires understanding more about the distribution of data than location and dispersion. A graphical approach can provide insight.

▼Histograms

One of the best ways to graphically describe a set of data is with a histogram chart. Many statistics texts describe a number of graphical techniques for describing data, but many of them, including stem-and-leaf charts and frequency polygons, are simply variations of histograms.

A histogram groups data into a relatively small number of intervals. A vertical bar chart shows the number of observations in each interval. Let's use Excel to produce a histogram chart of the data on median house value by state. We first must determine the intervals. Although Excel can automatically determine the intervals into which the data are grouped, doing that step manually may produce a better histogram.

From the descriptive statistics, we can tell that the minimum value in the data is 45200 and the maximum is 245300. The range is $245,300 - 45,200 = 200,100$. The intervals should be equally sized, but Excel's histogram tool always makes the first and last intervals open-ended (no minimum for the first, no maximum for the last). If eight intervals were used, each would be slightly over 25,000 ($^{200,100}\!/_8$). The intervals would be those shown in the table below.

Interval	More than...	But not more than ...
1	45,000	70,000
2	70,000	95,000
3	95,000	120,000
4	120,000	145,000
5	145,000	170,000
6	170,000	195,000
7	195,000	220,000
8	220,000	245,000

Since the largest value in this set of data is 245,300, it lies just above the upper bound of the largest interval. Since the difference is slight, including this value in the largest interval will bend the rules only slightly. Since

Excel makes the last interval open, we will simply make that interval contain all data values greater than or equal to 220,000.

For the Histogram tool to use the intervals (Excel calls them *bins*) that we have selected, the upper bounds of each interval, except the last, must be entered into a section of cells somewhere on the worksheet. Let's use the vertical section beginning with cell C18.

- Enter the label "Interval Upper Bound" in cell C18. Enter the values 70000 in cell C19 and 95000 in cell C20.

These are the upper bounds of the first two intervals.

- Use Excel's "fill" capabilities (see page 30) to complete the rest of the series (95000, 120000, 145000, 170000, 195000, 220000) in cells C20:C25. These values correspond to the values in the right-most column of the table above except that the last one is omitted.

Now you are ready to use the Histogram tool.

- Open the "Tools" menu on the Menu Bar and select "Data Analysis...."

- When the Data Analysis dialog window opens, select "Histogram." The Histogram dialog window will open.

- The first field of the dialog window is "Input Range," and an insertion point should already be in that field. You need to enter here the cell addresses that contain the state median housing values. Because of the length of the list (greater than can be shown on the screen without scrolling), you may find it awkward to use the normal mouse actions. Let's look at an alternative method for selecting a large number of cells.

▼ Selecting a Range of Cells with the Keyboard

It is possible to use the normal technique of selecting a range of cells by placing the mouse cursor on the first one, pressing and holding the mouse button, and dragging down the column. If you move the pointer below the last visible cell in the column, the worksheet will begin to scroll up. If you move the pointer back up into the cell area, the scrolling will stop. This scrolling can be hard to control, however.

When selecting large regions, it is often easier to use the keyboard than the mouse. Once a cell is selected (by any means) the selected region can be expanded by pressing a Shift key while using the cursor (arrow) keys. Here are step-by-step instructions for this case:

- Select *any* cell in column B. That cell's address will appear (as an absolute address) in the dialog window's "Input Range" field.

- Press the End key on your keyboard. Release the End key and press the up-arrow cursor key. The worksheet will scroll up, cell B1 will have a moving border, and $B$1 will appear in the "Input Range" field.

- Press and hold a Shift key on your keyboard. Press and release the End key on your keyboard. While holding a Shift key, also press the down-arrow key. The selected region will immediately move down to include all cells until an empty cell is reached. The cell addresses $B$1:$B$52 should appear in the dialog window's "Input Range" field.

The region is now selected, and we can turn our attention to the rest of the dialog window.

- The next field in the dialog window is "Bin Range." Click the mouse pointer in this field so that it will have an insertion point. The cell addresses that should go in the field are those containing the interval boundaries: C18:C25.

- Click "Labels" so a check appears in the small box.

Notice that when "Labels" is checked, Excel expects to find labels in both the "Input Range" and the "Bin Range." If labels are not included, the first value in the range is interpreted by Excel as a label rather than as data. It is not included in the determination of the histogram.

- Click the mouse pointer on the Output Range radio button and then click the mouse pointer in the "Output Range" field. Click the mouse pointer in cell C27 or enter that address directly in the field.

- Select "Chart Output" at the bottom of the dialog window by clicking the square just to the left of those words so that a check appears.

The histogram dialog window should look like that which appears on the next page. If you have entered any cell addresses directly, it is OK if they appear as relative rather than absolute addresses.

- Click the OK button.

You may need to scroll your worksheet in order to completely view the output. Two types of output will appear: a table and a chart. Both provide the same information; the chart is simply a graphic representation of the table. It's hard to clearly see the bars in the histogram because Excel has made the chart too short. Let's make it taller.

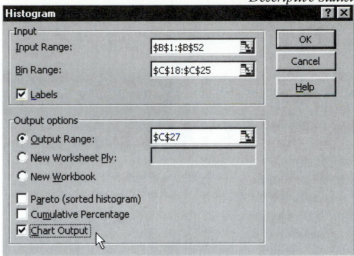

- Select the chart by placing the mouse pointer inside the chart on the white border away from any objects and click the (left) mouse button *once*. Small squares (called "handles") should appear at each of the four corners and in the middle of each of four sides. The one at the top of the chart should look like this: ▬█▬ . These handles confirm that the chart is selected and enable you to change its size.

- Place the mouse pointer directly over the handle on the middle of the top border of the chart. When it is in the correct position, the mouse pointer will change shape to an arrow with two heads pointing up and down: ⬍ .

- With the mouse pointer in the double-arrow shape, press the (left) mouse button and drag the mouse pointer up by four or five cell heights. You should see the boundary around the chart move with the mouse pointer.

- Release the mouse pointer. You have resized the chart to make it taller. It should look like the picture at the top of the next page.

Handles on the side of an object allow you to increase the object's size in only one direction. If you drag a corner handle, however, you can simultaneously make an object (like this chart) both taller and wider.

This histogram shows data that are *right-* or *positively skewed*. Most of the data are close to the lower bound, but there are a number of extremely high values. From the output of the Descriptive Statistics Tool, we know that the median for the data is $68,900. Since this value lies within the interval represented by the first bar, that interval must contain more than half of all state median housing values.

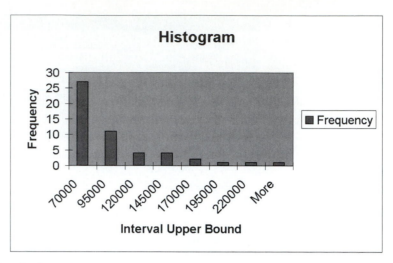

▼Printing the Worksheet

The process of printing a worksheet is very similar to that of printing a chart. If the amount of information on a worksheet is not too great, it is often useful to have Excel print the entire worksheet on a single sheet of paper. Excel will then reduce the size of charts and print so it will fit on a page. To avoid having Excel reduce things until they are too small, it is useful to have the information on the worksheet in as compact a rectangular area as possible.

To better examine the layout of the worksheet, you can have Excel reduce the size at which things on the worksheet are displayed on your monitor.

- If the chart is still selected (has handles), click the mouse pointer on any worksheet cell of the chart to deselect it.

- On the Standard Toolbar, click the down-arrow to the right of the Zoom control 100% ▾. A list of Zoom factors will open.

- Click on 75%. If you cannot see the entire list of states, change the Zoom factor to 50% or 25%. Do not worry if the words or numbers become unreadable.

In order to make the information on the worksheet more compact, you should move the histogram chart down and to the left. First "select" the chart.

- Place the mouse pointer approximately in the border of the histogram chart (not on a chart object) and click the mouse button once so that the handles appear in the chart's border.

- With the mouse pointer in the approximate center of the chart, press and hold the (left) mouse button. You can now drag an outline of the chart to a new location. When you release the mouse button, the chart will move to the new position.

- Move the chart down and to the left as shown in the illustration below.

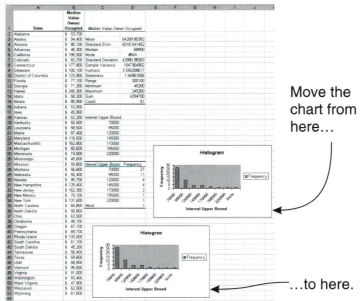

Move the chart from here…

…to here.

- Deselect the chart by clicking any worksheet cell.

- Open the File menu on the Menu Bar. Select "Page Setup."

- When the Page Setup dialog window opens, click the "Page" folder tab.

- You have a choice between two orientations: *Portrait* and *Landscape.* You should choose Portrait whenever the material you want printed will better fit the page in a vertical orientation than a horizontal orientation. That's the case here, so click the Portrait radio button.

- In the "Scaling" section, click the radio button to the left of "Fit to," and be sure the numbers in the following fields are both 1 (for pages wide and tall). This tells Excel to reduce the print so that everything will fit on one sheet. The dialog window should look like the picture at the top of the next page.

- Click the "Header/Footer" folder tab, put your name in the header, and eliminate the footer. Click the OK button.

- Click the Print Preview button to check what the printout will look like. You should see all of the state names (although they may be un-

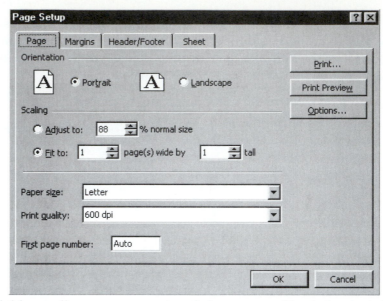

readably small on your screen) and the output of both Analysis Tools (including the histogram chart) on a single page.

- If the Print Preview checks out, click the Print button at the top of the Print Preview screen.

- When your screen returns to the worksheet, change the Zoom factor back to 100%.

Look at the table produced by the Histogram tool in your printout (cells C27:D35 of your worksheet). This table shows the number of observations in each interval. The first interval contains 27 observations, confirming that over half are in this interval. The extremely large values in the last interval increase the value of the mean but not the median. Finding that the mean is larger than the median (as in these data) is an indication of positive skew. Notice that the output of the Descriptive Statistics Tool includes a measure for skewness (1.84961606). For positively skewed data like these, the skewness measure will be positive.

▼Sorting the Data

The construction of the histogram will be clearer if you examine the state median housing data sorted by value. This is easy for Excel. Recall that we used the Sort button earlier. Now we look at another method of sorting which gives us a little more control than the Sort button.

- Select the range of cells including both the state names and the median housing values. Because of the amount of data, this is best done by using the keyboard method, the same as was done on page 71 but for a slightly different range. First select cell A1 by clicking the mouse pointer on that cell. Next, hold down a Shift key and press the right-arrow key once. This will extend the selected region one cell to the right to include cell B1. Continue pressing a Shift key and press in sequence the End key and the down-arrow key. The selected region will include all the cells in columns A and B down to the bottom of the list, row 52.

- With the region A1:B52 selected, open the Data menu on the Menu Toolbar and choose "Sort." The Sort dialog window will open.

The Sort dialog window enables you to specify multiple sort keys. In this case only one is needed. Excel will sort the entire selected region. The purpose of the dialog window is to tell Excel which column to sort the region by. The first column contains the state names and the second contains the median housing values. Sorting the region by the first column would alphabetize by state name (which is how it is currently ordered). Instead, we want it sorted by the second column.

At the bottom of the dialog window you will find two radio buttons allowing you to choose either Header Row or No Header Row. This determines whether the dialog window refers to the column by the column's letter (A or B) or the column label in the first row ("State" or "Median Value Owner Occupied").

- Select the Header Row radio button.

- Click the small down-arrow to the right of the top "Sort By" field. In the list that opens, choose the column containing the median state housing value. Your dialog window should look like the picture at the top of the next page.

- Click the OK button. Excel will sort the data. Scroll your worksheet so that you can examine the top of the list (cells A2 and B2 at the top of your screen).

Scroll down until you find a state whose median housing value exceeds $70,000. You have to go pretty far down in the list until you reach New Mexico, which has a median of $70,100. Continue scrolling down until you reach a state with a median value over $95,000. You need only look down a few states before reaching Vermont, whose median value is $95,500. Notice how few states you need to go down before reaching the next interval boundary, $120,000. Each $25,000 increase in median housing value requires moving down fewer states in the list. This confirms what the histogram tells us: Although the range of median housing

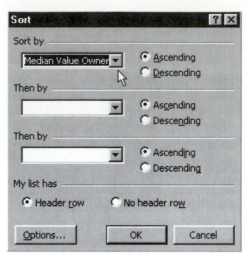

values is quite large, most of them are concentrated near the bottom, below $70,000.

▼Let Excel Choose the Intervals

It's much quicker and easier to let Excel choose the interval widths than to determine them yourself, but Excel's choices are often not ideal. Let's look at this with a different set of data.

- Click the "Deterg" worksheet tab to bring it to the front and make it active. This worksheet contains information on the cost per load of a number of different liquid and powder laundry detergents available for sale at a single supermarket.

- Sort the data on the worksheet (A1:C33) so that the detergent with the lowest cost per load is at the top and the one with the highest cost per load is at the bottom. First use the keyboard method to select the region. Once selected, sort it by choosing "Data...Sort..." on the Menu Bar.

- Choose "Data Analysis" from the Tools menu on the Menu Bar and select "Histogram."

- When the Histogram dialog window opens, enter the locations of the Cost/Load data in the input range, click the "Labels" and "Chart Output" boxes, and specify that the output should be placed beginning in cell D2. Clear the "Bin Range" field so that it is blank. The dialog window should look like the picture at the top of the next page.

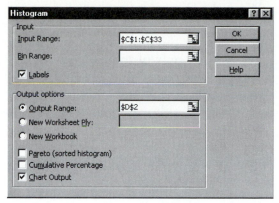

- Click the OK button. The results should look like this:

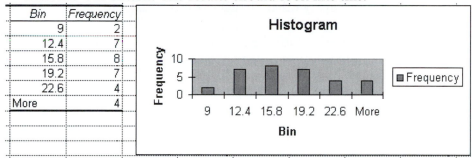

Bin	Frequency
9	2
12.4	7
15.8	8
19.2	7
22.6	4
More	4

- Compare this histogram with that for the housing data.

In this chart, most of the observations are in the middle rather than close to the lowest or highest values. This is reflected in the chart by the fact that the tallest bars are in the center rather than on one side. This distribution is less skewed, or more *symmetric,* than that of the housing data. If a distribution were perfectly symmetric, and you were to draw a vertical line in the center of the histogram chart, the portion of the chart to the left of the line would be a mirror image of that to the right. In such a case, the mean and the median would be the same value.

- Use the Descriptive Statistics Tool to calculate descriptive statistics for the detergent cost/load data. Have the output placed in the region beginning with D10. Adjust the column widths so the output is fully visible.

How do the mean and median compare? The median for these data is 15 while the mean is a bit more than 16.2. These are much closer together, although the fact that the mean is still greater than the median indicates some positive skew. This is confirmed by the positive coefficient of skewness, which is slightly over 0.50. Although positive, this is less than that of the housing data, which was just under 1.85. Perfectly symmetric data would have a skewness coefficient of zero, and negatively skewed data would have a negative coefficient of skewness.

When the Histogram tool chooses its own intervals, it forms six intervals, which is a reasonable number, but may not be the most logical grouping for the problem at hand. Unfortunately, the first interval usually consists only of those observations with the minimum value in the data set. For continuous data only one observation may have the minimum value. Excel's self-chosen first interval will thus often have only one observation, although there were two observations for these data.

▼Embellishing the Histogram Charts

You have already learned how to increase the height of the chart. There are many other changes you can make to the appearance of the chart. To change a chart element, you must first "activate" that element by clicking on it with the mouse pointer. When an element has been activated, it will be surrounded by an active mode boundary: ⬚⬚⬚.

- Place the mouse pointer on the title of the chart ("Histogram") and click the (left) mouse button once. An active mode boundary will surround it. When you move the mouse pointer into that boundary, it will change to an insertion point, allowing you to change the title.

- Change the title of the histogram chart to "Distribution of Detergent Costs per Load" (without the quotation marks).

- Change the horizontal axis label from "Bin" to "Cost per Load."

Clicking on other parts of the chart will enable you to make changes to those parts. Double clicking will typically cause a menu to appear, permitting you to change such characteristics as color.

If you print from Excel while a chart is selected (or an object on it is activated), only the chart will print, and it will fill the output page just as it did when the chart was placed on its own worksheet. This does not necessarily mean that the printed chart will be formatted exactly the same as it would have been had it been on its own worksheet. Printing a small chart that shares a worksheet, for example, often results in large letters in axis labels and titles.

When a chart has been selected, or an object on the chart has been activated, the Menu Bar items change. They become the same as they did when a chart was on a separate worksheet.

- With the histogram chart selected, open the Chart menu on the Menu Toolbar. Choose "Chart Type...." The Chart Type dialog window will open. Click the "Standard Types" folder tab. In the "Chart type" field choose "Line." In the "Chart sub-type" field, select the option in the upper left-hand corner. Click OK.

- Make the chart taller.

- Eliminate the legend by clicking on it (selecting it) and then pressing the Delete key.

- Make the chart wide enough so that the title is on a single line

- Add the note "Frequency Polygon Chart" to the top of the chart below the title (like a subtitle). Your chart should look like the picture below.

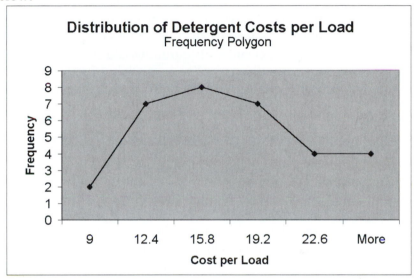

- Print the frequency polygon with your name on the right side of the header and nothing in the footer.

Your histogram chart has become a frequency polygon chart. It displays the same information as a histogram chart but in the form of a line chart rather than a bar chart. Some statisticians prefer a frequency polygon chart because it is more like the density function charts used to display distributions. We will examine these types of charts in later chapters.

▼Run Charts

The last descriptive statistic we will consider in this chapter is the run chart, which has important application to quality control. Although a run chart is a simple plot of a set of data, it incorporates additional information: order or time. Let's look at an example.

- Click the "Wait" worksheet tab to bring it into view.

This worksheet shows the waiting time spent by each of 36 patients in a physician's office on a single day. The data are ordered so that the first number represents the waiting time of the first patient. The second number is that of the second patient, and so on.

Suppose that we want to determine whether or not there appears to be a problem with the process that this physician uses to schedule his patients. Let's first use the tools already discussed to examine this issue.

- Use the Descriptive Statistics Tool to produce descriptive statistics on patient waiting time.

The mean waiting time for patients in this office is a little over 24.5 minutes, which may indicate a problem. The slightly lower median (23 minutes) suggests a slight positive skew, which is confirmed by the skewness coefficient. A histogram would show that waiting time was approximately symmetric, as might be expected. None of this establishes clearly whether or not there is a problem. Let's see what can be learned from a run chart.

- From the Menu Bar, open the Insert menu. Choose "Chart...." Note that this has exactly the same effect as clicking the Chart Wizard button on the Standard Toolbar.

- In the dialog menu for the first step of the Chart Wizard, choose "XY (Scatter)" as the "Chart Type." Under "Chart sub-type," select the one that marks each point with a dot and connects them with a line (as shown below). Notice that the sample plots show plots with two data series. For the run chart discussed here, only one data series (patient waiting time) will be shown. Click the Next button.

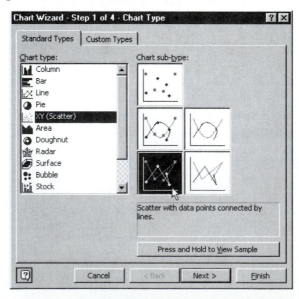

- The second-step dialog window is where you give Excel the location of the data to be plotted. Excel will first try to guess, which is sometimes correct.

- Be sure the window correctly shows whether the data are in rows or columns. If you are not sure, try one and look at the sample chart. The correct run chart should have only one plot on the chart. Click the Next> button.

Step 3 allows you to set certain options. We will change the titles, add axis labels, and remove the legend. A legend is useful only if a chart has more than one data series and more than one line. In such a case, a legend would tell which line went with which data series. Since only one data series is used in this case, the legend should be eliminated.

- Select the "Titles" folder tab. Change the chart title to "Patient Run Chart" (without the quotation marks). Label the horizontal axis "Patient Number" and the vertical axis "Waiting Time."

- Select the "Legend" folder tab. Set it so that no legend is showing. Click Next>.

- In the last dialog window, have the chart placed by itself on a new worksheet titled "Run Chart." Click the Finish Button. Your chart should look like the one below.

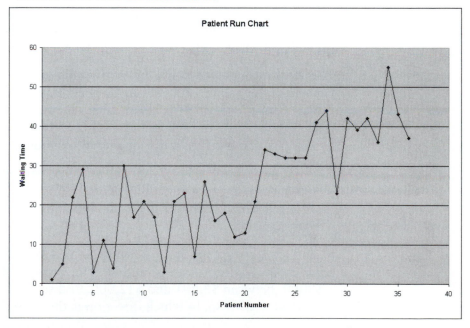

What does the run chart tell us that was not apparent from simply looking at the data? The large up-and-down movements of the graph suggest the physician often spends an amount of time with a patient that differs substantially from the amount of time scheduled for that patient. In addition, there is an overall pattern to the graph—as the graph moves to the right it has a tendency to move up. This indicates that the average wait for patients seen later in the day is greater than the average wait for patients seen earlier in the day. This suggests that the physician tends to spend a longer time with a patient than the scheduled time. Perhaps too many patients are being scheduled each day.

Univariate (one-variable) descriptive statistics does not reveal the problems with patient waiting time that are clear from the run chart. This is because a run chart shows a relationship between time or sequence (first, second, etc.) and the value of the variable to be analyzed while ordinary descriptive statistics cannot show this relationship. Run charts are used as an aid to understanding a repeated *process*. The manufacturing of a product is such a process, and run charts can be an important tool in quality control for identifying and diagnosing problems. A problem should be suspected whenever the run chart shows a clear pattern, such as a tendency to trend upwards (or downwards). Excessive variation can also be evidence of a problem.

▼Exercises

1. Use Excel to produce a frequency polygon chart of patient waiting time. Does the picture of the distribution appear symmetrical? Print the polygon chart with your name on the page header.

2. The worksheet named "GDP per cap" provides an international comparison of per capita GDP valued by purchasing power parity for OECD countries in 1991. This measures the value of economic production per person in each country adjusted for differences in prices by country and is an indicator of average economic well-being by country.

   • Sort the data by per capita GDP from lowest to highest so you can easily tell which countries are at the top and which are at the bottom.

   • Produce a histogram chart showing the number of countries with per capita GDP between $0 and $4,000, between $4,001 and $8000, between $8,001 and $12,000, and so on. Do the data appear skewed? If so, in which direction is the skew?

   • Calculate descriptive statistics for these data. Which statistics, if any, confirm the judgment you made above about direction of skew?

- Print the worksheet on a single sheet of paper showing the list of countries and GDP per capita sorted by GDP per capita, the descriptive statistics, and the histogram chart. Put your name in the header at the top of the page.

3. Amalgamated Hardware is a producer of specialty bolts for the automotive and aircraft industries. One of its products is a 20-centimeter high-strength bolt. The process used to manufacture that bolt is designed to produce bolts whose average length is 20 centimeters. The length of the bolts is carefully controlled, but some process variation is impossible to remove. When the process is operating normally, this variation is completely random. Amalgamated calculates the average length of a sample of the bolts produced each day. The worksheet "Bolt Length" contains the data for 100 consecutive samples. The average of these 100 numbers is 20.0063, which seems high to management.

   - Investigate the source of any possible problem by producing a run chart of the sample lengths. Do you see any pattern in the run chart that might indicate an equipment problem or other problem? If so, what is it?

Chapter 3

Discrete Random Variables and Probability Distributions

Random variables and their probability distributions are the basis of inferential statistics. In this chapter you will explore the relationship between the distribution of a random variable and the distribution of data. You will start with one kind of random variable—discrete—and one way of representing a probability distribution—a table. In later chapters you will learn how to work with discrete probability distributions represented as mathematical formulas or Excel formulas and how to work with continuous random variables. Understanding random variables and probability distributions will help you make sense of sampling distributions.

▼Probability Distributions

The value of a random variable can never be known in advance of its selection. If you toss a die, for example, you can't be certain before the toss what number will come up (assuming the die is not loaded!). You do, however, know the *set of possible values*. The toss of a die must result in an integer value between 1 and 6. The probability distribution of a random variable gives you this information and also provides you with the probability associated with each possible value.

Sometimes random variables have outcomes that are not quantitative. The outcome of a coin toss, for example, is heads or tails, not a number. The gender of a newborn child is also not a number. These nonquantitative outcomes must be represented as numbers to be usable in Excel. Usually, any integers will suffice, such as 0 for tails and 1 for heads.

Suppose your statistics professor assigns grades purely by chance. You have no idea what your grade will be, but you do know the probability distribution that is shown in the table on the next page:

Grade	Probability
4	.10
3	.20
2	.35
1	.25
0	.10

Remember that Excel's operations require the values of random variables to be numeric. Thus rather than represent the grades as A, B, C, D, and F, they are represented by integers with 4 for A, 3 for B, and so on.

- Start Excel with a new blank workbook.

- Enter this table into an Excel worksheet using columns C and D and rows 1 through 6. Put the labels "Grade" and "Probability" in cells C1 and D1, respectively. Your worksheet should look like the picture below.

	A	B	C	D
1			Grade	Probability
2			4	0.1
3			3	0.2
4			2	0.35
5			1	0.25
6			0	0.1

- Open the File menu on the Menu Bar and choose "Save As...." If you plan to use a diskette, select "3½ Floppy (A:)." Otherwise choose the folder where the data files for this book are located. When the dialog window shows the folders for each chapter, create a new folder by clicking the Create New Folder button at the top of the dialog window: 🗁. This will open the New Folder dialog window. Give the new folder the name "Chap_3" and Click OK. Double click the icon for the new folder so the workbook will be saved in it. Give the new file the name "Chapter 3.xls."

- An important property of a probability distribution is that the probabilities must all sum to 1.0. Check that this is true in your worksheet by selecting cell D7 and clicking the AutoSum button: Σ. Excel should respond by showing a formula to sum cells D2 through D6.

- Press the Enter key and the number 1 should appear in cell D7, confirming that the sum of the probabilities is 1.

▼Mean and Variance of a Probability Distribution

Let's have Excel calculate the mean and variance of this distribution. We will then explore the *meaning* of the mean and variance of a probability distribution. The formula for the expected value or mean of a probability distribution is

$$E(x) = \mu = \sum (x \cdot P(x))$$

where P(x) is the probability of the random variable having the value x.

When calculating a formula like this, it is often best to have Excel perform the calculations on the expression within the summation $(x \cdot P(x))$ for each x value and then sum the result of these calculations across all x values. This is the procedure used to calculate the variance and standard deviation of a sample in Chapter 2. This will be done by having cell E2 contain the product of the value of x in cell C2 and the value of P(x) in cell D2. Cells E3 through E6 will have the corresponding products for the values in those rows. The sum of these products will be the expected value.

- To document what you will be doing, enter the label "Mean" in cell E1 and the word "Variance" in cell F1.

The mean or expected value will be calculated in column E and the variance in column F.

- Select cell E2.

- Type an equal sign (=) to let Excel know that you are entering a formula.

- Move the mouse cursor to cell C2 and click the left mouse button. That cell address (C2) should appear after the equal sign in the formula in cell E2. Notice that this is a *relative* address, not an *absolute* address, since there are no $ signs in the address.

- Enter the Excel multiplication symbol (*), and then point to cell D2 and click the left mouse button. The formula appearing in cell E2 should be "=C2*D2."

- Press the Enter key or click the checkmark in the Formula Bar, and the formula should be replaced by its value, 0.4.

The next step is to copy this formula to the other cells in column E.

- Use the mouse cursor to select cell E2.

- Position the mouse cursor on the fill handle and drag the fill handle downward (while pressing the left mouse button) until the selection border surrounds cells E2 through E6.

- Release the mouse button.

Each cell in the selected region of column E should contain the product of the numbers in columns C and D for that row. Check this by selecting cell E5 and checking the Formula Bar. The formula that appears should be "=C5*D5."

The last step is to calculate the sum of the values in cells E2 through E6.

- Select cell E7 and use the AutoSum (Σ) button to have Excel automatically enter the formula summing cells E2 through E6. Press the Enter key, and the expected value of the probability distribution (1.95) should appear in cell E7.

We will explore the meaning of a probability distribution's expected value below. First, let's use Excel to calculate the variance of this probability distribution.

The formula for the variance of a probability distribution is the following:

$$\text{VAR}(x) = \sigma^2 = \sum (x - \mu)^2 \, P(x)$$

The structure of this formula is similar to that of the expected value—a summation of separate terms for each value of x. We will use the same strategy to calculate the formula as we used in that case. In cells F2 through F6 Excel will calculate the value of the expression within the summation (Σ) for the value of x for that row. In F2 we will put the formula to calculate this expression for $x = 4$. That formula will then be copied to cells F3 through F6, and cell F7 will sum these values.

- Select cell F2 and type an equal sign followed by a left parenthesis.

- Click the mouse pointer on cell C2 (the value of x for that row), and "C2" should appear after the left parenthesis in the formula in cell F2.

- Type a minus sign and click cell E7. Cell E7 contains the expected value, the "μ" in the formula. Since we will want to copy the formula in this cell to the cells below E2, this address must be made an absolute rather than a relative address. Do this by pressing the F4 function key once. This should change the E7 in the formula to $E$7.

- Type a right parenthesis.

The expression within the parenthesis, "=(C2-$E$7)," corresponds to the "$(x - \mu)$" in the formula for the variance.

- To square the quantity in parentheses, enter "^2" after the right parenthesis.

The formula now corresponds to the expression "$(x - \mu)^2$" in the formula for the variance. All that remains is to multiply this by the probability of x, $P(x)$.

- Enter the multiplication symbol, *, and click cell D2. The formula in cell F2 should be "=(C2-$E$7)^2*D2." Press Enter or click the checkmark in the Formula Bar and the value "0.42025" will appear in the cell.

- Copy the formula in cell F2 to cells F3 through F6.

- Check to be sure that the copying is correct by examining the value of cell F5. It should be "0.225625." If this is not the value, check the Formula Bar or double click cell F2 to see the formula in the cell. It should be "=(C5-$E$7)^2*D5."

If this is not the formula in cell F5, you probably entered the wrong formula in cell F2. Go back to cell F2 and be sure the formula there is "=(C2-$E$7)^2*D2," then recopy it to cells F3 through F6.

- Use the AutoSum button to place the sum of the values of cells F2 through F6 in cell F7. This is the variance of the distribution.

If you have done everything correctly, your spreadsheet should look like the picture below:

	A	B	C	D	E	F
1			Grade	Probability	Mean	Variance
2			4	0.1	0.4	0.42025
3			3	0.2	0.6	0.2205
4			2	0.35	0.7	0.00088
5			1	0.25	0.25	0.22563
6			0	0.1	0	0.38025
7					1.95	1.2475

Thus the mean of the probability distribution is 1.95 and the variance is 1.2475. But what is the connection between the mean and variance of a probability distribution and the mean and variance of a set of data? Let's examine that relationship.

▼ Probability Distributions and Data

If we choose one student at random from the class whose grades are described by the probability distribution, there is no way we can know for certain what grade that student will receive. If, however, many students are chosen, the distribution of those grades should be similar to that given by the probability distribution. We can see this by taking advantage of Excel's ability to choose random variables from a probability distribution, a capability provided by Excel's Analysis ToolPak.

- Select the Tools menu from the Menu Bar. Choose "Data Analysis..." from the menu that opens.

- Choose "Random Number Generation" from the list in the Data Analysis dialog window. You may need to scroll the list down before you see this choice. The Random Number Generation dialog window will open.

Let's start by having Excel draw one random number from the probability distribution on our worksheet.

The first two fields in the dialog window for which we must provide information are labeled "Number of Variables" and "Number of Random Numbers." You must enter a number in each field. The labeling of many of these fields is confusing. Despite the way the fields are labeled, the total number of random numbers Excel will draw is the *product* of the numbers you enter in these two fields.

Excel will put the random numbers in a rectangular array on your worksheet. The value you put in the "Number of Variables" field determines how many columns Excel will use for the random numbers. The value you put in the "Number of Random Numbers" field determines the number of rows Excel will use. The names Excel uses are consistent with standard statistical practice, where data are usually arranged in rectangular arrays with each observation in a separate row and each variable in a separate column.

- Since our first use of the random number generator will be to generate only one random number, enter the number 1 in both the "Number of Variables" field and the "Number of Random Numbers" field.

The third field in the dialog window is labeled "Distribution." It is here that you tell Excel what kind of random number you wish generated.

- Click on the small downward-pointing arrow, ▼, beside the "Distribution" field.

This will open a list of distributions.

- Choose the "Discrete" distribution.

The distribution you choose determines which fields appear in the dialog window. When "Discrete" is chosen, the fourth field in the dialog window is labeled "Value and Probability Input Range." In this field you must put the cell addresses of the probability distribution table showing each possible value for the random variable and the probability of that value.

- Click the mouse pointer in the field labeled "Value and Probability Input Range." An insertion point should appear in the field.

- Use the mouse or the keyboard to enter the cell addresses for columns C and D, rows 2 through 6. Note that you do not include the column labels in the first row. If you use the mouse, the cell addresses will appear as an absolute address, but you may enter a relative address with the keyboard.

- Click the radio button beside "Output Range:" and then click the mouse pointer in the adjacent field so that an insertion point will appear. Click the mouse button in cell A1. The absolute address $A$1 will appear in the field. An alternative to pointing at the cell is to type A1 directly into the field. When you have finished, the dialog window should look like the picture below:

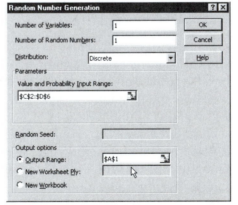

- Click the OK button. The dialog window will disappear and cell A1 will contain one of the integers 0 through 4. Since this is a random number, it is impossible to predict in advance what that number will be. Make a mental note of what the number is so that when you repeat this process you can observe how the value changes.

- Open the Tools menu again and again choose "Data Analysis."

- When the Data Analysis dialog window opens, notice that "Random Number Generation" is already chosen. Click the OK button. The Random Number Generation dialog window will open.

- Notice that the fields you previously filled out in the Random Number Generation dialog window retain those values. Again, simply click the OK button. A warning window will open.

Clippit will warn you that the new random number will destroy or *over-write* the value already in cell A1. This could be a mistake, but this time we know what we are doing. Click OK.

- Simply click the OK button on the warning window. A new value will be written to cell A1.

Is the new value the same as the old?

- Select a dozen different new random numbers by repeating this sequence: open the Tools menu, select "Data Analysis," and click the OK button in the next three windows that open. Try to predict which value will come up next. Tally the number of times each comes up in the table below by placing a mark in the "Tally" column below each time that value appears.

Value	Tally	Count
4		
3		
2		
1		
0		
	Sum	

- After you have chosen and tallied all 12 random numbers, enter the total number of times each value occurred. Check your answer by summing these numbers. They should sum to 12.

It is impossible to predict exactly how many times each grade appeared in your tally above. As the number of random values drawn increases, we expect the proportion of times each value appeared to become closer to the probability associated with each value. The number 2 probably occurred more often in your tally than either the numbers 0 or 4 because the probability associated with 2 is higher. This should be clearer if we choose many numbers.

Let's use Excel to automate the process of drawing many random numbers and tallying how many times each different value occurs.

- Recall the Random Number Generation dialog window (Tools, "Data Analysis," OK).

- Change the value in the "Number of Random Numbers" field from 1 to 1000. Click OK in Clippit's warning balloon.

Excel will generate 1,000 different random values and place them in column A (A1:A1000). This will, of course, take a bit longer than generating a single random number. You can tell Excel is still busy if the mouse pointer is in the shape of an hourglass.

The next step will be to look at the distribution of these random numbers. We will tally the number of 4s, 3s, 2s, 1s, and 0s and also determine the proportion of the total made up of each of these values. In addition, we will calculate the mean and standard deviations of this group of numbers and compare all this to the probability distribution. We will also look at how these proportions change as the number of random numbers increases.

The thousand values in A1:A1000 are, of course, a sample of 1,000 random numbers. Rather than generating more samples, we will take the 10 numbers in A1:A10 as a sample of 10 random numbers and the 100 numbers in A1:A100 as a sample of 100 random numbers.

Use columns G, H, and I in the same rows as the probability distribution, which will be used to count the number of times each value of the random variable occurs in each of the three samples we will look at.

- Label cell G1, H1, and I1 as shown below:

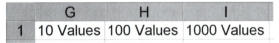

	G	H	I
1	10 Values	100 Values	1000 Values

In cell G2 we will have Excel put a count of the number of times the value "4" occurs in cells A1:A10. In cell H2 we will put a count of the number of times the value "4" appears in cells A1:A100, and in cell I2 we will put a count of the number of times the value "4" appears in A1:A1000. In cells G3, H3, and I3 we will put a count of the number of times the value "3" appears in each of the same ranges. Rows 4, 5, and 6 will contain similar counts for values "2," "1," and "0." Excel has a useful function named COUNTIF for just this purpose.

- Select cell G2. Click the Edit Formula button ▣. Open the list of recently used functions in the Formula Palette and choose "More functions...."

- In the Paste Function dialog window choose "Statistical" for function category and "COUNTIF" for function name. Click the OK button.

The COUNTIF function has two arguments: *Range* and *Criteria*. The *Range* argument is the cell addresses where you want Excel to determine the count for a specific value, and *Criteria* is the value you want counted.

We will first have Excel count the number of times the value "4" appears in the first 10 numbers. We will then extend this to have Excel count the other possible values the random variable can have (3, 2, 1, and 0) and do this count for the first 100 numbers and all 1,000 numbers as well as for the first 10.

- Move the dialog window for COUNTIF to the lower right of the screen so you can see all the data on the worksheet.

- Click the "Range" field and use the mouse to select the first 10 random numbers in column A. Press the F4 function key once to make the address absolute ($A$1:$A$10). The contents of this cell can then be copied without this address changing. This address is where COUNTIF will look for the value we want it to count.

- Click the mouse pointer in the criteria field and then click cell C2. The cell address, C2, will go in the field. C2 contains the value "4," which is the number we want counted.

- Press the F4 function key three times. The "C2" in cell G2 should become "$C2." This is a "mixed" address; the column is absolute but the row is not. If the cell containing this address is copied, the row part of this address will change to be the same as the cell to which the address is copied, but the column will always refer to C.

- Click the OK button. Check to be sure the value in cell G2 really is the number of 4s in cells A1:A10.

The next step will be to copy the formula in cell G2 to cells G3 through G6. The copied formula in each cell will be slightly different. The Range will always be $A$1:$A$10 (because it is absolute), but the Criteria will change to $C3, $C4, etc., because the row portion of the cell address is relative.

- Copy the contents of cell G2 to cells G3:G6. Check by clicking on cell G6 and verifying that the formula there is "=COUNTIF($A$1:$A$10,$C6)."

- Further check your results by using the AutoSum button in cell G7 to calculate the sum of the values in cells G2:G6. Since G2:G6 contain the counts of all possible values in the 10 cells, the sum of those values should be 10.

The formulas in cells H2:H6 should be just like those in G2:G6 except the range should be A1:A100 instead of A1:A10.

- Copy the formula in cell G2 to H2.

- Select cell H2. Click the Edit Formula button (=). The Formula Palette will open with the COUNTIF dialog fields containing the values currently in cell H2.

- Change the cell address in the range from $A$1:$A$10 to $A$1:$A$100. This will cause COUNTIF to count the number of times each value in the Criteria occurs in the first 100 cells rather than just the first 10.

Notice that the cell address in the criteria field is $C2, the same value you originally entered in cell G2. Copying from G2 to H2 didn't change this address because although G2 and H2 are in different columns, the "$" in front of the "C" in $C2 made the column part of the address fixed. Since G2 and H2 are in the same row, the row part of the address didn't change even though it is relative.

- Click OK. Cell H2 contains the number of times the value "4" appears in the first 100 random values.

- Copy cell H2 to H3:H6. Look at cell H6. What is the cell address of the Criteria of COUNTIF? As in the case of row G, copying the $C2 from cell H2 caused the row part of the address to change from 2 to 6 ("$C6"). What is in cell C6? The number 0. Cell H6 thus contains the number of times the value "0" appears in the first 100 random values.

- Use the AutoSum button in H7 to determine the sum of the values in H2:H6. If done correctly, the sum should be 100.

- Follow a similar procedure to put formulas in cells I2:I6. The formulas in column I should refer to A1:A1000 for their range.

- Check your work in column I by using I7 to sum the values of I2:I6. The sum should be 1,000.

You now have a table counting the number of times each value appears in the sample. There should be a relationship between the number of times each value occurs in a set of random numbers and the probability of that value occurring. The relationship will be clearer if we convert the number of occurrences to a proportion. That will be done next.

Let's make a comparison table in the region C9:G17.

- Copy the contents of cells C1:D7 to C9:D14. This will provide the first two columns of the new table giving the possible grade values and probabilities. The easiest way of copying a small number of cells is to first select the cells to be copied, place the mouse pointer on the cell boundary, and, while pressing the Ctrl key (PC) or OPTION key

(MAC), drag the selection outline to the location where you want the copy.

- Copy the contents of cells G1:I1 to D9:F9. This will give a row of labels across the top of the table.

- Enter the labels "Mean" in cell C15 and "Variance" in cell C16.

Cells D15 and D16 will contain the mean and variance of the probability distributions that are calculated in cells E7 and F7.

- Select cell D15 and enter the formula "=E7." Select cell D16 and enter the formula "=F7."

This section of your worksheet should look like the picture below. The probabilities of each grade value will be compared with the sample proportions that still need to be calculated.

	C	D	E	F	G
1	Grade	Probability	10 Values	100 Values	1000 Values
2	4	0.1			
3	3	0.2			
4	2	0.35			
5	1	0.25			
6	0	0.1			
7	Mean		1.95		
8	Variance		1.2475		

Next we will put formulas in cells E10:G14 that will calculate the proportion of each sized sample that is equal to the value given in the appropriate row of column C. For example, we want cell E10 to show the proportion of the first 10 random values that have the value "4." This would be calculated by taking the number of times the value "4" appears in the first 10 numbers (which is given in cell G2) and dividing it by the number of random numbers (10 in this case.)

The instructions below will demonstrate another use of a cell address that is "mixed." In this case the column portion will be relative and the line portion will be fixed.

- Select cell E10. Enter an equal sign to start the formula.

- Click cell G2. "G2" (which contains the number of "4"s in the first 10 random values) will be written in the formula. Enter the division symbol ("/" without the quotes). Click cell G7, the number of values being counted, and press the F4 function key twice, which should change the "G7" to "G$7." Check the Formula Bar to be sure the cell contains "=G2/G$7." Press the Enter or Return key.

Cell E10 converts the number of "4"s in G2 to a proportion by dividing it by 10. The next step is to similarly convert all of the other cells in G2:H6 to proportions.

- Copy the formula in E10 to E11:E14.

The "G2" in the formula in E10 will change to "G3," "G4," "G5," and "G6" as it is copied down because it is a relative address. The "G$7" divisor in G2 will not change because the cells you are copying to are in the same column as D10—which means the "G" part of the "G$7" won't change, and the "$7" part is an absolute address and thus can't change.

- Check the copying by clicking E13 and checking the Formula Bar. The formula should be "=G5/G$7." This converts the number of "1"s in G5 to a proportion.

- Select region E10:E14 again. Copy this region to F10:G14 by placing the mouse pointer on the Fill Handle and dragging it two columns to the right.

Copying the vertical region E10:E14 to the right has the same effect as if we first copied E10 to F10:G10 then copied E11 to F11:G11, E12 to F12:G12, and so on. Let's consider exactly what this does by looking at row 13 as an example.

- Compare the formulas in E13 and F13. Write them both down in the margin at the left.

Recall that E13 converts the number of "1"s in the first 10 values to a proportion. The formula in F13 is "=H5/H$7." The "G5" in E13 has changed to "H5." The numerator in F13 is the cell counting the number of "1"s in the first 100 values. The change from "G5" to "H5" increases the column part of the formula by one because, in copying from E13 to F13, we have moved one column to the right. There is no change in the row part of the formula because E13 and F13 are in the same row.

The "G$7" in cell E13 changes to "H$7" in F13. The denominator thus changes from "10" (in G7) to "100" (in H7). Since the column part of G$7 is relative, the copying changed it as it changed the numerator. Since the row part is fixed, it will remain "7" for all the values in the table.

The result is that F13 now contains the proportion of the first 100 random values that equal "1." Similarly, F14 will calculate the proportion of the 1,000 random values that equal "1." Each number in E10:G14 should be a number between 0 and 1. The sum of the numbers in each column (E10:E14, F10:F14, and G10:G14) should be 1.0 in each case. We will compare them to the corresponding probabilities in column D.

Next, put formulas in rows 15 and 16 to calculate the mean and variance of each set of numbers in column A. E15 will have the mean of the first 10 numbers, F15 will have the mean of the first 100 numbers, and G15 will have the mean of all 1,000 number in column A. Cells E16, F16, and G16 will have the variances for the first 10, 100, and 1,000 numbers in column A. These values will be compared to the mean and variance of the probability distribution in D15 and D16.

- Use Excel's built-in function (by using the Formula Palette) in cell E15 to calculate the average of cells A1:A10. Similarly, in cell F15 calculate the average of cells A1:A100, and in cell G15 calculate the average of A1:A1000. (Note: the Formula Palette initially assumes you want the average of the values above the cell where the average goes. This is *not* what you want, and you will have to change the "Number1" argument field in each case.)

- In cells E16, F16, and G16, use Excel's built-in function to calculate the sample variance (use VAR in the "Statistical" category) of A1:A10, A1:A100, and A1:A1000, respectively.

The table can be made more readable by formatting. Let's format the numbers so that all the proportions, probabilities, and summary statistics are displayed with three positions to the right of the decimal point.

- With the mouse select the region D10:G16. This is the region whose values are to be formatted.

- Click the Increase Decimal button on the Formatting Toolbar (🔲) twice. This should cause all of the values displayed in the table to be rounded to exactly three decimal places. Remember that although the values Excel displays are rounded, if the addresses of these cells were used in formulas in other cells, the values with all of Excel's precision would be used, not the rounded values.

For the proportion receiving each of the grade values and for the mean and variance, notice the pattern that exists as you move to the right. As the number of random numbers increases, the proportion that each value has is usually closer to the probability given by the probability distribution. Sometimes this doesn't happen. The exceptions generally occur when the smaller data set happened to have a proportion that was already very close to the distribution probability. Increasing the size of the data set might result in a proportion that was further from the distribution probability, but this is not what usually happens.

Similarly, as the size of a data set of random numbers increases, the mean and variance of those data generally approach the mean and variance of the probability distribution. In all cases, the values associated with 1,000 numbers should be quite close to those of the probability distribution. Increasing the number of values would bring them even closer, but it should be clear that there is not a lot of room for further improvement. Although a single value of a random variable cannot be predicted, the characteristics of a moderately large number of random variables can be predicted with a fairly high degree of accuracy.

Think of a probability distribution as representing an infinitely large set of values drawn from that distribution. The mean and variance of the probability distribution are the same as the mean and variance of that infinite set of data.

▼Turning Off Automatic Calculation

With this worksheet, it is easy to look at a different set of random numbers. Excel will, however, recalculate the values of all of the formulas in the workbook each time a single random number is generated. If you have a slow computer, the wait can be annoying. The process of picking new random numbers will be speeded up if we turn off Excel's automatic calculation.

- Open the Tools menu on the Menu Bar and choose "Options...." The Options dialog window will open.

- The Options dialog window has many folder tabs. Click on the "Calculation" folder tab.

- In the top left of the dialog window is a region titled "Calculation," with several radio buttons. Click the Manual radio button. The dialog window should look like the picture below.

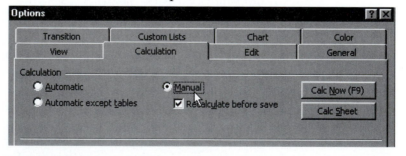

▼New Random Numbers

Let's generate a new set of random numbers.

- Open the Tools menu and choose "Data Analysis" and "Random Number Generation."

If you have done this chapter in a single session with Excel, the Random Number Generation dialog window will already have the fields filled out. If not, refer to the picture on page 92, except change the value in the "Number of Random Numbers" field from 1 to 1000.

- Click the OK button.

- Give Excel the OK to overwrite existing data.

Wait until the mouse pointer is no longer in the shape of an hourglass. (If your machine is fast, the mouse pointer may not have a chance to assume the shape of an hourglass.) Notice that because you set calculation to manual, neither of the tables summarizing the random numbers will have changed until you tell Excel to do a recalculation.

- Tell Excel to recalculate by pressing the F9 function key. You should see the values in the table change.

Look at the new table. You should, of course, see some differences, but the general pattern should be the same. The larger the sample of random numbers, the closer its distribution, mean, and variance will tend to be to those of the probability distribution. You can think of the probability distribution as a description of an infinitely large set of random numbers drawn from that distribution.

▼Probability Distributions and Business Decisions

Most business decisions must be made in an atmosphere of uncertainty—it is impossible to be certain about the consequences of each choice. For one class of business decisions, the concepts of the mean and standard deviation of a probability distribution can be helpful. This is the case when the outcome of a decision can be measured in terms of money (such as an investment decision), and we assume that outcome can be expressed as a probability distribution.

The latter assumption is a strong one. In order to represent the outcome of an investment decision as a probability distribution, we must know the set of all possible outcomes and the probabilities associated with each outcome. We never really have this kind of information about the future, but this assumption is certainly better than simply believing we know for certain what the future holds, since it incorporates some of the features of our ignorance of the future. Instead of viewing an investment as returning a known amount of money, we can view it as a fishbowl containing slips of paper with different amounts written on the slips. One slip is chosen and the amount written is the investment's return.

Choosing between two investments is like choosing between two fishbowls. How can we make that choice?

Two factors are involved in evaluating choices: the expected return and the risk associated with each choice. The *expected return* of a probability distribution with monetary payoffs is the mean (expected value) of that probability distribution. The *risk* can be measured by the variance of the probability distribution. In general, the best choice is the one with the highest expected value (mean) and lowest risk (variance). Thus if the distributions associated with two choices have the same variance, the better choice is the one with the higher mean. If the two choices have the same mean, the better choice is the one with the lower variance. Of course if one choice has both a higher mean and lower variance, it is clearly better.

What if the choice with the higher mean also has the higher variance? In this case the correct choice depends on the decision maker's *risk aversion*. A decision maker who is highly risk averse will tend to prefer the safer choice even if the expected return is much lower. One who has low risk aversion will put more weight on the expected return. It is possible that a decision maker could be a risk lover, and would prefer a choice with high variance even if it had a lower expected value. Businesses, however, almost always have some degree of risk aversion, although it may vary from business to business. Let's consider an example.

A manufacturing firm wants to expand production and is considering three different proposals which differ in flexibility and fixed costs. The outcome associated with each choice depends on how well the economy performs in the future, which the firm cannot know with certainty. After consulting a number of economic forecasts, it has determined the outcome expected by a plurality of forecasts. Some forecasters, however, are more optimistic, while others are more pessimistic. The firm wants to consider those minority positions in its decision and has decided on the probability of each possible economic outcome. Those probabilities, together with the profits expected from each different expansion choice in each outcome of the economy are summarized in the table below (this is sometimes called the payoff table).

State of the Economy	Probability	Profits from each Proposal (millions of dollars)		
		#1	#2	#3
Pessimistic View	.2	−$100	−$250	−$50
Plurality View	.5	$120	$250	$200
Optimistic View	.3	$300	$350	$160

Suppose the firm chooses the second proposal. If the pessimistic view turns out to be correct, the firm will lose $250 million. If the plurality *view is correct, the firm will make $250 million, and if the optimistic view is correct, the firm will make $350 million. Given the firm's chosen probabilities, which proposal should it choose?*

Each of the proposals is a random variable whose outcome is money. For example, proposal 2 has a probability of .2 of producing a $250 million loss, a probability of .5 of producing a $250 million profit and a probability of .3 of producing a $350 million profit. In order to compare the three proposals, calculate the expected value and standard deviation of each proposal. Your results should match those in the table below. If you have difficulty obtaining the same answers, examine the "Investment Expansion" workbook in the "Chap_3" directory of the data for this book.

	Mean	Variance
Proposal 1	130	19300
Proposal 2	180	48100
Proposal 3	138	9136

What can we conclude from these results? If we compare proposals 1 and 3, the latter is clearly preferable to the former. Not only does proposal 3 have a higher expected value (mean), it is less risky as indicated by the lower variance. What about proposals 2 and 3? Since proposal 2 has a higher expected value but is also riskier than proposal 3, the choice between these two will depend on the firm's risk aversion.

▼Exercises

1. Use the formatting buttons to enhance the appearance of the table in C9 through G16. Use formatting to set the row and column headings apart from the data in the table. Use font changes or style changes to further enhance the visual distinction between the headings and the data.

   When you are finished, print out the enhanced table with your name in the header. Here is how to print just the table on the worksheet.

   • Select the region C9:G16 (the new table).

   • Open the File menu on the Menu Bar and choose "Print...." The Print dialog window will open.

   • At the bottom left of the dialog window under "Print What," click the Selection radio button.

- Click the Preview button in the bottom-left corner of the window.

- Click the Setup... button at the top of the Print Preview screen.

- Use the "Page" folder in the Setup dialog window to shift the orientation from Portrait to Landscape. Increase the scaling to 200%. This will enlarge the selection to be printed so that it will fill more of the page.

- Use the "Margin" folder in the Setup dialog window to center the table horizontally and vertically.

- Use the "Header/Footer" folder tab to put your name and a title on the page header.

- Click the OK button in the dialog window.

- Click the Print... button at the top of the Print Preview page.

2. A manufacturing firm is considering expanding production of one of its three products. Because of financing constraints, production can only be expanded in a single product. The estimated profit from each product depends on a forecast of competitive conditions. Three possible scenarios are forecast. The probability of each scenario and the anticipated profits (in $1,000s) from each product under each scenario are given in the payoff table below.

| | | Product | | |
Scenario	Probability	A	B	C
I	.2	−$1,900	−$2,950	$4,000
II	.5	1,600	1,900	400
III	.3	2,000	2,200	500

Determine the expected value and variance associated with each product. How should the firm rank the three products if it desires the highest profit at the lowest risk?

3. An investor is considering purchasing shares of newly issued stock. Suppose many companies are issuing stock this year. The percentage one-year return to each stock can be treated as an independent random number following the same distribution as shown at the top of the next page.

Use Excel to calculate the mean and variance of this distribution.

Percentage Profit	Probability
-100	.10
-60	.20
-10	.15
+10	.15
+60	.25
+100	.15

Use Excel's Random Number Generator to simulate the one-year return to the following different portfolios consisting of stocks with the probability distribution shown above:

- a portfolio distributed equally among five different companies' stocks (select 5 numbers from the distribution).

- a portfolio distributed equally among 50 different companies' stocks (select 50 numbers from the distribution).

- a portfolio distributed equally among 500 different companies' stocks (select 500 numbers from the distribution).

For each portfolio determine the proportion of stocks providing each of the six levels of profit and the mean and standard deviation of each portfolio. Create a chart comparing these proportions and summary statistics with the probability distribution like the chart prepared in this chapter. Enhance the appearance of your chart, put your name and a title on the header, and print it out. What conclusions can you draw about the effect of buying more rather than fewer stocks?

4. A city street vendor with a stand outside a large office building must determine whether to sell ice cream or soda tomorrow. The vendor believes that the profit will depend upon the weather. The payoff table is as follows:

Event	Strategy	
	Sell Soda	Sell Ice Cream
Cool Weather	+$40	+$30
Warm Weather	+$55	+$65

Based upon her past experience and the best available weather reports, the vendor estimates the probability of warm weather is .40. (Assume the weather must be either warm or cool.) Determine the expected value and the standard deviation of selling soda and of selling ice cream. Which should she decide to sell? Explain.

5. An investor is considering investing $10,000 in three different portfolios for a five-year period. According to her analysis, if the economy's performance differs from the consensus expectations, the return on each portfolio will be as shown in the table below.

	Portfolio Return		
Performance of the economy:	A	B	C
Worse than expected	−$5,000	+$900	−$8,000
In line with expectations	+$1,500	+$1,000	+$500
Better than expected	+$6,000	+$1,100	+$9,000

The investor believes that the probability the economy will do worse than expected is .2, the probability the economy's performance will be in line with expectations is .5, and the probability that it will do better than expected is .3. Using these probabilities, determine the expected value and standard deviation of the return to each portfolio. If the investor seeks the highest return at the smallest risk, which should she choose?

Chapter 4

The Binomial Distribution

A number of probability distributions occur so often in practical situations that mathematical formulas for their distributions have been developed. These formulas make it easier to solve problems using these distributions, especially since Excel has built many of the most popular formulas into Excel functions. When a distribution is important enough to get this kind of special attention, it also gets a name. The distribution we will look at in this chapter is the *binomial* distribution. There is one mildly confusing feature in the way distributions are named. The name of a distribution is always singular. For example, the distribution we will look at in this chapter is always called *the* binomial distribution. In reality, however, the binomial distribution is not a single distribution in the same way as the distribution of grades discussed in a previous chapter was a single distribution. The binomial distribution is really a family of distributions. There are an infinite number of different binomial distributions. They all have certain characteristics in common, and they share a common formula.

A random number from the (or a) binomial distribution can be thought of as being generated by a random process that has two possible outcomes. One of the outcomes is of particular significance and is usually termed *success;* the other is termed *failure.* The random process occurs a fixed number of times. The probability of success each time is constant and independent of whether or not a success has occurred any of the other times. The binomially distributed random number is the count of the number of successes that have occurred.

Two things make one binomial distribution different from another. These are the probability that the random process will produce a success and the number of times that the process is repeated. These are the variables of the binomial distribution. Most statistics texts symbolize the probability of the random process resulting in success with p or π. Since the use of p may create confusion with the p value, a concept you will encounter in later chapters, the symbol used here will be π. The number of trials will be symbolized with n.

An example may make this easier to understand.

An automobile salesperson has discovered from experience that 2 out of every 10 persons she takes for a test drive in a new automobile eventually buy a car from her. Suppose one evening she takes five people for a test drive. What is the probability that none of them purchases a car from her?

The random variable here is the number of persons who purchase a car from the salesperson out of the 5 taken for a test drive. The random process here is the one determining whether or not a person taken for a test drive ends up buying a car. That process has two outcomes: The person buys a car or the person does not buy a car. The outcome we want to count is the first, so we will call the outcome "buying a car" a success. The question tells us that the probability of success is 2 in 10 or .20. In other words, $\pi = .20$. Furthermore, we know that five people are taken on a test drive, so $n = 5$.

Recall that a probability distribution tells us all the possible values that the random variable can equal and the probability associated with each of those values. What are the possible values for this random variable? In other words, what values are possible for the number of people who buy a car out of five who take a test drive? Clearly the lowest value is zero; it is possible that none of those who take a test drive will buy a car. The highest value is five; all of the people who take a test drive might buy a car. All of the integer values in between are also possible. The number of people who buy a car is thus 0, 1, 2, 3, 4, or 5. These are the possible values for the random variable (which we will symbolize as x). For this problem we are to determine the probability that $x = 0$.

Let's further explore this problem by using Excel to simulate the situation.

▼Simulating a Binomial Problem

- Start Excel and open a new workbook.

- Open the File menu on the Menu Bar and choose "Save As...." In the dialog window that opens, find the directory containing the files for this book or, if you are using a diskette, place the diskette in the A drive and select "3½ Floppy (A:)."

- Create a new folder named "Chap_4" by using the Create New Folder button (▣). Double click on this folder's icon after it is created.

- Save the workbook using the file name "Chap4.xls."

The Random Number Generation tool will be used to simulate the random process of a test driver deciding either to buy or not to buy a car. The first step is to enter a probability distribution for this random process. To buy or not to buy; that is the first question.

Since Excel requires that the outcomes of a random process be represented as numbers, we will use "0" to represent the outcome of *not* buying a car (*failure*) and "1" to represent the outcome of buying a car (*success*). The probability of "1" is .20; the probability of "0" is thus .80 (1.00 – 0.20 = 0.80).

- Enter the label "Outcome" in cell H1 and "Probability" in cell I1.

- In cell H2 enter the number "1" (without quotes), which stands for buying a car, and in I2 enter the number ".20" (without quotes), which is the probability that the person taking the test drive will buy a car. This is the value of π, the probability of success, just discussed.

- In cell H3 enter the number "0" (without quotes), which stands for not buying a car. The probability of not buying a car is $1 - \pi$. In this case that probability is .80, but instead of entering that number, enter the formula "=1-I2" in cell I3 so that later changes in π will cause this probability to be changed automatically. The displayed value should be "0.8."

Now let's use the Random Number Generation tool to simulate the outcome associated with *one* person taking a test drive.

- Open the Tools menu, select "Data Analysis...," and choose "Random Number Generation." The Random Number Generation dialog window will open.

- Enter "1" for both "Number of Variables" and "Number of Random Numbers."

- Choose "Discrete" for "Distribution." In the "Value and Probability Input Range" put the address for the cell range containing the probability distribution you just entered for whether or not a test driver becomes a buyer, H2:I3.

- Choose "Output Range," and have the Random Number Generation tool put the output in cell A1.

The completed dialog window should look like the picture at the top of the next page.

- Click the OK button in the dialog window.

Random Number Generation

Number of Variables:	1	OK
Number of Random Numbers:	1	Cancel
Distribution:	Discrete ▼	Help

Parameters

Value and Probability Input Range:

H2:I3

Random Seed:

Output options

◉ Output Range: A1

○ New Worksheet Ply:

○ New Workbook

Look in cell A1. Did the test driver buy the car (cell A1 has a "1") or not (cell A1 has a "0")?

- Try another customer by opening the Tools menu again, choosing "Data Analysis," and clicking OK in the next three dialog windows (the last may be Clippit's overwrite warning) that open. See how many times you have to do this before you find a test driver (or another test driver) who decides to buy (that is, before you get a "1" (or another "1") in cell A1.

Let's now simulate an entire evening of five test drivers.

- Open the Tools menu and choose "Data Analysis" again. Click OK to recall the Random Number Generation dialog window.

- Change the number "1" in the "Number of Variables" field to "5." Click OK, and then click OK again in the overwrite warning window.

Five numbers will fill the range A1:E1. How many of them are 1s? Although it is not difficult to spot and count the 1s among the 0s, let's have Excel do this for us automatically. One way would be to use the COUNTIF function. A perhaps simpler method would be to simply have Excel add all five numbers together. Since the numbers must each be either 0 or 1, the sum of the five numbers will always equal the number of 1s, the number of successes. It is this sum that is a binomially distributed random variable, the number of successes in five trials.

- Select cell F1.

- Click the AutoSum button (Σ). The formula to add A1:E1 will automatically be entered in cell F1. Press the Enter key.

Cell F1 now contains a count of the number of 1's in cells A1:E1. This number is a simulation of the number of people out of five test drivers who will buy a car. The possible values are the integers 0 through 5.

Try the simulation five to 10 times by opening the Tools menu, choosing "Data Analysis" and clicking the OK button in the next three dialog boxes. What is the largest number of buyers you get in these simulations? What do you think is the most likely number of buyers the salesperson will get after taking five people on test drives? Your experience should convince you that often none of the five test drivers will purchase a car. Car sales is a tough business.

Rather than repeatedly simulating the purchase decisions of five test drivers, let's have Excel do this for us.

- Recall the Random Number Generation dialog window and change "Number of Random Numbers" from 1 to 1,000. Click the OK button, and OK the overwrite.

After a delay, Excel will fill the range of cells A1:E1000 with 0s and 1s. We can interpret each row in this range as a separate simulation of the purchase decision of five test drivers.

The next step is to copy the formula in cell F1, which tells the number of 1s in row 1, down column F, until a similar sum is available for each row. This could be done by selecting cell F1 and dragging its fill handle down to cell F1000. This is tricky to do, however, because the region is so large. Here is an alternative.

- Click the mouse pointer in the Name Box. (See page 4 if you have forgotten where the Name Box is.) The current value will become highlighted, and you will be able to enter a new value.

- Enter "f1:f1000" (without quotation marks) in the Name Box. Press the Enter key.

The entire region F1:F1000 becomes selected.

- Open the Edit menu on the Menu Bar. Select "Fill." A cascade menu will open to the right, as shown on the next page.

- Select "Down" from the cascade menu. The menu will disappear, and the formula in F1 will be copied to all the cells in the selected region. Column F will provide the number of 1s in each of 1,000 rows. These values in column F are values for specific instances of the binomially

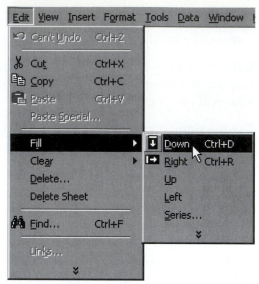

distributed random variable, the number of people who buy cars out of five who take test drives.

The next step is to count the number of times each possible different value occurs in column F, determine the proportion of times each value occurs and the average and standard deviation of the values, and compare these with the values given by the binomial distribution functions.

▼Counting the Number of Car Buyers

- Prepare labels for the first table in the positions shown in the picture below.

	H	I	J	K
6	x	Number	Proportion	Probability
7	0			
8	1			
9	2			
10	3			
11	4			
12	5			

- Select cell I7. Use the Formula Palette to select the COUNTIF function.

A useful trick which works with most Excel functions (but not the Data Analysis tool) is to select an entire row or column when there are data in only part of the row or column.

- Click the mouse pointer in the "Range" argument field and then click the F column header.

E	F	G
1	2	
0	0	
0	1	

Click mouse pointer here ⟶

The entire column will be selected, and the address which appears in the "Range" argument field is F:F, Excel's way of referring to the entire F column.

- In the "Criteria" argument field enter the relative cell address for the value of *x* for that row of the table, H7. Press the Enter key and cell I7 should display the number of times the value "0" appears in column F.

- Copy the formula in cell I7 to cells I8 through I12.

Since the address in the "Criteria" argument field is relative, when copied it will change to point to the value of *x* in column H of each row. Each cell in the table in column I should display the number of times that corresponding value appears in column F.

- Double-check the table by selecting cell I 13 and clicking the AutoSum button. After pressing the Enter key, the value "1000" should display. Since the only values that can appear in column F are the integers 0 through 5 in the first 1,000 rows, the sum of the times each value appears should be 1,000.

The next step is to convert the number of times each value occurred to a proportion which can then be compared to a probability.

- Click cell J7. Enter a formula which will divide the number of times the value 0 appears (cell I7) by the total number of cells (1,000, or cell I13). If you use the address of cell I13 in your formula, be sure to make that cell address absolute.

- Copy the formula in cell J7 down through cell J12. Each cell should show the value beside it in column H converted to a proportion. Double-check this by using the AutoSum button in J13 to verify that the values in cells J7:J12 sum to 1.

- Select the range J7:J12. Click the Increase Decimal ( ) and Decrease Decimal ( ) buttons so that each of the values show exactly four decimal places. The last place for all the numbers will be zero, but this will make it easier to compare these values with the probabilities which will go in the adjacent column.

The next step is to calculate the probabilities associated with each of the values 0 through 5 using the binomial distribution, which is built into Excel in the BINOMDIST function.

▼Using the BINOMDIST Function

As we have seen, if five people test drive a car, the number of those five who eventually buy one is a random number between 0 and 5. If we assume that the probability that any one person who test drives a car will buy is .20, and is constant and independent of the decisions of others, the distribution of that random number is binomial with $\pi = .20$ and $n = 5$. Cell K7 is to contain the probability that the random variable will equal 0.

- Select cell K7.

- Click the Edit Formula button. From the "Statistical" category choose the "BINOMDIST" function. Click the Next> button.

The BINOMDIST function has four arguments:

1. **Number_s**—short for number of successes. This is the value of the random variable for which we want a probability. Most textbooks symbolize this as x. For cell K7, this argument should be 0. Enter into this field the corresponding cell address of that number (H7).

2. **Trials**—This argument is the number of trials. Most textbooks symbolize this as n. This is one of the two variables distinguishing one binomial distribution from another. For cell K7 this value should be 5 because five people test drive a car in each evening. Enter the number 5.

3. **Probability_s**—short for probability of success. Most textbooks abbreviate this either as p or as π. This is the other binomial distribution variable. For cell L15 this value should be .20 because there is a .20 probability that any one test driver will purchase a car. Rather than enter this number directly, enter the address of cell I2 where the value "0.20" was entered for use by the Random Number Generation tool. This will allows us to easily look at other values for π by simply changing I2.

4. **Cumulative**—This argument determines whether Excel provides the probability that the random variable is *equal* to x (the value given in the first argument) or the probability that the random variable is *less than or equal* to x. The latter is commonly called the *cumulative probability*. As we will see, this is quite useful for dealing with many

binomial problems. For cell L15, however, we want the probability that the number of buyers is equal to 5, not less than or equal to 5 (which must be true). We tell Excel we don't want a cumulative probability by putting the word "false" (without quotes) or the number "0" into the argument field. If we did want a cumulative probability, we would put "true" or the number "1." We *don't* want a cumulative probability in this case. Enter the appropriate value for that in this argument field.

If the correct arguments are entered into the argument fields of the dialog window, the value "0.32768" will appear below and to the right of the last argument field. Click the OK button and that value will appear in cell K7.

- Enter formulas into cells K8:K12 which will calculate the binomial probabilities for the values in column H for each row (1 through 5). Use the AutoSum button in K13 to verify that the sum of the values in K7:K12 is 1.

- Select K7:K12 and use the Increase and Decrease Decimal buttons so that exactly four decimal places are displayed.

- Compare the proportions of the 1,000 simulated values in column J with the corresponding probabilities in each row in column K. The values should be similar. If significantly more than 1,000 simulations were done, we would expect the values to be closer.

▼The Binomial Mean and Standard Deviation

The last step is to compare the mean and standard deviation of the number of cars bought in the 1,000 simulations with the expected value and standard deviation given by the binomial distribution.

Enter labels for the comparisons as shown in the picture below.

	H	I	J
15		Simulated	Binomial
16	Mean		
17	Std Dev		

- In cells I16 and I17 enter formulas to calculate the mean and the standard deviation of the 1,000 simulated values in column F. Use the AVERAGE and STDEV functions and click the heading of column F (as shown on page 113) to enter the "F:F" address, which refers to the numbers in the entire column.

The formulas for the expected value and standard deviation of a binomial distribution with n and π representing the number of trials and the probability of success on a single trial are:

$$\text{expected value} = E(x) = \mu = n\pi$$
$$\text{standard deviation} = \sigma(x) = \sqrt{n\pi(1-\pi)}$$

For this worksheet the value of n is 5, and the value of π is given in cell I2.

- Enter the Excel formula in cell J16 to calculate the mean of the binomial distribution by multiplying the number 5 (n) by the value of cell I2 (π). The answer should be 1.

- Enter a formula in cell J17 to calculate the binomial standard deviation using the formula above, replacing n with the number "5" and π with a reference to cell I2. One way to do this is use the Formula Palette to get the dialog window for the SQRT function (Math & Trig category). In the single argument field for that function enter an expression which will calculate $n\pi(1-\pi)$: "5*I2*(1-I2)." The correct value is 0.894427.

- Select cells I16:J17 and use the Increase and Decrease Decimal buttons so that each number displays four decimal places.

- Save the workbook—now and often.

Compare the value in I16 with that in J16 and the value in I17 with that in J17. As the number of random values (1,000 in the current worksheet) increases, the mean and standard deviation of those values (I16 and I17) will converge to the mean and standard deviation of the binomial distribution (J16 and J17). Let's take a look at that by increasing the number of random numbers to 10,000.

Although we could simply recall the Random Number Generation tool and rerun it, you would likely find that it has become very slow. The reason is that each time a new random number is selected, Excel will perform all of the calculations to update the tables. It would be better if Excel waited until all the random numbers were selected before doing this. We can force Excel not to do the constant recalculation by switching it to manual recalculation.

- Switch to manual recalculation by opening the Tools menu on the Menu Bar and selecting "Options…" and the "Calculation" tab. For more details, see page 100.

Now we can simulate 10,000 nights of trying to sell a car. (*Whew!*)

- Recall the Random Number Generation tool by opening the Tools menu and clicking "Data Analysis...." The dialog window should already have all fields filled out, and the only change needed is that the "Number of Random Numbers" should be changed from 1,000 to 10,000. *(If you need to completely fill out the dialog window, refer to page 110—except change "Number of Variables" from 1 to 5 and "Number of Random Numbers" from 1 to 10,000.)*

- Click OK at the bottom of the window.

The last step is to extend the formulas in column F, which add the simulated purchases in each row of columns A through E, to include the additional 9,000 simulations.

- Open the Edit menu on the Menu Bar. Click "Fill," and then click "Down" on the cascade menu.

- Press the F9 key. This will cause Excel to recalculate the formulas in the spreadsheet.

Examine the table of proportions and probabilities. The values should be quite close. Also compare the average and standard deviation of the simulated number of purchasers with the mean and standard deviation of this binomial distribution. They also should be quite close.

The answer to the question given at the beginning of this chapter is that the probability that *none* of the five people test driving the car will purchase one from the salesperson is .3277 (in cell L20). This is the binomial probability of zero successes in five trials given a probability of success in each trial of .20.

▼Exploring Other Binomial Distributions

Let's use this worksheet to explore a different binomial distribution, one with a different value of π.

The great baseball player Babe Ruth came to bat 8,399 times in his illustrious career. He hit a home run 714 of those times. What is the probability that if the Babe came to bat five times in a game he would hit at least one home run?

To use the binomial distribution, we have to assume that the probability of the Babe hitting a home run was constant and independent and equal to $714/8399$. Counting a home run as a *success,* the probability is equivalent to the probability of one or more successes in five trials given a probability of success of $714/8399$ on each trial.

There are two differences between this problem and the previous car salesperson problem: The value of π has changed, and the values of x for which a probability is needed have also changed. In the car salesperson problem we wanted to determine the probability that $x = 0$ (no test driver would purchase a car). In this problem we wish to determine the probability that $x \geq 1$ (at least one home run will be hit). The value of n, however, is still 5.

We will use this worksheet not only to calculate the probability, but also to simulate the Babe's batting performance in a game.

- The value of π is in cell I2. There are two ways of entering the value in the cell. Excel will allow you to enter a fraction by entering a zero, followed by a space, followed by the fraction. To do this, select cell I2 and enter "0 714/8399" without the quotes and with a space after the "0." An alternative would be to have Excel do the implied division by entering the formula "=714/8399" (no quotes, of course).

If you enter the value as a fraction, when you press the Enter key, the fraction in its reduced form (4/47) will be displayed immediately (if the cell is selected, the decimal equivalent will appear in the Formula Bar). None of the other cells have changed their value, however, because the workbook is set for manual calculation. Cell I3, which is supposed to equal $1 - \pi$, still displays "0.8."

- Recalculate the workbook by pressing the F9 function key.

This changes not only the value of cell I3 (to 0.91499) but also the binomial distribution calculations in cells K7:K12. In fact, these values are sufficient to answer the question. Let's redo the simulation, however.

- Recall the Random Number Generation dialog window from the "Data Analysis" list chosen from the Tools menu.

If you are still in the same Excel session you were in when you generated the simulations for the car buyers, all the fields in the dialog window will already have the correct values. If they do not, look back at the illustration on page 110. Change the value in the "Number of Variables" field at the top to 5 and the value of the "Number of Random Numbers" field to 10,000.

- Click the OK button in the Random Number Generation dialog window. When the overwrite warning appears, Click OK.

- After the random numbers have been generated, recalculate the workbook by pressing the F9 function key. This will update the tables that determine the number and proportion of successes and the mean and standard deviation. Depending on the speed of your machine, it may take a while for the workbook to complete the recalculation. You can monitor its progress on the left side of the status bar below the worksheet tabs.

Look at the table again. Confirm the same general pattern you saw before. The proportions of times each simulated number of hits appears in column J should be close to the calculated probability of that number of hits in column K.

You might notice that the displayed value for the probability that the Babe would get five home runs is ".0000." Does that mean the probability is zero that he would hit a home run each time at bat? The answer is no. The probability is not zero, but it is so low that when rounded to four decimal places it displays as zero.

- Increase the width of column L to about twice its normal width.

- Click the Increase Decimal button nine times. The displayed probability in L15 is now clearly not exactly zero, but it is a small number.

- Click the UNDO button repeatedly until L15 again displays "0.0000."

What is the probability that the Babe would hit at least one home run? This probability is not directly available in the table, but it can be easily calculated. What needs to be determined is the probability that x is greater than or equal to 1 or $P(x \geq 1)$. This can also be stated as $P(x = 1$ or $x = 2$ or $x = 3$ or $x = 4$ or $x = 5)$. Since these outcomes are mutually exclusive, this probability can be calculated by adding $P(x = 1)$ plus $P(x = 2)$ and so on.

- Select cell L8. Click the AutoSum button, but do not press Enter.

When the AutoSum button is clicked, Excel makes a guess about which cells you wish to add. In this case, Excel assumes you want to add the row adjacent to cell L8 (H8:K8), which is wrong. Fortunately, Excel makes it easy for you to change the cells to be summed by "highlighting" them so that you need only enter the cell address range you want, and it will replace the one Excel guessed. In this case we want to add K8 (which is $P(x = 1)$) to K9, K10, K11, and K12.

- Select the range K8:K12 with the mouse pointer. You should see the formula in cell M19 change to "=SUM(K8:K12)."

- Now press the Enter key. The correct value, "0.3587," will be displayed in M19.

An alternative way of coming up with the same answer would have been to calculate $1 - P(x = 0) = 1 - .6413 = .3587$.

- Double click the "Sheet1" worksheet tab and change its name to "Simulate" (without quotes).

- Change Excel's calculation back to automatic. Open the Tools menu, choose "Options...," click the "Calculation" folder tab in the dialog window, and click the Automatic radio button in the upper left-hand corner. Click the OK button in the dialog window.

- Save the worksheet. Note: this worksheet should have a size of about 937 KB, which will almost fill a diskette. If you are saving to a diskette, look at Appendix F for information on how to compress the workbook so that it won't take up so much room. You may want to temporarily save it to a hard disk or network drive until you end your current session, at which point you would compress the workbook to fit on your diskette.

▼Using Excel to Solve Binomial Word Problems

Most statistics texts provide binomial tables for use in solving word problems involving the binomial distribution. With Excel, the BINOMDIST function takes the place of a table. Compared to a table, BINOMDIST is easier to use, more accurate, and can be used to solve a wider variety of problems than any binomial table. To solve a binomial word problem, however, you still must figure out what the problem is asking for, the same as you would if you were to use a table. First, you have to be sure the problem really is one requiring the binomial distribution. Next, you must come up with answers to the following three questions:

1. What is the value of π (the probability of success on a single trial) for the binomial distribution for this question?

2. What is the value of n (the number of trials) for the binomial distribution for this question?

3. For what value or values of x (the binomially distributed random variable) are you to determine a probability?

The third question is the one most likely to be answered erroneously. A systematic approach can help. Once you have determined the value of n (the answer to the second question), you know the set of possible values for x—the integers between 0 and n, including 0 and n. A useful visual aid is to write down the set of possible integers (assuming the set is not too large). Once that is done, determine which integers within the set satisfy the condition in the question for which you want to determine a probability.

The final step is to figure out how to convert the probability BINOMDIST can give you to the probability which will answer your question.

BINOMDIST provides two different probabilities depending on the value of the fourth argument ("Cumulative"), which can be set to either "true" or "false." This means any binomial problem can be solved at least two different ways with BINOMDIST. To make the best use of BINOMDIST, you need to understand when it is more appropriate to set this argument to "true," and when it is more appropriate to set it to "false." We first will explore in more detail how cumulative probabilities work.

▼BINOMDIST and Cumulative Probabilities

- Open a new workbook by clicking the New button (⬜). Save the workbook in the Chap_4 folder with the name "Chap4_2.xls."

- Open the Tools menu on the Menu Bar. Select "Options...," click the "Calculate" tab in the dialog window and click the Automatic radio button in the "Calculation" field. This will turn automatic recalculation back on for this workbook.

- Double click the "Sheet1" worksheet tab and change its name to "Cumulative."

The decision of whether to make the "Cumulative" argument "true" or "false" depends on the values of x for which you need to determine a probability. Let's examine this by first preparing a table showing the probabilities BINOMDIST provides for all values of x for a particular problem.

Consider the following binomial problem:

A service company provides in-home repair service for a large variety of major appliances. Experience has shown that 65% of service calls can be resolved in one hour or less. What is the probability that, of the next 12 calls, at least 10 of them can be resolved in one hour or less?

We will next set up a table which makes clear the relationship between cumulative and noncumulative probabilities and how each can be used to solve this problem.

- In cell A1 enter the label "pi," and in cell A2 enter the label "n" (both without quotes).

- In cells B1 and B2, enter the values for π and n, respectively, for this problem.

- In cell A4 enter the label "x." In cell B4 enter the label "P(x)," and in cell C4 enter the label "C(x)." These will label the columns for the noncumulative and cumulative probabilities, respectively.

- In cells A5:A17 enter all of the values x could possibly equal in this problem.

The least number of calls which could be resolved in one hour or less is none of them—0. This value ("0") should be in cell A5. The most number of calls which could be resolved in one hour or less is all 12 of them. That value should appear in A17. The other cells should contain the integers between those two values.

In column B we will enter the probabilities we get for each x value when the "Cumulative" argument is "false." In column C we will enter the probabilities when it is "true."

In cell B5 we will enter a formula using the Excel BINOMDIST function to calculate the noncumulative probability that 0 (the value in A5) of the service calls will be resolved in one hour or less, given the values of n and π in cells B1 and B2. The references to n and π will be absolute while the reference to x will be relative. When this formula is copied down, we want the value of x to change, but not the values of n and π.

- Select B5. Click the Edit Formula button and select the "BINOMDIST" function (Statistical group).

- Since we want a noncumulative probability, enter "false" in the "Cumulative" argument field.

- Enter the appropriate cell addresses for x, n, and π in the correct argument fields. If you have forgotten the meaning of the names of the arguments given in the dialog window, look at page 114. Remember that the reference to x should be relative while the others should be absolute. The dialog window should look like the picture at the top of the next page.

- Click the OK button.

The value which displays in cell B5 should be "3.37922E-06." If you don't have this value, be sure cell B1 contains .65 and cell B2 contains 12. If that still doesn't fix it, select cell B5. The formula in the formula bar should be "=BINOMDIST(A5,$B$2,$B$1,FALSE)."

This very low probability indicates it is very unlikely that in the next 12 service calls, none can be completed in one hour or less.

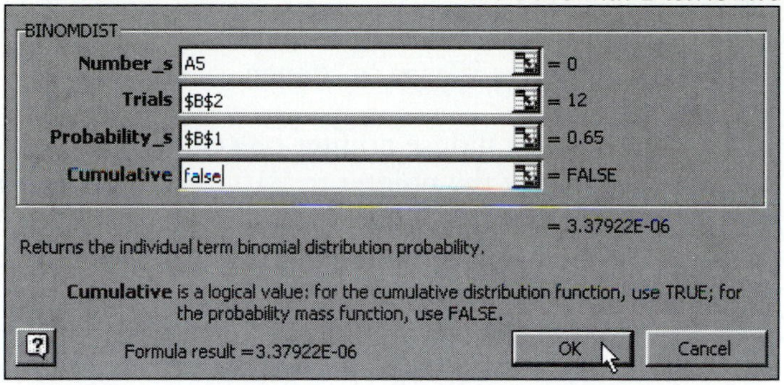
BINOMDIST
Number_s A5 = 0
Trials $B$2 = 12
Probability_s $B$1 = 0.65
Cumulative false = FALSE
= 3.37922E-06
Returns the individual term binomial distribution probability.
Cumulative is a logical value: for the cumulative distribution function, use TRUE; for the probability mass function, use FALSE.
Formula result =3.37922E-06
OK
Cancel

- Copy the formula in cell B5 to the rest of the column in the table: B6:B17. Check to be sure the value displayed in cell B16 is "0.036753." This is the probability that exactly 11 of the next 12 calls can be completed in one hour or less.

Now for the cumulative probabilities.

- Select cell C5. Click the Edit Formula button and select the "BINOMDIST" function. All of the argument fields should be filled out as they were in B5—a relative reference to the number of successes in A5 followed by absolute references to the values of n and π in B2 and B1. In the "Cumulative" field enter "true" (without quotes). Press Enter.

The value which displays in cell C5 should be the same as that displayed in B5.

- Copy the formula in cell C5 to C6:C17. Although the adjacent numbers in B5 and C5 are identical, the numbers below row 5 should be different. The value displayed in cell C17 should be "1." If this is not the case, compare the formulas in adjacent cells in the table. They should be identical except for the "Cumulative" argument, which is "FALSE" in column B and "TRUE" in column C.

▼Converting between Cumulative and Noncumulative Probabilities

The cumulative probability of a particular x value is the sum of all noncumulative probabilities for all values of x less than or equal to that particular value. For example, consider the value in cell C10 ("0.084632"). This is the cumulative probability of 5. It is equal to the sum of the noncumulative probabilities of 0, 1, 2, 3, 4, and 5.

- To see this select cell D10. Click the AutoSum button (Σ). This will automatically insert a formula to sum the values in A10:C10, which is not what we want. Since these values are already selected in the formula, this is easy to change.

- Place the mouse pointer on cell B5 and, while holding the (left) button, drag the pointer to B10, thereby selecting B5:B10. The formula in cell D10 should change to "=SUM(B5:B10)." Press the Enter key. The value displayed in cell D10 should be identical to that displayed in C10.

Clearly, if you have noncumulative probabilities, you can always get the cumulative probabilities by simple addition. It is also easy to go the other way. If you have cumulative probabilities, you can get noncumulative probabilities by simple subtraction. For example, suppose you wanted the (noncumulative) probability that exactly 9 of the next 12 service calls could be resolved in one hour or less, and the only available probabilities were those (cumulative) in column C?

Cell C14 contains the cumulative probability that 9 service calls will be resolved in one hour or less as given in the formula below.

$$C(9) = P(9) + P(8) + P(7) + P(6) + P(5) + P(4) + P(3) + P(2) + P(1) + P(0)$$

Similarly:

$$C(8) = P(8) + P(7) + P(6) + P(5) + P(4) + P(3) + P(2) + P(1) + P(0)$$

By substitution:

$$C(9) = P(9) + C(8)$$

Rearranging:

$$P(9) = C(9) - C(8)$$

The probability of exactly 9 successes is the probability of 9 or fewer successes ($C(9)$) minus the probability of 8 or fewer successes ($C(8)$).

- Select cell D14. Enter the Excel formula to take the value of C14 (which equals $C(9)$) and subtract the value in cell C13 (which is $C(8)$). The displayed value should be identical to that displayed in B14 (which is $P(9)$).

The fact that cumulative probabilities can be determined from noncumulative probabilities, and vice versa, means that either probability can be used to solve any problem. Although noncumulative probabilities might seem more straightforward, cumulative probabilities are often more versatile and easier, especially when large values of n are involved.

▼ Cumulative Probabilities and a Range of *x* Values

To determine the probability that at least 10 of the next 12 service calls can be resolved in an hour or less, we need to determine the probability that *x* equals 10 or 11 or 12. Determining this with noncumulative probabilities is easy to understand and, with such a short range, is easy to determine. For longer ranges, however, cumulative probabilities are easier to use. Although noncumulative probabilities may be the most practical method for this problem, it will serve as an example for the use of cumulative probabilities.

Since the outcomes of a binomial distribution are mutually exclusive, the probability that *x* will fall in a range of values is simply the sum of the probabilities that *x* will equal each value in the range.

- Select A19 and enter the label "noncumulative." Adjust the width of column A to hold the entire label. B19 will be used to calculate the probability of *x* being at least 10 using noncumulative probabilities.

- Enter "cumulative" in cell A20. B20 will be used to calculate the probability of *x* being at least 10 using cumulative probabilities.

- Select cell B19. Enter a formula to add the values of P(10), P(11), and P(12), which are in cells B15:B17. The displayed value in B19 should be "0.151288."

The answer to the question of what is the probability that at least 10 service calls can be resolved in one hour or less is 0.151288. To see how this answer can be determined using cumulative probabilities, consider the cumulative probability of the largest value in the range (12). The expression for this is given by the sum of all the individual probabilities from 12 to 0 as shown in the arithmetic expression below:

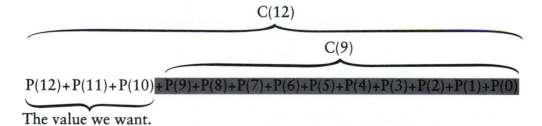

This expression includes the calculation we want, the sum of P(12), P(11), and P(10), but it also includes values (shaded gray) which we don't want. The way to eliminate the unwanted values is to subtract them from the cumulative probability of 12. The unwanted values consist of the sum of all probabilities for 9 or less—the cumulative probability of 9. We can get the answer we want by calculating the cumulative probability of 12 minus the cumulative probability of 9.

Since 12 is the maximum possible value for this binomial distribution, we don't need to get its value from Excel (although it is already in cell C17). The cumulative probability of the largest possible value is always exactly 1.

- Select cell B20. Enter a formula to calculate 4 minus the cumulative probability of 9 (which is in cell C14). The displayed value should be the same as that in cell B19.

To get the probability of x being between 10 and 12, we calculate the cumulative probability of 12 minus the cumulative probability of 9. In general, the probability of x falling within a range of values is the cumulative probability of the upper bound of that range minus the cumulative probability of *one less* than the lower bound. A common mistake is to subtract the cumulative probability of the lower bound rather than one less than the lower bound. This is incorrect because it excludes the probability of x equaling the lower bound, when it should be included.

This problem was a special case in which the upper bound was the maximum possible value, and this made it unnecessary to calculate the cumulative probability of the upper bound since it is known to be 1. Another special case comes when there is no lower bound, when the problem involves calculating the probability that x is less than or equal to a particular value. In this case there is no need to calculate a probability from the lower bound—the answer is simply the cumulative probability of the upper bound.

As we have seen, any binomial probability can be calculated by using BINOMDIST with either cumulative or noncumulative probabilities. Problems involving a single x value are clearly more easily solved with noncumulative probabilities, while problems involving a long range of x values are more easily solved with cumulative probabilities. My preference is to use cumulative probabilities for all cases in which the probability of a range of x values is desired, even if that range is not long.

▼Practice Binomial Problems

In solving any binomial problem you must determine the values of n and π. Let's set up a place in the worksheet for these two important numbers.

- Click the "Sheet2" worksheet tab. In cell A1 enter the label "n," and in cell A2 enter "pi."

Consider the following problem.

What is the probability that the toss of two dice will result in two 1s?

A "success" in this problem is getting a 1. The number of trials is two, since two dice are thrown. Therefore, $n = 2$. The probability of success on a single trial is the probability that a single die will have a 1 when tossed. Since there are six sides to a die, and only one side has a 1, the probability of rolling a 1 with one die is $\frac{1}{6}$. Therefore, $\pi = \frac{1}{6}$.

- Enter (without quotes) "2" in cell B1 and "0 1/6" (space after "0") in cell B2.

The next step is to determine the value or values of x for which we want a probability. In this problem there is only one value for the number of successes for which we want a probability—2. In other words, $x = 2$.

- Enter an "x" in cell A3 and the value of x for which we want a probability (2) in B3.

- Enter the label "Prob" in cell A4. The probability answer will be put in cell B4.

- Select cell B4. Click the Edit Formula button and select "BINOMDIST." Since we are seeking the probability for a single x value, enter "false" (without quotes) in the "Cumulative" field. This will cause BINOMDIST to give a noncumulative probability.

- Enter the values for n, x, and π in the appropriate fields. An explanation of Excel's names for the argument fields is on page 114. Click OK and the answer, "0.027778," will appear immediately in cell B6.

- Select A3:B4. Press the Delete key. The values of x and the way probabilities are calculated will differ in the following problem.

Consider this problem:

If a fair coin is tossed 10 times, what is the probability that the number of heads will be between four and six?

The biggest difference between this problem and the previous one is that this time we must determine the probability that x will fall within a range (a short range) rather than a single value. We will use cumulative probabilities to solve this. The first step, however, is to determine the values of n and π for this problem. The coin is tossed 10 times—$n = 10$. A success in this case is getting a head, and the probability of a head in a single toss is .5—$\pi = .5$

- Enter the values for n and π in the appropriate cells in B1:B2. Don't be surprised if the .5 displays as "½." To Excel, fractions are a format, and since the first value entered in B2 was a fraction, Excel has set the formatting of that cell to fraction and will use that to display any number. The cell format could be changed.

The range of *x* values for which we want a probability is 4 through 6. This can be determined using cumulative probabilities by taking the cumulative probability of the upper bound (six) and subtracting the cumulative probability of the lower bound minus one $(4 - 1 = 3)$.

- In cell A3 enter the label "x Range." In cell A4 enter "Upper." In cell A5 enter "Lower-1."

- In cell B4 enter the value of the upper bound of the *x* range (6), and in cell B5 enter the number which is one less than the lower bound.

- In cell C3 enter "Cumulative Probability." Select cell C4. Click the Edit Formula button and select the "BINOMDIST" function. Use absolute cell addresses for *n* and π and a relative address for the value of *x* in cell B4. Enter "true" in the "Cumulative" field. Click OK. The displayed value should be "0.828125," which is the probability of getting six or fewer heads in 10 coin tosses.

- Copy the formula in cell C4 down to cell C5. This should result in changing the value of the *x* argument to that in B5 without changing the other arguments. The displayed value should be "0.171875," the probability of getting three or fewer heads in 10 tosses.

- Select cell C6. Enter the formula which will subtract the value in cell C5 from that in C4. The displayed value should be "0.656250."

The probability of getting between four and six heads in 10 tosses of a fair coin is thus .65625.

Consider this similar problem:

If a fair coin is tossed 100 times, what is the probability that the number of heads will be between 40 and 60?

Notice the similarity between this question and the previous question. The number of coin tosses and the range boundaries have both been multiplied by 10. The proportion of possible values within the requested range is the same for both problems. Does it seem to you that the answer to this problem will be the same as that of the previous problem?

This problem can be answered with the same worksheet. The differences are in *n* and the upper and lower − 1 bounds.

- Enter these values in the appropriate places in the worksheet. The value displayed in C6 should now be "0.964800."

This much higher value indicates that it is far more likely that 100 tosses will result in the number of heads being between 40 and 60 heads than 10 tosses would result in between 4 and 6 heads. Why the difference? In the beginning of this chapter and in the previous chapter you saw that the larger a sample of random numbers, the more likely it is to resemble the probability distribution that generated the numbers. In both of these distributions, the probability of success is .5. Both problems essentially asked for the probability that the proportion of heads would be between .4 and .6. The larger the number of tosses, the more likely it will be that the proportion of heads is close to .5 and thus between .4 and .6.

• Delete the contents of A3:C6 in preparation for the next problem.

Typically, 10% of a particular brand of new car requires some warranty service during the first year. In a particular shipment of 200 cars, what is the probability that fewer than 15 would require warranty service during the first year?

• First determine the values of n and π for this problem and enter them in the correct cells in column B.

Cell B2's formatting may cause it to not correctly display its value. The correct value can be seen in the Formula Bar when B2 is selected. Let's change B2's formatting:

• Select B2. Open the Format menu on the Menu Bar. Select "Cells...." In the dialog window which opens, click the "Number" tab at the top. In the "Category" region on the left, select "General," which is the first choice. Click OK.

The next step is to determine the range of x values for which a probability is to be determined. This is given in the question as "fewer than 15." What then are the upper and lower bounds of this range? The largest value within the range is 14 since 15 is not "fewer than 15." The smallest value is 0. Since the lower bound is the smallest possible value in the distribution, we need only determine the probability that x is less than or equal to 14—the cumulative probability of 14.

• In cell A3 enter the label "x." In cell A4 enter the label "C(x)." In cell B3 enter the upper bound of the x range for this problem—14. In cell B4 enter the formula using BINOMDIST, which calculates the cumulative probability of the value in B4 given the values of n and π in B1 and B2. The displayed value should be "0.092946." This is the probability that fewer than 15 cars would require warranty service in the first year.

• Clear the values in A4:B4.

Let's consider one more problem:

A television manufacturer is considering purchasing a chassis component from an independent supplier. In order to test the supplier's quality, the TV manufacturer takes a random sample of 100 components and tests them to see how many are defective. Suppose the component manufacturer's process results in 99% of the chassis components being defect-free. What is the probability that none of the components in the sample chosen by the TV manufacturer will have a defect?

The wording of this problem is tricky and obscures exactly what should be considered a "success." The second sentence of the problem suggests that finding a part to be defective is what is to be counted, that is, a defective part is a "success." The next sentence, however, tells the probability of a part being defect-free. A part is either defective or defect-free. The question can be answered by taking either of these outcomes as a "success," although that decision affects the determination of the values of π and x.

Let's take the finding that a part is defective as a "success." The number of trials, n, is the number of parts the TV manufacturer tests, 100. The problem tells us that 99% of the parts are defect-free. Thus 1% are defective and the probability of a part being defective (a "success"), π, is .01. We are asked the probability that none of the parts have a defect, so the value of x for which we want a probability is 0.

- Enter the values for n and π in B1 and B2. Enter "0," the value of x, in cell B3.

In this problem x has only a single value, not a range of values, so a noncumulative rather than a cumulative probability is needed. Since no value of x can be less than 0, in this case the cumulative and noncumulative probabilities would be the same. Nevertheless, it's good to get in the habit of using noncumulative probabilities whenever the probability of a single x value is desired.

- Enter the label "P(x)" in cell A4. In cell B4 enter an Excel equation using BINOMDIST to determine the probability of getting exactly the number of successes shown in B3 (0) given the values for n and π shown in cells B1 and B2. Enter "false" in the "Cumulative" field. The displayed value should be "0.13398." This is the probability that none of the components in the sample will have a defect.

▼The Wording of Binomial Word Problems

As was mentioned at the beginning of the chapter, decoding the language of a binomial word problem is often the hardest part to solving the problem, especially when the problem is asking for the probability of a range of values for the random variable. This, of course, is not a computer problem or a statistics problem, it's an English problem. Most people taking a statistics course think English is the least of their worries, but when you are faced with solving a binomial word problem (especially on a test), it's the English that will often fail you.

The table below is meant to be an aid to help you decode word problems. When you try to solve a word problem, you must first determine the values of n, π and the upper and lower bounds for x. The table is designed to help you with the last determination.

What is the probability that in n trials with probability of success in each trial of π, the number of successes will be

	Lower Bound	Upper Bound
at least y.	y	n
at most y.	0	y
more than y.	$y + 1$	n
fewer than y.	0	$y - 1$
not fewer than y.	y	n
not more than y.	0	y

▼Exercises

1. Suppose the postal service has a delivery goal of delivering 90% of all first-class mail within the same city on the day after mailing. If this goal is achieved, and 100 items of mail are chosen at random to test delivery time, what is the probability that...

   (a) at least 90 will be delivered by the next day?

   (b) more than 95 will be delivered by the next day?

   (c) all 100 pieces will have been delivered by the next day?

(d) fewer than 90 will have been delivered by the next day?

2. Suppose the proportion of automobiles of a certain make that require warranty service is .15. If a particular dealer sells 500 cars...

   (a) what is the expected number of cars sold by that dealer which will require warranty service?

   (b) what is the standard deviation of the number of cars which will require warranty service?

   (c) what is the probability that the number of cars requiring repair will exactly equal the expected value?

   (d) what is the probability that the number of cars requiring repair will be within two standard deviations of the mean (more than the mean minus two times the standard deviation and less than the mean plus two times the standard deviation)?

3. A quality control inspector has drawn a sample of 45 light bulbs from a recent production lot. If none are defective, the lot passes inspection. Suppose 9% of the bulbs in the lot are defective.

   (a) What is the probability that the lot will pass inspection?

   (b) What is the expected value and standard deviation of the number of defective light bulbs in a sample of 45?

4. A manufacturer of integrated circuits is testing a new fabrication process designed to reduce errors in the manufacturing of the most complex integrated circuits (such as high-performance CPU chips). The new process is supposed to have a failure rate of .123, which can be regarded as the probability of any single chip being defective. Suppose the new process is tested by using it to manufacture 800 chips.

   (a) What is the expected value and the standard deviation of the number of those 800 chips which are defective?

   (b) What is the probability that at least 120 out the 800 chips manufactured would be defective?

5. When its process is working properly, the proportion of fluorescent lights produced by a particular process which is defective is .004. Suppose a batch consists of 1,000 fluorescent lights.

(a) What is the probability that a batch will contain at least one defective light?

(b) What are the expected value and standard deviation of the number of defective lights in a batch?

6. A telephone solicitor makes 180 "cold calls" each day trying to convince people to accept a free vacation at a resort in exchange for participating in a sales meeting. Over the long run, experience has shown that the proportion of calls which result in acceptances is .035.

(a) What are the expected value and standard deviation of the number of acceptances which the solicitor receives each day?

(b) What is the probability that the number of acceptances received in a single day will be within one standard deviation of the expected value (the expected value minus one times the standard deviation to the expected value plus one times the standard deviation)?

(c) What is the probability the solicitor would not receive a single acceptance on one day?

(d) One day the solicitor decides to try a new approach on her calls. On that day she receives 10 acceptances. Suppose the new approach was no more effective than the old and the probability of a single call resulting in an acceptance was unchanged. What is the probability that on one day the solicitor would get at least as many acceptances as she got the day she used the new approach?

7. A researcher wishes to conduct a study of the color preferences of new car buyers. Suppose that 40% of this population prefers the color red. If 12 buyers are randomly selected, what is the probability that between 2 and 4 (inclusive) buyers would prefer red?

8. A circuit board manufacturing process has a fault rate of .00025 (25 per 100,000) when it is operating normally. What is the probability that in a batch of 500 circuit boards under these circumstances there would be more than one defective board?

9. A multiple-choice exam has four choices for each question's answer. What is the probability that a student could get at least half the answers correct by guessing on a 30-question exam?

10. An electronic wholesaler has started a program to evaluate errors in the monthly orders received from retailers. The wholesaler has determined that the probability of any single order containing an error is .08. This error is the same for all retailers and independent of the results determined earlier. If each retailer places 12 orders per year, what are the expected number of errors and the standard deviation of errors for each retailer?

11. The Snowden Secretarial Service procures temporary office personnel for major corporations. They have found that 37% of their invoices are paid within 10 working days. A random sample of 18 invoices is checked. What is the probability that at most 4 of the invoices will be paid within 10 working days?

Chapter 5

The Normal Distribution

The normal distribution is important for two reasons. First, many real-world random variables are either normally distributed or have distributions that can be closely approximated by the normal distribution. Second, properties of the normal distribution place it at the foundation of traditional inferential statistics. Indeed, its importance is suggested by its name. (Another name for the normal distribution is the *Gaussian* distribution, crediting the mathematician who first worked with it.)

Like the binomial distribution (and all other named distributions), there is not a single normal distribution. There are an infinite number of normal distributions. Any binomial distribution could be identified by the values of its variables—the number of trials (n) and the probability of success on a single trial (π). Similarly, any normal distribution can be completely identified by the values of two variables—μ and σ. These are the same symbols used for the mean and standard deviation of a population (or probability distribution). They are used for the variables of the normal distribution because the mean of the normal distribution *is* the value of the first variable, and the standard deviation of the normal distribution *is* the value of the second variable. Using the same symbols makes that easy to remember.

An important difference between the normal distribution and the binomial distribution is that the normal distribution is *continuous* while the binomial distribution is *discrete*. A binomially distributed random variable must have an integer value; a normally distributed random variable can have noninteger values. Between any two integer values there are an infinite number of different values that a normally distributed random variable can equal. Like all continuous random variables, the probability that a normally distributed random variable will equal any *specific* value is zero. Nonzero probabilities can only be assigned to a *range* of values. It is thus not meaningful to ask the probability that a normally distributed random variable exactly equals 2, for instance, because 2 is a specific value and the probability of that specific value (2.000000... to infinite precision) occurring is zero. We could ask the probability that a normally distributed random variable has a value between 1 and 3 or between 1.99 and 2.01. The probability associated with these ranges of values would be nonzero. As the width of the interval around any value decreases, so does the probability of a random variable falling within that interval, since more values are included.

Continuous probability distributions are represented by a probability *density* function that differs from the probability *distribution* function used to represent discrete random distributions like the binomial. Probability density functions are often shown graphically. Like a discrete distribution function, the horizontal axis shows the set of values that the random variable could equal. Unlike a discrete distribution function, the vertical axis does not show probability; instead it shows density. A range of values of a continually distributed random variable would define a line segment on the horizontal axis. The *area* between the density function and that segment equals the probability that the random variable will equal a value within that range. The smaller the interval around any value, the smaller the area. Think of the probability of a single value as the area of an interval of zero width—a vertical line. The area of a line is zero as is the probability of a continuous random variable equaling a specific value.

Density functions are often represented graphically. Consider the graph of the "bell-shaped" density function shown below in which the peak is directly above zero on the *x* axis. Consider the probability of a random variable falling between –3.2 and –1.6 or between –0.8 and +0.8—two intervals with equal width—1.6.

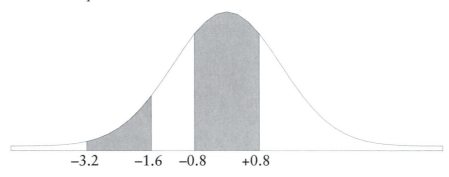

$$-3.2 \qquad -1.6 \quad -0.8 \qquad +0.8$$

The left region represents the interval from –3.2 to –1.6, while the central region represents the interval from –0.8 to +0.8. The central region, however, is taller and has a much greater area than the left region. Since the area of the region equals the probability of the interval, this means that a random variable with this distribution is much more likely to have a value within the range of –0.8 to +0.8 than it is to have a value within the range –3.2 to –1.6. The places where the density function is furthest above the horizontal axis correspond to the values on the horizontal axis that are most likely to occur. For a bell-shaped density function, the range of values around the central peak have the highest probability.

The area under any density function from the smallest possible value to the largest possible value must be 1. This corresponds to the probability of a random variable being between its smallest and largest possible value—a random variable *must* fall within that range and so the probability of its doing so is 1.

In addition to being continuous, the normal distribution (*all* normal distributions) is unbounded. This means that a normally distributed random variable could take on any value from $-\infty$ to $+\infty$. Even so, the area under the curve from $-\infty$ to $+\infty$ must be 1. As we will see, the probabilities associated with intervals far from the mean are very small. So small, in fact, that for practical purposes the distribution can be treated as bounded.

Before looking at how those calculations can be done in Excel, let's look at the shape of the normal density function and how that shape is affected by the values of the distribution's variables, μ and σ.

▼Graphing the Normal Density Function

In the days when the areas under density functions had to be determined using tables, the normal distribution had an important advantage. It is a simple matter to convert an interval of values from any normal distribution to a corresponding interval in another normal distribution which has the same density area (probability). This means that once the relationship between interval and area had been worked out for one normal distribution, it could be used to solve problems for all other normal distributions simply by converting the interval from any normal distribution to the "solved" normal distribution. Thus although there are an infinite number of normal distributions, problems with all could be solved with a single table—a luxury not available with other useful continuous distributions.

The normal distribution chosen to be represented in tables was the "standard" normal distribution, which has a mean equal to 0 and standard deviation equal to 1. Its importance comes from the ease with which intervals in other normal distributions can be converted to intervals in it.

The following directions will guide you in preparing a chart of two normal density functions. One will be the standard normal function, whose mean and standard deviation are fixed at 0 and 1, respectively. The other will be a general normal density function with values for the mean and standard deviation that are taken from worksheet cells and that you will be able to change. In this chart the unchanging standard normal distribution will provide a benchmark that makes it easier to see how changes in the mean and standard deviation of the general normal distribution affect the shape of the distribution.

Before the chart can be drawn, a table must be created giving a set of x values and the density values associated with each of these x values.

- Start Excel with a new blank worksheet and save it in a new directory named "Chap_5" as "Chap5.xls."

- In cell A1 enter the label "x." Column A will be used for the values of the random variables.

- In cell B1 enter the label "general." Column B will be used for the general normal density values.

- In cell C1 enter the label "standard." Column C will be used for the standard normal density values.

- Enter the label "mu" in cell D1 and "sigma" in cell D2.

- Enter the value "0" in cell E1 and "1" in cell E2. These cells will hold the variables for the general normal distribution.

These initial values for the mean and standard deviation of the general normal distribution will make it the same as the standard normal. By changing the values in these cells, however, we will be able to make our general normal distribution be any of the infinite number of normal distributions.

In column A, starting with cell A2, we will put the series of numbers starting with −5 and going to +5. Each time we move down a cell, the value will increment by 0.1. Thus cell A3 will be −4.9, cell A4 will be −4.8, and so on. How many cells will be needed? The general formula is to take the difference between the ending and starting value, divide by the increment, and add 1. Thus, if we were going from a to b by increment i, the formula would be: $\dfrac{b-a}{i}+1$. For this case: $\dfrac{5-(-5)}{0.1}+1=101$. Therefore, if the series starts in cell A2, it will end in cell A102.

There are a number of ways of having Excel create the series, but since over 100 cells are involved, using the mouse could be tricky. Try the following method instead.

- Enter "-5" in cell A2.

- Click the mouse pointer in the Name Box, and then enter "a2:a102." Press the Enter key and that region will be selected. The location of the Name Box is shown on page 4.

- Open the Edit menu on the Menu Bar. Click "Fill." A cascade menu will open. Choose "Series...." These menus are shown in the picture below.

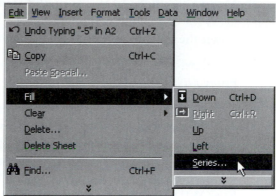

- The Series dialog window will open. This window allows you to specify how you want Excel to create a series. In this case you want a *linear* series, which means the increment value will be constant, and you want the increment to be 0.1. The increment is referred to in the dialog window as "Step value."

- Click the mouse pointer in the "Step value" field and enter the value "0.1." The window looks like the picture below.

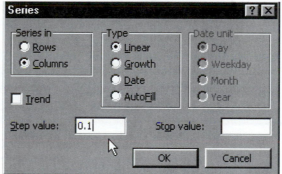

- Click the OK button and you should see the series in the selected region.

Next we will put the values for the density functions in columns B and C.

- Select cell B2. Instead of using the Formula Palette, click the Paste Function button on the Standard Toolbar: $f_\times$. In the "Statistical" category, choose the "NORMDIST" function, and click the OK button.

The NORMDIST function has three arguments:

1. **X**—the value of the random variable for which the density is to be determined. Enter a *relative* address for cell A2, which contains −5. The relative address will change to refer to the cell in the same row of column A when the formula is copied down the column.

2. **Mean**—the mean of the normal distribution. Enter an *absolute* address for cell E1, which contains a 0. When the formula is copied down the column, this reference to cell E1 will remain.

3. **Standard_dev**—the standard deviation of the normal distribution. Enter an *absolute* address for cell E2, which contains a 1.

4. **Cumulative**—Enter the word "false" (without quotes). This will cause the function to provide the density value. If the word "true" were entered, the cumulative probability would be provided. It is important to note that the density has little practical value—charting the density function (as we are doing here) is a rare exception. Unlike BINOMDIST, there are virtually no other useful situations where this argument should be "false."

The dialog window should look like the picture below.

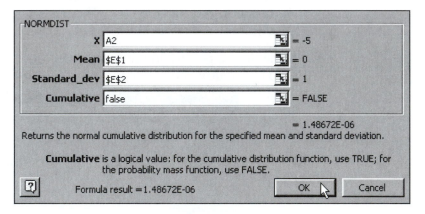

Click the OK button. The value that appears in cell B2 is "1.48672E-06," which could also be written as .00000148672. Remember that this very small number is *not* a probability.

The density values for the standard normal distribution will go in column C. The standard normal distribution is the normal distribution with $\mu = 0$ and $\sigma = 1$.

*   Select cell C2. Use the Formula Palette and choose "NORMDIST" again, which will appear as the most recently used function. Use the same values in the argument fields you used above *except* enter the number 0 in the "Mean" field and the number 1 in the "Stan-

dard_dev" field (as shown below). Click the OK button. The same value should appear in cell C2 as appears in cell B2.

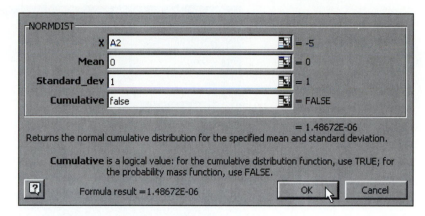

Next the formulas in cells B2 and C2 must be copied down the columns. Recall that the last value in column A is in A102. The formulas in B2 and C2 need to be copied down to row 102. The instructions which follow use a method similar to that used to generate the series in column A.

- Click the mouse pointer in the Name Box. Enter the range address "B2:C102." Press the Enter key, and the range will be selected.

- Open the Edit menu on the Menu Bar. Choose "Fill," and a cascade menu will open. Click "Down" on the cascade menu. These menus are shown on page 112. Check row 52. Column A should display a "0." Columns B and C should both display the value "0.39894228."

- Save your worksheet now and often!

The last part is to have Excel graph the density values in columns B and C against the x values in column A. The instructions will direct you to create a graph that will share your screen with the values of μ and σ in cells E1 and E2. This will enable you to change those values and immediately see the change in the density function without scrolling your screen or changing worksheets. In an earlier chapter you saw the Histogram tool place a chart on an existing worksheet. You can create your own chart on a worksheet by using the Chart Wizard button. It is often a good idea to select the data you want used in a chart before clicking the Chart Wizard button.

- Use the Name Box to select the region A1:C102.

- Click the Chart Wizard button, 📊.

- In the Step 1 dialog window for the Chart Wizard select an "XY (Scatter)" plot with the data points connected by lines without markers by making the choices shown in the picture below. Click the Finish Button.

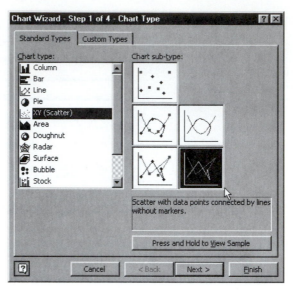

To best see how the mean and standard deviation affect the general normal distribution, let's increase the size of the chart and make some formatting changes.

- Using the Scroll Bars, scroll your worksheet so that cell D1 is in the upper-left corner of your screen. Columns A–C will not be visible.

- Select the chart (so that it has handles) unless it is already selected. Place the mouse pointer inside the chart boundary but not on any object in the chart. Press and hold the mouse button and slightly move the mouse. The pointer will change to a "drag" shape: ✛.

- Drag the chart so that the upper-left corner of the chart is near the upper-left corner of cell D3.

- Place the mouse pointer on the handle on the lower right-hand corner of the chart. The mouse pointer will change to the object-resize shape: ↖.

- Press and hold the (left) mouse button. Drag the handle to the lower right-hand corner of your screen. The object is to make the chart as large as possible on your screen without making it too large to be seen without scrolling and without covering the first two rows (1 and 2) of the worksheet.

Enlarging the graph has the unfortunate effect of enlarging the letters and numbers. We will reduce them next, and, while we are at it, we will make some changes in the way the chart handles axis values.

- Place your mouse pointer on the legend. Wait a second until a small window opens with "Legend," verifying the pointer is on the legend. Click the (left) mouse button. The legend should have handles indicating that it has been selected.

- Click to open the Format menu on the Menu Bar. When the menu opens, choose "Selected Legend...."

- When the Format Legend dialog window opens, click the "Font" folder tab at the top.

- On the right side of the dialog window is a field labeled "Size:," which controls the size of the fonts in the legend. Change the size from its present value to "8" either directly in the field or by selecting "8" from the list below the field. Click the OK button. The legend should appear visibly smaller.

- Place the mouse pointer on one of the numbers along the y (vertical) axis (such as the ".45" at the top). After a second, a small window should open with "Value (Y) Axis." Click the (left) mouse pointer. This will select the y axis, which you can verify by seeing the handles that appear at each end of the vertical axis (in the positions shown below).

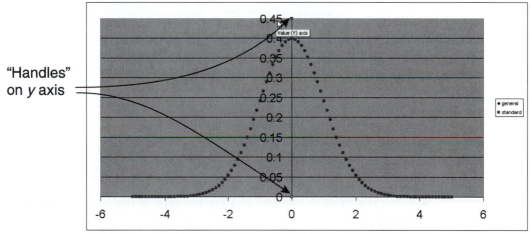

"Handles" on y axis

- Open the Format menu on the Menu Bar and click "Selected Axis...." Click the "Scale" tab. In order to ensure that the scale of the axis does not change when we change the general normal distribution curve, we want to disable the automatic determination of the axis scale. Along the left side of the dialog window is a set of check boxes that currently have checkmarks. Click the mouse pointer in each box so that the checkmarks are removed from all boxes.

- Click the "Font" tab. Change the font size to "8" as you did with the legend. Click the OK button.

The last step is to alter the x (horizontal) axis.

- Place the mouse pointer on one of the numbers for the x axis. A small window will open with "Value (X) Axis." Click the (left) mouse button to select the axis and verify that handles appear at each end of the horizontal axis.

- Open the Format menu on the Menu Bar and click "Selected Axis...."

In addition to preventing Excel from changing the values along the x axis, we will explicitly set those values to agree with the values used in the worksheet (from −5 to +5).

- Click the "Scale" folder tab. Change the values in the "Minimum:" and "Maximum:" fields to "−5" and "5," respectively. Change the "Major unit:" value to "1." This will result in values along the x axis at one-unit intervals. Remove all checkmarks in the window. The window should look like the picture below.

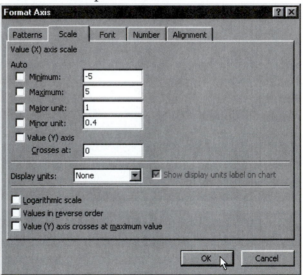

- Click the "Font" tab and change the size of the numbers to "8" as you did before.

There appears to be only one graph on your screen, but actually there are two identical charts, one on top of the other. Both are the standard normal distribution in which $\mu = 0$ and $\sigma = 1$. You may recognize the shape of the graph; it is often referred to as "bell-shaped." The peak of the graph occurs right above the value 0 on the horizontal axis.

Notice on your worksheet how close the density function is to the horizontal axis to the left of −3.5 and to the right of +3.5. There doesn't seem to be any space at all between the horizontal axis and the density function line. The area of the region for the interval between 3.5 and 5.0, for example, looks like it would be zero. In fact the density function line *is* above the horizontal axis and so the region would not be exactly zero. It *would* be so small that it could practically be taken as zero. Although the standard normal distribution is unbounded, the probabilities associated with any region to the left of −3.5 or to the right of +3.5 are so very small that they can practically be treated as zero. For practical purposes, then, the standard normal distribution can be regarded as bounded between −3.5 and +3.5. Other normal distributions will also have practical (but not theoretical) boundaries.

Let's examine the effect that changes in the values of μ and σ have on the shape of the general normal density function.

- Select cell E2 (the value of σ, the standard deviation of the general normal distribution) and change the value from 1 to 1.1. The two density functions are now both clearly visible. Look at the legend to determine which is the "general" normal density function. That is the one that has changed.

- Change cell E2 from 1.1 to 2 in steps of 0.1. Observe the change in the density function with each change in σ.

Increasing the standard deviation makes the curve more "spread out." It also causes the "peak" to be less high. This second change is necessary to keep the entire area below the entire curve at a constant 1.0.

- Change cell E2 back to 1. Now change it to 0.9. Continue decreasing the value of E2 to 0.5 in steps of 0.1.

Since we have indicated in the Chart Wizard that we do not want the *y* axis rescaled, as the peak of the general normal distribution increases, it moves off the top of the chart on the worksheet. If the chart were taller, we would see that the plot continues to have a bell shape.

Decreasing the standard deviation makes the curve higher and more "pinched." What is the meaning of these changes? A normally distributed random variable drawn from a distribution with small standard deviation is more likely to have a value near the mean than is a normally distributed random variable drawn from a distribution with a large standard deviation. The area of an interval around the mean (like the central region in the preceding picture) will be greater the higher the curve, which happens when the standard deviation is small. The area of an interval away from the mean (like the left region in the preceding picture) will be smaller if the curve is more "pinched," as also happens with a small standard deviation.

Observe now the effect of a change in μ.

- Change the value of E2 back to 1.

- Select cell E1, which contains the mean. Change it to 0.5. Continue increasing the value of E1 by steps of 0.5 to 4.0. Observe the chart. Then change it back to 0 and decrease it by steps of –0.5 to –4.0.

As you see, changing the value of μ shifts the curve right or left. The peak is always above μ, no matter what its value. Since the peak marks the value that the random variable is most likely to be close to, you can see that the mean is always the value that normally distributed random variables are likely to be close to.

- Double click the "Sheet1" worksheet tab and change its name to "Density."

- Save the workbook.

▼ Determining Probabilities from Intervals

Most problems involving the normal distribution fall into two categories: (1) determining the probability of a normally distributed random variable having a value within a given interval, and (2) determining an interval within which the value of a normally distributed random variable will fall with a given probability. The first type of problem will be considered first.

- Double click the "Sheet2" worksheet tab and change its name to "Probability."

The normal distribution has a property that made it a particularly convenient distribution to use in the precomputer days. If we want to find the probability of a randomly distributed variable having a value within a given interval, it is an easy matter to find a corresponding interval for a different normal distribution with the same probability. The importance of this property is that once the relationship between intervals and probabilities is worked out for one particular normal distribution (that is, one particular set of values for μ and σ), a problem involving another normal distribution can be easily transformed to the one for which the probabilities have been worked out. The distribution to which all intervals are converted is the standard normal distribution we have seen, where $\mu = 0$ and $\sigma = 1$.

Suppose we have a problem involving determining the probability of a normally distributed random variable having a value within a known interval. That interval will be defined by one or more boundary values. The process of transforming those boundary values to the equivalent values in the standard normal distribution is called the *z transformation* or *standardization*. If the normal distribution of concern in the problem has a mean equal to μ and a standard deviation equal to σ, the z transformation is given by the formula:

$$z = \frac{x - \mu}{\sigma}$$

Another name for the standard normal distribution is the *z* distribution, and the value of a standard normal interval boundary corresponding to the value of the interval boundary in a different normal distribution is called a *z* value.

With a computer program like Excel, it would be possible to avoid the *z* transformation. As you have seen, the NORMDIST function has arguments for the mean and standard deviation of the distribution that interests you. The *z* transformation is, however, easy, even trivial, in a spreadsheet. Furthermore, the use of *z* values and the *z* transformation is so deeply ingrained in modern statistical practice that the methods discussed in this book will involve calculating and using the *z* value. Its importance is sufficiently great that Excel provides separate functions for the standard normal distribution. Another reason for explicitly standardizing random variables is that it will be required for other probability distributions, and it makes sense to cover it now where its use is traditional.

The discussion below will first consider determining the probabilities associated with intervals in the *z* distribution. This will then be expanded to an interval for any normal distribution.

▼Determining Probabilities for *z* Intervals

The Excel function used for determining probabilities for the *z* distribution is NORMSDIST—different from NORMDIST by the "S" (for *standard*) in the middle. A typical problem will be to find the probability of a random variable falling between two values—let's call them z_1 and z_2. Look the probability density function for the standard normal distribution shown at the top of the next page.

The points corresponding to the boundaries of the interval—z_1 and z_2—are located on the horizontal axis. The probability of a random *z* variable falling between these two values equals the area below the density function curve and between the interval boundaries—the shaded region in the picture. We will use NORMSDIST to determine this area.

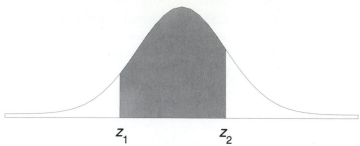

z_1 z_2

NORMSDIST has a single argument—*z*—and it returns the probability of a standard normal variable being less than the value of that argument. This corresponds to the area to the left of that argument. If, for example, we gave NORMSDIST the value of z_2 in the picture above, it would return a probability equal to the area below the density function to the left of z_2. That is a bigger area than we want, however. To get the area we want, we need to exclude the area to the left of z_1—the probability of a standard normal variable being less than z_1. This is done simply by subtracting the area to the left of z_1 from the area to the left of z_2:

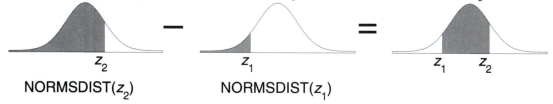

z_2 z_1 z_1 z_2

NORMSDIST(z_2)   NORMSDIST(z_1)

Let's determine the probability of a standard normal random variable having a value between −1.0 and 0.5

- Click the "Sheet2" worksheet.

- In cell A1 enter the label "z," and in cell B1 enter the label "Probability."

- In cell A2 enter the number "0.5" and in cell A3 the number "-1."

- Select cell B2. Click the Edit Formula or Paste Function (*fx*) button and select "NORMSDIST" from the "Statistical" category of functions. When its dialog window opens, click cell A2 to insert its (relative) address in the "Z" argument field. Click OK. The value "0.691462" should be displayed in B2. This is the probability of a standard normal variable being less than 0.5.

- Copy the function in B2 down to B3. Cell B3 should display "0.158655," the probability of a standard normal variable being less than −1.0.

- Select cell B4. Enter a formula which will calculate the value of cell B2 minus the value of cell B3. The displayed result should be

"0.532807." The probability of a standard normal variable being between -1.0 and 0.5 is a little over .53.

Using Excel to determine the probability of a standard random variable falling within a given interval is straightforward—simply use NORMSDIST to find the cumulative probability of the upper bound and subtract from that the cumulative probability of the lower bound.

This is similar to the method used with BINOMDIST to find the probability of a binomial variable falling within a specific interval, but there is one difference. With the discrete binomial distribution, we had to be careful with the interval boundaries. For example, if we wanted to calculate the probability of a binomial variable being between 10 and 12 we had to take the cumulative probability of 12 minus the cumulative probability of <u>9</u>, not 10 (see page 126). For a continuous random variable this adjustment in the boundary value is unnecessary. The reason is that with the binomial distribution we needed to subtract the probability of being less than 10 from the probability of being less than or equal to 12. Since cumulative probability is the probability of being less than or equal to a value—and not just less than that value—we had to use the cumulative probability of 9. If only integer values are possible, the probability of being less than 10 is the probability of being less than or equal to 9. In other words, $P(x \leq 10) \neq P(x < 10)$. The difference between the two is the probability that x exactly equals 10, which is not zero.

The difference with a continuous random variable is that the probability of being less than or equal to a given value is the same as the probability of just being less than that value. In other words, $P(z \leq -0.5) = P(z < -0.5)$. Think of the difference between the two as the probability that z exactly equals -0.5. That probability is 0 because the probability of any continuous random variable exactly equaling a specific value is 0. We don't need to worry about explicitly including the boundary values in the intervals because the probability the random variable will exactly equal a boundary value is 0.

There are two special cases to consider; both involve situations in which one side of the interval is unbounded, as shown in the picture below.

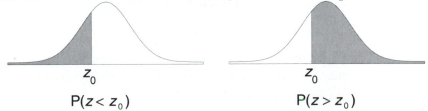

$$P(z < z_0) \qquad\qquad P(z > z_0)$$

The left picture show the case when there is no lower bound. In this situation no subtraction is needed. The probability of a standard normal variable being less than z_0 is simply the cumulative probability of z_0, NORMSDIST(z_0).

The right picture shows the case when there is no upper bound. Recall that the area under an entire probability density function is always exactly 1. To get the area of the shaded region in the right picture, calculate one minus the area of the unshaded region, which is the cumulative probability of z_0: $1 -$ NORMSDIST(z_0).

- In cell A6 enter the label "z," and in cells B6 and B7 enter the labels "Prob <" and "Prob >," respectively.

- Let's use the value –0.72 for the value of z_0 in the picture above. Enter this value in cell A7.

- Select cell B7. Click the Edit Formula button and select the "NORMSDIST" function. Click A7 to enter that address in the "Z" argument field. Click OK. Cell B7 should display "0.235762," which is the probability of a standard normal variable being less than –0.72.

- Select cell C7. Again click the Edit Formula button. Using the keyboard, enter "1-" (no quotes) and click "NORMSDIST" in the Function Box. When the NORMSDIST dialog window opens click cell A7 to enter its address in the "Z" argument field. The Formula Bar should show "=1-NORMSDIST(A7)." Click OK and the value "0.764238" should appear in C7. This is the probability that a standard normal variable will be greater than –0.72.

▼Determining Probabilities for Other Normal Distributions

The next step is to use NORMSDIST to determine probabilities for other normal distributions with any value for the mean and standard deviation. This is a two-step process. The first step is to convert the boundary value or values to z values using the formula on page 147. Once these boundaries have been converted to z values, NORMSDIST can be used to find the corresponding probabilities.

Consider the following problem:

Suppose Wednesday sales at a convenience store average $2,000 with a standard deviation of $500. What is the probability that sales for one Wednesday will be below $1,000?

It's always a good idea to sketch a picture of the distribution with the interval shown on the horizontal axis. This ensures that we have the interval correctly determined and can give us some idea of what the answer should be. For this problem, the picture is shown below. Since the area under the entire curve is 1, the area to the left of 2,000 is 0.5. The shaded area is only part of the area to the left of 2,000, so it must be less than 0.5.

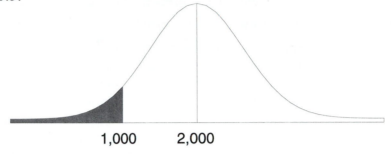

- Enter the following labels in cells A1:A5: "mu," "sigma," "x," "z," and "cumulative probability." Adjust the width of column A to accommodate the last label.

- Enter the values for μ and σ (2,000 and 500) of the distribution of daily sales in cells B1 and B2, respectively.

- In cell B3 enter the value for the interval boundary x (1,000) for which we want a probability.

Cell B4 will contain the formula which will convert that x value into its corresponding z value using the formula $z = \dfrac{x - \mu}{\sigma}$. Since an Excel formula must be on a single line, the calculation for $x - \mu$ must be placed in parenthesis to force it to be evaluated before the division by σ.

- Select cell B4. Begin entering an Excel formula by clicking the Edit Formula button or by pressing the equal sign key. Enter a left parenthesis. Click the cell containing the value for x (B3) to enter that address next, press the minus sign key, click the cell containing the value for μ (B1), and press the right parenthesis key. At this point the formula bar should contain "=(B3-B1)." Complete the formula by pressing the divides key (/) and clicking the cell containing the value for σ (B2). The formula in the Formula Bar should be "=(B3-B1)/B2." Press the Enter key or click the Enter Formula button (✔). The value displayed in B4 should be "-2," which is the z value corresponding to 1,000 in this problem.

- Enter a formula in cell B5 which will use NORMSDIST to determine the cumulative probability of –2.

The displayed value should be "0.02275," which is the probability that sales on a single Wednesday will be less than $1,000. As expected, this probability is less than 0.5.

- Select cells B1:B5. Press the Delete key to erase their contents.

Consider the following problem:

An automobile manufacturer has determined that the cars in a particular model line have fuel consumption that averages 27 miles per gallon with a standard deviation of 5 miles per gallon. What proportion of cars could be expected to have fuel consumption between 25 mpg and 30 mpg?

Sketch the distribution showing the area that corresponds to the probability which must be found. That sketch should look something like the picture below.

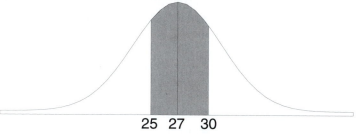

25 27 30

There are two *x* values in this problem. Each must be converted to a corresponding *z* value. The cumulative probability of each can then be determined using NORMSDIST. Finally, the difference between those two cumulative probabilities will give the value corresponding to the shaded region in the diagram.

- Enter the distribution's mean and standard deviation (27 and 5) in cells B1 and B2.

- Enter the two values for the two *x*'s (25 and 30) in cells B3 and C3.

- Enter formulas in B4 and C4 which will convert the *x* values in B3 and C3, respectively, to *z* values. The displayed values should be "-0.4" and "0.6," respectively.

- In cells B5 and C5, enter formulas using NORMSDIST which will calculate the cumulative probabilities of B4 and C4. The displayed values should be "0.34458" and "0.72575," respectively.

- In cell B6 enter a formula which will calculate the difference between the two cumulative probabilities in row 5. The displayed value should be "0.38117."

The expected proportion of cars with gas mileage between 25 and 30 mpg is 0.38117.

- Select cells B1:C6. Press the Delete key to erase the cell contents.

Try this problem:

A package delivery firm regularly sends trucks between two regional distribution centers. Through careful record keeping, it has discovered that the transit time is normally distributed with a mean of 10 hours and a standard deviation of 2.5 hours. What is the probability that a single truck would make the trip in less than 5 hours or more than 15 hours?

The interval described here is illustrated by the shaded areas in the diagram below.

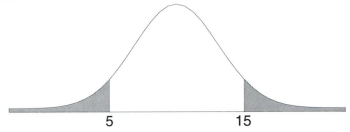

The shaded region in this diagram has two parts. Two approaches to determining the shaded area are possible:

1. The shaded region could be regarded as what's left over when the central region is taken out. Using this approach, you would determine the area of the region above the interval between 5 and 15 and subtract that from 1. The central area could be determined using the same method used in the previous problem. Another cell could be used to subtract that area from 1.

2. The shaded region could be regarded as the combination of two intervals, one to the left of 5 and the other to the right of 15. Using this approach, you would determine the area of the left-tail region bounded from above by 5 and add that to the area of the right-tail region bounded from below by 15. Do this addition in an available cell near that used above by using an Excel formula.

- Use both approaches to solve this problem. Verify that you get the same answer with each approach. The correct answer is .0455.

- Save your worksheet.

▼Determining Intervals from Probabilities

A different type of problem that arises with the normal distribution (and other distributions) is one in which you want to determine an interval within which a normally distributed random variable will fall with known probability. This type of problem is, in a sense, a backward version of the problems we have just looked at. Instead of determining the probability of a random variable falling within a defined interval, we are given the probability and must find the interval.

- Open the "Insert" menu on the Menu Bar. Click "Worksheet" on the open menu. A new worksheet will be created.

- Rename this worksheet "Find Interval." Move it to the end of the workbook by dragging the new worksheet tab to the right of the other tabs. (This is covered in more detail on page 28.)

Excel provides a function which is the inverse of the NORMSDIST function. NORMSDIST takes a z value and returns the probability of a standard normal variable being less than that value. NORMSINV takes a probability and returns that z value which has the property that the probability of a standard normal variable being less is exactly the given probability.

Consider the standard normal density function below.

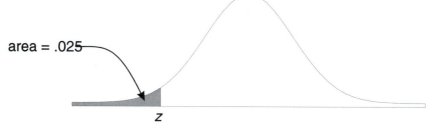

What z value has the property that the probability of a standard normal variable being less is exactly equal to .025?

- In cell A1 enter the label "Prob <" and in cell A2 enter "z."

- In cell B1 enter the probability ".025."

- Select cell B2 and click either the Edit Formula or Paste Function button. Select "NORMSINV" from the "Statistical" category.

- After the NORMSINV dialog window opens, move it and click cell B1 to enter that address in the "Probability" argument field. Click OK.

The displayed value in cell B2 should be "-1.95996." The probability of a standard normal variable having a value less than −1.95996 is .025. Let's use NORMSDIST to check this and to verify the inverse relationship between it and NORMSINV.

- Select cell B3. Click the Edit Formula button. Select "NORMSDIST," which, unless you have closed Excel since using it early in this chapter, should be the second function in the Function Box.

- Once the NORMSDIST dialog window opens, move it and click B2 to enter the −1.95996 in the "Z" argument field. Click OK and "0.025" will be displayed in B3.

NORMSDIST "undoes" NORMSINV by converting the z value back to its cumulative probability.

- Enter other values in cell B1. As long as the value entered is between 0 and 1, the same value will appear in B3. What happens if you enter zero or a negative value or a positive value greater than or equal to 1?

The value in B1 is a probability. NORMSINV will return an error code if it is given a value which is not a valid probability. Zero and 1 are, of course, valid values for probabilities, but the corresponding z values are −∞ and +∞, which cannot be represented as numbers in the computer. Also, if you enter values in B1 which are very close to 0 (e.g., .00001), the value in B3 will differ slightly because of rounding error.

Just as NORMSDIST could be used to find probabilities other than cumulative probabilities, NORMSINV can be used to find z values when the probability provided in a problem is not a cumulative probability. Generally, a probability will be one of the types represented by the shaded regions in the four density functions shown below.

| Less than z | Greater than z | Two-Tail | Central Region |
| z | z | z_1 z_2 | z_1 z_2 |

An important characteristic of the two-tailed region is that *the areas of the two tails are equal.* The central region has the property that it is centered directly over the mean of the distribution. As a consequence, the two tails that lie outside the region are again equal in area. Since the standard normal distribution is symmetric and centered on zero, for both the two-tail and central-region case z_1 and z_2 will differ in sign but have the same absolute value.

NORMSINV is most easily used when the probability we have is the probability that a standard normal variable is less than z. When the probability we have corresponds to one of the other three shaded regions, the first step is to determine the area to the left of z (or one of the z's in the cases where there are two).

Suppose, for example, that we want to determine the value of z such that the probability of a greater standard normal variable equals .2. This probability corresponds to the shaded region in the density function labeled "Greater than z." If the area to the right of z is .2, what is the area to the left of z? Remembering that the area under the entire density function is 1, the area to the left of z is $1 - .2 = .8$. We could thus determine the value of z by giving NORMSINV .8.

The other cases are only slightly more difficult.

- Enter the following labels in cells A5:A9: "central area," "2 tail area," "1 tail area," "left z," and "right z."

Consider the following problem:

What z value has the property that the probability of the absolute value of a standard normal variable exceeding that value is .42?

This probability corresponds to a two-tail area, and the z value asked for is the positive z, z_2 in the picture on page 155.

- Enter the probability ".42" in cell B6.

In cells B5 and B7 we will enter formulas to calculate the central area and the area of one tail from the value entered in B6.

- If the area of two tails is .42, The area of one tail is half that. Enter a formula in cell B7 which will divide the value in B6 by 2. The displayed value should be "0.21."

- If the area of the two tails is .42, and the area under the entire curve is 1, the central area must be one minus the area of the two tails. Enter a formula in B5 which will calculate one minus the value of B6. The displayed value should be "0.58."

We can now label all of the segments of the density with their areas as shown in the diagram on the top of the next page. This makes clear what the areas are to the left of z_1 and z_2, which are the values required by NORMSINV to provide the values of z_1 and z_2

- Select cell B8. Click the Edit Formula button and click "NORMSINV" in the Formula Box. The area to the left of the left z (z_1) is the area of one tail. Click cell B7 to enter this area in the "Probability" argument of NORMSINV. Click OK. The value "-0.80642" will be displayed.

- The area to the left of z_2 is the central area (.58) plus the left tail (.21). Select cell B9. Click the Edit Formula button and "NORMSINV" in the Formula Box. When the dialog window opens, move it out of the way.

- Click the cell containing the central area, B5. Press the plus key and then click the cell containing the area of the left tail, B7. The "Probability" argument field should contain "B5+B7." Click OK. The value "0.806422" should be displayed.

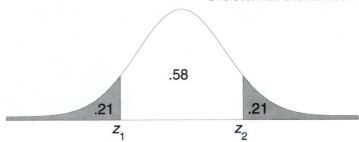

As expected, z_1 and z_2 have the same absolute value but different signs. The slight difference between the values displayed in B8 and B9 is due to the fact that the absence of the minus sign allows Excel to display the value of B9 with an additional digit of significance. Remember that the values displayed are always a rounded version of the values stored internally for each cell.

The answer to the problem is the value of z_2. Since z_1 and z_2 have the same absolute value, the easiest way to determine z_2 may be to simply determine the value of z_1 and change the sign to positive.

- Select cells B5:B9 and press the Delete key to empty the cells.

Consider the following problem:

Within what region, symmetrically distributed about the mean, will a standard normal variable fall with probability .9?

The probability given in this problem corresponds to the central area shown in the diagram on page 155. To find the z values, we must convert this to the area to the left of each z.

- Select cell B5. Enter the probability value, ".9."

- Select cell B6. Enter a formula which will calculate the area of the two tails given the value of the central area in B5. The displayed value should be "0.1."

- Select cell B7. Enter a formula which will calculate the area of a single tail given the area of both tails in B6. The displayed value should be "0.05."

The density function with the area of each region is shown at the top of the next page.

- Select cell B8. Enter a formula using NORMSINV which will calculate the value of z_1. The displayed value in B8 should be "-1.64485."

- Select cell B9. Enter a formula using NORMSINV which will calculate the value of z_2. This value should be "1.644853."

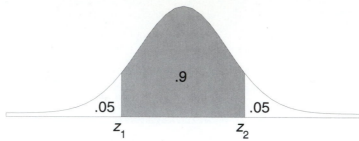

There is a .9 probability that a standard normal variable will have a value between −1.64485 and +1.64485.

Next let's extend this technique to determine intervals corresponding to given probabilities for any normal distribution, not just the standard normal distribution.

▼Going from a Standard Normal Boundary to a General Normal Boundary

Recall that the steps involved in determining the probability of a normal variable falling within a given interval were first to convert the interval boundaries to the corresponding z values, then to use NORMSDIST with those boundaries to determine cumulative probabilities, and finally to convert those cumulative probabilities to the probability for the desired interval.

The process of going from probability to interval traces these steps backward. First we convert the probability given to cumulative probabilities. Next we use NORMSINV to get the values of the interval boundaries for the z distribution. Finally the z values are converted to the corresponding values in the problem's normal distribution. The conversion used to go from x value to z value is given by the equation on page 147. For this type of problem we must convert from z to x. If the equation given on page 147 is solved for x it provides a form useful for this conversion:

$$x = \mu + z\sigma$$

Consider the following problem:

The time required for a package delivery firm to deliver a package is normally distributed with a mean of 10 hours and a standard deviation of 3 hours. What delivery time will be beaten by only 2.5% of all deliveries?

The first step is to determine exactly what probability is given by the problem and what steps might be necessary to convert it to the cumulative probability required by NORMSINV. The object of the problem is to find a delivery time, x, which is "beaten" by 2.5% of all deliveries. If a delivery time "beats" x, it is less than x. So the problem is to find a delivery time such that 2.5% of all delivery times are less than x. If 2.5% of all delivery times are less than x, the probability of a randomly chosen delivery time being less than x is .025. This situation is depicted in the graph below.

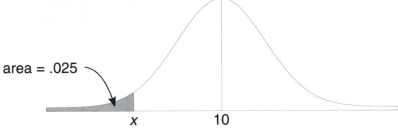

area = .025

x 10

The .025 probability *is* a cumulative probability, and NORMSINV can be used directly to determine the z value corresponding to x.

- Select cell B7. Enter the probability ".025."

- Select cell B8. Enter a formula using NORMSINV which determines the z value corresponding to x. The value displayed in that cell should be "-1.95996."

The next step is to convert this z value to an x value for the distribution of delivery times ($\mu = 10$, $\sigma = 3$).

- In cells A10:A12 enter the labels: "mu," "sigma," and "left x."

- In cells B10 and B11 enter the values for μ and σ for the distribution of delivery times.

- Select cell B12. Enter the Excel formula that will take the mean in cell B10 and then add the product of the z value in cell B8 and the standard deviation in cell B11. The displayed value should be "4.120117."

Only 2.5% of all deliveries will be less than about 4.12 hours.

- Select cells B7:B12 and press the Delete key to erase the cell contents.

Now consider this problem:

A tire manufacturer produces a particular model tire whose tread wear life is normally distributed with a mean of 39,000 miles and a standard deviation of 5,300 miles. The manufacturer wishes to provide a guaranteed tread life for this model which would be exceeded by 98% of all tires. What tread life would meet this requirement?

If the guaranteed tread life is x, the probability that a randomly chosen tire will have a tread life greater than x is .98. This means that x must be less than the average tread life (which would be exceeded only with probability .5). The graph is shown below.

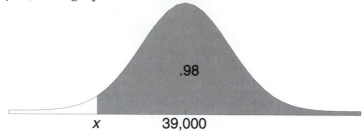

In order to use NORMSINV to find the z value corresponding to x, it must be given the cumulative probability of x, corresponding to the area to the left of x in the density function.

- Enter the label "right area" in cell A4. Enter in cell B4 the probability corresponding to the area to the right of x in the diagram above, ".98."

- Select cell B7. Enter the Excel formula which will calculate the area to the left of x given the area to the right in B4. The displayed value should be "0.02."

- Select cell B8. Enter the Excel formula which will calculate the z value corresponding to x given the cumulative probability in B7. The displayed value should be "-2.05375."

- Enter the mean and standard deviation of the tread life in cells B10 and B11, respectively.

- Enter the formula in B12 which will take the value of z in B8 and convert it to the corresponding value of x given the values of μ and σ in B10 and B11. The displayed value of B12 should be "28115.13."

Ninety-eight percent of all tires could be expected to have tread lives which exceeded slightly over 28,115. If the company rounded the guaranteed tread life to 28,000 miles, slightly more than 98% of all tires' tread lives would exceed this.

- Select B4:B12 and press the Delete key.

The last problem in this group concerns a central area:

The mechanical process which fills 10 pound bags of dog food is subject to random fluctuations in the amount placed in each bag. The amount placed in each bag is approximately normally distributed with a mean of 170 ounces and a standard deviation of 4.3 ounces. Determine an interval centered on the mean such that the weight of the contents of 99% of the bags will fall within that interval.

The diagram for this distribution is shown at the top of the next page.

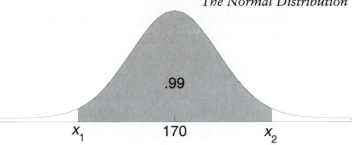

- Select cell B5 and enter the probability corresponding to the central area for this problem (".99").

- Select cell B7. Enter a formula to calculate the area of each of the two unshaded tails in the diagram above by taking one minus the central area (which equals the area of both tails) and dividing this difference by 2. The displayed value should be "0.005."

- Select cell B8. Enter a formula using NORMSINV to determine the z value corresponding to x_1. The displayed value should be "-2.57583."

- Select cell B9. Enter a formula to determine the z value corresponding to x_2. The displayed value should be positive but with the same absolute value as B8.

- Enter the mean and standard deviation of this distribution in cells B10 and B11, respectively.

- Enter the label "right x" in cell A13. In cells B12 and B13 enter formulas which will convert the z values in B8 and B9, respectively, to x values using the values for μ and σ in B10 and B11. The values displayed in B12 and B13 should be "158.9239" and "181.0761," respectively.

Ninety-nine percent of the dog food bags will contain between approximately 159 and 181 ounces of dog food.

▼The Normal Distribution as an Approximation to the Binomial

One of the reasons for the popularity of the normal distribution is that it can approximate many other distributions, including distributions that are inconvenient to work with without a computer. One of the distributions that has traditionally been approximated by the normal distribution is the binomial distribution. This approximation underlies the traditional approach to making statistical inferences about a population proportion. Although the use of computer programs like Excel makes this unnecessary, this approach still dominates in introductory statistics textbooks. In this section we will use Excel's graphics to compare various binomial probability distribution functions with their approximations using the normal distribution.

The variables of the binomial distribution are n and π (or p), the number of trials and the probability of success on a single trial, respectively. These must be converted to values for the normal distribution's μ and σ using the formulas for the mean and standard deviation of the binomial distribution:

$$\mu = n\pi$$

$$\sigma = \sqrt{n\pi(1-\pi)}$$

We will proceed by creating a binomial table for the case when $n = 100$ and $\pi = .2$, add the corresponding normal approximation for each value of x, and then graph the two distributions.

- Open the "Insert" menu on the Menu Bar and select "Worksheet." When the new worksheet is created, change its name to "Binom Approx." Move it to the end of the workbook.

- Place the following labels in the newly renamed worksheet.: "x" in A1, "Binomial" in B1, "Normal" in C1, "n" in D1, "pi" in D2, "mu" in D3, and "sigma" in D4.

- Enter the initial value for n ("100") in cell E1 and the initial value for π (".2") in cell E2.

- Enter the Excel formula in cell E3 to calculate μ as shown in the formula above.

- Enter the Excel formula in cell E4 to calculate σ as shown in the formula above. You will need to use the SQRT function, which can be found in the "Math & Trig" category.

At this point your worksheet should look like the one below. Be sure E3 and E4 contain formulas (and not just numbers), because we will be changing the values of n and π, and μ and σ need to automatically recalculate.

	A	B	C	D	E
2	x	Binomial	Normal	n	100
3				pi	0.2
4				mu	20
5				sigma	4

The values of x (which go from 0 to n) are to be placed in column A.

- Place the series of integers from 0 to 100 in the range A2:A102. The easiest way to do this is to first enter a "0" in A2, then select the region A2:A102 using the Name Box, then open the Edit menu on the Menu Bar, choose "Fill," then "Series...," and select a "Step Value" of 1. This same procedure was used earlier and described in more detail on page 138.

Each cell in column B will contain the binomial probability of getting the number of successes indicated by the value in that row in column A given the value of n in cell E1 and the value of π in cell E2. This is most easily done by entering a formula in B2 that uses a relative address to refer to x and absolute addresses to refer to n and π. The formula can then be copied to cells B3:B1001.

- Select cell B2.

- Click the Paste Function button. Choose the "BINOMDIST" function in the "Statistical" category.

- The "Number_s" argument is x and should have a *relative* address reference to cell A2.

- The "Trials" argument is n and should have an *absolute* address reference to cell E1.

- The "Probability_s" argument is π and should have an *absolute* address reference to cell E2.

- Enter the word "false" in the "Cumulative" argument field so Excel will provide the probability for a single x value.

- Click the OK button.

The value appearing in cell B2 should be "2.03704E-10." This is a very small number, reflecting the fact that it is extremely unlikely that no success would occur in 100 trials if the probability of success in each trial were .2.

- Copy the formula in cell B2 down through cell B102. The easiest way to do this is to use a method similar to that used to generate the series in column A. Select cells B2:B102 using the Name Box. Open the Edit menu on the Menu Bar, and choose "Fill." Select "Down" (instead of "Series...").

Examine the probabilities. As you move down the list, the probabilities should first increase. The largest probability will correspond to a value for x of 20 (in cell B22). That probability is "0.099300215." Check to be sure you have this value in your worksheet. If you do not, then you have made an error somewhere and need to recheck and redo the values in columns A and B.

Since the normal distribution is continuous, the probability of a normally distributed random variable equaling any specific value is always zero. In order to approximate a single binomial value, the corresponding range of values from the previous integer to the desired integer is used. For example, if we wanted to approximate the probability of getting exactly 15 successes, we would use the probability of a normally distributed random variable having a value between 14 and 15. This can be implemented using Excel's cumulative distribution functions by calculating the cumulative probability of 15 minus the cumulative probability of 14. The approximation could be improved (but seldom is) by using the correction for continuity, which would approximate the probability of 15 successes by calculating the cumulative normal probability of 15.5 minus the cumulative probability of 14.5. This is discussed in an exercise at the end of the chapter.

In order to enter a formula in which Excel subtracts the probability of a value being less than $x - 1$ from the probability of a value being less than x, we will start with cell C3. This is the first cell for which there is a value in the worksheet for $x - 1$. This cell will contain the probability of a normally distributed random variable (with the same values for μ and σ as the binomial distribution being approximated) having a value between 0 and 1.

We want to be careful in the use of *relative* and *absolute* cell addresses so that the formula in cell C3 can be copied down to the other cells in column C. The references to the "x" values should be relative, since we want those to differ for each formula in column C. The references to μ and σ, however, should be absolute. The mean of the normal distribution is in cell E3 and the standard deviation is in cell E4, and those addresses must be fixed for all the formulas in column C.

Since the formula we want to enter must calculate the difference between two normal probabilities, the Paste Function must be used *within* an equation rather than as the whole equation.

- Select cell C3. Click the Edit Formula button. Select the "NORMDIST" function.

- Set the "X" argument to be a *relative* reference to cell A3.

- Set the "Mean" argument to be an *absolute* reference to cell E3, and the "Standard_dev" argument to be an *absolute* reference to cell E4.

- Enter the word "true" in the field for the "Cumulative" argument.

- Click the mouse pointer to the right of the formula being written in the Formula Bar. With the insertion point on the right of the formula, enter a minus sign.

- Click the NORMDIST button on the Formula Palette again. A new dialog window will open. Enter the same arguments as you did previously except the "x" argument should be a relative reference to cell A2. Click OK.

The *value* displayed in cell C3 will be "7.31223E-07," but the *formula* in the Formula Bar should be "=NORMDIST(A3,$E$3,$E$4,TRUE)-NORMDIST(A2,$E$3,$E$4,TRUE)." This calculates the probability of being less than 1 (in A3) and subtracts the probability of being less than 0 (in A2). This is the probability of a normally distributed random variable with mean 20 and standard deviation 4 having a value between 0 and 1. This value like the value it approximates in cell B3, is very close to 0.

- Copy cell C3 to cells C4 through C102. Like other massive copies, this is best done by entering the range C3:C102 in the Name Box and then using the "Edit...Fill...Down" menus sequence. Check the formula by verifying that the value displayed in cell C22 ($x = 20$) is "0.098706274."

The easiest way to evaluate the approximation is to look at a graph that charts both the values in column B and those in column C.

- Click the Chart Wizard button.

- In the Step 1 dialog window, select the "Custom Types" folder tab. In the "Chart Type" list select "Line - Column" (you will have to scroll down the list to see this choice). This choice will make the binomial distribution a vertical bar chart with the normal approximation superimposed as a line chart. Click the Next> button.

- In the Step 2 dialog window, we need to tell the Chart Wizard which data to use in the chart. Click the "Data Range" folder tab (it may already be on top) and replace the values in the "Data range:" field with the address for the data in columns B and C. Do this by first making sure the field is selected and then entering "B1:C102," which are the cells containing both the binomial distribution and the normal approximation.

We haven't told Excel what to put on the x axis. Without that information, Excel will simply sequentially number the values. This is almost what we want, but not quite. The problem is that Excel's numbering starts with 1, while the first x value on the chart should be 0.

- Select the "Series" tab at the top of the dialog window. At the bottom of the window is a field labeled "Category (X) axis labels:." The values we want to appear as labels on the x axis are in A2:A102. A quirk in Excel prevents us from simply entering that address. Select the field and then click on cell A2. Hold the Shift key, then press and release the End key and the down-arrow key. This will enter "='Binom Approx'!$A$2:$A$102" in the field. Click the Finish Button.

Excel has placed the chart too low on the worksheet.

- Move the chart so that its upper left-hand corner is in cell D5. Here's one way to do this. With the chart selected, click the Cut button (✂). This will erase the chart. Select cell D5 and click the Paste button (📋).

- Scroll your worksheet so that cell D1 is in the upper-left corner (columns A–C should not be visible). Place the chart so that it is on the left side of the screen just below row 5. Increase the height and width of the chart so that it extends to the lower-right corner of your screen.

Your screen should look like the picture at the top of the next page.

Unfortunately, as you can see, Excel has put so many labels on the x axis that it is impossible to read any of them. This can be fixed.

- Place the mouse pointer some place on the jumble of numbers below the x axis. You've got the right place if, after the pointer has rested a second, this small window opens below it: `Category Axis`. Double click the (left) mouse button. This will open the Format Axis dialog window.

- On the top of the dialog window click "Scale." In the field labeled "Number of categories between tick-mark labels" change the value to "5" (without quotes). Click OK.

The axis labels should now be quite readable.

If the approximation were perfect, each point on the line would lie on the top of a bar. A close inspection should convince you that the line plot looks as if it had been shifted slightly to the right of the bar chart.

- Select cell E2 (which contains the value of π). Change the ".2" to ".5." Notice how this changes both the graph and the values of μ and σ (in cells E3 and E4).

- Experiment with other values of π, going from very small values (such as .001) to very large values (.999). Notice the extent to which the normal line closely follows the binomial bar chart.

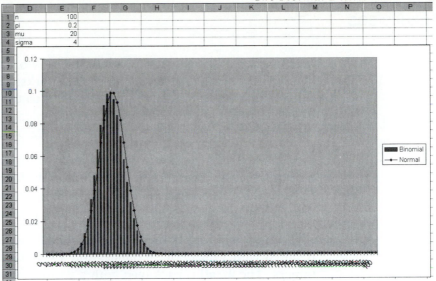

The normal distribution generally does a better job of approximating the binomial distribution the closer π is to .50. It also works better for larger values of *n*.

Try now an even smaller value for *n*.

- Change the value of π to .5, and change the value of *n* to 20.

- Correct the horizontal dimension of the chart by selecting the chart (single click the mouse button with the mouse pointer inside the chart boundary on the white margin) and then click the Chart Wizard button. Click the Next> button to go to the Step 2 dialog window.

- Look in the "Data Range" field. In the early version of Excel 2000 available when this was written the following appeared: "='Binom Approx'!$A$1:$C$102." The "102" at the end should be changed to "22." At the time this was written, an apparent bug in the early version of Excel 2000 caused the data to begin in column A instead of column B, as was originally entered. Unless this has been corrected in your version, change the "A" in "$A$1" to "B" and click the "Series" tab at the top.

- Click the "Category (X) axis labels:" field and use the mouse to select cells A2:A22. This should enter "='Binom Approx'!$A$2:$A$22" into the field. Click Finish.

For smaller sizes of *n* the normal distribution is a poorer approximation of the binomial.

- Experiment with different values for π when *n* = 20. Verify that the approximation seems best when π is close to .5.

▼Exercises

Answer problems 1 through 4 on a new, blank worksheet. The objective of the lesson was not to provide you with a worksheet to use to solve these problems but to enable you to learn how to use Excel to implement standard statistical concepts. In answering problem 5, however, you should use the "Binom Approx" worksheet developed in the lesson.

1. The scores on an exam are approximately normally distributed with a mean of 75 and a standard deviation of 10. If the professor wants 10% of the class to receive the grade of A, then what is the minimum score a student can get and receive an A on the exam?

2. The weight of a loaf of bread produced by a bakery is normally distributed with a mean of 18 ounces and a standard deviation of .9 ounces. The bread is packaged with a wrapper that describes it as weighing 16 ounces. What proportion of the loaves of bread can be expected to weigh less than the amount shown on the package?

3. A company that produces fasteners for the automotive industry is evaluating a new bolt-making machine that makes a particular style bolt with a weight that is normally distributed with a mean of 28 grams and a standard deviation of 1.16 grams. Within what interval, symmetrically distributed about the mean, will the weight of 95% of the bolts fall?

4. The speed of cars traveling a section of the interstate was found to be normally distributed with a mean of 62 mph and a standard deviation of 4.8 mph. What is the probability that a single car is exceeding the posted speed (55 mph)?

5. In examining the normal distribution as an approximation for the binomial, we did not use the correction for continuity. To approximate the binomial probability of receiving exactly x successes, the normal probability of getting a value between $x - 1$ and x was calculated. This was done by subtracting the cumulative probability of $x - 1$ from the cumulative probability of x. If the correction for continuity were used, the binomial probability of receiving exactly x successes would be approximated by the normal probability of getting a value between $x - 0.5$ and $x + 0.5$.

   Print the chart you got showing the relationship between the binomial and normal approximations distributions *without* using the correction for continuity when $n = 10$ and $\pi = .2$. Put headings on the printout that identify this printout as *not* using the correction for continuity.

Consider the formula in cell C3. It currently calculates the cumulative normal probability of 1 (in cell A3) or less and subtracts the cumulative normal probability of 0 (in cell A2) or less. Thus the approximation of the binomial probability that x equals 1 is the normal probability that x is between 0 and 1. The correction for continuity would instead use the normal probability that x is between ½ and 1½. Instead of using A3 and A2 in the "X" field of NORMDIST, use A3 + 0.5 and A3 − 0.5 to incorporate the correction for continuity. Similarly, change the other formulas in column C. Print the resulting chart, this time with a heading that identifies it as using the correction for continuity. What difference does the correction for continuity seem to make? (To print only the chart, first select it, then click the Print Preview button: 🔍).

Chapter 6

The Sampling Distribution of the Mean

Sampling distributions are the foundation of inferential statistics. The object of inferential statistics is to take data from a sample and gain knowledge about the population from which the sample was drawn. A good example is a TV rating service, such as Nielsen, which tracks the TV watching behavior of a sample of viewers and makes inferences about the popularity of shows to all television viewers. A potential problem with this, which has occurred to anyone whose favorite show was canceled because of "low ratings," is that the sample might somehow not be "representative" of the population. How sure can we be that a couple of thousand viewers are going to be similar to the population of millions of television viewers? It's an obvious question. The answer comes from understanding sampling distributions.

What we want to know about a population is usually a descriptive statistic, such as the mean or the proportion of the population that fits into a certain category. A population descriptive statistic is called a *parameter*. A parameter is a number. It's easy to imagine calculating this descriptive statistic if all the population data were available. Because of difficulty or expense, collecting all the population data is not done. Instead, a sample is drawn from the population, and a descriptive statistic is calculated from the sample data. In the jargon of inferential statistics, the number calculated from the sample is a *statistic*. Once a sample is drawn and a statistic is calculated from the sample, that statistic becomes an *estimator* for the population parameter that we want to know. Since a sample may not be representative of the population, we need to know whether the sample statistic is likely to be a good estimator of the population parameter.

In order to understand the relationship between a sample mean and a population mean, we need to think about the *sampling distribution of the mean*, which describes the set of all possible sample means drawn from a population. This is a difficult concept for most beginning students of statistics. Much of this chapter will be devoted to a simulation in which we will look at the distribution of a large number of means taken from samples of different shapes. One of the foundations of inferential statistics is the Central Limit Theorem, which essentially states that regardless of the population distribution, the distribution of the means of sufficiently large samples will be approximately normal. We will use simulation to investigate how sample size and population distribution affect the sampling distribution of the mean.

▼Sampling Techniques

There are a number of techniques for selecting samples from a population. Unfortunately, many methods are not statistically valid in the sense that a statistic calculated from a sample should not be used to make an inference about the population parameter. Among those sampling techniques from which valid inferences can be made, the simplest is known as *simple random sampling*. In this technique, all items in the population have an equal probability of being chosen. Depending on the nature of the data to be analyzed, other valid techniques, such as stratified sampling, may make it possible to make equally valid inferences from smaller samples. They sometimes complicate the mathematics of the analysis, however, and for introductory statistics it is best to keep things as simple as possible.

With simple random sampling (or any other valid sampling technique), any value taken from a member of a sample is a random number since that member is chosen by a random process. Any sample statistic calculated from the sample values is also going to be a random number. A random number has a distribution. If we knew that distribution, we would have good information on the likelihood of a sample statistic being a good estimator of a parameter.

Sampling can be done *with replacement* and *without replacement*. When a sample is drawn with replacement, once an item is chosen for the sample from the population, that same item is replaced before a second item is selected for the sample. It is possible that the same population item might be chosen twice for the sample. When sampling is drawn without replacement, this cannot happen. If the population is very large compared to the sample, both techniques result in essentially equivalent samples, but this is not the case if the sample is close in size to the population. Suppose a sample of 10 people were chosen from the entire U.S. population. It wouldn't matter if the sampling were done with or without replacement, because there is almost no chance that the same person could be chosen twice even if sampling were done with replacement. On the other hand, if a sample of 10 people were chosen from a class of 30, it is very likely that someone would be chosen more than once if sampling were done with replacement. In practice, sampling is almost always done without replacement. With small populations this permits smaller samples to be used to make equally valid inferences. The simplest analysis, however, occurs if sampling is done *with replacement.* So that technique will be the one we will assume is used whenever it might make a difference.

▼Simulating the Sampling Distribution of the Mean

Most people find the concept of a sampling distribution a little tricky when they first encounter it. It often seems a little nebulous or abstract. It is really a very concrete concept, however. We will investigate it here by using Excel to help us look at a specific sampling distribution of the mean.

Ideally, this would be done by calculating a mean from every possible sample that could be drawn from a population. Unfortunately, even if the sample size and population size are not particularly large, the number of possible samples is astronomical. For example, suppose we were interested in estimating the average lifetime of a specific lot of 100 light bulbs by choosing and testing a sample of 10 light bulbs. How many different samples are there in total?

How many different choices do we have for the first member of the sample? Any of the 100 bulbs in the population could be chosen. What about the second member? If the sampling is done with replacement, there are 100 choices for the second as well. The total number of distinct samples would be the product of 100 multiplied by itself 10 times, or 100^{10}. This is a huge number, which could be written as a 1 followed by 20 zeroes! If we correct for the fact that some of these samples would be identical except for order, we still would have left so many samples that their number would have 14 digits to the left of the decimal point. If the sample size or population sizes were larger, the number of samples would grow even faster.

Our approach will be to look at the means of a large enough number of samples that we can get a good notion of what the distribution of all sample means would look like.

▼Drawing Samples with Excel

Excel has a sampling tool included with its Analysis Tools. Unfortunately, this tool will not take multiple samples. Taking a thousand samples one at a time is impractical. By installing the Excel Add-Ins included on the data diskette for this book (see Appendix C), you will add this capability to your Excel.

- If you have not already done so, start Excel with a new blank workbook. If the workbook that displays is not empty, click the New button on the Standard Toolbar: ⬜.

- Save the new workbook in a file named "Chap6.xls." (Note: this file should be saved on a hard disk or network drive; it will become too large for a diskette. For a method of storing it on diskette at the end of your session, see Appendix F.)

- In cell A1, enter the label "Population."

- In cells A2 through A6, enter five different numbers. Use any numbers you like, but be sure all five are different.

- In cell C1, enter the label "Samples."

For the purposes of seeing how a sample can be chosen, the five numbers you have entered in cells A2 through A6 will be regarded as a population, and we will see how the Excel Add-In can be used to select values from this population.

- Open the Tools menu on the Menu Bar. Select "Learning Business Statistics." A submenu will open (as shown below). Select "Multiple Random Samples." If "Learning Business Statistics" does not appear on your Tools menu, you have not installed the Add-Ins for this book. Follow the instructions in Appendix C before proceeding.

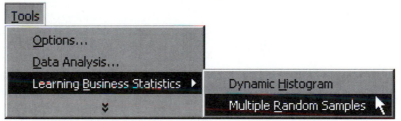

- The Multiple Random Samples dialog window will open. In the "Population Range:" field, enter the range address of the population values you have entered. In the "Sample Size:" and "Number of Samples:" fields, enter the number "1." In the "Output Range:" field, enter "C2." Click the OK button.

Cell C2 should now contain a value chosen randomly from the five values in column A.

- Recall the Multiple Random Samples dialog window and click the OK button. Try this several times, observing the value in cell C2.

Sometimes the same value will be chosen twice, but usually you should see a new value in cell C2 each time the Multiple Random Samples tool is run.

- Recall the Multiple Random Samples dialog window. Change the value in the "Sample Size:" field from "1" to "5." Click the OK button.

- Rerun the Multiple Random Samples tool several times and observe the changes in the sample.

When a sample contains more than one value, the Multiple Random Samples tool places the sample values in a row. Your observation should confirm that the sampling is done with replacement since the samples will usually include at least one value more than once.

- Recall the Multiple Random Samples dialog window and change the "Number of Samples:" field from "1" to "3." Click OK and observe the values written by the tool.

When more than one sample is drawn, each sample is written in a separate row. The random samples each contain five values (the length of a row) and there are three samples (the number of rows).

We are now ready to use the Multiple Random Samples tool to investigate the sampling distribution of the mean.

▼Setting Up a Uniform Population

- Double click the "Sheet2" worksheet tab and change its name to "Population."

Once we have the workbook set up, it will be easy to change the population from which the samples will be drawn. To begin with, a very simple population will be used—all of the numbers divisible by 0.5 between 0.5 and 100.

- Enter the number ".5" in cell A1.

- Enter the number "1.0" in cell A2.

- Select the region A1:A200. Probably the easiest way to do this is to enter "a1:a200" in the Name Box and press the Enter key.

- With A1:A200 selected, open the Edit menu on the Menu Bar. From the menu that drops down, select "Fill." A cascade menu will open. Select "Series…" from that menu. The Series dialog window will open.

- Look in the "Step" field and verify that it contains "0.5." Verify that under "Type" the button beside "Linear" is chosen.

Unless explicitly told otherwise, Excel assumes you want a *linear* series—where each value is calculated by adding the step value to the previous value. Excel set the "Step" value by looking at the difference between the two values you placed in A1 and A2. Had you omitted the value in A2, Excel would have assumed a "Step" value of 1. This could, of course, have been changed in the dialog window, and the final result would have been the same.

- Click OK. The selected region, A1:A200, should automatically fill with the series of numbers from 0.5 to 100, with each cell having a value that is 0.5 greater than the cell above it.

The same result could have been achieved by selecting A1:A2 and using the mouse to drag the fill handle to A100. This can be tricky to do when it involves moving the mouse pointer to cells which are off screen, because of the difficulty of controlling Excel's scrolling.

▼Setting Up a Dynamic Histogram

In order to better see the shape of the distribution of the population we have just created, it would be useful to have a histogram. In Chapter 2 you learned how to use the Histogram tool. That is the simplest way of producing a histogram in Excel. Like all the output prepared by the Analysis Tools, the Histogram tool is *static*—changes to the data are not immediately reflected in the histogram. To see the effect of changes in the data, the Histogram tool would have to be rerun.

Instead of using the Histogram tool, the Add-Ins included with this book provide a Dynamic Histogram tool. It is very similar in use to the Histogram tool but has a few differences. For example, you must provide a "Bins" range for the Dynamic Histogram tool. The Dynamic Histogram tool does not produce a "More" bin. A chart is always produced. The major difference, however, is that the relationship between the histogram (both chart and table) and input data is *dynamic*. If the input data change, the histogram will automatically reflect those changes.

The first step is to set up the "bins," the intervals that each bar in the histogram will represent. Since the population values all fall between 0 and 100, let's use 10 intervals whose upper bounds are 10, 20, 30, etc.

- In cells B1 through B10, enter the values "10, 20, 30, …, 100." Remember that one easy way of doing this is to enter "10" in cell B1 and "20" in cell B2. Then use the mouse to select cells B1:B2. After the two cells are selected, the fill handle can be dragged down to cell B10. When it is released, the series will be completed.

- Open the Tools menu, click "Learning Business Statistics," and select "Dynamic Histogram."

- In the "Input Range" field, enter the address of the data that the histogram is to summarize: "A1:A200."

- In the "Bin Range" field, enter the address of the bins: "B1:B10."

- In the "Output Range" field, enter "B4" (which will overwrite the bin values). Click the OK button.

The histogram for this population should consist of 10 bars of equal height with that height corresponding to 20. To see how this histogram is "dynamic," do the following:

- Select cell A1. Change the "0.5" to "95." Notice that the leftmost bar on the histogram is now shorter and the rightmost bar taller than the others, reflecting that the change in the value of A1 reduced the number of cells with values less than or equal to 10 and increased the number of cells with values more than 90 but less than or equal to 100.

- Change the value of A1 back to "0.5." Observe that all the bars in the histogram have returned to being the same height.

The last thing to put on this worksheet is the population mean and standard deviation.

- Delete the values in cells B1:B3

- Enter the label "Mean" in cell B1 and "Standard Deviation" in cell B2. Adjust the width of column B.

- Enter the formula in cell C1 to calculate the mean of the numbers in column A. The Excel function has the name "AVERAGE." The value displayed should be "50.25."

- Enter the formula in cell C2 to calculate the standard deviation of the numbers in column A. Since these numbers constitute a population, you need to use the population standard deviation formula rather than the sample standard deviation formula. The Excel function to calculate a population standard deviation is STDEVP. The value displayed should be "28.86715."

- Save your workbook, now and often!

▼Drawing the Samples

Double click the "Sheet3" worksheet tab and change its name to "Samples." On this worksheet we will have Excel draw 1,000 samples of different sizes, initially of size 5 from the population of 200 on the "Population" worksheet.

Open the Tools menu on the Menu Bar. Select "Learning Business Statistics" and then click "Multiple Random Samples."

- In the "Population Range:" field, you should enter the address of the population on the Population worksheet. This is best done with the mouse since the worksheet name must be part of the address, and this is done automatically when you use the mouse.

- Enter "5" for "Sample Size" and "1000" for "Number of Samples."

- Click the "Output Range:" field so an insertion point is visible and click cell A1 on the Samples worksheet. The dialog window should look like the picture below. Notice how Excel includes the worksheet name in the name range. Click the OK button.

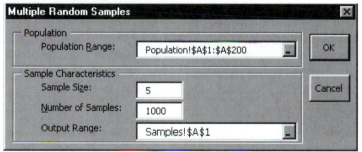

▼Calculate the Sample Means

The Samples worksheet now has 1,000 rows of numbers, each of which is five numbers long. Each row is a separate sample drawn from the population on the Population worksheet. The next step is to calculate the mean of each of the 1,000 samples.

- Click the Insert menu on the Menu Bar and select "Worksheet." Change the name of the new worksheet to "Sample Means" and move it to the end of the workbook.

This sheet will contain the means of all the samples on the Samples sheet and information about the distribution of the sample means.

- Select cell A1. Click the Edit Formula or Paste Function button and select "AVERAGE." With the insertion point in the "Number1" field, click the "Samples" worksheet tag and click the row heading for the first row (see picture below). The "Number1" field in the AVERAGE dialog window should contain "Samples!1:1." Click OK.

Click here

	A	B
1	16.5	93
2	91	56.5

Cell A1 on the Sample Means worksheet now has the mean of the first sample. By copying this formula down each cell below it will have the average of the corresponding row of the Samples worksheet.

- Use the Name Box to select A1:A1000. Open the Edit menu on the Menu Bar. Choose "Fill" and then, on the submenu, "Down."

Since we will be looking at different sample sizes, we need a measure of that on the Sample Means worksheet.

- Enter the label "n" in cell B1. Select cell B2. Click the Edit Formula or Paste Function button and choose "COUNT" from the "Statistical" category. When the dialog window appears, select the "Samples" worksheet and click the row heading for the first row as you did with the AVERAGE function. The Formula Bar should show cell B2 containing "=COUNT(Samples!1:1)," and the value "5" should display in the cell.

The COUNT function counts the number of numeric values in the range given in its argument fields. By clicking the row heading for the first row of the Samples worksheet, we get a count of the number of numbers in that row, the first sample. Since all of the samples on that worksheet will always have the same size, B2 will indicate the size of all the samples.

▼The Theoretical Distribution of Sample Means

We now have a set of 1,000 sample means. With a population of 200 and a sample size of 5 (sampling with replacement), there are 200^5 different samples. The distribution of all 200^5 (320 billion) means would be the sampling distribution of the mean. (Eliminating the samples which differ only in the order of the sample values reduces the number to over 2.5 billion.) The 1,000 means we have generated can be thought of as a sample drawn from the entire population of samples. It's a big enough sample so that by looking at the distribution of the 1,000 numbers we have, we should get a pretty good idea of the characteristics of the distribution of all sample means, but it is certainly not going to be the same.

Statistical theory tells us that the distribution of sample means should have a mean that is itself equal to the population mean:

$$\mu_{\bar{x}} = \mu$$

and a standard deviation that is related to the population standard deviation by the following formula:

$$\sigma_{\bar{x}} = \frac{\sigma}{\sqrt{n}}$$

Note that n is the size of each of the samples, not the total number of samples. For our case, $n = 5$ (*not* 1,000).

The preceding two equations hold strictly for the entire set of sample means. The mean and standard deviation of the 1,000 values we have drawn might differ. Still, it would be interesting to see how close the mean and standard deviation of the sample means just generated are to the values that theoretically would hold for the entire set of sample means. Let's create a table for these values.

- In cell C1 enter the label "Sampling Distribution." In cell C3 enter the label "Theoretical." In cell C4 enter the label "These Samples."

- Increase the width of column C so that it is wide enough to hold the label in C4.

- In cell D2 enter the label "Mean," and in cell E2 enter the label "Standard Deviation."

- In cell D3, enter a formula that reads the population mean from the Population worksheet. Do this by making D3 active. Then enter an equal sign to tell Excel you are beginning a formula. Then click the "Population" worksheet tab with the mouse pointer. Then click the cell containing the population mean (C1). Press the Enter key.

Pressing the Enter key will cause your display to shift back to the Samples worksheet with the value "50.25" displayed in D3.

- Again make D3 active and observe the formula in the Formula Bar. Verify that it is "=Population!C1."

Once again we see the use of a worksheet name in a cell range address, necessary if the range is not on the current worksheet. If you were to change the name of a worksheet, Excel would automatically change all formulas in the workbook that referred to cells on that worksheet.

The next step is to enter the formula that will calculate the theoretical standard deviation of sample means from the population standard deviation. This requires taking the population standard deviation and dividing it by the square root of the size of the samples. The sample size for the samples just generated is 5, but when that changes, the correct value will always be in cell B2

- Select cell E3. Click the Edit Formula button. An equal sign will appear in the Formula Bar.

- Switch to the Population worksheet and click the cell with the population standard deviation. The Formula Bar should now have "=Population!C2," which represents the population standard deviation. We must complete the formula by telling it to divide this by the square root of the sample size.

- Enter the division symbol ("/"). It should appear at the end of the Formula Bar, which now should be "=Population!C2/."

- Click the arrow to the left of the Formula Bar, which opens the list of recently used functions. Click "SQRT" if it appears on the list. If it does not, click "More Functions…" and select "SQRT" from the "Math & Trig" category. The SQRT dialog window will open with an insertion point in the "Number" argument field.

- Click cell B2 to enter that address in SQRT's "Number" argument field.

- Click the OK button. Cell D3 should display the value "12.90978," and the Formula Bar should show the formula in D3 as "=Population!C2/SQRT(B2)." 12.90978 is the theoretical value of the standard deviation of the means of samples of size 5 selected from the population on the Population worksheet.

The standard deviation of sample means is very important in inferential statistics since it essentially measures how much sample means vary from the population mean. It is important enough to have its own name, the *standard error of the mean* or just the *standard error*.

The next step is to add the formulas to calculate the mean and standard deviation of the sample means that are in the cell range A1:A1000. We expect these values to be close to the theoretical values for the mean and standard deviation in D3 and E3, respectively. They won't be exactly the same because the 1,000 sample means on this worksheet are only a sample of the (huge) set of all possible sample means.

- Select cell D4. Enter the Excel formula that calculates the average of the numbers in column A. Use the AVERAGE function and click the column heading for column A (whose location is shown on page 12).

- Select cell E4. Enter the Excel formula that calculates the standard deviation of the numbers in column A. In this case you should use the *sample* standard deviation (STDEV) because the 1,000 sample means represent a sample of the huge set of all possible sample means. Use the column heading to generate the A:A address in STDEV.

The theoretical mean and standard deviation should be very close (but not identical) to the mean and standard deviation of the 1,000 sample means. An increased number of samples (more than 1,000) should result in values even closer to the theoretical values.

▼Examining the Distribution of Sample Means

We will use a histogram to investigate the distribution of the 1,000 sample means. Their distribution will be compared to what would be predicted by the normal distribution by modifying the histogram to show a superimposed normal distribution, similar to the one used in Chapter 4.

In order to provide more detail, 20 bars will be used for the histogram of sample means compared to the 10 bars used for the population histogram. This means 20 "bins" (or categories) must be created. Cells C6:C25 will be used for this. These bins will go from 5 to 100 by 5.

- Enter the series of numbers "5, 10, 15, ..., 100" in C6:C25. This is easiest if you use the fill handle or the Fill menu.

- Select "Learning Business Statistics" from the "Tools" menu and click "Dynamic Histogram."

- In the "Input Range" field put the range address of the 1,000 sample means on your worksheet.

- In the "Bins Range" field, put the range address of the bin values you have just entered: "C6:C25."

- Enter "C6" in the "Output Range" field. This will cause the histogram table to overwrite the bin values you previously entered, but since the table shows those values, nothing will be lost. Click the OK button.

- Change cell D6 so it contains "Sample Means" rather than "Frequency."

Compare the histogram of the 1,000 sample means on the Samples worksheet with the histogram of the population on the Population worksheet. Clearly their shapes are very different. The "bell" shape shows the tendency of the sample means to cluster around their mean.

The fact that all the bars are clustered together provides visual confirmation that the standard deviation of sample means (the standard error) is less than the standard deviation of the population.

▼The Normal Distribution and the Central Limit Theorem

According to the Central Limit Theorem, the distribution of sample means should be approximately normal if the samples are large enough. The size of the samples required for this depends on the population distribution. Essentially, the greater the difference between the distribution of the population and the normal distribution, the larger the sample size required.

We will look at that by comparing the distribution of sample means with that which would occur if the sample means were normally distributed. Since the 1,000 sample means we are looking at are a tiny proportion of all the sample means, some mismatch between the actual distribution of the 1,000 sample means and the number predicted by the normal distribution is to be expected.

The range E7:E26 will be used for the values predicted by the normal distribution. In each cell we will calculate the probability of a normally distributed random variable, whose values for μ and σ are given by the values in D3 and E3, falling within an interval whose upper limit is the bin value in that row in column D. This probability will be multiplied by 1,000, giving the expected number of the 1,000 samples falling within the bins interval.

Since we have to calculate normal probabilities for a *range* of values, the first normal probability will be calculated for the *second* bin. Cell E8 will take the probability of a normal random variable being between the values in C7 and C8, calculated as the cumulative probability of C8 minus the cumulative probability of C7, multiplied by 1,000. By the judicious use of absolute and relative addresses, we will be able to copy C8 through the rest of the range.

The probabilities will be calculated using Excel's NORMDIST function, which (unlike the NORMSDIST function) allows us to specify a value for the mean and standard deviation. An argument value controls whether this function provides the density or cumulative probability. We will use it to provide cumulative probability.

- Move the histogram chart to the right, if needed, so that it does not cover column E. Enter the label "Normal Expected" in cell E6. This, and the label in D6, will show up in a chart legend.

- Select cell E8. Click the Edit Formula button. Enter "1000*(" in the Formula Bar.

This will multiply the probability to be entered by 1,000. Inside the parenthesis just opened we will calculate the probability of a normal variable being less than the bin value in C8 minus the probability of a normal variable being less than the bin value in C7.

- Click the downward-pointing arrow on the Formula Palette, which opens the list of recently used functions. The function you want is NORMDIST (*not* NORMSDIST). If it is not on the list, select "More functions…" and look for it in the "Statistical" category.

- The value for the "x" argument is the value in cell C8. Be sure to use the *address* C8 (and not just the displayed value). Be sure the address is relative.

- Cells D3 and E3 contain the theoretical mean and standard deviation of the distribution of sample means. Put these addresses in the argument fields for "mean" and "standard_dev," respectively. These addresses should be *absolute*. Enter the word "true" in the "cumulative" argument field.

Look at the Formula Bar. At this point it should contain "=1000*(**NORMDIST(C8,$D$3,$E$3,true**)." The NORMDIST function in this formula will determine the probability of a normal random variable being less than the bin value in C8. We need to subtract from that the probability of a normal variable being less than the bin value in C7.

- Click the mouse pointer in the Formula Bar to the right of its current contents. An insertion point should appear. Enter a minus sign ("-"). As soon as you enter it, the NORMDIST dialog window will close.

- Since NORMDIST was the most recently used function, its name should appear in the Function Box to the left of the Formula Bar. Click it and a new NORMDIST dialog window will appear.

- This time the "x" argument field should contain the relative address C7. The "mean" and "standard_dev" argument fields should contain absolute addresses for D3 and E3, respectively, as before. Again enter the word "true" in the "cumulative" argument field.

- Click the mouse pointer on the right side of the Formula Bar so that an insertion point appears. Enter a right parenthesis (")"). This closes the parenthesis entered after the "1000*" within which the difference between the two normal probabilities was calculated. Click the OK button on the Formula Palette.

The value "0.682861" should be displayed in cell E8, and the Formula Palette should contain "=1000*(NORMDIST(C8,$D$3,$E$3,TRUE)-NORMDIST(C7,$D$3, $E$3,TRUE))"

- Copy the formula in E8 to E9 through E26. The value displayed in cell E16 should be "150.149."

If the actual distribution of the sample means were approximately normal, the expected values displayed in column E would be close to the actual counts in the same rows in column D. The relationship between the values in these two columns is easy to see graphically.

▼Adding the Normal Expected Values to the Histogram

We already have a chart showing the distribution of the actual 1,000 sample means—the histogram chart. Excel makes it easy to modify this chart so that it also shows the normal expected values.

- Select the region E6:E26. This contains the normal values and the heading.

- Click the Copy button on the Standard Toolbar: 🖺.

- Place the mouse pointer in the center of the histogram. You can put it either in the gray plot area or directly on one of the bars. Click the (left) mouse button so that either the plot area or the bars are selected.

- Click the Paste button on the Standard Toolbar: 🖺.

You should immediately see a new set of bars on the histogram, and the chart should be selected. These two bars chart the normal expected values. The comparison can be made clearer by changing the chart type.

- Open the "Chart" menu on the Menu Bar. Select "Chart Type...."

- In the Chart Type dialog window, click the "Custom Types" folder tab. Scroll down through the list of chart types until you find ▦ Line - Column. Select it by clicking the mouse pointer directly on it. Click the OK button.

- If you have room, enlarge the chart to make it easier to examine.

As indicated by the legend, the values predicted by the normal distribution are represented by dots connected by a line. The actual values in the 1,000 samples are shown by bars. If the actual values were precisely predicted by the normal expected values, each dot would lie exactly on the top of a bar.

Remember that the Central Limit Theorem is about the distribution of *all* sample means, and this chart shows the distribution of only 1,000 sample means, a tiny proportion of the total. This will prevent the distribution of the sample means in this chart from ever exactly following the normal distribution regardless of the sample size. Although samples of size 5 are generally regarded as too small for the Central Limit Theorem to apply, larger samples would not appreciably result in a better "fit" between the distribution of sample means and the normal distribution than you see here.

Let's look at a different set of sample means.

• Click a cell off the chart to be sure the chart is not selected. Open the Tools menu, click "Learning Business Statistics," and choose "Multiple Random Samples" again. When the dialog window opens, all the fields should contain the values previously entered.

• Click the mouse pointer in either the "Sample Size" or "Number of Samples" field. This will switch the top worksheet back to Sample Means. Move the dialog window (if needed) so that you can see the chart. Click OK.

It's a simple matter to look at the means of larger samples.

• Recall the Multiple Random Samples tool. Change "Sample Size" from "5" to "30." Click OK.

The most noticeable change in the distribution of sample means is that it is now even more clustered around the mean. Most of the values along the horizontal axis show no bars at all, and those that are present are pretty much concentrated between 30 and 80. Although it is not visually apparent, the vertical axis automatically rescaled. Had it not done so, the bars in the middle would be so tall they would go through the top of the chart.

All of this reflects that the means of large samples are likelier to be close to the population mean than are means of small samples (drawn from the same population). Another way of saying it is that the standard error of large samples is less than the standard error of small samples.

A problem with having relatively few bars of nonzero height is that it is more difficult to judge the fit between the bars and the curve. One way of fixing this is to change the range of values along the horizontal axis. As long as the total number of values (20) remains unchanged, this can be done on the worksheet without redrawing the chart. The instructions below will change the horizontal axis so that instead of going from 5 to 100, it will go from 31 to 69.

- Enter "31" in cell C7 and "33" in cell C8. Select C7:C8 and drag the Fill Handle down to cell C26. This will change the range of values in C7:C26 so that it goes from 31 to 69 in steps of 2. As soon as this is done, the change will be reflected in the chart, which should now show a bell-shaped curve filling the chart.

- Rerun the Multiple Random Samples tool to look at the means of other sets of 1,000 samples of size 30.

As was the case of the means of samples of size 5, different sets of 1,000 means of samples of size 30 will have slightly different distributions. Were we to look at the set of all possible sample means (which would be an astronomically large set of numbers), its distribution would appear much closer to the normal distribution than would the distribution of any of the subsets.

▼A Nonuniform Population

Let's now look at the distribution of sample means from a very different population distribution. The distributions of the sample means we have looked at so far have tended to be bell-shaped, which means most of the means have been close to the mean of the population. What would be the distribution of sample means drawn from a population in which no value of the population was close to the mean?

In order to avoid having to redo the histograms for both the population and the sample means, we are going to look at populations whose range of values is not greater than that of the first population (about 0 to 100) and whose mean is fairly close to the mean of the first population (about 50). We will look at a population in which all values of the population are either between 0 and 20 or between 80 and 100. The mean of this population will be in the middle (close to 50), and the population will be approximately symmetric, but every single value in that population will be far from the mean.

Before doing this, we need to do some "housekeeping" on the workbook. This includes restoring the range of the values on the horizontal axis of the sample means and erasing the existing samples.

- Change the range of values in C7:C26 back to the series 5, 10, 15, ... , 100.

- Select the Samples worksheet. Click the Select All button at the insertion of the row headings and the column headings (see below).

Click the
"Select All"
button here. —

Clicking that button will select the entire worksheet. Press the Delete key. This will erase the contents of all cells in the worksheet.

- Click the "Population" worksheet tab.

The first 100 elements of the population will consist of the numbers between 0.2 and 20, and the second 100 elements will consist of the numbers between 80.2 and 100. There will be no values between 20 and 80.2.

- Enter ".2" in cell A1.

- Select the first 100 cells in column A by entering "A1:A100" in the Name Box. Press the Enter (or Return) key and those cells will be selected.

- Open the Edit menu on the Menu Bar. Select "Fill" and then click "Series...."

- In the Series dialog window locate the "Step value" field on the bottom left. Change the value in that field from "1" to ".2." Leave "Type" selected on "Linear." Click OK.

- Enter "A100" in the Name Box and press the Enter key. Verify that the value in that cell is "20."

- Select cell A101 and enter the value "80.2."

- Using the Name Box, select the region A101:A200.

- Open the Edit menu and select "Fill" and "Series...." Again change the "Step value" from "1" to ".2." Click OK.

The population should now consist entirely of numbers less than 20 and numbers between 80 and 100. The histogram chart should look like the picture at the top of the next page.

The values of the population mean and standard deviation are automatically updated on both the Population and Sample Means worksheets. Let's now compare the distribution of sample means for different-size samples drawn from this population.

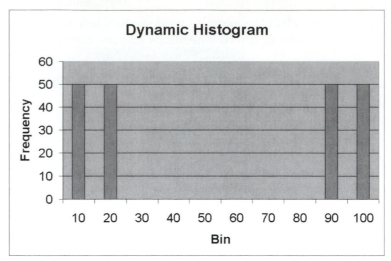

- Select the Sample Means worksheet. Because the values on the Samples worksheet have been erased, this worksheet will be filled with error values. This will change once the new samples are drawn.

- Open the Tools menu on the Menu Bar, select "Learning Business Statistics," and click "Multiple Random Samples."

- If you are in the same Excel session as when you last ran the Multiple Random Samples tool, the fields in the dialog window will already be filled out. In this case, change the value of "Sample Size" to "5." If all the fields are empty, look at the picture on page 177 to see what values should be entered.

- If you select either the "Population Range" or "Output Range" fields, the top worksheet will switch to the one whose cells are shown in the field you select. If you are no longer at the Sample Means worksheet, click the mouse pointer in either the "Sample Size" or "Number of Samples" field, and the Sample Means worksheet will return to the top.

- Move the Multiple Random Samples dialog window so you can see the sample means histogram chart. Click the OK button.

It should be apparent that the distribution of these sample means is not close to the normal distribution. There are few values close to the mean of about 50. The tallest bars are likely for the intervals whose upper bounds are 45 and 60, and the two bars between those are short.

- Rerun the Multiple Random Samples tool several times to get a feel for how different sets of 1,000 samples differ in the distribution of their means. When the dialog window first appears, the top window will shift to the Population worksheet. Click the mouse pointer in the

"Sample Size" field to switch back to the Sample Means worksheet and move the dialog window so you can see the histogram chart change when the new samples are drawn.

Different sets of samples will differ somewhat in the distribution of their means. All (or nearly all) will have the characteristics described above, and none will be close to the line showing the normal distribution.

Lets next look at the distribution of the means of larger samples.

- Recall the Multiple Random Samples tool, change the "Sample Size" to "15" and Click OK. Try this several times.

The means of samples of size 15 are closely approximated by the normal distribution. Different sets of samples will differ somewhat from each other and none will exactly follow the normal distribution line—partly because 1,000 is such a tiny portion of all the possible samples. Nevertheless, the fit for these sample means should be about as good as it was for the previous population.

- Clear the Samples worksheet by selecting that worksheet. Unless all cells on the worksheet are already selected click on the Select All button (shown on page 187). Press the Delete button.

▼Skewed Population

The population shape most resistant to producing sample means which are normally distributed is a skewed shape. We will look at this by using a simulated population which has an extremely strong positive skew.

- Select the Population worksheet. In cell A1 enter the value ".5."

- Select the cell range A1:A200.

- Open the Edit menu. Choose "Fill" and then "Series."

We have used the Series dialog window to create linear series, where each value was calculated by taking the previous value and adding a fixed constant. This time we will create a growth series in which each value is calculated by taking the previous value and multiplying that by a fixed constant.

- Under "Type" click the "Growth" button. In the "Step value" field enter "1.033." The window should look like the picture on the next page.

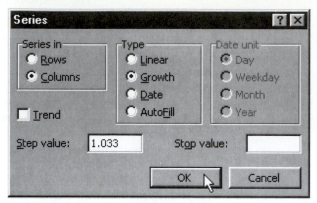

- Click OK. The histogram should look like the picture below, showing a set of data with a very strong positive skew.

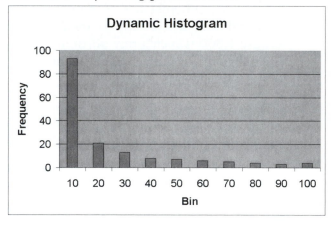

This histogram, in fact, does not show all of the data, since the maximum value (in cell A200) is over 319. Let's correct this by changing the bin values in B13:B22.

- Enter "35" in cell B13 and "70" in cell B14. Select B13:B14 and drag the fill handle down to B22. This should produce the series of values in which each cell is 35 more than the cell above, with the value 350 in cell B22.

Our conclusion about the shape of the population remains unchanged: It has a fierce positive skew. Now let's look at the distribution of sample means for samples of different size.

- Switch to the Sample Means worksheet and recall the Multiple Random Samples tool. If you haven't started a new Excel session since the last time you used the tool, all the fields will already have the correct value except for "Sample Size," which should be changed to "5." If the dialog window is blank, you want it to have the same values shown in the picture on page 177. Move the dialog window so that it does not cover the sample means histogram. Click OK.

- Repeat the process a few times so you can see the distributions of different sets of 1,000 sample means.

The Sample Means histogram should look approximately like the picture below. Yours should not be exactly the same since every set of random samples is likely to be different.

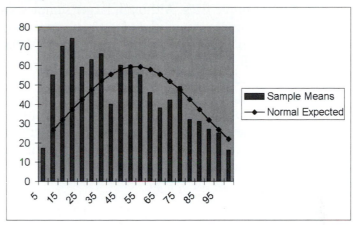

A few of the sample means may exceed 1,000 and thus not be shown on this histogram. Increasing the range of the horizontal axis would not change the fact that this distribution also has a strong positive skew, although not as strong as that of the population. The bars to the left of the center all tend to be above the normal distribution curve, while those to the right tend to be below. Clearly, the distribution of these sample means is *not* approximately normal.

Now let's try larger samples.

- Recall the Multiple Random Samples tool. Change the sample size to 15. Move the dialog window so you can see the histogram and Click OK. Repeat this several times.

Increasing the sample size will make the distribution of the sample means more symmetric and closer to the normal distribution. Even though the skew has been reduced, it should still be apparent. Bars to the left of the mean should have a clear tendency to be taller than the normal curve, while bars to the right should be shorter. Although closer, this distribution still cannot be regarded as approximately normal. Let's try samples of size 30.

- Recall the Multiple Random Samples tool and change the sample size to 30. Again, run the tool several times and look carefully each time for signs of positive skewness.

Although the skewness of the distribution of sample means has again been reduced (and the distribution is closer to the normal prediction), you should see clear evidence that the skewness is persisting. Although there is a general rule of thumb that samples of size 30 are large enough to assume that the sampling distribution is normal, that is not the case for this population.

If you have the patience (and a fast-enough computer), you can try even larger sample sizes. Although larger samples always bring the distribution of sample means closer to the normal, you will find that even with samples of size 100, evidence of a slight (perhaps negligible) positive skew will still be present. Fortunately, it is almost unheard of for real-world data to have as extreme a skew as does this population, and, in general, large sample sizes (over 30) provide reasonable assurance that the distribution of sample means will be approximately normal. For data which are symmetric, or approximately symmetric, even relatively small sample sizes will produce a sampling distribution of the mean which is approximately normal.

▼The *t* Distribution

In the great majority of situations where the sampling distribution of the mean is applied, the population standard deviation is unknown. Instead, the standard deviation of a single sample must be used. Although the *expected value* of a sample variance is the population variance, a sample standard deviation is a random number, and its use can be thought of as adding uncertainty to the sampling distribution.

In the early part of the century William S. Gosset, a British industrial research scientist who worked for the Irish brewer Guinness, showed that better results were obtained when the sampling distribution of the mean was treated not as following the normal distribution but as following a similar distribution, which he termed the *t* distribution. The use of a different probability distribution in Excel would cause little difficulty except for the fact that Excel is inconsistent in its treatment of continuous probability distributions.

As you know, the normal distribution has two variables, μ and σ. An important property of that distribution is that a problem involving any normal distribution can be converted to a problem involving the standard normal distribution (which has $\mu = 0$ and $\sigma = 1$) by using the standardization formula (which converts x to z, or vice versa).

The *t* distribution is used in place of the *z* distribution when the population standard deviation is unknown. While the *z* distribution is a specific instance of the normal distribution, the *t* distribution has a variable called the *degrees of freedom* or *dof*. For problems involving the sampling distribution of the mean, the value of the degrees of freedom is $n - 1$, where n is the size of the sample from which the standard deviation was calculated.

Before using the t distribution, the value of the sample mean must be transformed in a way identical to that used to standardize the sample mean to a z variable: Subtract the population mean and divide by the standard error (calculated, in this case, from the sample's standard deviation). The transformed value can be treated as a random variable following the t distribution with $n - 1$ degrees of freedom.

Excel provides four functions to handle the normal distribution: NORMDIST, NORMSDIST, NORMINV, and NORMSINV. The first two are probability distribution functions, and the second two are inverse distribution functions. The two with an "S" in the name are for the standard normal distribution, while the other two work for any normal distribution (and require that the values for μ and σ be given as arguments). All of these functions are cumulative; the probability they associate with a value for the random variable is the probability of a random variable being less than or equal to that value.

By contrast, there are two functions for the t distribution, TDIST and TINV. The first is a probability distribution function and the second is an inverse distribution function. Both provide a relationship only for standardized t values. They both take the value of the degrees of freedom as an argument. Neither of them is cumulative. Furthermore, both handle only positive t values. Despite these differences, we can get the same information from these two functions as we did from the normal functions. We just have to keep in mind how what we want relates to what the functions provide.

Consider the diagram on the next page showing the density function for a standard t distribution. TDIST has three arguments. If the first argument of TDIST is set equal to the value of t in the diagram, and the second is set equal to the value of the degrees of freedom, TDIST will return either the area of both shaded regions or the area of just the shaded region to the right, depending on the value of the third argument. Notice that the two regions are always equal in size, so that if TDIST is asked to give the area of both regions, the result is exactly twice what it would be if TDIST were asked to give the area of just one region. The value of t must be positive, a negative value for t will result in an error message. Since the t distribution is symmetric (and has mean 0), the value for the upper boundary of the left tail will have the same absolute value (but negative sign) as the lower boundary of the right tail.

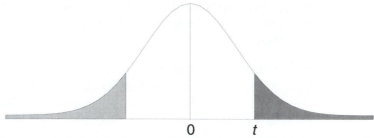

TINV, by contrast, has only two arguments. The first is set equal to a probability, and the second to the degrees of freedom. TINV interprets the probability as the area of *both* tails, and it returns the value of *t* shown in the diagram. Unlike TDIST, TINV has no argument allowing us to indicate that our problem involves only the area of one tail. Since the area of one tail is always merely half the area of two, this is not a serious problem. Notice that the *t* value returned is always positive.

▼Looking at the *t* Distribution

In order for you to get a visual sense of the relationship between the *t* distribution and the *z* distribution, a workbook has been prepared and is included with the data set for this book that contains a chart combining both distributions.

- Click the Open button on the Standard Toolbar (🖾). Navigate to the diskette or other location where you have placed the data sets for this book. In the Chap_6 folder open the "t and z distributions.xls" file.

Column A contains values of the random variable (both *t* and *z*). Column B contains probabilities for the *z* distribution.

- Examine the formula in cell B3 by selecting it and looking in the Formula Bar. It calculates the cumulative probability of –3.9 in A3 minus the cumulative probability of –4 in A2.

Each cell in column B contains the probability that a standard normal random variable will fall between the value in the same row in column A and the value in the previous row in column A. Thus cell B3 contains "1.64295E-05," which is the probability of a *z* value falling between –3.9 and –4.

The formula to calculate the probabilities for the *t* distribution is slightly more complicated because of the way the TDIST works.

- Examine the formula in cell C3.

The formula is similar in concept to that used in B3. The degrees of freedom is taken from cell E1. The Absolute Value function (ABS) is used to ensure that the *t* value passed to TDIST is nonnegative. It also is used to be sure the probability returned is positive. Note that this formula would not work to determine an interval in which one boundary is negative and the other is positive. This is avoided on the worksheet by having 0 as a boundary.

The chart graphically displays the values in columns A through C.

- Move the chart so that the upper-left corner is in cell D2. Scroll your screen so that cell D1 is in the upper-left corner. Select the chart (unless it is already selected) so that it is surrounded by "handles." Drag the lower-right handle to the lower-right corner of your screen. The objective is to make the chart as large as possible but small enough to view without scrolling and small enough so that cells D1 and E1 are also visible.

- Change the value of the degrees of freedom by changing the number in cell E1. Start by reducing the value to 8, then to 5, then to 2, then to 1. Does reducing the value of the degrees of freedom make the two plots more alike or less alike?

- Increase the value of the degrees of freedom. Try 20, 100, 1000, 10,000, and 100,000. It may seem that the line for the *z* plot completely disappears. Actually, it is simply becoming better covered by the *t* plot line. Look carefully at the places where the plot curves most sharply and you may see indications that the two lines are not perfectly superimposed. If you can't tell a difference, scroll the worksheet back to where you can see the numbers in columns B and C. If the two plots were identical, the numbers would be identical. If you can't see a difference between the numbers in columns B and C, increase the widths of those columns. This will enable Excel to display the numbers with more precision, making the (slight) difference clearer.

As you can see, as the degrees of freedom increases, the *t* distribution becomes more like the normal distribution.

- Change the degrees of freedom back to 1.

When the degrees of freedom is 1, the *t* distribution is most unlike the normal. The difference is similar for other values of the degrees of freedom. The tails are "fatter" for the *t* distribution than they are for the normal. The *t* distribution appears more spread out than the normal distribution. Since the tails are higher and the peak is lower, how would the width of an interval symmetrically distributed around the mean with given area compare for the standard t and z distributions? This issue will be discussed again below.

▼ Using Excel to Solve Distribution of Sample Means Problems

Solving distribution of sample means problems is important not because these problems are useful. It is important to help you connect an understanding of the normal distribution with an understanding of confidence intervals and hypothesis tests, highly useful tools of statistical inference. There are two classes of problems concerning the distribution of sample means: those for which the population standard deviation (or variance) is known, and those for which only a sample standard deviation is known. The first class of problems is solved much like the very similar normal distribution problems. The primary difference is that the standard error (standard deviation of sample means) must be calculated from the equation $\sigma_{\bar{x}} = \dfrac{\sigma}{\sqrt{n}}$. Consider the following example:

A soft-drink bottling machine fills each bottle with an average of 2.05 liters with a standard deviation of .03 liters. Within what region symmetrically distributed around the mean will 95% of the means of samples of 50 bottles fall?

- Double click the "Sheet2" worksheet tab. Change its name to "Sigma Known."

- Enter the following labels in cells A1:A9: "Mu," "Sigma," "n," "Standard Error," "Prob," "zL," "zH," "x bar L," and "x bar H."

- Enter the values from the problem above in cells B1:B3 adjacent to the labels in column A.

- Enter an Excel formula in cell B4 that will divide the value of the standard deviation by the square root of n. The displayed value should be "0.004243."

- Enter the number ".95" in cell B5.

- Using the same technique used in Chapter 5, enter the formulas in cells B6 and B7 that will display upper and lower z values for the central interval with area .95. This will require using the NORMSINV function. B6 will display "-1.95996," and B7 will display "1.959961."

- Enter the formulas in cells B8 and B9 that will convert the z values in cells B6 and B7 to $\bar{x}$ values. This conversion should be done using the following formula:

$$\bar{x} = \mu + z\sigma_{\bar{x}}$$

The difference between this formula and that used in Chapter 5 is that the z value is multiplied by the standard error rather than by the population standard deviation. The displayed value for cell B8 should be "2.041685," while that for B9 should be "2.058315." Thus 95% of the means of samples of size 50 will lie between 2.041685 and 2.058315.

Now consider the following problem:

A soft-drink bottler has selected a random sample of 10 bottles from a bottle-filling machine designed to fill bottles with an average of 2.05 liters. The average fill in the sample was 2.00 liters with a standard deviation of .12 liters. If the machine was actually putting an average of 2.05 liters in all bottles, what is the probability that a sample of 10 bottles could be selected with a sample average of 2.00 or less?

This problem requires the t distribution because the only standard deviation known is that of a single sample.

- Double click the "Sheet3" worksheet tab to display this blank worksheet. Change its name to "Sigma Unknown."

- Enter the following labels in cells A1:A8: "Mu," "s," "n," "Standard Error," "x bar," "t," "TDIST," "Answer."

- In cells B1:B3 enter the population mean (2.05), the sample standard deviation (.12), and the sample size (10). In cell B5 enter the value for $\bar{x}$ (2.00). These are the data provided by the problem.

- In cell B4 enter the formula that will calculate the standard error. The standard error is calculated from the sample standard deviation just as it was from a population standard deviation; divide the standard deviation by the square root of n. The displayed value should be "0.037947."

- In cell B6 enter the formula that will standardize the number in cell B5. The formula to standardize the x value is the same as that used in the previous problem, although the symbols are usually slightly different:

$$t = \frac{\bar{x} - \mu}{s_{\bar{x}}}$$

The symbol t is used instead of z because sample means will be treated as following the t distribution. The symbol for the denominator is $s_{\bar{x}}$ instead of $\sigma_{\bar{x}}$ to indicate that the standard error used here is derived from a sample standard deviation (s) instead of a population standard deviation (σ). When the correct formula is entered in B6, it will display the value "-1.31762."

Before using TDIST, it is helpful to have a clear picture of what area in the density function corresponds to the probability we want to determine. For this problem, the density function and the area are shown below:

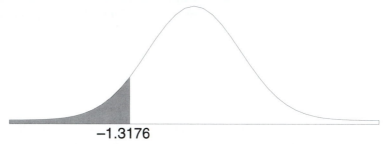

$$-1.3176$$

Compare this diagram with that shown on page 194. If we give TDIST the absolute value of −1.31762 and ask for the one-tail probability, it will return the area of the tail to the right of (+)1.31762. But the area of this tail is the same as the one above, which we want.

- Select cell B7, click the Edit Formula button, and choose "TDIST."

- In the "X" argument field, enter the expression that will take the absolute value of the number in cell B6.

- In the "Deg_freedom" argument field, enter an expression that will subtract 1 from the number in cell B3. The degrees of freedom equals $n − 1$.

- Enter the number "1" in the "Tails" argument field. The number "0.11009272" will appear immediately as the "Formula Result." Click the OK button, and the same number will appear in cell B7.

- Since this is the value we want, enter a formula in cell B8 that will make the contents of that cell equal the value of cell B7. The probability of a sample of 10 bottles having an average fill less than 2.00 liters is .110093.

Consider this problem:

A soft-drink bottler has selected a random sample of 12 bottles from a bottle-filling machine. The average fill in the sample was 2.00 liters with a standard deviation of .09 liters. What is the probability that the average fill for a sample of 12 bottles will be within .05 liters of the actual average fill for all bottles?

A diagram of the density function with the relevant area is shown at the top of the next page. The smallest value a sample mean can have and be

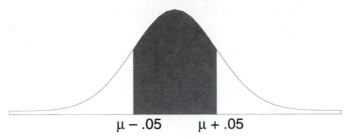

μ − .05   μ + .05

on the boundary of the area is μ − .05. The largest value a sample mean can have is μ + .05.

In this problem we are given a value for *s* and *n*, but we don't have a numeric for the two $\bar{x}$ values, and we don't have a value for μ. The expressions that are given for $\bar{x}$ (μ ± .05) will enable us to find the corresponding *t* values because the values for μ will cancel out.

- Enter the values for *s* and *n* in the appropriate places on the worksheet. The standard error will be calculated automatically from these values and should be displayed as 0.025981.

The calculation of the *t* value corresponding to the *x* value of μ + .05 is:

$$t = \frac{\bar{x} - \mu}{s_{\bar{x}}} = \frac{(\mu + .05) - \mu}{s_{\bar{x}}} = \frac{.05}{s_{\bar{x}}} \, .$$

Notice that μ is not present in the final expression.

- Select cell B6. Enter the formula that will divide the number .05 by the standard error in cell B4. The displayed value should be "1.924501."

How do we use TDIST with this problem? Compare the diagram above with the one showing the probability given by TDIST on page 194. The center region above is the complement of the two shaded tails shown on page 194. The shaded area above can be calculated by having TDIST determine the two-tail probability associated with the positive *t* value and subtracting that probability from 1.

The formula currently in cell B7 determines the one-tail area associated with the *t* value. Let's change it to the two-tail area:

- Select cell B7. Click the Mouse pointer on "TDIST" in the Formula Bar. Click "TDIST" on the most recently used function button. The TDIST dialog window will appear with the argument fields filled out as they were when the formula in B7 was created.

- Change the "1" in the "Tails" argument to "2." Click the Finish Button. The value displayed in cell B7 should be "0.080535."

- Select cell B8. Enter the Excel function that subtracts the value in cell B7 from 1.

The answer to the problem, as displayed in cell B8, shows that the probability that the mean of a sample of 12 bottles will be within .05 liters of the mean of all bottles is ".919465."

Let's examine the use of the TINV function to solve a couple of problems:

An advertising agency wants to determine whether a new campaign for Crunch-O cereal has increased consumption among 8- to 12-year-olds who eat cold cereal. Prior to the campaign, those in the population group consumed an average of 12 oz of Crunch-O per month. If the campaign had no effect, average consumption would remain at 12 oz. A sample of 15 children was chosen whose consumption after the campaign averaged 13.9 oz with a standard deviation of 3.1 oz. Assuming the campaign had no effect (and the population average remained at 12 oz), what sample average would be exceeded by only 5% of all samples?

A diagram of this situation is shown below. The shaded area to the right has a given area of .05. The problem is to determine the boundary value, $\bar{x}$ for that area. This is done by first using TINV to determine the value of t such that the probability of a standard t having a greater value is .05, and then converting that t value to an $\bar{x}$ value.

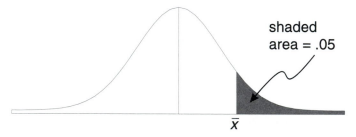

- Enter the following labels in cells D1:D8: "Mu," "s," "n," "Standard Error," "Upper Tail," "TINV Prob," "t," "x bar."

- In cells E1:E3, enter the values given in the problem: $\mu = 12$, $s = 3.1$, and $n = 15$.

- In cell E4 enter the formula to calculate the standard error. The displayed value should be "0.800417."

- Enter the upper tail area, ".05," in cell E5.

Refer back to the picture on page 194. In order to use TINV, we must determine the *two-tail* probability which would give us the t value corresponding to the $\bar{x}$ value in the picture above. If we were to add a left tail to the picture corresponding to the area to the left of $-\bar{x}$, the area of that tail would also be .05 because of the symmetry of the t distribution. Thus the two-tail area is exactly twice the one-tail area.

- Enter the formula in cell E6 that will double the value in cell E5. The displayed value should be "0.1."

- Select cell E7. Click the Edit Formula button. Select TINV from the "Statistical" category. Move to the TINV dialog box.

- In the "Probability" argument field, put the address for the two-tail probability you have just calculated. In the "Deg_freedom" argument field, enter an expression that will subtract 1 from the value in cell E3. Click the Finish Button. The displayed value should be "1.761309." This t value needs to be converted to an $\bar{x}$ value.

The formula for converting a t value to an $\bar{x}$ value is very similar to that used to convert a z value to an x value:

$$\bar{x} = \mu + ts_{\bar{x}}$$

- Enter the formula in cell E8 that will add the mean (in cell E1) to the product of the t value (in cell E7) and the standard error (in cell E4).

The answer, 13.40978 oz, is the sample average amount of cereal that would be exceeded by only 5% of the sample of 15 children, assuming that the average amount eaten by all children was 12 oz.

Let's consider a slightly different version of the problem:

An advertising agency wants to determine whether a new campaign for Crunch-O cereal has increased consumption among 8- to 12-year-olds who eat cold cereal. Prior to the campaign, those in the population group consumed an average of 12 oz of Crunch-O per month. If the campaign had no effect, average consumption would remain at 12 oz. A sample of 15 children was chosen whose consumption after the campaign averaged 13.9 oz with a standard deviation of 3.1 oz. Assuming the campaign had no effect (and the population average remained at 12 oz), within what interval, symmetrically distributed about the mean, would 95% of sample means fall?

The diagram for this problem is shown at the top of the next page. The shaded central region has an area of .95, and the values of $\bar{x}_L$ and $\bar{x}_H$ must be determined.

- Since the mean, sample size, and standard deviation for this problem are the same as those for the previous problem, copy the region D1:E4 to G1:H4. An easy way to do this is to select D1:E4, place the mouse

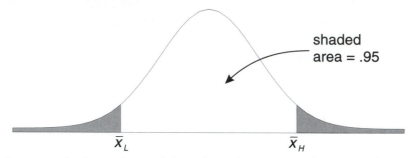

shaded
area = .95

$\bar{x}_L$ $\bar{x}_H$

pointer on the boundary of the selected region, and press and hold the Ctrl key while dragging the boundary to the new location.

- Add the following labels to cells G5:G10: "Mid Prob," "TINV Prob," "t," "x bar L," "x bar H," and "Width."

- In cell H5 enter the given probability of a sample mean having a value in the central region, .95.

Compare the shaded region shown in the diagram above with that required by TINV (shown in the diagram on page 194). The probability required by TINV is the *complement* of that given in the problem, and is shown in the diagram above by the nonshaded region under the density function. Since the area under the entire density function is 1, the area of the nonshaded region is 1 minus the area of the shaded region.

- Enter the formula in cell H6 that will calculate 1 minus the value in cell H5. The displayed number should be "0.05."

- Select cell H7. Click the Edit Formula button. Select "TINV" and go to the dialog window.

- In the "Probability" field enter the address for the TINV probability, H6. In the "Deg_freedom" field enter the expression that will subtract 1 from the value given in the cell displaying the number of observations (H3). Click the Finish Button. The value displayed in H7 should be "2.144789."

This *t* value is the *t* value corresponding to $\bar{x}_H$. There is also a negative *t* value corresponding to $\bar{x}_L$. Since both have the same absolute value, the negative *t* value must be –2.144789.

- Enter the formula in cell H9 that adds the product of the positive *t* value (in H7) and the standard error (H4) to the mean (H1). The displayed value should be "13.71672."

- Enter the formula in H8 that will do the same as the one in H9, except with the negative *t* value. Since the standard error is (always) positive, adding the product of the negative *t* value and standard error is the same as subtracting the product of the positive *t* value and standard error. The displayed value should be "10.28328."

- In cell H10 enter the formula that will calculate the difference between the value in cell H9 and that in cell H8. The displayed value should be "3.433449."

The answer to this problem is that 95% of the means of samples of size 15 will be between 10.28328 and 13.71672.

Let's consider the effect of the degrees of freedom on the width of this interval by determining the change in the width of the interval that would occur if the sample had a size different from 15 (but with the same standard deviation).

- Change the value of *n* (H3) to 10. Observe what happens to the *t* value (H7), the standard error (H4), and the interval width (H10). (With a sample of size 10, the interval width should be 4.435216.) Switch the value in H3 back and forth between 15 and 10 until you have determined the way all three of these values change.

When the sample size goes down, the degrees of freedom also decreases. This causes the *t* value to increase (to 2.262159 when *n* is 10). Refer again to the diagram on page 194. As the value of *t* goes up, the boundary moves further from the mean, 0, of a standard *t* distribution. Since the *t* value of the boundary for the left tail has the same absolute value (but negative sign), it too moves away from the mean and the interval becomes larger. Conversely, if the sample size (and degrees of freedom) becomes larger, the width of the interval containing the central 95% of *t* values decreases. Since the *z* distribution is the limit of the *t* distribution as the degrees of freedom increases toward infinity, the width of the interval containing 95% of *z* values must be narrower than the corresponding interval for any *t* distribution.

When the number of observations goes down, the standard error goes up. This reinforces the effect of the change in the *t* value caused by the change in degrees of freedom. Conversely, an increase in sample size causes the standard error to go down, which reduces the width of the central interval. The impact of the change in the standard error is much larger than the impact of the change in the degrees of freedom of the *t* distribution.

▼Exercises

1. A bottle-filling machine is designed to fill bottles with an average fill of 2.02 liters. A sample of 20 bottles is selected. The average fill of

the bottles in the sample is 1.99 liters, and the standard deviation is .09 liters. Assume that the machine is operating properly and really is filling *all* bottles with an average fill of 2.02. What is the probability that a random sample of 20 bottles could have a sample average fill of 1.99 or less? Assume that the filling process is normally distributed.

2. For the question above, determine an interval symmetrically distributed about the population mean of 2.02 liters within which would fall 90% of the means of samples of 20 bottles.

3. The average time required for students to complete the registration process at a university has been 55 minutes. A university administrator is trying a new procedure. Under this procedure, the registration times of 25 randomly selected students are recorded, resulting in a sample mean of 50.2 minutes and a sample standard deviation of 8.7 minutes. Assuming that there has been no improvement in the average time with the new procedure, determine the probability that the mean time for 25 students would be 50.2 minutes or less. Assume that student registration times are normally distributed.

4. A bolt-making machine is designed to produce bolts whose length is normally distributed with an average of 2 inches and a standard deviation of .1 inches. If the machine is working properly, what is the probability that a sample of 10 bolts would have an average length of 2.05 inches or more?

5. For the problem above, determine the value of the length of the bolts such that only 5% of the samples of 20 bolts would have means less than that length.

6. Recent graduates from an information technology program have received starting salaries which average $44,000 with a standard deviation of $4,700. If samples of 25 graduates are chosen, within what region, symmetrically distributed around the mean, will 95% of the sample means fall?

7. When it is working properly, a soft-drink bottle-filling machine fills bottles with an average of 3.1 liters of product. As part of a quality control program, the bottling company selects a sample of bottles and carefully measures the amount of soft drink in each bottle. The data are as follows: 2.94, 3.10, 3.02, 3.23, 3.45, 2.99, 2.88, 3.03, 2.73, 3.64, 2.51, 2.67, 3.12, 2.72, 2.98, 3.13, 2.83, 3.21, 3.04, 3.12, 3.10, 2.98, 3.08, 3.26, 2.86, 2.95, 3.17, 3.01, 2.97, 3.06, 3.29, 2.77, 3.25, 2.96, 3.36, 3.19, 2.86, 3.16, 2.66, 2.76, 2.75, 3.04, 3.16, 3.14, 2.83, 3.12, 2.65, 3.09, 3.45, 3.03. (These data are also in the "Exercises" workbook for this chapter.) Assuming the machine is working

properly ($\mu = 3.1$), what is the probability that a sample the size of this sample could be chosen with a sample mean as low or lower than this sample's mean?

8. Using the data from the above problem and again assuming the machine is working properly ($\mu = 3.1$), within what region, symmetrically distributed about the mean, would 95% of sample means fall?

9. Decreasing the number of degrees of freedom causes the shape of the standard t density function to change. The function goes up in the tails and down in the middle. This change is similar to that which happens with the normal density function when the value of the standard deviation is increased. Is it the same? Investigate this by changing the "t vs z" worksheet. Change column B so that NORMDIST is used rather than NORMSDIST so that you can vary the value for the standard deviation. Use a low value (1 to 4) for the degrees of freedom of the standard t distribution. Now change the standard deviation of the normal curve so that the tops of the two curves are the same height. Are the two curves identical? If not, describe the differences. Print the plot showing the two curves with the same heights. Put your name on the header and use the title to document the value for the dof of the t curve and the value of σ for the z curve.

Chapter 7

Confidence Intervals on a Population Mean

Inferential statistics generally involves a straightforward application of the concepts of a sampling distribution. One of the techniques of inferential statistics is interval estimation. Suppose you need to know the mean of a population, but only data from a (properly drawn) sample is available. How can you take information from a sample and use it to *infer* information about a population? The best single-value (or *point*) estimate you can give for a population mean is the sample mean. It is best in the sense that no other calculation can be made of the data in the sample yielding a single number that is likely to be as close to the population mean as is the sample mean.

Using the sample mean as an estimate of the population mean has one drawback—it is certain to be wrong! A sample mean, as we saw in the previous chapter, is a continuous random variable. A population mean, on the other hand, is not a random variable. It is a fixed value, even though it is unknown. The probability that a continuous random variable will ever precisely equal a fixed value is zero. Therefore, the probability that any sample mean will ever precisely equal the population mean is zero. Clearly statistics needs a technique for providing estimates of a population mean that can sometimes be correct.

The sampling distribution of the mean provides a technique for determining intervals within which a sample mean may lie with nonzero probability. These problems, examples of which were worked in the previous chapter, are worded like this, "Find an interval symmetrically distributed around the population mean that will contain $x\%$ of sample means." By using the t distribution, it is possible to use a sample standard deviation to solve this type of problem. The interval boundaries are found by evaluating the following expression:

$$\mu \pm ts_{\bar{x}}$$

The center of this interval is μ, the population mean. The lower bound is below μ by an amount equal to $ts_{\bar{x}}$, while the upper bound is above μ by the same amount. The value of t is determined by the size of the $x\%$ in the problem and by the size of the sample (degrees of freedom). The value of the standard error, $s_{\bar{x}}$, is determined by the sample standard deviation (s) and the sample size (n).

In most situations the value of μ is unknown. If we knew μ, there would be no point to estimating it with a sample! If we don't know the value of μ, there's no way we can calculate the boundaries of an interval symmetrically distributed around μ, which contains a given percentage of sample means. Even though its value is unknown, both μ and the interval around μ still exist. If we pick a sample, there is no way of knowing whether or not the mean of that sample lies within the interval. But we do know the *probability* that it lies within the interval. How can this be used? Consider the diagram below of a density function of a sampling distribution of the mean.

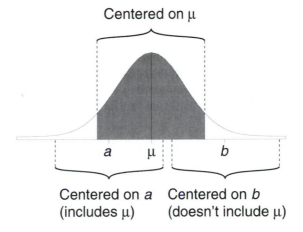

Centered on μ

a μ b

Centered on *a*   Centered on *b*
(includes μ)   (doesn't include μ)

Suppose the shaded central region, which is centered on μ, has an area of .95. The portion of the horizontal axis below the shaded region represents the range of values, symmetrically distributed about the mean, within which a single sample mean has a .95 probability of falling. If we know nothing about the population, then we can't know the actual values of the boundaries of that range. If a sample is drawn and its mean is calculated, we cannot know for sure if that mean lies within the range of values (as does *a* in the diagram) or outside the range (like *b*). But we know it has a 95% chance of being inside the range and only a 5% chance of being outside the range.

Suppose we construct an interval of the same width as the unknown interval around this sample mean. We can do this by adding and subtracting $ts_{\bar{x}}$ from the sample mean, which we can calculate entirely from the data of the sample. This value, $ts_{\bar{x}}$, is called the *sampling error*. Notice that if the sample mean lies within the range containing 95% of the sample means (like *a*), the interval centered on it will include μ. If the sample mean lies outside the range containing 95% of the sample, then the interval centered on it will not contain μ. Since there is a 95% probability that the sample mean does lie within the range, there is a 95% probability that this interval centered on the sample mean will include the unknown value of μ. Such an interval is called a *95% confidence interval*. Intervals can be constructed to other confidence levels, such as 80%, 90%, or 99%, by using the appropriate value for *t* in the expression for the sampling error.

▼Using Excel to Determine Confidence Intervals

- Start Excel with a new blank workbook and save it in a file named "Chap7.xls."

- Double click the "Sheet1" worksheet tab and change its name to "CI on Mu."

Consider the following problem:

A manufacturer wants to test a batch of light bulbs for lumen output. A sample of light bulbs was tested with the following results:

1326, 1336, 1351, 1365, 1209, 1343, 1259, 1365, 1308, 1349

Determine a 95% confidence interval estimate for the mean lumen output of all light bulbs in the batch. The lumen output of all bulbs can be assumed to be normally distributed.

- In cell A1 enter the label "Data." In cells C1:C9 enter the following labels in the order given: "n," "mean," "std dev," "std err," "conf level," "t," "samp error," "lower bnd," "upper bnd."

Column D will contain the statistics given by the labels in the same row of column C.

- In cells A2:A11, enter the data from the problem.

- Use the Excel functions COUNT, AVERAGE, and STDEV to determine the values in cells D1:D3, respectively. For the first argument of each of these functions, refer to the entire column A by clicking the column heading (shown on page 12), which will enter the address "A:A." All of these functions know to look only at the numbers in the column. The values which display in D1:D3 should be "10," "1321," and "50.38397," respectively.

- Enter the formula in cell D4 to calculate the standard error. Recall that the standard error is the standard deviation (in cell D3) divided by the square root of the sample size (in cell D1). The value displayed in D4 should be "15.93281."

- Enter "95%" in cell D5. Be sure to enter the percent symbol: "%."

Excel regards the percent symbol as a type of cell format. Entering a number followed by a percent sign is equivalent to first entering the number as a proportion between 0 and 1 and then clicking the Percent Style button to set that cell's format.

- To see the effect of the percent style, select D5 again and click the Comma Style button: ▪. The cell will display "0.95," the actual value in the cell. Select the cell again and click the Percent Style button: %. Now it again displays "95%." When this cell is used in a formula, the value Excel will use in calculations is 0.95.

The formula to be entered in cell D6 will determine the t value corresponding to the level of confidence (.95 for this problem) and the degrees of freedom. The TINV function will convert a probability to a t value, but the probability it expects is not the area of the central region corresponding to the confidence level. Refer to the diagram on page 194. TINV must be given the two-tail probability represented by the two shaded regions. The confidence level corresponds to the area of the unshaded region in the center. These two areas are complementary; they must sum to 1. To determine the tail areas, simply subtract the confidence level from 1.

- Select cell D6. Click the Edit Formula button and select the "TINV" function.

- In the "Probability" argument field, enter an expression that will subtract the confidence level in cell D5 from 1. Check the value displayed to the right of the argument field. It should be "0.05."

- In the "Deg_freedom" argument field, enter the expression that will subtract 1 from the sample size in cell D1. The value displayed to the right of the field should be "9." Click the OK button. The value displayed in cell D6 should be "2.262159."

- Enter the formula in cell D7 to calculate the sampling error. The sampling error, $ts_{\bar{x}}$, is the product of the t value and the standard error. The displayed value should be "36.04255."

- Enter the formulas in cells D8 and D9 to calculate the lower and upper bounds of the confidence interval. The lower bound is the sample mean minus the sampling error while the upper bound is the sample mean plus the sampling error. The displayed values should be "1285.057" and "1357.143," respectively.

The 95% confidence interval on the population mean can be written as

$$1285.057 < \mu < 1357.143$$

You can determine the 80% confidence interval on the mean by entering ".80" (or "80%") in cell D5. You should get this result:

$$1299.064 < \mu < 1343.136$$

Similarly the 99% confidence interval should be

$$1269.321 < \mu < 1372.879$$

Notice that the higher the level of confidence, the lower the value of the lower bound and the higher the value of the upper bound. Higher levels of confidence are associated with larger sampling errors and wider intervals than lower levels of confidence. It is desirable for a confidence interval to have as high a level of confidence as possible, but it is also desirable for it to be narrow. What answer do you get from Excel when you ask for a 100% confidence interval? (The correct answer is $-\infty < \mu < +\infty$.)

▼Using Excel to Determine Required Sample Size

The only practical way of reducing the sampling error without decreasing the level of confidence is to increase the size of the sample. As *n* increases, the standard error will decrease. The higher degrees of freedom will also slightly reduce the *t* value associated with a particular confidence level. Larger samples are more expensive to collect and thus some trade-off between the sample size and the size of sampling error is often needed. In order to investigate that trade-off, users of confidence intervals will often want to determine the sample size needed to obtain a target sampling error. Since the sampling error, $ts_{\bar{x}}$, requires a standard deviation, it is not really possible to determine the relationship between sample size and sampling error before drawing a sample. It's tough to draw a sample before knowing the sample size required. This problem is so important, however, that we have to assume that some information about the population standard deviation is known. Perhaps historical data can be used or a pilot sample drawn. Assuming that we know something about the *population* standard deviation also sidesteps another issue. If we don't know the size of the sample, what value for the degrees of freedom should be used for the *t* in the sampling error? Using a value for the population standard deviation enables us to use the *z* distribution rather than the *t* distribution for the distribution of sample means. The sampling error in this case is $z\sigma_{\bar{x}}$ rather than $ts_{\bar{x}}$. If we symbolize the sampling error as *e*, this equation can be written as

$$e = z\sigma_{\bar{x}}$$

$$= z\,\frac{\sigma}{\sqrt{n}}$$

Solving for *n* yields

$$n = \left(\frac{z\sigma}{e}\right)^2$$

If the value for *n* is not an integer, the convention is to round *up* to the nearest integer.

- Double click the "Sheet2" worksheet tab and rename it "n" (the symbol for the size of a sample).

Consider the following problem:

Owners of a fast-food restaurant want to estimate the average amount spent by customers during the lunch hour. A 92% confidence interval is desired with a sampling error of no more than $2.00. Based on past experience, they believe the standard deviation of customer expenditures is no more than $5.00. What sample size is needed to achieve this sampling error?

- Enter the following labels in the range A1:A6 of your worksheet: "samp error," "conf level," "z," "sigma," "n1," and "n."

- In cell B1 enter the desired sampling error from the problem, "2." In cell B2 enter the desired confidence level, ".92" (or "92%"). In cell B4 enter the assumed value for σ, "5."

Cell B3 must contain the *z* value corresponding to the confidence level in B2. This will involve using the NORMSINV function, which converts a *left-tail* probability to a *z* value. Furthermore, if you convert the area of the central region corresponding to a confidence interval to the area of the tail to the left of the central region, the *z* value you get will be negative. You want the value displayed in cell B3 to be positive. Refer to Chapter 5, particularly the section beginning on page 164, to review the technique for determining the *z* value you need.

- Enter the formula in cell B3 to convert the confidence level in cell B2 to the appropriate positive *z* value. When the correct formula is entered, the displayed value corresponding to a 92% confidence level is "1.750686."

- Enter the Excel formula in cell B5 that will calculate the value for *n* given in the formula on page 211. Recall that "^" is the Excel symbol to raise a number to a power. The expression to square the value of cell B3 would be "B3^2." When the correct formula is entered, cell B4 should display the value "19.15564."

- Round the number in cell B5 *up* to the next integer and enter the result in cell B6. Although there are Excel functions which will do this (such as ROUNDUP), do this by hand and simply enter a number in B6. That number should be 20.

This worksheet allows us to easily investigate the trade-offs between decreased sampling error and increased sample size. Suppose, for example, that we wanted to reduce the sampling error by half.

- Change the desired value of the sampling error in cell B1 from "2" to "1." This should cause the required sample size (n) to be 77.

Reducing the required sampling error by half more than tripled (or almost quadrupled) the required sample size.

- Reduce the desired sampling error again by half, from ±1.00 to ±0.5. This should cause the needed sampling size to nearly quadruple again, to 307.

As the sampling error gets smaller, it becomes increasingly more expensive (in terms of sample size) to achieve additional reduction.

▼Simulating the Accuracy of Confidence Intervals

In order to better understand the accuracy of confidence intervals, we will look at the results of drawing 1,000 samples from a known population and constructing a confidence interval from each sample. Of course, when confidence intervals are actually used, the population is never known, otherwise there would be no point in estimating the population mean—we could calculate it directly. As a result, we never know for sure whether a confidence interval is really correct or not. Although artificial, this exercise will give us better insight into the meaning of "confidence level."

- Save and close the Chap7.xls worksheet.

Consider the following problem:

A large woodworking company is offered the opportunity to purchase a lot of 1,275 radial saw blades from a new supplier at what seems like a very good price. Critical to the decision of whether or not to buy the blades is their quality, and a critical aspect is the blades' useful lifetime, since a low price on a blade that won't last is no bargain. The only way of determining the lifetime of a blade is to destructively test it—use it to cut wood in a testing situation until it wears out. Clearly a sampling procedure is necessary, and the company has decided to estimate a 95% confidence interval of the average life of the blades in the lot.

- Open the workbook SawBlades.xls located in the Chap_7 folder of the data set for this book. If that file is on a diskette, open the File menu on the Menu Bar and click "Save As...." Save the workbook on a hard disk or network drive because it will become too large to fit on a diskette.

There are three worksheets in this workbook: Population, Samples, and Conf Intervals. The Population worksheet shows the actual lifetime of each of the 1,275 blades. In a real-life situation this information would be unknown, or, if known, there would be no reason to estimate μ with a confidence interval. With this information we will be able to determine whether or not a confidence interval estimated from a sample is correct—that is, whether it really includes 0.

We will use the Multiple Random Samples tool to draw 1,000 samples and place them on the Samples worksheet. There are already three samples there that we will use to develop the confidence interval calculations. The actual confidence intervals will be calculated on the remaining worksheet. Let's do this now for the first sample provided.

- Click the "Conf Intervals" worksheet tab and select cell A2. We will enter a formula to calculate the mean of the first sample here.

- Click the Edit Formula button. Select the "Average" function ("Statistical" category). With an insertion point in the "Number1" field, click the Samples worksheet.

- Move the Formula Palette down so that you can see the second row on the worksheet. Click the row header for the second row. In the "Number1" field you should see "Samples!2:2." This form of address refers to the entire second row of the Samples worksheet. Since all cells in that row are blank except for the sample values, this address will work for all of the functions calculating sample statistics. Click the OK button. The value displayed in cell A2 of the Conf Intervals worksheet should be "98.93333."

- Select cell B2. Enter a formula which will calculate the sample standard deviation of all values on row 2 of the "Samples" worksheet. The displayed value will be "17.87843."

- Select cell C2. Enter a formula using the COUNT function that will determine the number of values on row 2 of the Samples worksheet. The displayed value should be "15."

- Enter a formula in cell D2 to calculate the standard errors, using relative addresses for B2 and C2. This displayed value should be "4.61619."

- The confidence level is in cell K1. Use an absolute address to that location. Enter a formula in cell E2 which will calculate the *t* value for that confidence level and for the sample size given in C2. Be sure the reference to K1 is absolute. The displayed value should be "2.144789."

- Use relative addresses to calculate the sampling error in cell F2. The displayed value should be "9.900751."

- Use relative addresses to calculate the upper and lower bounds of the confidence interval in cells G2 and H2. The displayed values should be "89.03258254" and "108.8340841," respectively.

Based on this sample, the 95% confidence interval on the mean is $89.0326 < \mu < 108.8341$. Is this correct? A common error in confidence intervals is to say that this statement has a 95% probability of being correct. Probability can only be used when discussing random variables. The boundaries of the confidence interval of this sample are not random numbers—we have determined exactly what their value is. The population mean is also not a random number, although we haven't figured it out yet. Let's do that now.

- Switch to the Population worksheet. In cell G1 enter the label "Mu." In cell G2 enter a formula to calculate the average of the population numbers in A2:E256. The displayed value should be 100.

- Switch to the Conf Intervals worksheet.

Does the confidence interval contain the true population mean? The answer is yes. There is no probability associated with it. If we were to draw another sample, would it also contain the true population mean? Of that we cannot be certain. The confidence interval boundaries of a new sample are random numbers (until the sample is drawn). We therefore can speak of the probability that those boundaries will bracket the true population mean. What is that probability? Is it 95%? We will examine this by drawing 1,000 samples and determining the proportion of the 1,000 resulting confidence intervals that do correctly bracket the population mean. The expected value of that proportion is the probability of a sample having correct confidence interval boundaries. Of course, it is likely the proportion will differ somewhat from its expected value, but it should be close.

Before drawing the 1,000 samples, let's put a formula in cell I2 that will automatically tell us if the confidence interval is correct. We can use Excel functions to display the word "Yes" if the confidence interval is correct and "No" if it is not. This formula will have to examine the values in G2 and H2 and display "Yes" if and only if the value in G2 is less than the population mean and the value in H2 is greater than the population mean.

- Select cell I2. Click the Edit Formula button. Choose the "IF" function ("Logical" category).

The IF function has three arguments. In the "Logical_test" argument field, we will put an expression that is either true or false. If the expression is true, the IF function will display the value of the "Value_if_true" argument field. Otherwise, it will display the value of the "Value_if_false" argument field. The expression we want is one that says that the value of G2 is less than the population mean *and* the value of H2 is less than the population mean. The fact that we have two conditions, both of which must be true, means we have to use another Excel function.

- With the insertion point in the "Logical_test" field, open the list of functions and select the "AND" function from the "Logical" category.

The AND function has two or more arguments. Each argument must contain an expression that is either true or false. If all arguments are true, the AND function returns the value of "true." If any argument is false (even if others are true) the AND function returns the value "false." In the "Logical1" argument field we will enter an expression that the value of G2 is less than the population mean, and in the "Logical2" argument field we will enter an expression that the value of H2 is greater than the population mean. The AND function (and the value of the IF function's "Logical_test" argument) will thus be true if and only if the confidence interval correctly brackets the population mean.

- With the insertion point in the "Logical1" argument field, click the mouse pointer in cell G2. This address should be *relative*. Enter the "less than" symbol ("<"). Click on the Population worksheet and then click on cell G2, where the true population mean is. Make this address *absolute*. The argument field should contain "G2<Population!$G$2." Immediately to the right of the argument field you should see "=TRUE" for the value of the field.

- Click the "Logical2" argument field to put the insertion point there. Click cell H2 on the Conf Intervals worksheet. Enter a "greater than" symbol (">"). Click cell G2 on the Population worksheet and make the address *absolute*. The field should contain "H2>Population!$G$2." To the right of the field you should see "=TRUE," and just below you should also see "=TRUE" for the resulting value of the function. The Formula Bar should contain "=IF(AND(G2<Population!$G$2,H2>Population!$G$2))."

- Click the mouse pointer on the "IF" in the Formula Bar. The IF function dialog window should reappear with the "Logical_test" argument field filled.

- Enter the word "Yes" in the "Value_if_true" argument field and the word "No" in the "Value_if_false" argument field. Click the OK button. The word "Yes" should display in cell I2, and the formula bar should show "=IF(AND(G2<Population!$G$2,H2>Population!$G$2),"Yes","No")."

- Test the worksheet by copying the formulas in row 2 (A2:I2) down to rows 3 and 4. Check the displayed results with the picture below. If your values are not the same, change only the formulas in row 2 and recopy those formulas to rows 3 and 4 until your results agree.

	A	B	C	D	E	F	G	H	I
1	Mean	Std Dev	n	Std Err	t value	Samp Err	Lower Bound	Upper Bound	Correct?
2	98.93333	17.87843	15	4.61619	2.144789	9.900751	89.03258254	108.834084	Yes
3	105.8	16.83194	15	4.345989	2.144789	9.321227	96.47877269	115.121227	Yes
4	91	14.14719	15	3.652788	2.144789	7.834457	83.16554284	98.8344572	No

Let's now check the accuracy of 1,000 different confidence intervals.

- Open the Tools menu on the Menu Bar. Select "Learning Business Statistics" and "Multiple Random Samples." If "Learning Business Statistics" is not on the Tools menu, you haven't installed the Add-Ins for this book. See Appendix C.

- Use the mouse to enter the address of the population (to ensure the worksheet name is included). Enter "15" for the sample size and "1000" for the number of samples. Click the "Output Range:" field and then click the mouse pointer in cell A2 of the Samples worksheet. The dialog window should look like the picture below.

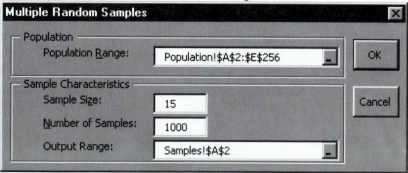

- Click the OK button. Note that this will replace the three samples already on the worksheet, as well as generate 997 additional samples.

- Switch to the Samples worksheet and verify that all the rows between 2 and 1001 contain numbers.

- Switch to the Conf Intervals worksheet. Select the region A2:I1001. This is probably most easily done using the Name Box.

- Open the Edit menu on the Menu Bar. Select "Fill" and then "Down." This should copy the formulas in the first row to the next 999.

- Look at the values displayed on the worksheet. Since the samples have all been separately drawn, you should see different numbers as you look down each column, with the exception of columns C and E. Most of the cells in column I should display "Yes," but you should find a few "No's" as you scroll down through the column.

In order to more easily determine the number of confidence intervals that are correct and incorrect, we will construct a table in which Excel will automatically tabulate the number of times "Yes" and "No" appear in column I.

- In cells J4:J6 enter the labels "Correct," "Incorrect," and "Total." In cells K3:L3 enter the labels "Number," and "Percent."

Excel has a function, COUNTIF, that will scan a range of cells and count the number of times a particular value (including a particular word) appears.

- Select cell K4. Click the Edit Formula button and choose the "COUNTIF" function from the "Statistical" category.

COUNTIF has two arguments: "Range," where the range address to be scanned is entered, and "Criteria," where a value can be put that is to be counted.

- With the insertion point in the "Range" argument field, click the header for column I. "I:I" will appear in the argument field. Enter "Yes" in the "Criteria" argument field. Click the OK button. Cell K4 will display a number which should not be greater than 1,000 and should be close to 950. This is the number of times the word "Yes" appears in column I.

- Select cell K5. Enter a formula using COUNTIF, which will count the number of times "No" appears in column I.

- Select cell K6. Click the AutoSum button on the Main Toolbar: **Σ**. Press the Enter key. K6 should display "1000."

- Enter formulas in L4 and L5 that will take the corresponding numbers in K4 and K5 and convert them to proportions by dividing by the number in K6.

- Select L6 and enter the formula that will sum the numbers in L4 and L5. The displayed value should be "1."

- Select cells L4:L6. Click the Percent Style button (%️)to display the proportions as percentages. Then click the Increase Decimal button (🔳) so that the percentages show two values to the right of the decimal points.

Recall that when the confidence level is increased, the sampling error (and the width of the confidence interval) increases. Every sample whose 95% confidence interval included the mean will still include the mean when the confidence level increases to 99%. Some of the samples whose 95% confidence intervals did not include the mean will now include the mean because those intervals are wider.

- Experiment with lower confidence levels, including 80%, 50%, and 25%. Compare the value of the confidence level with the percentage of the 1,000 samples whose confidence intervals are correct.

The confidence level and the percentage of the 1,000 samples with correct confidence intervals should always be close in value, regardless of the value of the confidence level. So what does the confidence level mean? If we choose a sample and construct a 95% confidence interval from that sample, is it correct to say that there is a 95% chance that the population mean lies within the confidence interval?

No. Once a sample is chosen, a 95% confidence interval either contains the population mean or does not contain the population mean. Since we usually don't know the population mean (and wouldn't need a confidence interval if we did) we don't know whether the interval does contain the population mean. Not knowing doesn't change the fact that everything is determined and a probability statement is inappropriate.

The confidence level tells us the probability that a randomly chosen sample will have a correct confidence interval. If we construct a 95% confidence interval, there is a 95% probability that we will choose a sample whose confidence interval will be correct. The distinction here is subtle. It is the sample and the confidence interval boundaries calculated from that sample that are random. The confidence level tells us the probability that the confidence interval procedure will result in a correct interval. Once a particular interval is calculated, its boundaries are no longer random; they are fixed. The population mean is also not random; it too is a fixed value. Before the sample was chosen, there was a probability, given by the confidence level, that that sample would result in a correct confidence interval. After the sample is chosen, the confidence interval is either correct or incorrect, and our ignorance of that state does not make the issue random or probabilistic.

▼Exercises

Close your worksheets before doing the exercises. Your objective in using Excel to determine confidence intervals is not to use the worksheets you have developed in this lesson but to understand the process of forming confidence intervals well enough that you can always develop your own worksheet in response to any problem you encounter.

Sometimes the data we wish to analyze are provided on a diskette or in another form that can be directly read by a computer. It is a good idea to have Excel read such data because it reduces the chance for error. Data provided on a diskette can come in a variety of formats. The easiest for Excel is data in the form of an Excel workbook. Other formats are common, however, and we often have no control over the formats in which data we want to use are provided.

Besides Excel workbooks, Excel has no difficulty reading data provided in the formats of competing spreadsheet products like Quattro Pro and Lotus 1-2-3. The format used by early versions of 1-2-3 has become a popular way to distribute data because this format can now be read by most spreadsheet programs. Files written in this format typically have names which end in .WKS or .WK1.

The most universal format for data is ASCII text. Data in this form can be read by most computer programs. Data in this form can be in a file with any name, although common endings for files with ASCII data include .TXT, .DAT., and .PRN. There is nothing in the ASCII format that corresponds to the notion of spreadsheet cells. Although Excel can read ASCII text, it needs help determining exactly what items go into individual cells. In most cases, this is easily done.

In these exercises we will use a set of data collected by a battery manufacturer testing the life of a particular model battery. These data are in the file named "Battery.txt," and instructions will be given on how to read them. The first step is the same as that used for reading an Excel workbook.

- Click the Open button (⬚) and display the directory where the data files for this book are located (in Chap_7).

The Open dialog window will initially show only files containing Excel workbooks (and directories or folders). To get the window to show other files (including ASCII files) a setting must be changed.

- Near the bottom left of the Open dialog window, locate the field named "Files of type:". Click the small downward-pointing arrow to open the list, as shown by the picture below. Select "All Files (*.*)" The list will close and "All Files (*.*)" will appear in the field.

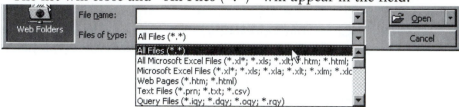

This setting will cause the Open dialog window to show all of the files in the displayed directory.

- Select "Battery.txt" from the list of files and click the Open button on the right side of the dialog window.

Excel will recognize that the data in the file are in the ASCII format. Because this format can be harder for Excel to interpret than other formats, Excel automatically starts the Text Import Wizard and opens the first dialog window. You will notice that the window shows some of the first few lines of the data. Most of the difficulties with using ASCII files occur when there is more than one number in each line. With this file, however, each line has only a single number. Excel has no difficulty with such a file.

- Click the Finish Button.

Excel tries to treat the ASCII file as a workbook. If you look on Excel's Title Bar you will see the name "Battery.txt." Notice that the workbook has only a single worksheet. If you were to make changes on that worksheet and then try to save them, Excel would do its best to write the changed workbook as an ASCII file and would replace the existing "Battery.txt" with the file it wrote. To avoid this, it is necessary to do the following.

- Click File on the Menu Bar. Select "Save As…." The Save As dialog window will open.

- At the bottom of the window is a selection field titled "Save File as Type." You will probably recognize it as similar to the "List Files as Type" field in the Open dialog window.

- The current selection is "Text (Tab delimited) (*.txt)." Click the down-arrow to the right of the field and choose "Microsoft Excel

Workbook (*.xls)." Notice that the name of the file in the "File Name" field changes from "BATTERY.TXT" to "BATTERY.xls."

- Click the Save button. This will save the file in the same folder as "Battery.txt." Notice that the Excel Title Bar now has the name "BATTERY.xls."

1. Based on the data in the worksheet, calculate a 95% confidence interval on the average battery life of all batteries of this type.

2. Suppose the manufacturer wanted future 95% confidence intervals to have a sampling error of, at most, 0.5 hr. Assuming that future population variances are the same as the current sample variance, determine how large a sample would be needed to achieve this sampling error.

3. Produce a chart that shows the relationship between sampling error and required sample size, assuming the population has the same standard deviation as this sample of batteries. Do this by creating a series of numbers that goes from 2 to 0.1 by increments of –0.05. In an adjacent column, determine the sample size required to achieve that sampling error with a 95% confidence interval. Produce a line plot with desired sampling error on the *x* (horizontal) axis and required sample size on the *y* (vertical) axis. Give the chart an appropriate title and print it. Be sure your name is in a header or footer. Describe in words the relationship the chart shows between reduced sampling error and increases in the required sample size.

4. Develop a chart showing the relationship between confidence level and sampling error for a confidence interval of the population mean battery life. First add a new worksheet to your workbook by opening the Insert menu on the Menu Bar and selecting "Worksheet." A new worksheet will be created with the name "Sheet2," although Excel will place it in front of the existing "Sheet1." Copy cells A1:A36 from Sheet1 to the new worksheet. Copy also the cells you used in answering problem 1 to the new worksheet. Create a column with the series of confidence levels from 10% to 95% with increments of 5%. In a column to the right enter the formula which will calculate the sampling error associated with each confidence level. Plot this relationship on a line chart with confidence level on the *x* axis and sampling error on the *y* axis. Print the chart with an appropriate title and your name in either the header or footer. Describe this relationship and contrast it with the relationship between sampling error and sample size you determined in response to problem 3.

5. Use the Descriptive Statistics tool to analyze the battery life data. In the "Output Options" area select "Summary Statistics" and "Confi-

dence Level for Mean" and put "95%" in the field to the right. The output written by the tool will include a number labeled "Confidence Level(95.0%)." What name has been used in this chapter for that number?

The data for the following problems can be found in the workbook Exercises.xls in the folder containing the data for this chapter.

6. A detergent-box filling machine fills empty boxes with detergent. A sample of boxes filled by the machine was selected, and the weight of the detergent (in ounces) placed in each box was measured. The measurements are:

   55.67, 47.28, 54.55, 48.19, 46.94, 52.34, 49.62, 51.48, 49.77, 49.71, 48.09, 49.78, 48.39, 49.81, 53.83, 48.41, 47.30, 46.68, 48.40, 48.85, 47.97, 49.98, 51.20, 51.57, 55.81

   Determine a 95% confidence interval for the mean amount of detergent placed in all boxes. How large a sample would you estimate would be required to reduce the sampling error to 0.75 ounces?

7. A bank office wishes to estimate the amount of time required to approve a home equity line of credit measured from the original application. A sample of applications was selected, and the amount of time (in working days) required to approve each application was determined. The values are:

   8, 16, 17, 12, 11, 16, 16, 21, 18, 11, 16, 18

   Determine a 90% confidence interval for the average amount of time required to approve all home equity lines of credit. How large a sample do you estimate would be required to reduce the sampling error to 1 day?

8. A ball-bearing manufacturer wants to determine the diameter of a particular ball bearing. A sample of bearings was selected and the diameter of each bearing (in cm) was measured. Those numbers were:

   9.66, 8.34, 11.09, 9.53, 9.22, 10.10, 11.51, 10.13, 8.62, 9.62, 9.29, 10.66, 12.28, 10.06, 11.63, 9.42, 9.24, 9.31, 9.29, 11.75

   Determine the sampling error associated with 99%, 95%, and 90% confidence intervals of the mean. How large a sample would you estimate would be required for a 99% confidence interval sampling error of 0.50 cm?

9. A large university offers many sections of undergraduate statistics. A sample of sections for the past five years was chosen, and the section GPA was calculated. These data are:

1.8, 1.8, 2.2, 2.4, 3.2, 1.6, 3.1, 3.0, 1.5, 2.4

Based upon these data, determine a 95% confidence interval for the average section GPA for all sections for the past five years. How large a sample would you estimate would be required to reduce the sampling error to 0.1?

10. A manufacturer of aircraft control cable makes a particular cable designed to have a breaking strength of 1,000 kg. A sample of cable was chosen and tested to determine breaking strength. The measured breaking strength of the sample cables (in kg) were:

996, 993, 990, 1010, 995, 989, 999, 1011, 981, 1000, 980, 994, 1003, 990, 999

Based upon these data, determine a 90% confidence interval estimate for the mean breaking strength of all cable. How large a sample would you estimate would be required to reduce the sampling error to 2 kg?

Chapter 8

Understanding Hypothesis Testing

Hypothesis testing is a technique that lets sample data be used to determine whether or not a characteristic of a population is true. It is used when the need is to answer a yes/no question about the population rather than to determine an estimate of a population parameter. This arises, for example, in quality control when the yes/no question may be, "Is our production system operating properly?" It is used in marketing when the yes/no question might be, "Does the proposed new package lead to higher sales than the old package?"

Hypothesis testing often seems confusing at first to the beginning student, although it is as straightforward an application of sampling distributions as confidence intervals. This chapter will give you a better sense of what hypothesis testing is and what it does. You will use Excel to explore the relationship between the characteristics of a population and those of samples within the framework of hypothesis testing in a way that could not easily be done without a computer. The example used here will be a hypothesis test on a population mean, but the concepts apply equally to all hypothesis tests. The next chapter will deal with the ways you can use Excel to solve hypothesis-testing problems and should be read only after you understand what hypothesis testing is about.

There are several steps to solving the typical hypothesis-testing word problem. The first step requires setting up the Null and Alternate Hypotheses and determining the appropriate sample descriptive statistics to use in the later calculations. This is often the hardest step, because it is difficult to set up the two hypotheses before you fully understand what hypothesis testing is and what its capabilities and limitations are. Once you understand how hypothesis testing works, you will find it easier to formulate Null and Alternate Hypotheses.

Consider the following quality control example. This problem is a little simpler than the typical hypothesis-testing problem in most textbooks, but it's a good starting point to see how hypothesis testing works.

A division of a cereal manufacturer is responsible for packaging the product. When the packaging process is working correctly, the amount of cereal in each box is normally distributed with an average fill of 16 ounces and a standard deviation of 0.50 ounces. In order to check the fill of a large shipment sent to a grocery store chain, a sample of 10 boxes is chosen, and the average weight of the 10 boxes is 15.43 ounces. Does this provide evidence that the packaging process is working incorrectly?

Although it is unrealistic to assume that we could know anything about the distribution of the weights of *all* the cereal boxes, this example will be easier to explore if we take the population standard deviation as 0.50 ounces and the population distribution as normal. The question to be determined through hypothesis testing is whether or not the population mean is really 16 ounces.

▼The Population and the Null Hypothesis

For this particular problem, the Null Hypothesis is: $H_0 : \mu = 16$, and the Alternate Hypothesis is $H_A : \mu \neq 16$. The Null and Alternate Hypotheses are always statements about a population parameter; they are never statements about a sample statistic. They are always constructed so that one of them *must* be true and the other *must* be false. The Null Hypothesis *always* contains an equal sign (including $=$, $\leq$, or $\geq$). The Alternate Hypothesis *never* contains an equal sign. The relational symbol in the Alternate Hypothesis must be $\neq$, $<$, or $>$.

The object of the hypothesis test is to decide whether or not the Null Hypothesis is true. Let's begin by provisionally assuming that it *is* true, and the average fill of all boxes is really 16 ounces. We'll then look at the characteristics of the samples you could expect to get from the population described by the Null Hypothesis by having Excel simulate the choosing of such samples. Finally, we'll decide whether or not the sample described in the problem (with a sample mean of 15.43) is like those samples. If it is, that's evidence that the sample in the problem is *consistent* with the Null Hypothesis. If it's not, that indicates the sample is *inconsistent* with the Null Hypothesis and provides evidence that the Null Hypothesis is not true.

When we say the average fill is 16 ounces, we're making a statement about the population—all the boxes being filled (which we generally cannot measure directly). The statement also tells something about the weight of any single box of cereal we might measure. If the average weight of all the boxes is 16 ounces, we *expect* the weight of any randomly chosen box to also be 16 ounces. The word "expect" is used here in its statistical sense, not its everyday sense. There is going to be some variation in the weight of individual boxes; no box-filling process can be absolutely perfectly precise. If we regard the actual weight of any box of cereal to be a continuous random number, then the probability is 0 that a single box will turn out to have a fill that exactly equals 16 ounces. Most boxes will have a fill close to 16 ounces, and the average fill of boxes chosen will tend to be closer to 16 ounces as the number of boxes chosen increases.

Similarly, if the average weight of all boxes filled is 16 ounces, we *expect* the average weight of a random sample of 10 boxes to also be 16 ounces. Just as in the case of an individual box, the average fill of a sample will almost certainly differ from 16 ounces just because of the random nature of the filling process. Finding a sample whose average fill differs a little from 16 does not provide evidence that something has gone wrong with the average fill of all boxes. Finding a sample whose average is very far from 16 would, however, be suspicious. As we saw in Chapter 6, the distribution of sample means has the same mean as the population but a smaller standard deviation. It is thus unlikely that the difference between a sample mean and the population mean will be great. A small difference could well be due to normal random fluctuations, but a large difference probably indicates some problem with the population.

▼Formulating the Null and Alternate Hypotheses

To solve a typical hypothesis-testing word problem, you have to first determine the Null and Alternate Hypotheses. One principle to keep in mind is that the Null Hypothesis must describe the population and must give an expected value for the sample. A Null Hypothesis must have an equal sign (=); it cannot have a not equal (≠) or a greater than (>) or a less than (<) sign. Most statistics texts formulate one-tailed Null Hypotheses with greater than or equal to (≥) or less than or equal to (≤) signs. In practice, these are treated as equal signs when the tests are performed (a few statistics texts use equal signs even in one-tailed Null Hypotheses). The reason for these restrictions on the relationships expressed by the Null Hypothesis is that the Null Hypothesis must tell what the population *is*, not what it *is not*. It would have been impossible to generate the simulated samples in this chapter without a specific value from the Null Hypothesis for the average fill of all boxes.

If a problem asks for evidence of a particular situation, that situation is formulated as the *Alternate* Hypothesis. This is because you only come to a conclusion in hypothesis testing when you *reject* the Null Hypothesis. If you reject the Null Hypothesis, you have evidence of the Alternate

Hypothesis. For this reason, many students find it easier to formulate the Alternate Hypothesis first, and the Null Hypothesis as the logical opposite of the Alternate Hypothesis.

▼How Small a Difference Is Small?

In the example given here, the sample of 10 boxes had a mean of 15.43 ounces. This differs from the expected amount by 0.57 ounces. Is this the kind of small difference we expected to happen by chance in a sample of boxes chosen when the average of all (population) is 16? Or is 0.57 ounces too large a difference to explain by chance variability? A small difference would be *consistent* with a population mean of 16, while a large difference would be *inconsistent* with a population mean of 16. If we decide that 0.57 ounces is large, we will conclude that the average fill of all the boxes is not 16. In that case something is wrong with the box-filling process, and it will have to have attention.

Let's examine the question by taking a population of boxes in which the filling process *is* working properly and drawing several samples of 10 boxes and determining the sample average for each sample. By doing this, we will be able to see whether or not a sample whose average differs from 16 by 0.57 ounces (or more) is unusual. In other words, we will be able to determine if 0.57 is a large difference.

• Start Excel if you have not already done so, and open the workbook in the file named "Cereal.xls" (in the Chap_8) folder. If that file is on a diskette, open the File menu on the Menu Bar, click "Save as...," and save the workbook on a hard disk or network drive because it will grow too large to fit on a diskette. Appendix F provides instructions for storing the large file on a diskette at the end of your computer session.

• Select the Population_1 worksheet. In cell F1, enter the label "Mu." In cell G1 enter the formula that will calculate the average of the values on this worksheet (A2:E256). The average is 16.

• Switch to the Samples_I worksheet. One sample is already present on the worksheet.

• In cell K2 enter the formula to calculate the sample mean (use relative addressing). In cell L2 enter the number "16" just determined and shown in cell G1 of the Population_1 worksheet. In cell M2 enter a formula that will calculate the absolute value of the difference between the values displayed in cells K2 and L2. Cells K2:M2 should display "15.90," "16," and "0.103." If cell M2 displays "-0.103," correct the cell's formula so that it takes the *absolute value* of the difference.

- Open the Tools menu on the Menu Bar, select "Learning Business Statistics," and click "Multiple Random Samples." If "Learning Business Statistics is not on your Tools menu, refer to Appendix C.

- Fill out the dialog window of the Multiple Random Samples tool so that it will select values from the population on the Population_1 worksheet (A2:E256), select samples of size 10, select 1,000 samples, and will write the samples on the Samples_I worksheet beginning in cell A2 (thus overwriting the sample already there).

- Copy the formulas you entered in cells K2:M2 to all the cells below them through row 1001. (Enter "K2:M1001" in the Name Box, then click the menus "Edit"…"Fill"…"Down.") The values displayed in columns K and M will differ, but column L should display "16" in all cells.

Column M shows the amount each sample mean differs from 16. Since there are 1,000 different sample means, looking through them all to find those that exceed 0.57 would be a little tedious. One way of making this easier would be to resort the samples on the worksheet by the value in column M.

- Select the region A1:M1001. Open the Data menu on the Menu Bar and select "Sort…." The Sort dialog window will open.

In the dialog window we will tell Excel which column to sort the region by. We also will ask for a descending sort. This will put the samples with the largest differences at the top since those are the ones we are most interested in.

- At the bottom of the dialog window there is a region titled "My list has" with two choices selected by radio buttons. Select "Header row." This will cause the columns to be identified by the labels in the first row rather than by the column letter.

- Open the list under "Sort by" and choose "Absolute Difference," which will be at the bottom of the list. Click the "Descending" radio button. The dialog window should look like the picture at the top of the next page. If so, click the OK button.

Arrange your worksheet so that you can see the values at the top of column M, the difference column. In the entire set of 1,000 samples that Excel simulated, the one with the mean furthest from 16 is now in row 2. The difference between that sample's mean and 16 is shown in cell M2. Is it greater than or equal to 0.57? If not, then none of the 1,000

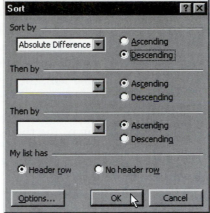

samples had a mean that differed from 16 by as much as the one in the problem. Perhaps the value in cell M2 is greater than 0.57. If so, see how many of the values in cells below M2 are also greater than 0.57. It is very unlikely (though not impossible) that there are more than 3 or 4 samples out of 1,000 with means which differ from 16 by as much as 0.57, and it is very likely that none of the 1,000 samples had a mean that differed from 16 by so much.

▼An Unusual Sample or a Process Gone Bad?

What has this exercise shown? If the average fill were 16 and 1,000 samples of 10 boxes were chosen, none or few of the samples would have means that differed from 16 by 0.57 or more. Thus a difference in a sample mean of 0.57 is *not* the kind of difference you would expect from a randomly drawn sample. It is not a small difference. It is a large difference—one very unlikely to occur by chance. A sample of 10 boxes having a mean of 15.43 is thus *not* consistent with all boxes being filled, on average, with 16 ounces.

Knowing this, what do we conclude if, one day, a sample of 10 boxes is drawn with a mean of 15.43? Although it is *possible* that the difference is due to chance, the probability of this is very low. There is another explanation, however. If something has gone wrong with the filling process, the population mean might no longer be 16. If the population mean had fallen, say, to 15.40, a sample mean of 15.43 might not be surprising at all. In this case, of course, something has gone wrong that needs correcting. Since a sample mean of 15.43 is so unlikely if nothing has gone wrong, it would be reasonable to conclude from such a sample mean that something has gone wrong. In this case we would *reject* the Null Hypothesis that the population mean (μ) equaled 16, and conclude that the Alternate Hypothesis ($\mu \neq 16$) is correct.

Suppose the sample of 10 boxes instead had an average weight of 15.89 ounces? The difference from 16 in this case is 0.11. Scroll through the values in column M until you find a value less than 0.11. What row is this value in? All of the numbers above it are greater than 0.11. Since the largest number is in row M2, the total number of values in column M that exceed 0.11 is the row number of the first number less than 0.11 minus 1. How many of the thousand samples have means greater than 0.11? What proportion of the thousand samples does that represent?

This proportion is liable to be at least .40, probably more. This shows that there is a high probability that a sample mean can differ from 16 by 0.11 or more. This is a difference that could likely occur by chance; it is thus a *small* difference that is *consistent* with all boxes being filled, on average, with 16 ounces. With such a sample we would *not* conclude that something has gone wrong with the process. We would *fail to reject* the Null Hypothesis.

▼Summary

Here's a quick summary of the steps we went through in determining that something had gone wrong with the process of filling cereal boxes:

1. The Null Hypothesis was assumed to be correct ($\mu = 16$).

2. Excel simulated the drawing of 1,000 samples from a population in which the Null Hypothesis *was* correct—population mean is 16.

3. The mean of each sample was calculated.

4. The difference between each sample mean and the *expected* value of the sample mean (16) was calculated.

5. The differences were sorted from highest to lowest so we could easily determine how many of the samples had means that differed from the population by at least as much as the sample described in the problem.

Had we calculated the proportion of the 1,000 samples with differences at least as great as that of the sample in the problem (0.57), we would have been approximating a probability, and that probability would have been close to 0. This is the probability that a single sample of 10 boxes chosen when the process was working perfectly would have a mean further from 16 than the sample mean given in the problem (15.43). This probability, called the *p* value, can be calculated precisely from the distribution of sample means using the techniques used in Chapter 6, and it is a far easier process than generating a thousand samples.

▼Determining the *p* Value

The diagram below shows the distribution of the means of samples of size 10 drawn from a normally distributed population with mean 16 and standard deviation 0.05. The shaded areas show the probability that a sample mean will differ from 16 by at least as much as 15.43 differs from 16. This combined area equals the *p* value.

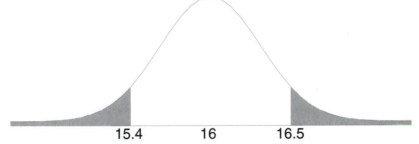

Since we know the population standard deviation, the normal distribution should be used for the distribution of sample means. In most hypothesis-testing problems we will *not* know the population standard deviation and instead will know the standard deviation of a single sample. In that case (which we will consider below), the *t* distribution will be used.

- Switch to the Population_1 worksheet. In cells F2:F7, enter the following labels: "sigma" "n," "standard error," "x bar," "z value," and "p value." Adjust the width of column F.

- In cell G2 enter a formula that will calculate the standard deviation of the population data on the worksheet (A2:E256). Be sure not to use the sample standard deviation function! The displayed value should be "0.5." (0.500196 is wrong!)

- In cell G3 enter the sample size (10—remember *n* is the size of each sample, *not* the number of samples), and in cell G4 enter the formula to calculate the standard error from the population standard deviation and the sample size. The displayed value should be "0.158114."

- In cell G5 enter the sample mean for this problem ("15.43") and in cell G6 enter the formula that will convert this value to a *z* value using the mean and standard deviation of the distribution of sample means. The displayed value should be "-3.605." Recall that the mean of this distribution is the same as the population mean and that the standard deviation is the standard error.

The result in cell G6 means that the z value corresponding to the sample mean value of 15.43 in the diagram on page 231 is –3.605 and the z value corresponding to 16.57 is +3.605

- Use the NORMSDIST function in cell G7 to calculate the p value. Remember that the p value equals the area of both shaded tails in the diagram on page 231. The displayed value should be "0.000312."

This p value means that if a sample of size 10 were drawn from the population on the Population_1 worksheet, the probability that the mean of the sample would differ from 16 by as much as 15.43 differs from 15 is .000312. This is less than 1 in 1,000—a bit more than 3 in 10,000. You shouldn't be surprised if none of the 1,000 samples you drew had a sample whose mean differed from 16 by 0.57 or more; if one or more of your samples had such means you were lucky. This confirms our finding that a sample mean of 15.43 is *not* consistent with the claim that all the cereal boxes, on average, are filled to 16 ounces. With this sample we would *reject* the Null Hypothesis.

Suppose the sample mean had been 15.89 rather than 15.43? What would the p value have been then? You can quickly determine this by replacing the 15.43 in cell G5 with 15.89. The p value becomes .486616. In other words, if all boxes were filled with an average of 16 ounces, just under half of all samples of 10 boxes would have means that differed from 16 by as much or more as 15.89 differs from 16. Is this close to the proportion you determined for your 1,000 samples? This is a high proportion and makes it reasonable to conclude that the average fill of all boxes might really be 16 and that the sample's average of 15.89 was due to chance. In this case, we would *fail to reject* the Null Hypothesis. Note that this is not the same as concluding that the Null Hypothesis is true. The fact that the sample is consistent with the Null Hypothesis does not mean that we have shown that it is true, a point that will be explored more later.

▼From *p* Value to Conclusion

Hypothesis testing is essentially a process that determines whether or not the sample selected has characteristics that make it likely to have been drawn from a population described by the Null Hypothesis. The p value quantifies this relationship between the sample and the Null Hypothesis.

A small p value is evidence that the sample is not the kind of sample that would be expected from the population described by the Null Hypothesis. This leads to the conclusion that the population must be different from that described by the Null Hypothesis. The Null Hypothesis is rejected.

Since chance can often cause small differences between the actual and expected value of a sample statistic, a small difference could occur by chance with a large probability. The p value for a small difference between the analysis sample's mean and the Null's expected mean would be large. A *small* difference can occur with a *large* probability.

A large p value is evidence that the difference between the sample and population mean is the kind likely to have occurred by chance. In that case the Null Hypothesis would not be rejected. Instead we would conclude that the difference between the analysis sample's actual mean and the expected mean given by the Null Hypothesis could well be due to chance. The Null Hypothesis is *not* rejected.

The p value provides a measure of the difference between the actual sample statistic of the test sample and the expected value of the sample statistic implied by the Null Hypothesis. The p value is the probability that if the Null Hypothesis were true, another sample of the same size as that used for the analysis would, by chance, have a statistic (such as sample mean) at least as different from the population parameter (population mean) as the analysis sample.

Whether or not a sample leads to rejection of the Null Hypothesis depends on how low the p value is. In the example given here, the p value was extremely low. In many, perhaps most, problems, the question is bound to arise of how low the p value must be before the Null Hypothesis is rejected. In many of the hypothesis-testing problems that beginning students encounter, the problem will provide a significance level, also referred to as α. For that problem, the significance level is the threshold. If the p value is less than the significance level, the Null Hypothesis is rejected. If the p value is greater, the Null is not rejected. Providing a significance level neatly solves the problem of how low a p value is low, but it begs the larger question of what the value of the significance level *should* be.

▼The Consequences of Error—Type I versus Type II

Hypothesis testing can never be an infallible method of determining the characteristics of a population. Depending on a sample to provide evidence about a population is always risky since we can never be certain the sample isn't unrepresentative. It's good to remember that the benefit of hypothesis testing also comes from the fact that it depends on a sample, because analyzing the entire population may be impossible or prohibitively expensive. Hypothesis testing is often the only practical way of investigating a population. The investigator using it, however, must explicitly consider the consequences of the unavoidable error that might occur with a hypothesis test.

Consider the problem just analyzed. A cereal packaging division wants to be sure that the average fill of cereal in all boxes is exactly 16 ounces. They monitor this process by selecting a sample and performing a hypothesis test. If the hypothesis test reveals a problem, the company does whatever is necessary to correct the problem. Suppose the hypothesis test gives them the wrong answer? What impact does that have?

There are two types of wrong answers. One possibility is that the filling process is working properly, but by sheer bad luck the company happens to select a sample that is not representative and which leads to the erroneous conclusion that something is wrong. The consequence of this error is needless expense. Equipment may be taken out of service for expensive testing; perhaps the production of cereal may be stopped or slowed until the cause of the problem is determined. The company's revenue may suffer. These costs would be gladly paid to fix a problem, but if there is no problem they are needless. Concluding that there is a problem when, in fact, there is no problem, is an example of *Type I* error.

The other possibility is that the filling process has broken, and the average fill of cereal boxes is either too high or too low, but again by sheer bad luck the company happens to select a sample that is not representative and that leads to the erroneous conclusion that something is *not* wrong. In this case, the company continues to incorrectly fill the boxes, unaware of the need for correction. Depending on whether the boxes are underfilled or overfilled, this could result in product waste, higher-than-expected production costs, regulatory troubles, or loss of confidence by consumers. These are potentially costly problems that the company also wants to avoid. Concluding that there is no problem when one really exists is an example of *Type II* error.

Ideally, of course, the company wants to avoid, or at least minimize, both types of error. The only way to reduce the likelihood of both types of error is to collect more data and use larger samples. This is itself a costly action. If Type I and Type II errors are very rare, it may make more sense to accept the risk of bearing the costs associated with them than to bear the costs of additional testing. We will assume that the company has decided that it can't afford to test samples of more than 10 boxes, although the cost of additional data collection should be balanced against the costs of errors. In this chapter you will explore the relationship between the significance level and the balancing of Type I and Type II errors.

▼Simulating Type I Errors

We will explore Type I and Type II errors by looking at the accuracy of hypothesis tests in a way similar to that used in Chapter 7 to look at the accuracy of confidence intervals. Just as for a confidence interval, when a hypothesis test is done on an unknown population there is no way to be certain whether the outcome of the test is correct or not. We will look at the accuracy of hypothesis testing by selecting samples from known populations. The first population will be the one on the Population_1 worksheet just used.

For all the populations we will do the same hypothesis test, "Is there evidence that the population mean differs from 16?" This also is the same test just considered, and the Null and Alternate Hypotheses are:

$$H_0 : \mu = 16 \text{ and } H_A : \mu \neq 16$$

This time, however, all the data used in the test will come from the sample. This means that the standard error will be calculated from the sample standard deviation rather than from the population standard deviation. The t distribution will then be used instead of the z distribution for the distribution of sample means.

We know that the mean of Population 1 is 16. A sample drawn from that population will have a correct hypothesis test if the test fails to reject the Null Hypothesis and concludes there is no evidence the population mean differs from 16. If a sample results in a hypothesis test that rejects the Null and concludes that there *is* evidence the population mean differs from 16, the test will be in error, and the error will be Type I error.

- Select the Summary worksheet. Information common to the tests on all populations will be placed here, as will a table summarizing the results of all the hypothesis tests.

- Cell B1 is to contain the significance level. Recall that the significance level sets how low the p value must be to conclude the sample must not have been drawn from a population described by the Null Hypothesis (reject the Null Hypothesis). Enter the value ".05" in B1 for the initial value.

- Switch to the Type_I worksheet. This worksheet contains three samples. The first sample will be used to develop the hypothesis testing formulas and the others will be used to test those formulas.

- In cells K2 and L2 enter formulas to calculate the sample mean and standard deviation for the sample in row 2. Use relative addressing.

The displayed values should be "15.969" and "0.450443," respectively.

- In cell M2 put the size of the sample in row 2 (10).

- Enter a formula in cell N2 to calculate the standard error from the sample standard deviation and sample size. Use relative addresses. The displayed value should be "0.142443."

- Enter a formula in cell O2 to calculate the sample *t* value. The *t* value is calculated from the formula $t = \dfrac{\bar{x} - \mu}{s_{\bar{x}}}$. The value of $\bar{x}$ is the sample mean given in cell K2. The value of μ is the *hypothesized* population mean given the Null Hypothesis shown on page 235. The denominator, $s_{\bar{x}}$, is the standard error calculated from the sample standard deviation in N2. The Excel equation appearing in the Formula Bar should be "=(K2-16)/N2." The displayed value should be "-0.21763."

- Enter the formula in cell P2 to calculate the (two-tail) *p* value. Use the TDIST function. Remember that you must use the ABS function to ensure that the *t* value used in TDIST's X argument is positive. The degrees of freedom is sample size minus 1. The displayed value should be "0.83257."

- Enter a formula in cell Q2 using Excel's IF function to display "Reject the Null" if the *p* value in cell P2 is less than the significance level in cell B3 of the Summary worksheet, and "Fail to Reject" if it is not. The "Logical_test" field in the IF dialog window should be " P2<Summary!B" The cell should display "Fail to Reject."

- Copy the formulas in the range K2:Q2 down to rows 3 and 4. If you use the fill handle, Excel will put "10," "11," and "12" in row M instead of simply copying the "10." Make sure all the cells in row M have "10." Check the other displayed values with the picture below. If the values in your worksheet differ, change only the formulas in row 2. If column Q is the only one which differs, check to be sure you used absolute addressing in the "Logical_test" reference to the significance level.

	K	L	M	N	O	P	Q
1	Sample Mean	Sample Standard Deviation	Sample Size	Standard Error	Sample *t* Value	*p* Value	Conclusion
2	15.969	0.45044	10	0.14244	-0.21763	0.83257	Fail to Reject
3	16.425	0.46417	10	0.14678	2.89545	0.01773	Reject the Null
4	16.149	0.63063	10	0.19942	0.74715	0.47404	Fail to Reject

Now let's look at the results of hypothesis tests on 1,000 different samples drawn from this population.

- Use the Multiple Random Samples tool to draw 1,000 samples of size 10 from the Population_1 worksheet (A2:E256) and write the samples beginning in cell A2 of the Type_I worksheet. This will overwrite the three samples previously there and change the values in the cells in the previous picture.

- Copy the formulas in cells K4:Q4 down to row 1001. Adjust the width of column Q so that it is wide enough to hold the displayed text.

Column P shows the p values for each of the 1,000 hypothesis tests, and column Q shows the conclusion we would draw from each test at the .05 level of significance. Although it should be clear that far more samples result in "Fail to Reject" than in "Reject the Null," the exact number in each category will change when we change the significance level. Since the number falling into each category depends in part on the significance level, we will construct a table that will provide a count of the samples resulting in each conclusion.

- Enter the labels shown in the picture below in the range R1:T4.

	R	S	T
1		Count	Proportion
2	Reject the Null		
3	Fail to Reject		
4	Total		

- Enter a formula in cell S2 that will provide a count of the number of times "Reject the Null" appears in cells Q2:Q1001. Use the COUNTIF function in the "Statistical" category. In the "Criteria" field put "Reject the Null" *and use quotation marks* in the field. If the displayed value is 0, your formula has not been correctly formed.

- Enter a similar formula in cell S3 that will provide a count of the number of hypothesis tests with "Fail to Reject."

- Use the AutoSum button in cell S4 to add the values in cells T2 and T3. The displayed value should be "1,000."

- Use cells T2:T3 to convert the values in S2:S3 to proportions by dividing each number by the total in S4. Use the AutoSum button in S4 to verify that the two proportions sum to 1.

▼Significance Level and Type I Error

Since the Population I data has a population mean exactly equal to 16, a sample's hypothesis test is correct if the conclusion is "Fail to Reject." Those samples that conclude "Reject the Null" have Type I error. Thus the proportion of samples with Type I error is the value displayed in cell T2.

- Switch to the Summary worksheet.

Since the Null Hypothesis ($\mu = 16$) is *correct* for Population I, we will put the results of the 1,000 hypothesis tests in cells B5 and B6.

- Select cell B5 and enter an equal sign. Switch to the Type_I worksheet, click cell T3 (the proportion of tests which "Fail to Reject" and press the Enter key. You should see displayed in cell B5 of the Summary worksheet this same proportion, which is the proportion of tests with the correct result for Population I.

- Select cell B6, enter an equal sign, switch to the Type_I worksheet, click cell T2, and press the Enter key. Now you should see in cell B6 the proportion of tests with the erroneous result.

- Remember that the current significance level is .05. Note the current proportion of Type I error. Change the significance level (on the Summary worksheet) to the following values: .01, .10, .20, .25 and note in each case the proportion of samples with Type I error (cell B6). What is the relationship between the significance level and the proportion of samples with Type I error?

As the significance level increases, so does the proportion of samples with Type I error. In fact, the two should be approximately equal. The *expected* proportion of samples with Type I error is the same as the significance level.

If we *knew* that the Null Hypothesis test were true, then choosing a very small significance level would increase the likelihood that a hypothesis test would yield the correct conclusion. Of course, if we *knew* the Null Hypothesis were true, there would be no reason to use a sample to test it! What if the Null Hypothesis were false or unknown?

- Change the significance level on the Summary worksheet back to .05.

▼Simulating Type II Errors

A Type II error can occur only if the Null Hypothesis is wrong. The Null Hypothesis specifies a particular value for a population mean ($\mu = 16$ for the case we have been considering). If the population parameter is any other value, the Null is wrong, and any test that fails to reject the Null Hypothesis will have Type II error.

We can simulate Type II error by simply drawing samples from a different population—one in which we know the mean does not equal 15. The simulation will be easy compared to the one for Type I errors because we have already entered all the formulas required to do hypothesis tests.

- On the Type_I worksheet, select cells K1:T4. These contain the labels and formulas to perform hypothesis tests on the first three samples and the table counting the results of the tests.

- Copy the contents of K1:T4 to cell K1 on the Type_IIL worksheet. One easy way of doing this is to click the Copy button ( ) on the Standard Toolbar after selecting the cells on the Type_I worksheet to be copied. Then select cell K1 on the Type_IIL worksheet and click the Paste button: .

- Adjust the width of columns Q and R. Range K1:T4 should look like the picture below. Pay particular attention to the numbers in K2:P2. The error codes in rows 3 and 4 are there because there are no sample values in that row.

	K	L	M	N	O	P	Q	R	S	T
1	Sample Mean	Sample Standard Deviation	Sample Size	Standard Error	Sample *t* Value	*p* Value	Conclusion		Count	Proportion
2	15.178	0.42869	10	0.13556	-6.0636	0.00019	Reject the	Reject the Null	1	1
3	#DIV/0!	#DIV/0!	10	#DIV/0!	#DIV/0!	#DIV/0!	#DIV/0!	Fail to Reject	0	0
4	#DIV/0!	#DIV/0!	10	#DIV/0!	#DIV/0!	#DIV/0!	#DIV/0!	Total	1	

- Use the Multiple Random Samples tool to draw 1,000 samples of size 10 from the Population_2 worksheet (A2:E256) to the Type_IIL worksheet (A2), overwriting the sample currently there. The error codes in rows 3 and 4 will be replaced.

- Copy the formulas in row 4 of columns K through Q down to row 1001. The table in R1:T4 will automatically update and the value in S4 should be "1,000." Look at the values in this table.

Unlike the table in the Type_I worksheet, the great majority of samples from Population 2 should result in rejection of the Null Hypothesis. In other words, most of the samples would lead to the conclusion that there *is* evidence that the population mean differs from 16. A few samples, however, should lead to the opposite conclusion that there is *not* evidence that the population mean differs from 16. Which conclusion is correct?

- Switch to the Population_2 worksheet. In cell G1 enter a formula that will calculate the mean of the data on the worksheet. The displayed value should be "15.3."

Since the population mean is 15.3 (and not 16), the Null Hypothesis is *incorrect*. Therefore hypothesis tests that reject the Null Hypothesis are correct while those that fail to reject are in error, Type II error in this case. Based on our examination of Population 1 and Population 2, it seems that the result of hypothesis testing is very likely to provide the correct result. Unfortunately, this is not always the case.

▼ Significance Level and Type II Errors

Next, we will copy the results of these tests to the Summary worksheet so that we can examine the effect that significance level has on the probability of Type II error. In this case, the correct result is "Reject the Null," and the error result is "Fail to Reject." As we have seen, the actual mean of the population from which these samples were drawn is 15.3. The hypothesized (given by the Null Hypothesis) population mean is 16. This difference (0.7) is one which we will characterize as "large." Column C on the Summary worksheet will hold the results of the tests based on the samples from Population 2.

- Click the Summary worksheet tab and select cell C5. In this cell will go the prorportion of results which are correct. Enter an equal sign, then switch to the Type_IIL worksheet and click cell T2. Press the Enter key and the proportion of the 1,000 tests on Population 2 which had the correct result will appear in cell C5.

- Select cell C6, enter an equal sign, switch back to the Type_IIL worksheet, click cell T3, and press the Enter key. The proportion of the 1,000 tests on Population 2 which had the erroneous result will appear in cell C6.

- Select cell B1. Change the significance level to .01. Then change it to .05, .10, .20, and .25. Each time you change it, pay attention to the error result for Type II errors (cell C6). What happens to the accuracy of the test as the the significance level goes up? How does this compare to the error result for Type I error (cell B6) which you looked at before?

Recall that in the case of Type I errors, there is a simple relationship between the significance level and the probability of Type I error—they are equal (and approximately equal to the proportion of erroneous tests for the 1,000 test on Population 1 in B6). For the Type II errors in cell C6, the relationship is inverse—a higher significance level leads to a lower proportion of error results. In other words, the higher the significance level, the lower the probability of Type II error. Furthermore, there is no simple relationship between the significance level and the probability of Type II error as there was with Type I error.

Increasing the significance level makes it easier to reject the Null Hypothesis since the *p* value doesn't have to be so low to be less than the significance level. At the same time, increasing the significance level makes it harder to fail to reject the Null Hypothesis because the *p* value has to be that much larger in order to fail to reject. If the Null Hypothesis is rejected, the only possible error is Type I. It makes sense that making it easier to reject the Null is going to increase the only error associated with that conclusion. Similarly, the only error which can be made if the Null is not rejected is Type II error, and making it harder to reject the Null will reduce the probability of that error.

The significance level should be set before a test is performed—before we know the *p* value. When a hypothesis test is actually performed, we don't know what the true value of μ is. If we did, there would be no reason to do a hypothesis test. There is, therefore, no simple answer to the question of whether significance levels should be large or small. That decision depends on the relative cost of a Type I error versus a Type II error.

Select cell B1. Change the value of the significance level back to .05.

▼Hypothesis Testing—A Difficult Population

Let's take a look at one last population, the one in the Population_3 worksheet. We will use the Type_IIS worksheet to hold samples from that population and tabulate the results of hypothesis tests from those samples. The procedure is very much like that we have just used.

- Copy the formulas in K1:T4 of the Type_IIL worksheet to cell K1 of the Type_IIS worksheet. Adjust columns Q and R. The displayed values should be as shown at the top of the next page.

- Use the Multiple Random Samples tool to select 1,000 samples of size 10 from the Population 3 worksheet. Have the tool write the samples starting in cell A2 of the Type_IIS worksheet.

	K	L	M	N	O	P	Q	R	S	T
1	Sample Mean	Sample Standard Deviation	Sample Size	Standard Error	Sample *t* Value	*p* Value	Conclusion		Count	Proportion
2	15.983	0.32578	10	0.10302	-0.165	0.87258	Fail to Reject	Reject the Null	0	0
3	#DIV/0!	#DIV/0!	10	#DIV/0!	#DIV/0!	#DIV/0!	#DIV/0!	Fail to Reject	1	1
4	#DIV/0!	#DIV/0!	10	#DIV/0!	#DIV/0!	#DIV/0!	#DIV/0!	Total	1	

- Copy the formulas in K4:Q4 down through row 1001. The table in R1:T4 will update and cell S4 should display "1000." Examine the table.

Most of the samples should result in "Fail to Reject," but a fairly large minority of samples should result in "Reject the Null." Since most samples indicate that the Null should not be rejected, isn't it reasonable to believe that the population mean probably is 16 as indicated by the Null Hypothesis?

- Switch to the Population_3 worksheet and enter a formula in cell G1 to calculate the mean of the data on that worksheet. The result should be 15.8.

Is the Null Hypothesis correct? No. The population mean is 15.8, not 16. Certainly 15.8 is closer to 16 than is 15.3, the mean of the Population 2 worksheet, but the assertion that the mean is 16 is wrong in both cases. The correct conclusion in both cases is to reject the Null, and those samples that fail to reject have Type II error. The data in Population 3 are troublesome because *most* of the samples result in error. What effect does significance level have on this error?

▼Significance Level and Type II Errors Revisited

Once again let's copy the results of this set of tests to the Summary worksheet. The difference between the hypothesized population mean (16) and the actual population mean (15.8) is small in this case, so we will put the results in column D.

- Select cell D5 on the Summary worksheet. Enter an equal sign, then switch to the Type_IIS worksheet and click cell T2. Press the Enter key and the (small) proportion of the 1,000 tests which gave the correct result will appear in cell D5.

- Select cell D6. Enter an equal sign, click cell T3 on the Type_IIS worksheet, and press the Enter key. The (large) proportion of incorrect tests on Population 3 should appear in cell T3.

- Select cell B1, change the significance level to .01, then change it to .05, .10, .20, and .25. Observe the change that occurs in each case in cell D6, the proportion of erroneous results. What happens as the significance level increases?

As is the case with the previous Type II error (C6), an increase in the significance level reduces the proportion of erroneous tests. The difference in this case is that, regardless of the significance level, the proportion of erroneous tests remains very high. Nearly half or more of all tests result in a failure to reject the Null Hypothesis. Why is that?

The problem is that hypothesis testing rejects the Null Hypothesis if the sample mean is far from the hypothesized population mean and fails to reject if the sample mean is close to the hypothesized population mean. This works well if the actual population mean is far from the hypothesized population mean (as was the case with Population 2), but it does not work well if the actual population mean is close to, but different from, the hypothesized mean (Population 3). Samples drawn from Population 3 are very likely to have means close to 16 because the expected value of those means is 15.8, which is close to 16. Had we drawn our samples from a population whose mean was even closer to 16 (like 15.9), the accuracy of the hypothesis testing would have been even worse.

▼ Type II Errors and the Power of a Test

For the Type_IIL population, the hypothesis test on a sample of size 10 was quite accurate in its ability to reject an incorrect Null hypothesis. For the Type_IIS population, however, the same test did a very poor job of rejecting an incorrect Null. The ability of a hypothesis test to come to the correct conclusion, including rejecting an incorrect Null Hypothesis, is termed the *power* of the test. When the Null is wrong, a test's power depends on (among other things) the difference between the value of the population parameter hypothesized by the Null and the population's actual value for that parameter. Tests of incorrect Nulls are always more powerful when the population is very different from the Null Hypothesis than when it is similar. We considered two populations in which the Null Hypothesis was incorrect. These are two of a potentially infinite number of populations, since there are an infinite number of possible values the population mean can have not equal to the hypothesized mean.

How can the power of a hypothesis test be improved? The best way of improving the power of a hypothesis test is to increase the size of the sample.

- Switch to the Resize worksheet. Open the Tools menu and run the Multiple Random Samples tool. Use the data in the Population_3 worksheet for the population, select 30 for the sample size, 1,000 for the number of samples, and cell A1 on the Resize worksheet for the output range. Click OK.

You will likely notice that it takes longer to select samples of size 30 than it did to select samples of size 10.

- Switch to the Power_Test worksheet. The formulas on this sheet have already been entered, but are quite similar to those on the three previous sample worksheets you have examined. Look at the table in cells H1:J4.

The correct conclusion for these tests is "Reject the Null." For samples of size 10 (on the Type_IIS worksheet), you found that a small proportion of the 1,000 tests came to the correct conclusion. For samples of size 30, this worksheet should show that most (probably around 60%) of the 1,000 tests came to the correct conclusion. Even larger samples would increase the power of the test more. If, for example, the sample size were 100, then about 98% of the tests should give the same result (try it).

Samples of size 100 do a good job determining that Population 3 does not have a mean of 16. Even samples of 100 would have had difficulty had the population mean been even closer to 16, such as 15.95. It is never possible to establish an upper bound to Type II errors. Regardless of the sample size, it is always possible to find a population whose mean is very close to the hypothesized value of μ on which hypothesis tests will perform badly.

As we have seen, tests of incorrect hypotheses are less likely to be accurate if the population differs only slightly from the value hypothesized by the Null than if the population differs significantly. It may be that, for a given situation, this will not be unacceptable. Consider the case we have been investigating. Suppose the process the cereal packaging division is using to fill packages is not, in fact, filling boxes with an average of exactly 16 ounces. What is the consequence? As discussed before, this probably depends on whether the boxes are being overfilled or underfilled, but, in either case, it is reasonable to expect that those consequences are less severe if the error is slight than if it is large. Some increased inaccuracy in a test's ability to detect small errors may be acceptable. In a case where this issue is important, a complete analysis of a test's power for different values of μ is the best way to determine the appropriate sample size required to achieve an acceptable level of power.

▼Failing to Reject versus Accepting a Null Hypothesis

The two standard conclusions arising from a hypothesis test are to *reject* the Null Hypothesis or to *fail to reject*. These are not, of course, exact opposites. The opposite of rejecting the Null would be to *accept* the Null. Why isn't that wording used?

- Switch to the Summary worksheet.

If you Reject the Null, and are wrong, you have Type I error. If you Fail to Reject the Null, and are wrong, you have Type II error. Although you can never be sure you have come to the correct conclusion in either case, you do have control over the probability a sample will lead to Type I error—the significance level. This is shown by the tendency on the Summary worksheet for B1 (the significance level) and B6 (the proportion of samples with Type I error) to be equal. Remember that cell B6 has the only error result when the conclusion was Reject the Null. If you Fail to Reject the Null, you may be in the situation shown by cell C6 (if you are lucky), or by D6 (if you are unlucky), or by a situation in which the probability of error is even higher than that shown by D6.

The problem is that Fail to Reject simply does not provide evidence that the Null is correct. It means the sample you have chosen is consistent with the Null Hypothesis being correct, but it is also consistent with the Null Hypothesis being incorrect—if the true value of μ is close to that given by the Null.

This also is the reason why, in formulating the Null and Alternate Hypotheses, you want the Alternate Hypothesis to state what you are looking for evidence of. You really only have good evidence from a simple hypothesis test if the only error you could be making is Type I error. The only way to be in that situation is to Reject the Null. Therefore the Null Hypothesis needs to be formulated as the *opposite* of what you are looking for evidence of. You will have the evidence if you reject the Null, subject to the (controlled) possibility of Type I error.

▼Exercises

In performing the first hypothesis test discussed in this chapter, we were concerned with the probability that the mean of a sample of 10 boxes would differ from 16 by more than 0.57 (the amount by which the sample mean given in the problem, 15.43, differed from 16). That probability was estimated empirically by actually looking at 1,000 sample means and seeing how many had means that differed from 16 by more than 0.57. It was also determined analytically by calculating the p value.

1. If another 1,000 samples were drawn, what is the probability that the number of means that differ from 16 by more than 0.57 would be exactly 0? Exactly 1? Exactly 2? Three or more? Given these answers, do you think your set of 1,000 samples was typical of all the possible sets of 1,000 samples? Why or why not? (Hint: Use the binomial distribution to answer this question. The number of trials is 1,000, and the probability of success is the p value.)

2. Using the Population 1 sheet of your workbook, find a value for the sample mean (cell G5) that will produce a p value of exactly .01. Start with 15.4, and increase the digit in the tenths place (initially "4"—the digit just to the right of the decimal point) until the p value switches to a value greater than .01. Then reduce the tenths place by one so the p value is again less than .01 and add a "5" to the hundredths place (the digit just to the right of the tenths place). Adjust the "5" up and down until you find the value for the hundredths place that keeps the p value just below .01. Then add a "5" to the thousandths place (just to the right of the hundredths) and make the same adjustment, continuing to the right until the p value that appears in your worksheet displays exactly as .01. What is the z value associated with this sample mean? This z value is the *critical z* for a significance level of .01. Suppose you were given a problem just like that given at the beginning of this chapter, but with a different sample mean. What values for that sample mean would result in a p value less than .01? Explain.

3. (Advanced) Use NORMSINV to determine the precise z values that would produce a p value of .01. Using the population mean and the standard errors, convert the z values to critical values. One will be the same as the one determined in response to problem 2. The other one will be greater than 16. What will its value be?

4. Produce a table showing the results on your Summary worksheets for significance levels of .01, .05, and .10. Do the first one by entering the label in cell A10 "Significance=.01." Next, copy the labels in A5:A7 to A11:A13. Set the significance level (B2) to .01. Select cells E5:G8 and click the Copy button on the Standard Toolbar. Select cell B11. Open the Edit menu on the Menu Bar. Select "Paste Special...." When the Paste Special dialog window opens, click the Values radio button under "Paste." Repeat the "Paste Special" operation and paste "Formats." This creates a table for a significance level of .01 which will not change when you change the value of cell B2. Use a similar method to create labeled tables for significance levels of .05

and .10. Print the three tables together and alone on a single sheet of paper by first selecting the region containing the three tables. Open the File menu on the Menu Bar and select "Print...." Under "Print what" click the Selection radio button and then click the Preview button. Add a heading with an appropriate title and your name.

5. (Advanced) Use the distribution of sample means to determine precisely the probability of Type II error for samples of 10 drawn from Populations II and III. Use a significance level of .05. To do this you will need to first determine the population standard deviation. Then determine the critical values for the test ($H_0 : \mu = 16, H_A : \mu \neq 16$). Finally, use the actual population mean to determine the probability of a sample mean falling between the two critical values.

Chapter 9

Hypothesis Testing of a Population Mean

Excel provides powerful tools that make it easy to perform hypothesis tests on a population mean. This chapter will provide you with instructions and exercises to help you gain proficiency in using Excel for this, but it does assume you have a basic understanding of the procedures involved in performing a hypothesis test. The chapter will provide examples of problems for which the t distribution is appropriate and problems for which the z distribution is appropriate. Examples of tests of both one- and two-tail hypotheses will be given. In addition, the use of critical values as well as p values will be discussed.

Excel's tools make it possible to virtually automate the process of hypothesis testing. Be careful; Excel is really no more than a calculator. You will be given step-by-step instructions on creating worksheets to test hypotheses. You haven't learned hypothesis testing if you simply plug in numbers to those worksheets. Test your abilities by working problems in which you start with a new, blank worksheet. If you have a good understanding of hypothesis testing, reconstructing a worksheet for the test should be easy.

▼ Classifying the Problem

When you face a statistical problem, you need to determine the type of problem you are facing before you start to solve it. Since we are dealing in this chapter with hypothesis tests on a population mean, it is reasonable to conclude that all problems here will be of that type. Once you consider other types of hypothesis-testing problems, however, you will have to determine exactly which population parameter is to be tested. Once a problem is identified as one requiring a hypothesis test of a population mean, you still have other issues to resolve.

1. **Will the test be one- or two-tailed?** A one-tailed test is one in which you are concerned with the question of whether the population mean exceeds a particular value or is less than a particular value. A

two-tailed test is one in which you are concerned with whether the population mean simply differs from a specified value; it does not matter if the mean is above or below that value. The hypothesis tests done in the previous chapter were two-tailed.

This determination must be made before the Null and Alternate Hypotheses can be specified, and they determine the relational symbols used. For a two-tailed test, the Null Hypothesis always has an equal sign (=) and the Alternate Hypothesis always has a not equal sign (≠). For a one-tailed test, the Null Hypothesis will always have a greater-than-or-equal sign (≥) or a less-than-or-equal sign (≤). The Alternate Hypothesis will have either a greater-than or less-than sign (> or <).

2. **Should the *z* or *t* distribution be used?** If you know the standard deviation of the population, it is appropriate to treat the distribution of sample means as following the *z* distribution. If you only know the standard deviation of a sample, the *t* distribution should be used.

   Because traditional *t* tables are less satisfactory than *z* tables, traditional statistical practice has favored using the *z* distribution as a substitute for the *t* distribution in situations where large samples (and thus a large value for degrees of freedom) were used, even if the only known standard deviation came from a sample. The *t* distribution with a large value for the degrees of freedom is very close to the *z* distribution and using it will introduce very little error. With computers (and Excel), the advantage of the *z* distribution disappears, and it is always appropriate to use the *t* distribution when the population standard deviation is unknown. For practical problems, it is very unusual to know the population standard deviation. For this reason, the *t* distribution is usually the appropriate one for hypothesis tests on a population mean.

3. **Should the decision be made with critical values or the *p* value?** This decision is primarily one of taste. The critical value approach is more traditional and will be preferred by those who are used to using it. Some day you may work with people with that preference. One characteristic of that approach is that it is often more suited to be used with statistical tables than the *p* value approach. The use of computers has greatly increased the popularity of the *p* value approach because it is easier for computers to report. A *p* value's magnitude is more intuitive than that of a critical value. Since both methods give the same answer, choose the method you prefer and use it consistently. We will cover both methods in this chapter, but unless there is a good reason, pick one method and just use it. It's usually a good idea to use the method you feel you understand best.

▼Two-Tail Tests on a Population Mean, σ Known

Consider the following problem:

A manufacturing firm purchases sheet metal from a supplier who maintains that the average thickness of the metal sheets is 15 mils and that the standard deviation of the metal sheets is .1 mils. The manufacturing firm selects a sample of 50 sheets and determines that the sample mean is 14.982 mils. At the .05 level of significance, is there evidence that the population average claimed by the supplier is incorrect?

Since the supplier's claim is incorrect if the population mean is either more or less than 15 mils, a two-tailed test is appropriate. The Null Hypothesis must have an equal sign, and the Alternate Hypothesis must have a not equal sign.

We are asked to look for evidence that the supplier is incorrect, and the assertion that he is incorrect becomes the Alternate Hypothesis. The Null Hypothesis is: $H_0 : \mu = 15$, and the Alternate Hypothesis is $H_A : \mu \neq 15$. We will find evidence that the supplier is incorrect if the Null Hypothesis is rejected.

No sample standard deviation is given by the problem. Instead we have the claim of the supplier that the population standard deviation, σ, equals .1. This is a two-tailed test using the z distribution. We will prepare a worksheet with labels for this type of problem.

- Open Excel with a new blank workbook.

- Under the File menu choose "Save As," and save the worksheet as "Chap9.xls."

- Double click the "Sheet1" worksheet tab at the bottom of the Excel window and rename it "2-Tail, Sigma Known."

The first step in setting up a worksheet is to enter labels for the data provided by the problem and for the values that will be calculated from that data. There are three types of data that the problem must provide: data about the population, data about the test sample, and the significance level. The objective of the calculations is to determine if a sample whose mean differs from the hypothesized population mean by as much or more as the test sample's could be drawn from this population with a probability less than the significance level. If the answer is "yes," we conclude that the sample could not have been drawn by chance. It is inconsistent with the Null Hypothesis, and we Reject the Null Hypothesis. If the answer is "no," we conclude the sample is consistent with the Null Hypothesis and Fail to Reject it.

In performing a hypothesis test, we always assume the Null Hypothesis is true. This assumption provides one piece of data about the population, the population mean. In this problem we also know the population standard deviation.

We have two pieces of information about the test sample: the sample mean and the sample size.

From the sample size and the (population) standard deviation, we will calculate the standard error. The standard error is actually the standard deviation of all sample means. In a sense it is data about neither the population nor the test sample; it is a measure of the population of samples. We will include it under the category of test statistic since it is integral to the calculation of that statistic.

After the standard error is calculated, it is used with the population mean to convert the sample mean to a *z* value. This *z* value is the *sample z*. The larger the absolute value of the sample *z*, the lower the probability that a sample could be drawn by chance with a sample mean differing from the hypothesized population mean by as much as the test sample's. To determine whether that probability is less than the significance level, we can either convert the sample *z* to a probability and compare it with the significance level, or we can convert the significance level to a critical *z* and compare it with the sample *z*. Both methods are discussed below.

Enter the labels in the worksheet shown in the picture below. The large labels are 14 point. First enter the label and reselect the cell containing the label. Click the arrow to the right of the font size tool on the Formatting Toolbar (10 ▾) and select "14." You can make the *z*'s and *p*'s italic by selecting them in the Formula Bar and then clicking the Italic button on the Formatting Toolbar.

	A	B	C	D	E	F	G	H
1	Population Data			Sample Data			Test Statistic	
2	Hypothesized Mean			Mean			Standard Error	
3	Standard Deviation			*n*			Sample *z*	
4								
5	Significance Level			p Value			Critical *z* Values	
6	Alpha			2 Tail			Upper	
7							Lower	

Next enter the data values from the problem.

- In cell B2, enter the population mean given by the Null Hypothesis.

- In cell B3, enter the population standard deviation.

- In cell E2, enter the sample mean, 14.982.

- In cell E3, enter the size of the sample, 50.

- In cell B6, enter the significance level (α), .05.

The remaining cells contain formulas performing calculations on these values.

The formula for the standard error is

$$\text{SE}(\bar{x}) = \sigma_{\bar{x}} = \frac{\sigma}{\sqrt{n}}$$

- In cell H2 enter the Excel formula to calculate the standard error. The displayed value should be "0.014142."

- The formula for the sample z is

$$z = \frac{\bar{x} - \mu}{\sigma_{\bar{x}}}$$

In cell H3, enter the Excel formula for the sample z. The displayed value should be "-1.27279."

This sample has a mean of 14.982. Is that close enough to 15 that it is reasonable to believe the difference is due to chance, or is it so far from 15 that such a sample is unlikely to have been drawn from a population with mean 15? To reject the Null Hypothesis, the probability of a randomly chosen sample having a mean that differs from 15 by at least as much as 14.982 differs from 15 must be less than the significance level (.05 in this case). In that case we decide the difference is too great to be due to chance and the difference must be due to the population mean being different from 15. If the probability is greater than the significance level, we conclude that the Null Hypothesis could be true and the different sample mean could be the result of chance.

The decision of whether or not to reject the Null Hypothesis thus involves a comparison between the sample z and the significance level. Before this comparison can be done, either the sample z must be converted to a probability (the p value approach), or the significance level must converted to a z value (the critical value approach).

▼The *p* Value Approach

The p value approach involves converting the sample z to the probability that a z value will have an absolute value that exceeds the absolute value of the sample z. For this problem, that probability is represented by the shaded area in the density function depicted in the picture below.

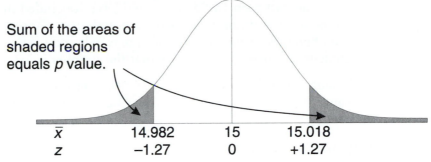

Sum of the areas of shaded regions equals p value.

$\bar{x}$	14.982	15	15.018
z	−1.27	0	+1.27

Excel's NORMSDIST function can be used to determine this area. NORMSDIST has a single argument and provides the probability of a standard normal variable having a value less than that argument. This is represented as the area to the left of the argument on the probability density function. If the argument for NORMSDIST were −1.27279 (the sample z for this case), the area of the left shaded tail in the density function above would be returned. If NORMSDIST were given the positive value 1.27279, the area to the left of that value would be returned. This would be equivalent to 1.0 minus the area of the right shaded tail. What we want here is the area of *both* shaded tails. An easy way to get that would be to double the value NORMSDIST would return if given a negative parameter, −1.27279 in this case.

Although the sample z in this case *is* a negative number, the formula for the p value should be one that would work even if the sample z were positive. A way to ensure that the parameter given NORMSDIST is negative is to take the negative of the absolute value of the sample z.

- Select cell E6. Click the Edit Formula button. Since we want to double the value that will be returned by NORMSDIST, enter "2*" and then select "NORMSDIST" ("Statistical" Category). When the NORMSDIST dialog window appears, enter a minus sign in the "Z" argument field. Use the recent function button to select "ABS" ("Math & Trig"). In the "Number" field enter the address of the sample z. Click the OK button. The displayed value will be "0.203092."

The p value is over .20, clearly greater than the significance level. That means that the test sample might well have been drawn by chance from a population whose mean was 15. The sample is consistent with the Null Hypothesis. We will fail to reject the Null and conclude that there is not evidence that the supplier is incorrect.

What if the mean had been further from 15? Select cell E2 and enter "14.95," which is further from 15 than is 14.982. Notice how the value of the sample z increases (in absolute value) to -3.53553, and the p value decreases to .000407, which is less than the significance level. If the sample mean had been 14.95, we would have concluded that the sample could not have been drawn from a population whose mean was 15. The Null Hypothesis would have been rejected, and we would have concluded that there was evidence that the supplier is incorrect.

Change the value of E2 back to 14.982. Let's now consider how Excel can be used to test a Null Hypothesis using the critical z approach.

▼The Critical Value Approach

Rather than converting the sample z to a probability, the critical value approach converts the significance level to a z value. These z values define "rejection regions," as shown in the diagram below.

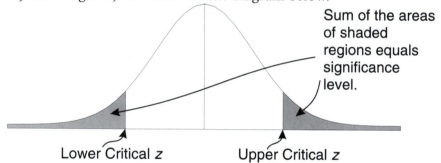

Sum of the areas of shaded regions equals significance level.

Lower Critical z Upper Critical z

The rejection regions are those z values that are greater than the upper critical z or lower than the lower critical z. The probability of a z value falling within the rejection region is equal to the shaded area that is equal to the significance level. Notice that the area of each tail for a two-tail critical region is half the significance level.

The difference between the area which defines the p value and that which defines the critical z is that the former involves finding a probability associated with the sample z, while the latter involves finding a probability associated with the significance level. A sample z can take on almost any value, since it is determined by the sample data. Significance levels, by contrast, are determined by the researcher and traditionally are just a few values (.01, .05, and .10 are the most common). When tables were used to convert between values of random variables and probabilities, the critical value approach could be supported by a much shorter and simpler table than could the p value approach.

With Excel, the determination of a critical value requires an inverse distribution function. For the z distribution this is NORMSINV. We will look at the lower critical z first since it is slightly easier.

- Select cell H7 and click the Edit Formula button. Select the "NORMSINV" function ("Statistical" category).

The dialog window for the NORMSINV function has only one parameter, "Probability," the probability of getting a z value less than the value the function returns. For the lower critical z in the diagram above, that probability is the area of the left tail. Since the area of both tails is given by the significance level (in cell B7), the correct probability for the lower critical z is half that.

- Enter in the "Probability" field of the dialog box an Excel expression that will divide the value of cell B6 by 2. Click the OK button. The lower critical z value, "-1.95996," should appear in cell H7.

- Select cell H6. Enter an Excel formula to determine the value of the upper critical z. There are several acceptable ways of doing this. All will result in cell H6 displaying a positive number with the same absolute value as that displayed in H7.

Since it is always the case that the upper and lower critical z's have the same absolute values, it is common for just the positive value to be referred to as the critical z in two-tail tests.

We can now determine whether or not to reject the Null Hypothesis by comparing two z values, the test statistic and the critical z. If the test statistic lies within the critical region, the Null Hypothesis is rejected. The test statistic will lie within the critical region if its absolute value exceeds the absolute value of a critical z (both of which have the same absolute value). The sample z, -1.27279, does *not* lie within the rejection region since it is not to the left of the lower critical z (-1.95996). We thus fail to reject the Null Hypothesis and conclude that there is not evidence that the supplier is incorrect. This, of course, is the same conclusion arrived at with the p value.

Again, change the sample mean in cell E2 from 14.982 to 14.95. The test statistic changes to -3.53553. This value *does* lie within the rejection region since it lies to the left of the lower critical z, which remains unchanged. In this case we would reject the Null Hypothesis and conclude that there *is* evidence that the supplier is incorrect. The critical value approach will always give the same answer as the p value approach.

- Click the column heading for column B and press the Delete key. Do likewise with columns D and H. This will prepare the worksheet for the next problem while leaving the labels.

Consider the following problem:

A quality control inspector wants to check the manufacturing process in a plant that makes scales for home use. The scales are tested by having them weigh a precise reference weight, which weighs 120 pounds. When the manufacturing process is working properly, the measured weight given by all scales averages 120 pounds with a standard deviation of .015 pounds. The inspector chooses 30 scales and weighs the reference weight with each of them. The average weight reported by this sample of scales is 120.01 pounds. Does the inspector have evidence at the .01 level of significance that the manufacturing process is not working properly?

The first step is to determine the Null and Alternate Hypotheses. Remember to make the Alternate Hypothesis the situation for which you are looking for evidence. The Null is the opposite—finding evidence must involve rejecting the Null. Remember also that the Null must include "equals." Since the inspector is looking for evidence that the process is not working properly, and it is working properly when the average is 120, the Alternate Hypothesis is $H_A : \mu \neq 120$. The Null Hypothesis is then $H_0 : \mu = 120$.

- Enter the hypothesized population mean, population standard deviation, sample size, sample mean, and significance level in the appropriate cells.

- Enter the formula to calculate the standard error. When the correct formula is entered, cell H2 will display "0.002739."

- Enter the formula to calculate the sample z in cell H3. The displayed value should be "3.651484."

- To complete the test using the p value approach, select cell E6 and enter a formula to calculate the p value from the sample z in H3. This will involve using NORMSDIST to get the area of one tail and multiplying that area by 2. Keep in mind that in this problem you have a positive sample z, while in the previous problem the sample z was negative. You will have to modify the formula used before to account for this difference. The displayed value should be "0.000261."

- To complete the test using the critical value approach, select first cell H6 and enter a formula which will determine the upper critical value from the significance level in cell B6. Since this is a two-tail test, the upper critical z will be that value such that the area to the right is half the significance level (as shown in the chart on page 254). The displayed value should be "2.575835." Enter a formula for the lower critical z which simply displays the negative of the value in cell H6.

Using the p value approach, the Null Hypothesis would be rejected because the p value, .000261, is less than the significance level, .05. Using the critical value approach, the Null Hypothesis would be rejected because the sample z, 3.651484, has a larger absolute value than the critical z, 2.575835. Both methods mean that this sample is sufficiently unlikely to occur (less than 5% chance) if the Null were true that we conclude the Null Hypothesis must be false. Yes, the inspector does have evidence that the manufacturing process is not working properly.

▼One-Tail Tests on a Population Mean, σ Known

- Double click on worksheet tab "Sheet2" and rename it "1-Tail, Sigma Known."

Consider the following problem:

A mail-order furniture company has been receiving complaints from customers concerning delays in receipt of merchandise shipped to them. The furniture company suspects the fault lies with the trucking firm it employs to ship the furniture to its customers. The trucking firm assures the furniture company that the average time from shipment to delivery is no more than 15 days, with a standard deviation of 4 days. The furniture company decides to check this by selecting a random sample of 50 shipments and determining the precise time between shipment and delivery. The furniture company decides that a significance level of .02 is appropriate for this issue.

The concern here is that the average delivery time may exceed the 15-day standard. There is no concern that the average may be less than 15 days. This makes a one-tail test appropriate here. When the furniture company takes its sample, it will calculate the sample mean. If the sample mean is less than 15 days, there would be no reason to do any further calculations. A sample mean that is less than 15 cannot possibly provide evidence that the population mean exceeds 15. If, however, the sample mean exceeds 15, a procedure is followed to determine if the high sample mean could be due to chance.

Many statisticians would formulate the Null and Alternate Hypotheses as follows:

$$H_0 : \mu \leq 15$$
$$H_A : \mu > 15$$

Other statisticians, however, while keeping the Alternate Hypothesis the same as that shown above, would formulate the Null Hypothesis as:

$$H_0 : \mu = 15$$

If it is necessary to calculate a test statistic, the value for the population mean (μ) used in the calculation would be the one given by the second form of the hypothesis test. In other words, for the purposes of calculating a test statistic, an inequality in the Null Hypothesis is treated as an equality. As will be discussed in more detail below, in one-tail tests some samples will lead to a failure to reject the Null solely on the basis of their mean. I think this is clearer when an inequality is used in the Null Hypothesis, and this is the procedure I will follow.

Suppose the furniture company selects a sample, and the sample mean is 17. Since this value exceeds 15, further computation is necessary to determine if chance can be excluded as an explanation for the high sample mean. The data and calculations for this problem are so similar to those for the previous problem that we will copy the labels and formulas from that worksheet.

- Copy the range A1:H7 from the 2-Tail, Sigma Known worksheet to cell A1 of the 1-Tail, Sigma Known worksheet. Adjust the width of columns A and G.

- Erase all entries and formulas leaving just the labels. Here is one way to do this. Click the column B column heading. Press and hold the Ctrl key and click the column headings for columns E and H. This will result in all three columns being selected. Press the Delete key to erase their contents.

Change the data in the worksheet to reflect the values for the current problem:

- In cells B2:B3 enter the hypothesized population mean and the population standard deviation given in the problem.

- In cell E2 enter the sample mean, 17.

- In cell E3 enter the sample size, 50.

- In cell B7 enter the significance level, .02.

- Select cell H2 and enter the formula for the standard error. The displayed value should be "0.565685."

- Select cell H3 and enter the formula for the sample z. The displayed value should be "3.535534."

The differences between a one-tail and a two-tail test are in the formulas for the p value and for the critical z values. One label also needs to be changed.

- Change the label "2 Tail" in cell D7 to "1 Tail."

- To determine the *p* value, select cell E7. Sketch a picture of the *p* value, which should look like the picture below.

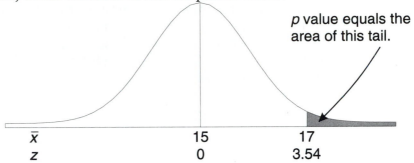

p value equals the area of this tail.

x̄	15	17
z	0	3.54

- Use NORMSDIST to determine the probability of a *z* value exceeding the value of the sample *z*. Remember that without modification, NORMSDIST will give you the area to the left, which is not what you need in this case. The displayed value should be "0.000204."

The critical *z* values for a two-tail test divide the significance level into two parts. The two critical *z* values define two tails whose *combined* areas equal the significance levels as shown in the picture below.

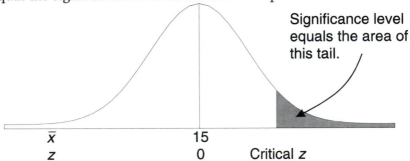

Significance level equals the area of this tail.

x̄	15	
z	0	Critical z

- Select cell H6. Enter a formula which will determine the critical *z*, that is, the value which has the property that the probability of a greater *z* value exactly equals the significance level. Use NORMSINV for this, but remember that NORMSINV interprets the probability argument as the area to the left of the *z* value it returns, while the significance level in this case is the area to the right. The displayed value should be "2.053748."

A one-tail critical statistic can be negative, in which case the significance level would equal the tail to the left of that critical value. Once you have determined that the sample mean is not consistent with the Null Hypothesis, the critical *z* will have the same sign as the sample *z*.

The formulas for the decision rules are the same for one- and two-tail tests. The *p* value is much lower than the significance level, and the absolute value of the sample *z* exceeds the absolute value of the critical *z*.

The Null Hypothesis is rejected. This result indicates that the furniture company should conclude that the trucking firm's claims are not accurate and that the average delivery time for all shipments exceeds 15 days. If the population mean were 15, the probability of a random sample of 50 deliveries having a mean delivery time of 17 or more is low enough (less than .02) that chance is excluded as an explanation for the high sample mean. If the sample mean were closer to 15, this would not have been the case.

Change the value of cell E2 to 16 (be sure to press the Enter key). The p value increases to .03885, greater than the significance level of .02. The sample z falls to 1.767767, less than the critical z and no longer in the rejection region. A sample mean of 16 is close enough to 15 that it could have happened by chance and the trucking firm's claim cannot be rejected. What would happen if the significance level were .05? The result would clearly change since the p value is below the significance level. To see how this would work with the critical value approach, change cell B7 to .05 and observe the effect on the critical z. Change B7 back to .02 before proceeding.

▼A Warning About One-Tail Tests

Recall that the Null Hypothesis is always a statement about a population parameter (μ, in the cases we have considered). Since we expect (in the statistical sense) a sample mean to equal the population mean, the Null Hypothesis also tells us what to expect from a sample. In order to reject the Null Hypothesis, it is necessary for the sample not be what the Null says to expect: The sample must be inconsistent with the Null. In a two-tail test, the Null Hypothesis always contains an equal sign. For a sample mean to be consistent with the Null Hypothesis, the sample mean would have to exactly equal the value given in the Null Hypothesis for the sample to be consistent with the Null. A sample mean is a continuous random variable, and the value given in the Null Hypothesis is a fixed value. The probability of a sample mean happening to exactly equal the value given in the Null Hypothesis is essentially zero.

The situation is different with a one-tail test. In this case, the Null Hypothesis contains an inequality ($\geq$ or $\leq$). It is certainly possible that a sample mean might be consistent with the Null and either less than or greater than the value given in the Null Hypothesis.

Consider, for example, the possibility that the average delivery time for the sample of 50 chosen by the furniture company was 13 days.

- Enter the value 13 for the sample mean in cell E2. The *p* value in cell E6 is over .99. If this had been a left-tail *p* value, the formula would have differed slightly. Select cell E6 and delete the minus sign in front of "H3." Now the *p* value is very low, much less than the significance level. Should the Null Hypothesis be rejected?

Which *p* value is correct? Although some statisticians would maintain the first one is correct, I believe careful consideration of what a *p* value measures will make clear that neither is correct. The *p* value measures the probability that an unexpected sample could have occurred by chance if the Null Hypothesis were true. A sample mean of 13 days is *consistent* with the trucking firm's claim that the average of all delivery times is less than 15 days. That assertion cannot be rejected by a sample that is consistent with the claim. For such a sample, no calculations of *p* values or critical *z* by Excel are needed. You should Fail to Reject the Null Hypothesis because the sample is consistent with the Null.

▼Hypothesis Tests on a Population Mean When σ Is Unknown

In the great majority of real hypothesis tests on a population mean, no information about the population, including the population standard deviation, is available. In these cases a sample standard deviation, *s*, must be used, and the *t* distribution is used instead of the normal distribution (although the error in using the normal distribution is minuscule when the sample size is large).

Textbook problems concerning hypothesis tests on a population mean when σ is unknown sometimes provide the sample mean and standard deviation, but sometimes the sample data are provided instead. Determining the mean and standard deviation becomes part of the problem—a more realistic situation. Excel can, of course, easily determine these sample statistics. Some textbooks provide the data for problems on a diskette or CD. In this section we will cover the use of such data.

Although you have produced separate worksheets for the one- and two-tail tests for the case when σ was known, you have seen that the differences were very small. We will combine one- and two-tail tests in a single worksheet by including both one- and two-tail *p* values and critical *t*'s. Keep in mind that Excel cannot determine for you whether a one-tail or two-tail test is appropriate for a particular problem. Furthermore, in a one-tail test, Excel cannot determine for you if the sample is inconsistent with the Alternate Hypothesis. As you saw earlier, if the sample is inconsistent with the Alternate Hypothesis, calculated *p* values and critical values are incorrect, and it would be incorrect to reject the

Null Hypothesis. The use of Excel, or any other computing tool, can never substitute for an understanding of basic statistical principles.

- Double click the worksheet tab "Sheet3" and rename it "Sigma Unknown."

- Return to the previous worksheet, 1-Tail, Sigma Known.

- Copy cells A1:H6 from this worksheet to the the Sigma Unknown worksheet. Adjust the widths of columns A and G.

Several modifications need to be made in the new worksheet. Either select each cell in turn and make the changes in the Formula Bar or double click and make the changes in the cells.

- Change the "z" in cells G3 and G5 to "t."

- Select cell A5. From the Insert menu choose "Rows." One blank row will be inserted in your worksheet below row 5. This will move the text "Significance Level" from row 5 to row 6.

Since the standard deviation will come from a sample rather than from a population, move the contents of cell A3 to D4. You can move a cell by using the drag-and-drop method (page 32) or by using Cut and Paste (buttons on Edit menu of Standard Toolbar). Enlarge column D so it will hold the contents of D4.

- Change the text in cell D7 to "1 or 2 Tail."

- Copy D7 to G7

Your worksheet should look like the picture below:

	A	B	C	D	E	F	G	H
1	Population Data			Sample Data			Test Statistic	
2	Hypothesized Mean			Mean			Standard Error	
3				n			Sample t	
4				Standard Deviation				
5								
6	Significance Level			p Value			Critical t Values	
7	Alpha			1 or 2 Tail			1 or 2 Tail	

Consider the following problem:

The average balance in a particular type of savings account in a large, multibranch bank has been $2,500. A new branch has opened, and the manager wants to determine if the average balance for this type of account in the branch differs from $2,500. A random sample of 30 accounts is chosen. The sample mean is $2,399, and the sample standard deviation is $250. At the .05 level of significance, does the manager have evidence that the average balance at the new branch differs from $2,500?

As always, the first step is to determine the Null and Alternate Hypotheses. Since we are looking for evidence that the average balance differs from $2,500, the Alternate Hypothesis will express this: $H_A : \mu \neq 2,500$. The Null Hypothesis will be the opposite: $H_0 : \mu = 2,500$. This is a two-tail test.

- Enter the hypothesized population mean, $2,500, in cell B2.

- Enter the sample data (mean = $2,399, $n = 30$, and standard deviation = $250) in the appropriate cells in column E. Note that it is perfectly acceptable to enter numbers with dollar signs and commas ($2,399 and 2399 are both acceptable).

- Enter the significance level, .05, in cell B7.

- Enter the formula in cell H2 to calculate the standard error. The formula is really the same as was used in the case when σ was known, except the sample s is used: $s_{\bar{x}} = \dfrac{s}{\sqrt{n}}$. The displayed value should be "45.64355."

- Enter the formula in cell H3 to calculate the sample t, $\dfrac{\bar{x} - \mu}{s_{\bar{x}}}$. The displayed value should be "-2.2128."

- If you want to use the p value approach, enter the formula to calculate the p value in cell E7. Since this is a two-tail test, you want to determine the sum of the areas to the left of -2.2128 and to the right of $+2.2128$ under the t density function:

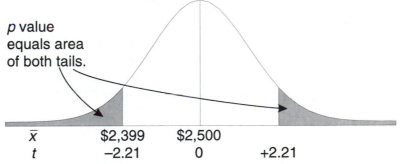

Use the TDIST function. Since the sample t is negative, put a negative sign before its cell address in the "X" argument field. TDIST won't accept a negative t value. The degrees of freedom equals $n - 1$, and the number of tails is "2.". The displayed value should be 0.034939.

- If you want to use the critical value approach, enter the formula in cell H7 to determine the critical value. The critical value will be that t

value which has the property that the area in the *t* density function to the right of positive *t* plus the area to the left of negative *t* exactly equal the significance level:

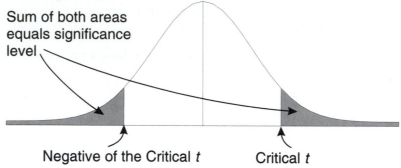

Use TINV to determine the critical *t*. The probability argument should be the significance level (B7) and the degrees of freedom is $n - 1$. The displayed value should be "2.045231."

Whichever method you use, you will conclude that this sample is too unlikely to be drawn from the population described by the Null Hypothesis to believe that this is what happened. So Reject the Null Hypothesis and conclude, "Yes, there is evidence that the average balance at the new branch differs from $2,500."

▼Using Sample Data to Test a Hypothesis

Consider the following problem:

The manager of a firm in the business of telephone solicitation is interested in determining if the installation of new telephone equipment has increased the average sales per worker. Last year, average sales per worker for the month of July were $3,987. As soon as the month of July ended this year, the manager selected a sample of 10 workers and determined the level of sales per worker. These were

$2,958, $3,816, $4,146, $5,325, $4,400, $2,085, $5,435, $2,218, $3,341, $5,124

Based on this sample, does the manager have evidence, at the .05 level of significance, that average sales for all workers this July exceeded the average of July of last year?

The correct test for this problem is one-tail, and the Null and Alternate Hypotheses are

$$H_0 : \mu \leq \$3,987$$
$$H_A : \mu > \$3,987$$

- Open the Insert menu on the Menu Bar and click "Worksheet." A new worksheet, Sheet4 will be added to your workbook.

- Rename the Sheet4 worksheet as "Sample Data."

- Move the Sample Data worksheet to the end of the worksheets by first placing the mouse pointer on the worksheet tab (where its name is). Details on how to move a worksheet are given on page 28.

- Enter the sample data in column A of the Sample Data worksheet.

- Enter the label "x bar" in cell B1.

- Enter a formula in cell C1 which will calculate the mean of the values in column A. Use the AVERAGE function. It is a good idea to give the function the entire column in its "Number1" argument either by clicking the column heading for column A or by entering the address "A:A." The displayed value should be "3884.8."

This is a one-tail test. Once you have the sample mean, you should determine if the sample is consistent with the Null Hypothesis. The Null Hypothesis is $\mu \leq 3987$. If the Null is true, the expected value of $\bar{x}$ is also less than or equal to 3987. For this sample, $\bar{x} = 3884.8$, which is less than 3987. The sample, therefore, is consistent with the Null Hypothesis.

No further calculation is needed to conclude that we must Fail to Reject the Null Hypothesis because the sample is consistent with the Null. It would be a waste of time to calculate a p value and might result in error. The answer to the question is, "No, the manager does not have evidence that average sales for all workers this July exceeded the average of July of last year."

Suppose that the manager chose a larger sample than indicated in the problem. Suppose that the sample was of size 15, and, in addition to the 10 values given above, the following 5 values were also chosen:

$$\$4,011, \$3,900, \$4,511, \$4,400, \$4,518$$

- Select the Data worksheet, and add these five values in column A *after* the 10 values already there. The new values should go into cells A11:A15.

- If cell C1 has a formula referring to all of column A, the addition of the extra values will automatically update the average, and the displayed value in C1 will now be "4012.533." If your worksheet does not display this number, change the formula in cell C1 to calculate the average of all 15 numbers.

The current sample is no longer consistent with the Null Hypothesis because $\bar{x}$ is now larger than 3987. If the Null Hypothesis were true, this is an unexpected sample. There are two possible explanations for an unexpected sample. One possible explanation is luck. An unexpected sample may have been chosen simply by chance. The other possible explanation is that the Null Hypothesis is wrong. We choose between these two explanations by determining whether the probability of a sample as or more unexpected than this one is less than the significance level. If the answer to this is "yes," then we conclude that luck does not explain the unexpected sample, and the Null Hypothesis must be wrong.

- Enter the labels "s" and "n" in B2 and B3. Enter formulas in cells C2 and C3 to calculate the sample standard deviation and sample size, respectively. The displayed values should be "1012.543" and "15."

- Enter the label "Standard Error" in B4, "Hypothesized Mu" in B5, and "Sample t" in B6. Adjust the width of column B6 to hold these labels.

- Enter a formula in cell C4 to calculate the standard error. The displayed value should be "261.4374."

- In cell C5 enter the value of μ given by the Null Hypothesis, "3987."

- In cell C6 enter a formula to calculate the sample t. The displayed value should be "0.097665."

- If you want to use the p value approach, enter the label "p value" in B7 and the formula to calculate the p value in C7. Keep in mind that this is a one-tail test and TDIST must be told to calculate the area of one tail. The displayed value should be "0.461791."

- If you want to use the critical t approach, enter the label "significance level" in B8 and "critical t" in B9. Enter the significance level (".05") in C8.

- Enter the formula to calculate the critical t in C8. To calculate the critical t, you will need to use TINV. Since TINV expects a two-tailed probability, and the significance level in this case is one-tail, you must give TINV a probability which is twice the significance level (see the picture below). The displayed value should be "1.761309."

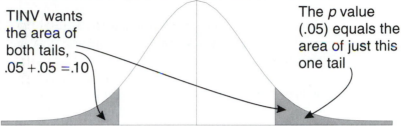

TINV wants the area of both tails, .05 + .05 = .10

The *p* value (.05) equals the area of just this one tail

Both approaches show that the probability of getting a sample like this (as, or more, unexpected than this) is greater than .05. The *p* value makes clear that this probability is, in fact, very high—over .4. We would thus Fail to Reject the Null Hypothesis and conclude again that there is not evidence (at the .05 level of significance) that averge sales this July exceeded the average for July of last year.

▼ Using Data on a Diskette

You can also read data from a file and bring the file into the worksheet. The simplest way of doing this is to read the file into a workbook and then copy the data from that workbook to the current one.

Consider the following problem:

A car manufacturer has launched a special ad campaign for a particular model car. The manufacturer wants to determine if average sales per dealer for this model exceed 60 during the month following the campaign. A random sample of dealers was surveyed. Respondents were asked how many of that particular model were sold in the month. The responses were coded and are available in the file cars.txt.

Based on the response to the survey, does the manufacturer have evidence (at the .05 level of significance) that average sales for all dealers during the month exceeded 60?

You don't need sample data to formulate the Null and Alternate Hypotheses. The test for this problem would be one-tail. The Null and Alternate Hypotheses are

$$H_0 : \mu \leq 60$$

$$H_A : \mu > 60$$

- Click the Open button on the Standard Toolbar. A dialog window will open where you will locate the cars.txt file.

There are two fields that you need to adjust: "Look in:," (at the very top of the dialog window) and "Files of type" (at the very bottom of the window).

- First find the directory containing the data. To the right of "Look in:" is a field which shows the current directory. On the right side of that field is a box with a downward-pointing arrow (▾) Click it and look for the storage device on which you have put the data files for this book. For example, if they are on a diskette, be sure the diskette is in your computer's reader and click "3½ Floppy (A:)."

- Choose the "Chap_9" folder. Change the "Files of type" (at the bottom of the window) from "All Microsoft Excel Files ..." to "All files (*.*)" Double click "cars.txt," which should be in the list of files. Excel will open the first Text Import Wizard dialog window.

- As you will see in that first window, this file contains only one data number per line with a label on the first line. Since the label has three words with spaces, we do not want Excel to regard the space character as a delimiter.

- Click the Next> button. Be sure the small square to the left of "Space" in the group of delimiters *does not* have a check in it. Click the Finish Button.

Excel will create a new workbook with the name (on the Name Bar) "cars.txt." The data will be in column A with the label in the first row. We will do the calculations for the hypothesis test right on this sheet.

- In cell C1 enter the label "x bar." In cell D1 enter a formula to calculate the mean of all the data in column A. The displayed value should be "62.64."

Is this sample consistent with the Null Hypothesis? If it were, the sample mean would be less than or equal to 50. Since it is not, we must continue the calculation to determine how the probability of a sample with $\bar{x} \geq 62.64$ drawn from a population with $\mu = 50$ compares with the significance level of .05.

- In cells C2:C4 enter the following labels: "s," "n," "standard error," "hypothesized mu," "sample t." Adjust the width of column C to hold these labels.

- In cells D2:D4 enter formulas to calculate the statistics indicated by the labels in column C of each respective row. The correct statistics are: $s = 8.900264$, $n = 50$, and $s_{\bar{x}} = 1.258687$.

- The hypothesized value of μ is given by the Null Hypothesis by changing the relational operator to equals. Enter "60" in cell D5.

- Enter the formula in D6 to calculate the sample t. The cell should display "2.097423."

- If you use the p value approach, enter the label "p value" in C7 and the formula to calculate the (one-tail) p value in D7. The value displayed in D7 should be "0.020569."

- If you use the critical value approach, enter the labels "significance level" and "critical t" in cells C8 and C9. In cell D8 enter the significance level for this test, .05. In cell D9 enter the formula to determine the t value whose upper tail exactly equals the significance level. The displayed should be "1.676551."

Both the p value and critical value approach show that if the Null were true ($\mu = 60$) the probability of drawing a sample this size with a sample mean greater than or equal to 62.64 is less than .05. The p value shows it to be only slightly more than .02. Therefore we conclude that we cannot accept luck or chance as an explanation for this sample.

The Null Hypothesis is rejected. Yes, there is evidence at the .05 level of significance that the average sales for all dealers that month exceeded 60.

▼ Exercises

Close the worksheet you have developed in this chapter before working the problems below. Use a new, blank worksheet with them. For each problem, state the Null and Alternate Hypotheses and determine the p value or critical t. State whether you Reject or Fail to Reject the Null Hypothesis and give a yes or no answer to the question asked. Copies of the data for the problems can be found in the workbook Exercises.xls.

1. A milk bottle-filling machine is operating properly when the average amount of milk placed in each bottle is exactly 1 gallon with a standard deviation of .02 gallons. A random sample of 50 bottles was chosen, and the average amount of milk in the sample was 1.01 gallons. At the .01 level of significance, is there evidence that the machine is not working properly?

2. A testing agency wishes to test the effectiveness of a new brake design in a particular automobile. The brakes are claimed to be able, with an average driver, to stop an automobile traveling at 40 mph in less than 50 feet. A random sample of drivers is chosen to test the brakes, and the stopping distances are as follows:

49, 42, 46, 29, 48, 55, 43, 48, 50, 46, 41, 46, 37, 40, 39

Based on this sample, is there evidence at the .05 level of significance that the average stopping distance for all drivers is less than 50 feet?

3. The director of retail operations wants to assign enough tellers to a group of bank branches so that the average amount of time any customer will have to spend waiting in line will be less than 120 seconds during peak hours. A random sample of customers was chosen during those peak hours, and the amount of time spent waiting in line by each customer was carefully measured in seconds. The data are coded in the file bank.txt. Based on these data, is there evidence at the .01 level of significance that the average amount of time spent by all customers is less than 120 seconds?

4. A random sample of students from a local college was selected and each person's height was measured. The results (in inches) were

62, 59, 73, 56, 71, 68, 54, 53, 64, 69

Is there evidence (at the $\alpha = .05$ level of significance) that the average height of all students is less than 68 inches?

5. A winery claims that the acidity level of a particular wine is normally distributed with an average pH level of 6.10. A random sample of 10 bottles is selected and the sample average acidity level as measured by pH is 6.03 with a sample standard deviation of .125. Is there evidence that the claim of an average pH level of 6.10 is not valid? Use $\alpha = .01$.

6. A random sample of students from a local college was selected and each person's height was measured. The results (in inches) were

62, 59, 73, 56, 71, 68, 54, 53, 64, 69

Is there evidence (at the $\alpha = .05$ level of significance) that the average height of all students is more than 68 inches?

7. A random sample of students from a local college was selected and each person's height was measured. The results (in inches) were

62, 59, 73, 56, 71, 68, 54, 53, 64, 69

Is there evidence (at the $\alpha = .05$ level of significance) that the average height of all students differs from 68 inches?

Data for the following problems are only available in the Exercises.xls workbook.

8. A firm manufactures rope used for mountain climbing. According to specifications, the average strength of this particular rope must be at least 20 kn. As part of its quality control process, a sample of rope for each production batch is selected and, using destructive testing, the strength of each rope in the sample is determined. Based on this sample, is there evidence at the .05 level of significance that the average strength of all rope is below specification?

9. In the problem above, explain the consequences of Type I and Type II error in this case. Which error might you have made, given your answer to the previous question?

10. A company which manufactures liquid dishwashing detergent want to check the average amount of the product put in each of a particular size bottle. When working properly, the filling process places an average of 32 ounces in all bottles. A sample of bottles was selected, and the amount of detergent (in ounces) in each bottle was determined. Is there evidence (at the .05 level of significance) that the average fill of all bottles differs from 32 ounces?

11. The pH of a particular brand of wine is supposed to average 6.7 at the time the wine is first produced (before aging). In order to determine whether this value has changed for wines produced from grapes from a new vineyard, a sample of barrels of new wine from the new area is selected and the pH of each barrel is measured. At the .05 level of significance, is there evidence that the average pH of all wine newly produced from grapes from the new vineyard differs from 6.7?

12. A manufacturer of mountain climbing equipment has begun production of a newly designed carabiner supposed to have a strength of at least 35 kilonewtons (gate closed). A sample of the new production was selected, and the strength of each carabiner was determined through destructive testing. The results are shown on the Carabiner worksheet. At the .05 level of significance, is there evidence that the average breaking strength of all the newly produced carabiners is less than 35 kn?

13. The registrar of the local state university wants to see if a new computer system using the World Wide Web will enable the average student to complete registration in less than 15 minutes. In order to determine this, a sample of students was chosen and asked to register

using the new system. Based on these data, is there evidence (at the .05 level of significance) that the average time required for all students would be less than 15 minutes?

14. A medical products firm produces a 2% saline solution used as a carrier for the intravenous administration of a number of drugs for seriously ill patients. Quality control requires that in addition to other things, the amount of salt in solution be very carefully controlled. A sample of solution is selected from each production batch, and the quantity of salt is very carefully measured. Using hypothesis-testing procedures, the firm makes a statistical inference about the average level of salt in all solution produced in each batch by using the Null Hypothesis: $H_0: \mu = 2\%$. Explain the meaning and consequences of Type I and Type II error. What characteristic of the hypothesis test determines the relative levels of these two errors? How can the firm reduce Type II error by increasing Type I error? How can the firm reduce both errors?

Chapter 10

Inferences on a Population Proportion

Some types of data cannot be averaged. In the period prior to an election, polls are taken to measure support for the various candidates. Imagine that you are involved in conducting such a poll for a particular candidate who is hoping to win an election. The first step would be to select a random sample. Once the sample is selected, data would be collected from each person in the sample to determine whether or not that person intends to vote for your candidate. The simplest type of data we might have for each member of the sample is a "yes" or "no." The entire set of data would be a collection of yes's and no's. How can you take an average of data like these? You can't. Instead, you describe the sample by calculating the proportion of people in the sample who said "yes." You can then use the sample proportion to make inferences about the proportion of people in the population who support the candidate, much as you used sample data to make inferences about a population mean when the data were of the type that could be averaged.

Once you have a basic understanding of confidence intervals and hypothesis tests of a population mean, you are most of the way to also understanding inferences on a population proportion. The concepts are the same, but some of the mechanics are a little different. Inferences on a population mean are based on the distribution of sample means. Inferences on a population proportion are based on the distribution of sample proportions.

Inferences on proportions are made on "binomial" data—the same kind of data encountered with the binomial distribution. Each individual observation can have only two values, traditionally called "success" or "failure." When the proportion of a sample that falls into a certain category is calculated, an observation in that category is a "success." The rest are "failures." Even though an election (and a poll) may have more than two choices, whenever the proportion favoring a certain outcome is determined, an observation either favors that outcome or does not favor that outcome.

273

▼Sampling Distribution of the Proportion

The sampling distribution of the proportion comes directly from the binomial distribution. In the binomial distribution, the random variable is the "number" of successes. In the sampling distribution of the proportion, the random variable is the "proportion" of successes. When a sample is chosen from a population, the sample size, n, can also be thought of as the binomial n trials. The population proportion of successes (π) is also the probability that a single observation selected from the population will be a success and is thus the same as the binomial π. The binomial random variable—number of successes, or x—is converted to the proportion of successes (p_s—not to be confused with the p value) by dividing by n.

The simple conversion of the binomial random variable to the sample proportion of successes makes it easy to determine the mean and standard deviation (standard error) of sample proportions. The mean of sample proportions is the binomial mean divided by n, and the standard deviation of sample proportions is the binomial standard deviation divided by n, which results in the following:

$$\mu_{p_s} = \pi$$

$$\sigma_{p_s} = \sqrt{\frac{\pi(1-\pi)}{n}}$$

As we saw in Chapter 4, under certain conditions (large n, π not too far from 0.50), the normal distribution approximates the binomial distribution. Subject to the same limitations, it also approximates the distribution of sample proportions and is traditionally used for this. As we will see, in the case of hypothesis testing it is possible to use the binomial distribution directly, which will give somewhat more accurate results.

▼Confidence Intervals on a Population Proportion

As was noted in Chapter 7 (see the discussion beginning on page 206), determining a confidence interval is closely related to the sampling distribution problem where an interval symmetrically distributed around the mean containing a given percentage of sample values is determined. For example, suppose we knew the population π and wanted to determine the interval around π which would contain a desired percentage of all the sample p_s's. Using the normal approximation, the boundaries would be

$\mu_{p_s} \pm z\sigma_{p_s} = \pi \pm z\sqrt{\dfrac{\pi(1-\pi)}{n}}$. If we wanted the interval containing 95% of the values of sample proportions, the appropriate z value would be approximately 1.96.

A confidence interval on a population proportion would be centered on a single sample proportion, but would have the same width ($\pm z\sigma_{p_s}$) as the interval above. There is, however, a problem. The value of σ_{p_s} is dependent on π, and π is unknown (its value is being estimated with the confidence interval). The traditional solution is to substitute the value of p_s from the sample. One justification for doing this is that the value of $\pm z\sigma_{p_s}$ is not highly sensitive to small changes in the value of π (a proposition that will be explored more in an exercise). Therefore, if p_s is reasonably close to π, using it in place of π to calculate σ_{p_s} should be acceptable. The formula for a confidence interval on π is thus:

$$p_s \pm z\sqrt{\dfrac{p_s(1-p_s)}{n}}$$

This can be easily implemented with Excel.

- Start Excel with a new blank workbook and save it as "Chap10.xls."

- Change the name of the Sheet1 worksheet to "CI on Pi."

- Enter labels so that your worksheet looks like the picture below. The larger labels are 14-point font and the smaller are in 10-point font. Adjust the column width so that the columns are wide enough to accommodate the 10-point labels. Allow the larger labels to continue to the unused adjacent cells.

	A	B	C	D	E
1	Sample Data			Confidence Interval	
2	n			standard error	
3	number of successes			confidence level	
4	proportion of successes			z value	
5				sampling error	
6				lower bound	
7				upper bound	

Consider the following problem:

A candy manufacturer wants to estimate the impact of an advertising campaign in a metropolitan area by measuring brand recognition for a new confection marketed for children. A random sample of 350 children from the area was chosen, and the children were asked if they knew of the new brand. Of these, 112 recognized the new brand. Based on this sample, provide a 95% confidence interval estimate of the proportion of all children in the area who would recognize the new brand.

- Enter the value of *n*, 350, in cell B2 and the number of successes, 112, in cell B3.

- Enter a formula in cell B4 that calculates p_s by dividing the number of successes by *n*. The diplayed value should be "0.32."

- Enter the formula in D2 to calculate the standard error as $\sqrt{\dfrac{p_s(1-p_s)}{n}}$. One way of doing this is to use the Edit Formula button and display the dialog window from the SQRT function ("Math & Trig" category). Enter the expression for $\dfrac{p_s(1-p_s)}{n}$ in the "Number" argument field. Be sure to include the parentheses, and remember that multiplication must be shown explicitly with "*." If the formula is entered correctly, the displayed value will be "0.024934."

- Enter "95%" (without quotes) in cell E3. Be sure to include the percent sign, which will cause Excel to interpret the value as 0.95.

The *z* value in cell E3 is the absolute value of the boundaries of a region in the center of the standard normal distribution whose area is given in cell E2. This is illustrated in the picture below. The shaded central region has an area equal to the confidence level. The two boundaries are labeled *z* and –*z*. Both have the same absolute value, and it is the positive value that is needed in E3.

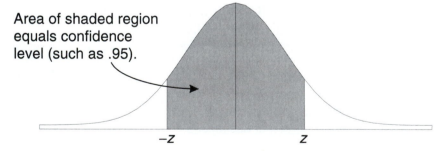

Area of shaded region equals confidence level (such as .95).

–z   z

Determining the *z* value requires using the NORMSINV function. Remember that the "probability" argument wants that probability corresponding to the area to the *left* of the *z* value the function returns and provides the *z* value for which the area to the left in the density function equals the "probability" argument. There are two different ways of doing this. One way would be to enter an expression for the "probability" argument that would calculate the area of the left tail from the value of E2. This is a simple expression, but the value returned by NORMSINV would be –*z*, a negative number. This means the formula in

E4 would have to convert the negative value provided by NORMSINV to a positive value, perhaps by using another negative sign in front of NORMSINV. Another way would involve putting an expression in the "probability" argument that adds the area of the central region to the area of the left tail. That sum is the area to the left of the positive z value on the right in the picture. With this area for a probability, NORMSINV would return the positive z value.

- Enter a formula in cell E4 that will determine the z value for the confidence level in E3. With 95% in E3, the displayed value will be "1.959961." Be sure this is displayed as a positive number.

- The sampling error is the product of the z value (in E4) and the standard error (in E2). Enter the formula in E5 to calculate this. This displayed value will be "0.04887."

- The lower bound is the value of p_s minus the sampling error, and the upper bound is p_s plus the sampling error. Enter the formulas in cells E6 and E7, respectively. The displayed values will be 0.27113 and "0.36887."

The 95% confidence interval on the proportion of all children in the area who recognize the brand name is between 0.27113 and 0.36887.

▼Determining Sample Size for a Desired Sampling Error

Larger samples generally result in narrower confidence intervals. Although it's desirable for confidence intervals to be as narrow as possible, sample size is usually the primary factor determining the cost of a statistical study. As a result, it is not uncommon for researchers to want to know how big a sample will be required to obtain a confidence interval of a certain width or a certain sampling error (the sampling error is half the width of the confidence interval).

The formula for the sampling error is $e = z\sqrt{\dfrac{\pi(1-\pi)}{n}}$, although p_s must ultimately be used in place of π. Solving for n yields: $n = \pi(1-\pi)\left(\dfrac{z}{e}\right)^2$.

When the value of n obtained from this formula is not an integer, the convention is to round *up* to the next larger integer.

Since the sample size determination must be made prior to selecting the sample, we generally do not have a value for π or even a value for p_s. This situation is analogous to that faced when determining the sample size required for a given confidence interval on a population mean. In that case, it was σ that was unknown. The problem here turns out not to be as difficult as it was in that case, however. Unlike σ, π is bounded—its value must be between 0 and 1. Once the confidence level (which determines z) and the desired sampling error are determined, the value of n is determined by $\pi(1 - \pi)$. The closer π is to 0.50, the larger this expression.

If we have no idea of the actual value of π, we simply use the value 0.50. The sample size we would calculate from this value might be too large—which means the actual sampling error obtained from the sample cannot possibly be larger than the desired value. It's better to discover that your estimate is more accurate than you expected rather than less accurate. On the other hand, if we are certain that π cannot possibly equal 0.50, choosing another value which is still closer to 0.50 than π will reduce the calculated value of n (thus saving money), and *still* ensure a sampling error no larger than the desired level.

- Change the name of the Sheet2 worksheet to "n" and switch to it.

- Enter labels in your worksheet so that it looks like the picture below.

	A	B	C
1	Sample Size Determination		
2	guess pi		
3	confidence level		
4	desired sampling error		
5	z		
6	n1		
7	n		

Consider the following problem:

A computer manufacturer wants to survey individuals who have bought a new model of a home computer to determine the proportion who report that they are satisfied with their purchase. For past models, the proportion has always been at least 80%. The manufacturer has strong reason to believe that no fewer than 70% could possibly report being satisfied. If the manufacturer wants to be able to estimate a 99% confidence interval with a sampling error of ±2%, how big a sample would be required?

Since the data in this problem are expressed as percentages, we will enter them in Excel as percentages. Remember that to Excel the difference between a percentage and a proportion is formatting, so that entering a number with a percent sign causes the actual number stored in the cell to be the corresponding proportion.

The value used for π should be that value which is reasonable and closest to .50. Based on the information in the problem, it appears that values between .7 and .8 (or more) are reasonable. Of these, .7 is the closest to .5.

- Enter "70%" as the value of π in cell B2 and "99%" as the confidence level in cell B3. Enter "2%" for the sampling error in cell B4.

The z value needed in cell B5 is the same type of z value used in the previous worksheet. It is the absolute value of the boundaries of the central region of a normal density function whose area equals the confidence level.

- Enter a formula in cell B5 that will determine the z value for the confidence level in B3. With 99% in B3, cell B5 should display the value "2.575835."

Cell B6 will contain the formula for n shown on page 277. The value obtained from this formula will not be an integer, although the sample size must be an integer. We will put the next larger integer in B7.

- Enter the Excel formula that will calculate $\pi(1-\pi)\left(\dfrac{z}{e}\right)^2$. In place of π, z, and e, you will use cell references to their locations in the worksheets. Remember that you must explicitly tell Excel where to multiply by using Excel's multiplication symbol ("*"). To square a number (or raise it to any other power), you use the exponentiation symbol, "^." The value that should be displayed in B6 is "3483.335."

- Enter the next larger integer in cell B7. That should be "3484." There are functions in Excel which will automatically round a number up to the nearest integer. If you want to experiment with one, try the ROUNDUP function ("Math & Trig" category). The "Num_digits" argument refers to the number of digits to the right of the decimal point to which you want the number rounded. To round up to the next integer, this value should be 0.

Remember that the sample size is the primary factor determining the cost of a statistical study. Let's see how some of the factors determined by the computer manufacturer in this problem affect the sample size.

What effect does the sampling error have on the sample size? Smaller sampling errors mean more precise estimates, so the computer manufacturer would like them to be as small as possible.

- Change the sampling error from 2% to 1%. The needed sampling size will shoot up to 13,934.

Reducing the sampling error by half approximately quadruples the sample size. The value of n (before rounding up) will exactly quadruple.

- Change the value of π from 70% to 30%. Notice this has no effect on the size of n.

Since π enters the determination of n only through the expression $\pi(1-\pi)$, there is no difference between using 70% (.70) and 30% (which is $1-.70$). In both cases the value .70 will be multiplied by the value .30.

Change π to 50%. The required size of n will increase. Can you find another value for π that will increase n further?

- Change the confidence level from 99% to 90%. The lower confidence level reduces the required sample size by more than half to 6764 ($\pi = 50\%$).

▼Hypothesis Tests on a Population Proportion

When the normal approximation is used for the distribution of sample proportions, hypothesis tests on a population proportion are very similar to hypothesis tests on a population mean. Somewhat greater accuracy can be achieved by converting a hypothesis test on a population proportion to a binomial problem and using the binomial distribution. Without computers it would be quite difficult to use the binomial approach, and few textbooks cover it for this reason. With Excel, the binomial distribution is no more difficult to use than any other probability distribution. Since it is the traditional approach, the normal approximation for the distribution of sample proportions will be explored first.

▼Hypothesis Tests on π Using the Normal Approximation

- Switch to the Sheet3 worksheet and change its name to "Hyp Test on pi."

- Put labels on your worksheet as shown in the picture at the top of the next page.

Let's consider the following problem:

An airline has established an on-time goal that requires that at least 95% of its flights will arrive on time. A random sample of 120 flights for the current week was chosen, and 110 of those flights arrived on time. Is there evidence at the .05 level of significance that the goal is not being met?

	A	B
1	x	
2	n	
3	ps	
4	Hypothesized pi	
5	standard error	
6	sample z	
7	approx p value	
8	significance level	
9	critical z	

The first step, as in all hypothesis-testing problems, is to formulate the Null and Alternate Hypotheses. As before, the Alternate Hypothesis expresses the situation for which you are looking for evidence:

$$H_0 : \pi \geq .95 \text{ and } H_A : \pi < .95$$

This is a one-tail test. The next step is to determine whether the sample is consistent with the Null Hypothesis. It would be consistent if the proportion of planes that arrived on time in the sample were greater than or equal to .95.

- Enter the number of successes (110) for this problem in cell B1 and the value for *n* (120) in cell B2.

- Enter the formula in cell B3 which will calculate $p_s = \dfrac{x}{n}$. The displayed value should be "0.91667."

Since .91667 < .95, the sample is *not* consistent with the Null Hypothesis. We must then determine whether this low sample proportion might reasonably be due to chance. Similar to the case of a hypothesis test on a population mean, this is done by determining the answer to the following question: "If the Null Hypothesis were true, what is the probability that a sample this size would have a sample proportion at least as far from what was expected as this sample?" If that probability is low (less than the significance level), we conclude that chance is not a reasonable explanation, and the Null Hypothesis is rejected. If that probability exceeds the significance level, we conclude that chance might be the explanation and fail to reject the Null Hypothesis. In assuming that the Null Hypothesis is true, we assume that $\pi = .95$, since this is the value given by the Null most likely to result in a sample proportion less than .95. If $\pi = .95$, we would also expect (in the statistical sense) that $p_s = .95$.

- Enter the value for the population proportion assuming the Null Hypothesis is true in cell B4.

- Enter the formula in cell B5 that will calculate the standard error, the standard deviation of sample proportions, σ_{p_s}, using the formula on page 274. Since this is the standard error assuming the Null Hypothesis is true, use the hypothesized population proportion in B4 for π rather than the sample proportion. The displayed value should be "0.0199."

- In cell B6 calculate the sample z from the formula $z = \dfrac{p_s - \mu_{p_s}}{\sigma_{p_s}}$. As shown by the formula on page 274, $\mu_{p_s} = \pi$. Use the hypothesized value for π in cell B2. The displayed value should be "-1.67542."

The p value is the probability that a standard normal random variable will have a value less than -1.67542. NORMSDIST is the correct function to use here. Recall that NORMSDIST takes a z value and returns the area to the left, which, since the z value is negative, is the one-tail p value.

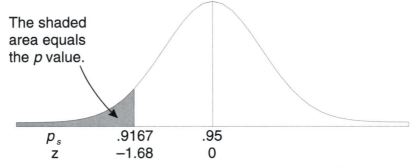

The shaded area equals the p value.

p_s	.9167	.95
z	−1.68	0

- Enter the formula in cell B7 to calculate the p value. The displayed value should be "0.04693."

- To use the critical value approach, enter the significance level, .05, in cell B8. In cell B9 enter a formula which will determine the value that has the property that the probability of a z value being smaller exactly equals the significance level. The displayed value should be "-1.64485."

Based on the information on the worksheet, it appears that if the Null Hypothesis were true, the probability of picking a random sample of flights with such a low proportion of on-time flights is less than the significance level. Since the (one-tailed) p value is less than the significance level, the Null Hypothesis should be rejected. The same result can be deduced from the fact that the absolute value of the sample z exceeds the (one-tailed) critical z. Our conclusion is, "Yes, there is evidence at the .05 level of significance that the airline's on-time goal is not being met."

This conclusion that there is evidence the airline is not achieving 95% on-time performance is based on the normal distribution approximating the binomial, and the approximation could be a source of error. The fact that the p value is so close to the significance level (which also means that the absolute value of the sample z is so close to the critical z) is a source of concern. This sample is so close to the "Reject"/"Fail to Reject" margin, that we cannot have great confidence in any conclusion. We can, however, eliminate the error associated with the normal approximation by using the binomial distribution to analyze this problem.

▼Using the Binomial Distribution to Test Hypotheses on π

Reread the problem on page 280. If $\pi \geq .95$, the number of on-time flights is unexpectedly low. The p value should tell us the probability that, if the Null were true, a sample of this size could be chosen at random with a number of on-time flights as unexpected or more unexpected than the number in this sample. In other words, if the probability of a single flight being on time is .95, what is the probability that in 120 flights the number of on-time flights would be 110 or less?

If the probability of a flight's being on time is independent (which was implicitly assumed in using the normal approximation), the number of on-time flights in a sample of 120 is binomially distributed. If the normal distribution is used to approximate the binomial, the probability is 0.046926, the same as the one-tail p value obtained using the normal distribution as an approximation for the distribution of sample proportions. Suppose we use the binomial distribution directly.

- Enter the label "exact p value" in cell A10.

Excel's BINOMDIST function gives us probabilities for the binomial distribution. In this particular problem, since the sample x is lower than the Null Hypothesis would have led us to expect, the p value is the probability of the number of successes being less than or equal to the sample x. In other words, it is the cumulative probability of x.

- Select cell B10. Enter a formula using BINOMDIST. The number of successes should refer to the sample x (110 in B1). The number of trials should refer to the sample n (120 in B2). Since we always calculate the p value assuming the Null Hypothesis is true, the probability of success on a single trial is the hypothesized value of π (.95 in B4). The "Cumulative" argument should be set equal to "true," since we want the cumulative probability of 110. Click OK. The displayed value should be "0.07863."

The value displayed in cell E14 is the exact (one-tailed) p value for this problem.

In some hypothesis tests of a population proportion, the expected number of successes will be less than those obtained in the sample. Assuming the sample is not consistent with the Null Hypothesis, a one-tail p value would be the binomial probability that another sample would have a number of successes greater than or equal to the number in this sample. To enable this worksheet to be used for these problems it will be necessary to calculate that binomial probability. This can be determined by calculating one minus the cumulative probability of the number of successes being one less than the number of successes in this sample. In other words, the probability of 110 successes *or more* is one minus the probability of 109 successes *or less*.

- Enter the formula in cell E15 that will calculate the binomial probability of a number of successes greater than or equal to the value given in cell B14. The number of trials and the probability of success on each trial are the same for this calculation as they were for the previous calculation. The value displayed in cell E15 should be "0.96155."

The one-tail p value for any problem will be either the value in cell E14 or the value in cell E15. How can we know which is the correct one? Unless the number of successes in the sample happens to be exactly the expected number, one of those two values will be less than .5 and the other will be greater than .5. If the number of successes in the sample is not consistent with the Null Hypothesis, the p value must be less than .5. As was the case with hypothesis tests on a population mean, the worksheet can't determine if the sample is or is not consistent with the Null. If the sample is consistent, there is no need to calculate a p or critical value because the Null Hypothesis cannot be rejected. Our calculation of the p value can, therefore, reasonably assume that the sample is *not* consistent with the Null Hypothesis.

- Enter a formula in cell H14 that gives that cell the value in E14 if E14 is smaller than E15, and the value in E15 otherwise. The value displayed in cell H14 should be ".07863." This is the exact one-tail p value for this problem.

What is our conclusion with this p value? Unlike the approximate p value obtained with the normal approximation, the exact p value exceeds the significance level. Therefore we would fail to reject the Null Hypothesis and conclude, "No, there is not evidence that the proportion of all planes arriving on time is less than .95."

▼Which Approach Is Correct, Binomial or Normal?

With different results from the binomial and normal approximation, it is natural to ask, "Which approach is correct?"

The answer, of course, is that the p value determined by the binomial approach, .07863, is correct, not the p value determined by the normal approximation approach, .046926. The latter value is an *approximation* of the former, not a very good approximation since the error is over half the approximate value. Why was the error so bad?

As we explored in the chapter on the normal distribution, the normal distribution approximates the binomial best if n is large and if π is close to 0.5. The value of π for this problem, 0.95, seems far from 0.5, but many textbooks give the rule of thumb that it is safe to use the normal approximation if $n \times \pi > 5$ and $n \times (1 - \pi) > 5$. The values for this problem met that test.

Another factor that caused the normal approximation to lead to the wrong conclusion in this problem is that the p value is close to the significance level. Had the p value been further in value from the significance level, the error involved with the normal approximation might not have mattered.

In most cases, using the normal approximation will result in the correct conclusion in hypothesis tests on a population proportion. The reason that approximation has been so widely used is that, prior to the computer, statisticians had to rely on tables to convert between values of a random variable and a probability, and the normal (z) tables are generally far more complete and shorter than binomial tables. With computers (and programs like Excel), it is an anachronism to continue using the normal approximation when more precise answers can be obtained from the binomial distribution.

▼Determining Other p Values from the Binomial Distribution

The use of the binomial distribution to calculate the p value for a hypothesis test on a population proportion will fall into one of three different categories:

1. One-tail p value when the Null Hypothesis has a "$\geq$." In this case, if the sample is inconsistent with the Null, it will be because the sample x is smaller than the Null Hypothesis would have led us to expect. In

this case, the p value is the cumulative probability of x. This was the case for the problem just discussed.

2. One-tail p value when the Null Hypothesis has a "≤." In this case the sample x will be larger than the Null would have led us to expect. The p value in this case will be the probability of drawing a sample the same as the sample in hand and having a number of successes which is greater than or equal to the sample x.

3. Two-tail p value when the Null Hypothesis has a "=." In this case you must determine whether the sample x is unexpectedly large or small. Then calculate a one-tail p value as in the first or second case above. That value is then doubled to give a two-tail p value.

Let's look at examples of these cases. In these problems will we focus on using only BINOMDIST to determine the exact p value.

• Click the colum B column heading and press the Delete key. This will erase all of the entries in column B.

Consider this problem:

A manufacturer of circuit boards has a quality goal requiring that the proportion of manufactured boards which are defective be .005 or less. As part of ongoing testing, 800 boards were selected. Of these, 8 were found to be defective. At the .05 level of significance, is there evidence that the proportion of all boards which are defective exceeds .005?

The Null and Alternate Hypotheses are:

$$H_0 : \pi \le .005$$

$$H_A : \pi < .005$$

• Enter the values for x and n in B1 and B2. Enter the formula in B3 to calculate the value of p_s. The displayed value should be ".01." Enter the hypothesized value for π (.005) in B4.

Since .01 > .005, this sample is not consistent with the Null Hypothesis. Therefore we must calculate the p value. In this case the value of the sample x is higher than would be expected if the Null were true. A more unexpected sample would have an even larger x value. Therefore we must calculate $P(x \ge 8)$. This can be done using cumulative probabilities using a technique that was explored in the section beginning on page 125. A cumulative probability tells us the probability that x is less than or equal to a given value. It can be used in this case by calculating one minus the appropriate cumulative probability. If x is not greater than or equal to 8 it is less than 8. But to use a cumulative probability, we must use what x is less than or equal to, not what it is less than. Since x must be an integer, if it is less than or equal to 8, it is less than 7.

- Select cell B10. Enter the Excel formula to calculate one minus the cumulative probability of seven using BINOMDIST. Use the sample values of x and n and the hypothesized value of π. The displayed value should be "0.05069."

Fail to Reject the Null Hypothesis because the p value exceeds the significance level. No, at the .05 level of significance there is not evidence that the proportion of all boards which are defective exceeds .005.

- Click column B's heading and press the Delete key to prepare the worksheet for the next problem.

Consider this problem:

Twenty years ago a large state university administered a math proficiency exam to its incoming freshmen and determined that the proportion who entered with a knowledge of calculus equal to that of students who had taken one semester of college calculus was .098. This year the college has decided to test a sample of 156 randomly chosen freshmen to see if there is evidence that this proportion had changed. Of the 156 freshmen, 20 scored as high on the test as the average student who completed one semester of college calculus. At the .05 level of significance, is there evidence the proportion of all freshemen with this level of calculus knowledge differs from .098?

If π represents the proportion of all entering freshmen whose knowledge of calculus is equivalent to a one-semester college course, the Null and Alternate hypotheses are:

$$H_0 : \pi = .098$$
$$H_A : \pi \neq .098$$

- Enter the sample values of x and n in cells B1 and B2. Enter the hypothesized value of p in B4. Enter the formula in B3 which will calculate p_s. B3 should display "0.12821."

Since this is a two-tail test, it is highly unlikely the sample will be consistent with the Null Hypothesis. Is x higher or lower than expected? Since p_s is greater than the hypothesized p, x must be higher than expected. To calculate the p value, we must determine the probability a sample of this size would have a value of x greater than or equal to this sample's (20) and then multiply that probability by 2.

- Select cell B10. Enter a formula which starts "=2*(" Inside the parenthesis just opened, enter an expression to determine $P(x \geq 20)$.

This will be calcuated as one minus the cumulative probability of 19. The displayed value should be "0.25972."

Since the p value exceeds the significance level, we conclude that the large x value could have happened by chance and fail to reject the Null Hypothesis. No, there is not evidence at the .05 level of significance that the proportion of all freshmen who enter with a calculus knowledge equal to one class in college calculus differs from .098.

▼Exercises

For the hypothesis-testing questions, state the Null and Alternate Hypotheses and determine the approximate p value using the normal distribution as well as the precise p value using the binomial distribution. Indicate whether or not you reject the Null Hypothesis and provide a "yes" or "no" answer to the question asked.

1. A large magazine wants to estimate the proportion of readers who are female. How large a sample would be needed to provide a 95% confidence interval estimate with a sampling error of ±1.00%?

2. A surreptitious survey at a convenience store revealed that out of 120 persons purchasing cigarettes, 43 appeared to be under the age of 27. Using these data as a random sample, calculate a 90% confidence interval estimate on the proportion of all cigarette purchasers at the store who appear to be under 27.

3. A political polling firm has conducted a poll to measure support for the incumbent political candidate. Out of 1,243 randomly selected voters likely to vote in the next election, 560 indicated an intention to vote for the candidate. Based on this survey, provide a 95% confidence interval estimate of the proportion of the entire electorate who will vote for the incumbent. What sample size should the firm choose next time if they wished to reduce the sampling error to ±1.5%?

4. A soft-drink manufacturer is considering introducing a new soft drink by dispensing free samples at grocery stores. Some grocery store shoppers, however, are known to refuse to accept free samples. The manufacturer wants to determine if there is evidence of a difference between the proportion of weekday shoppers who will accept free samples versus the proportion of weekend shoppers who will accept samples. A random sample of 375 weekday shoppers are selected and 290 are found to accept free samples. A random sample of 346 weekend shoppers are selected and and 284 are found to accept free samples. Construct a 95% confidence interval of the proportion

of all weekday and all weekend shoppers who will accept samples. Based on these intervals, would you say there is good evidence of a difference between the proportion of the two groups of shoppers who accept free samples?

5. A grocer wants to determine the proportion of apples in a shipment which have spoiled and cannot be sold. He randomly selects 250 apples from the shipment and finds 42 to be spoiled. Determine a 99% confidence interval estimate of the proportion of apples in the entire shipment that have spoiled. Suppose he wished to reduce the sampling error to ±.05. Estimate the required sample size.

6. The tourist office of a Caribbean island wants to issue tourists a guarantee that in a 14-day stay, at least 12 days will be sunny. To determine if this is feasible, 150 days during the tourist season are monitored. 125 of them were sunny. Determine a 90% confidence interval estimate for the proportion of all days during the tourist season that are sunny.

7. The management of a baseball stadium is interested in determining whether or not a new ad campaign has been successful in convincing more than 20% of people attending a game to purchase hot dogs. A sample of 200 people at the game was surveyed, and 33 reported having bought hot dogs. At the .05 level of significance, is there evidence that the ad campaign was successful?

8. An advertising firm wants to determine the proportion of children aged 10 to 15 who report that Coke is their favorite soft drink. They want to be able to develop a 95% confidence interval estimate on this proportion with a sampling error of at most ±.015. The firm is uncertain about what that proportion will be; past studies have found values ranging between .40 and .70. How large a sample should the firm choose? Report the effect of the assumed value of the true proportion by answering this question for the following assumed values for π: .40, .50, .60, and .70. If the firm has no idea which value is correct, which would you recommend they use and why?

9. An administrator of an institution that was previously a women's college and is now coeducational claims that at least half of the current students are male. A random sample of 200 students was selected, and 90 of them were male. At the .05 level of significance, is there evidence that the administrator's claim is invalid?

10. A city council wants to estimate the impact that a local professional hockey team has on the local economy by estimating the proportion of fans attending a game who live outside of the county in which the city is located. A random sample of 150 fans was chosen, and 25 of

these were found to live outside the county. Based on this result, provide a 99% confidence interval estimate on the proportion of all fans who live outside the county.

11. A manufacturing firm's quality control process involves measuring the proportion of product coming off a particular assembly line that is defective. Quality standards require that that proportion be no higher than .005. If evidence indicates that the proportion of defectives is higher than that amount, the equipment used on that assembly line may be failing and the line must be stopped and the equipment must be inspected. A random sample of 500 product items was taken off the line, and four of them were found to be defective. At the .05 level of significance, should the firm stop the line and inspect its equipment?

12. A confidential survey of all seniors attending a particular university 20 years ago found that 29% of them admitted to having cheated at some point in their college career. In order to determine if there has been a change in behavior, the student newspaper interviewed a random sample of 120 seniors and found that 24 of those admitted to having cheated at some point in their college career. At the .05 level of significance, is there evidence that the proportion of seniors who admit to having cheated has changed from the value found 20 years ago?

13. The management of a baseball stadium is interested in determining whether a new ad campaign has been successful in convincing more than 20% of people attending a game to purchase hot dogs. A sample of 200 people at the game were surveyed and 49 reported having bought hot dogs. At the .05 level of significance, is there evidence that the ad campaign was successful?

14. An automobile manufacturer wants to determine if the proportion of new car customers who would be willing to spend $500 for side impact air bags differs from .40. A sample of 185 new car customers were chosen; 61 of them were willing to spend $500 for side impact air bags. Does this provide evidence at the .05 level of significance that the proportion of all new car customers willing to spend $500 for side impact air bags differs from .40?

15. A light bulb supplier guarantees that no more than 1% of the bulbs it sells are defective. When a new manufacturer offers to provide bulbs at a good price, the supplier selects a random sample of 300 of the manufacturer's bulbs and tests them. Six are found to be defective. At the .05 level of significance, does the supplier have evidence that more than 1% of all the manufacturer's bulbs are defective?

Chapter 11

▼

Inferences on a Population Variance

In Chapter 7 we considered the problem of determining the required sample size to achieve a desired sampling error for a confidence interval on a population mean. In order to determine the sample size, it is necessary to have some information about the population standard deviation. One way this might be done is through a pilot study. In such a study a sample is drawn and from that sample an inference about the population standard deviation is made. (Since the standard deviation is simply the square root of the variance, the same inferences can be applied either to a population variance or standard deviation.)

Quality control is another area where inferences about a population variance are important. In any production process some degree of process deviation is inevitable. Maintaining high quality requires that variability be kept within acceptable limits. Consider, for example, a firm that manufactures cables used in airplanes to control the flight control surfaces, such as the ailerons, rudder, and elevator. If one of these cables were to break, it could have serious consequences for the pilot's ability to control the airplane. We would naturally expect that an important dimension of quality in these cables would be their strength. The manufacturer of the cables will undoubtedly have an ongoing quality control program involving sampling cable from the manufacturing process and testing the strength of the sample cable. From such a sample, inferences on the mean strength of all cable can be made, ensuring that the average strength of all cable is sufficient for the job.

Ensuring that the cable is sufficiently strong, *on average*, is not enough. Even if the average strength is sufficient, if the variance in the strength of the cable is large, some of the cable that is manufactured will be far stronger than needed, while other cable will be too weak. If your airplane happened to be the one whose cables broke because they were too weak, you would probably not be consoled by the knowledge that the *average* strength of all the cable made by that manufacturer was sufficient! The way for the manufacturer to avoid this is to monitor not only the average strength but also the *variance* of the strength of the cable being manufactured. If the variance is kept low enough (and the mean is kept high enough), the manufacturer can be reasonably assured that *all* the cable is strong enough to depend on.

The standard procedure for inferences on a population variance differs from the others we have seen. Rather than being based on the sampling distribution of the variance, it is based on the sampling distribution of another statistic. This statistic is called the "chi-square" statistic and is calculated according to the following formula: $\chi^2 = \dfrac{(n-1)s^2}{\sigma^2}$.

In this formula, s^2 is a sample variance, which, like all sample statistics, is a random number. Since s^2 is random, so is χ^2. Under the restrictive assumption that the population is normally distributed, the distribution of the χ^2 random number is easier to work with than would be the distribution of the s^2 random number, and this is the reason for its use. Notice that χ^2 cannot be negative, since both s^2 and σ^2 must be positive and, since n cannot be less than 1, $(n-1)$ must also be positive.

If the population is normally distributed, the chi-square statistic follows a distribution that is called the *chi-square* distribution. The same term is used to refer to the statistic and to the distribution. The chi-square distribution has only a single variable—the degrees of freedom. The degrees of freedom for the problems we will be concerned with will always be $n-1$, where n is the size of the sample.

Excel has two built-in functions for using the chi-square distribution, CHIDIST and CHIINV. CHIDIST converts a value of the chi-square statistic to a probability, and CHIINV converts a probability to a value of the chi-square statistic. In this way they are like the NORMSDIST and NORMSINV functions (and TDIST and TINV). Unlike the normal distribution functions, the two chi-square functions are not cumulative. Whereas the NORMSDIST function gives the probability of a standard normal variable being *less than* the value given in its argument, the CHIDIST function gives the probability of a chi-square variable with the specified degrees of freedom being *greater* than the value given in its argument. Similarly, the NORMSINV function returns a z value for which the probability of a standard normal variable being *less* equals the probability given in the function's argument. The CHIINV function returns a χ^2 value for which the probability of the chi-square variable being *greater* equals the probability given in the function's argument.

There are a few other differences between using the chi-square distribution and the other continuous distributions we have investigated. Some of these differences will be easier to understand after examining the shape of the density function. We can do this by having Excel prepare a chart of the distribution function for very small intervals. This has the same shape as the density function.

- Start Excel with a new workbook and save it as "Chap11.xls."

- Rename the Sheet1 worksheet "Chart."

- Enter the series of numbers "0, 1, 2," etc., up to "100" in column A.

- Enter the label "DOF" in cell D1. Cell E1 will be used for the chi-square distribution's only variable, the degrees of freedom.

- Enter the number "25" in cell E1. This will be the first value for the degrees of freedom we will try.

Column B will be used to enter the probability of a chi-square variable having a value between the value given on the same row of column A and that of the previous row. For example, row 6 has "5" in column A. In column B we will enter a formula that will display the probability of a chi-square variable having a value between the "5" in A6 and the "4" in A5. One way of doing this is to subtract the probability of a chi-square variable being less than 4 (that is, the cumulative probability of 4) from the probability of a chi-square variable being less than 5. The difference is the probability of being between 4 and 5.

The CHIDIST function, however, is not cumulative. Rather than provide the probability of a chi-square variable being *less* than the value we give it, it provides the probability of a chi-square variable being *greater* than the value we give it. The probability that CHIDIST returns for the chi-square value of 4 will be greater than the probability it returns for the chi-square value of 5. To get the probability of being between 4 and 5, we do the opposite of what would be done with a cumulative probability function; that is, we subtract the probability associated with 5 from the probability associated with 4. Let's start with the value 1.

- Select cell B2. Click the Edit Formula button. Select the "CHIDIST" function ("Statistical" category).

The function has two arguments: "X" is the value for which the function will provide the probability of a chi-square variable being larger, and "Deg_freedom" is the degrees of freedom of the chi-square distribution for which we want the probability.

- In the "X" argument field enter a *relative* address reference to the cell in the previous row in column A. That cell contains a zero. In the "Deg_freedom" argument field, enter an *absolute* address reference to the cell where we have placed the degrees of freedom (initially, 25).

Notice that the function result, shown in the dialog window below the argument fields, is "1." The probability of a chi-square variable being greater than 0 is 1. Remember that a chi-square variable must be positive.

- Click the mouse pointer in the Formula Bar to the right of its current contents so that an insertion point appears at the end. Enter a minus sign.

- Click the CHIDIST button (most recently used function). A new CHIDIST dialog window will appear.

- This time, enter a *relative* address reference to the cell in the same row in column A (which contains the number "1"). Enter an *absolute* reference to the cell containing the degrees of freedom, as in the previous case. Although the value given this time ("1") is different from that given last time, the probability appearing in the "Value" field will again be "1." That value is actually very slightly less than 1, but so slight that Excel expresses it as a 1. Click the OK button. The value "6.36158E-14" will display in B2. This is an extremely small number, but still greater than 0.

- Copy the formula in cell B2 down to cell B101. Since the two uses of CHIDIST in the formula in cell B2 have relative addresses for "X," those addresses should change as the formula is copied. The address of the degrees of freedom, however, should not change since an absolute address was used in the "Deg_freedom" argument. If error values appear in the cells to which you copied the formula, check to be sure you have the correct cell references in B2.

We can treat the values in column A as chi-square values, and we will next chart the probabilities in column B against those values.

- Select the range A1:B101. Click the Chart Wizard button. Select "XY (Scatter)" from the "Standard" chart types. Choose the subtype shown on the bottom right, which will connect the data points with lines and without markers. Click the Next button twice.

- Use the Chart Wizard to add the title "chi-square Distribution" to the chart and to eliminate the legend. Click Finish.

- Position and resize the chart so that it lies just below the first row (so that you can see and change the value in E1 and so that the chart fills as much of the screen as possible). Reduce the font size of the values shown on the axis and of the title so as to increase the size of the plot.

Your worksheet should look much like the picture on the next page.

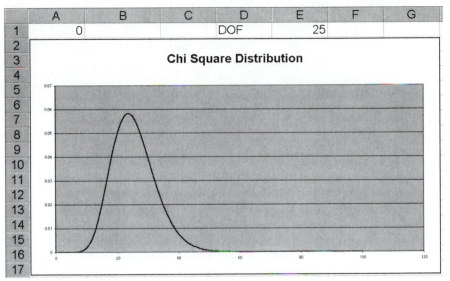

Notice that although the graph is bell-shaped, it is not symmetric. The degrees of freedom of the chi-square distribution is also the mean. The mean of the distribution on your screen is, therefore, 25.

Where exactly is the point on the graph directly above the mean? In the case of the normal and *t* distributions, the peak of the graph lies directly above the mean. To check whether this is also true of the chi-square distribution, let's have Excel put the vertical axis on the value 25.

- Click the mouse pointer on one of the values on the horizontal axis so as to select the horizontal axis. (When it is selected there will be "handles" on each end of the axis.) Open the Format menu on the Menu Bar (or click the right mouse button) and choose "Selected Axis."

- Click the "Scale" file folder tab.

- Change the "0" in the field labeled "Value (Y) Axis Crosses at " to "25." Set the "Maximum" value (in the second field) to "100." Click the OK button.

With the *y* axis drawn directly above 25, it is clear that the point on the graph directly above the mean is not at the peak but to the right of the peak. The positive or right skew of the chi-square distribution causes the extreme positive values to pull the mean to the right.

- Change the value for the degrees of freedom to other values. Try a number of values between 2 and 90. Change the position of the *y* axis so that it lies above the mean (the degrees of freedom) in each case. Pay attention to the effect these changes have on the apparent skewness of the chart and to the range of values for which the probabilities are clearly nonzero. You will notice that for larger values, not all of the density function will appear on your graph, given the range of chi-square values we are showing. The mean should always appear to the right of the plot's peak, but as the degrees of freedom increases, it should be closer.

The fact that the density function of the chi-square distribution is not symmetric and is not centered on zero will affect the nature of confidence intervals using this distribution.

▼Confidence Intervals on a Population Variance

- Rename the Sheet2 worksheet to "CI on Var" and switch to it.

- Enter labels so that your worksheet looks like the picture below.

	A	B	C	D
1	n			
2	s			
3	confidence level			
4				
5		chi square	variance	stdev
6	boundary 1			
7	boundary 2			

Consider the following problem:

A large bakery produces a national brand of cookies. Experience has shown that the temperature at which the cookies are baked affects their taste. It is important to maintain as little variation as possible in the baking temperature so as to maintain the consistency required of a national brand. A random sample of 25 batches of cookies was selected, and the standard deviation of the temperature at which those cookies were baked was 2.13°F. Based on this result, and assuming the distribution of temperatures is normal, construct a 95% confidence interval on the standard deviation in the baking temperature of all batches of cookies.

- Enter the values for *n*, the sample standard deviation, and the confidence level (as a proportion or with a percent sign) in cells B1:B3, respectively.

When we determined a confidence interval from a statistic that followed the normal or *t* distribution, the first step was to determine the *z* or *t* values corresponding to the confidence level desired. Similarly, when determining a confidence interval for a population variance or standard deviation, the first step is to determine the χ^2 values corresponding to the confidence level. For the *t* and *z* distributions, the two values always had the same absolute values and differed only in sign. This is not the case with the chi-square distribution, however.

Consider the chi-square density function in the illustration below, which shows the two values as χ_1^2 and χ_2^2. If these correspond to the values for the 95% confidence interval, the area of the white region between them must be .95. The area of each shaded tail region is .025. Unlike the case with the t and z distributions, the two values are not equidistant from the mean because the distribution is not symmetric.

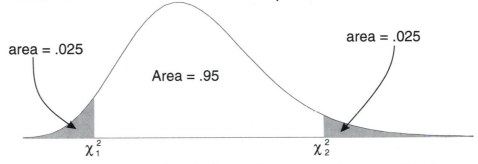

To find the values for χ_1^2 and χ_2^2, use the CHIINV function. This function requires that we provide it with the area to the *right* of the value it returns. For the 95% confidence interval, the area to the right of χ_2^2 is .025, and the area to the right of χ_1^2 is .95 + .025 = .975. We will need to provide CHIINV with expressions that will work even if the confidence level in cell E2 is changed. The central area is always equal to the level of confidence (expressed as a proportion). The sum of both tail areas is one minus the central area, and each tail is half the sum. The area to the right of χ_2^2 is the area of one tail. The area to the right of χ_1^2 can be calculated either as the area of the right tail plus the central area or as one minus the area of the left tail.

- Select cell E3, which will contain the formula to determine the value of χ_2^2. Click the Edit Formula button and select the CHIINV function in the "Statistical" category.

- The dialog window shows two arguments. In the "Probability" argument field, enter an expression that will calculate the area of the right tail in the picture on this page, given the confidence level (the area of the central region).

- In the "Deg_freedom" argument field, enter an expression that will subtract one from the sample size given on the worksheet. Click the OK button. The displayed value in cell E3 should be "39.36406."

- Select cell E4, click the Edit Formula button, and again select CHIINV. Enter an expression in the "Probability" argument field that will calculate the area to the right of from the confidence level in the worksheet. Enter the same expression in the "Deg_freedom" argument field used in E3. Click Finish. The value displayed in E4 should be "12.40115."

Taking the formula for the chi-square statistic on page 292 and solving for σ^2 gives: $\sigma^2 = \dfrac{(n-1)s^2}{\chi^2}$.

The sample data in the numerator of this formula are known for this problem. The confidence interval on σ^2 is found by evaluating the formula for each of the two chi-square values corresponding to the confidence level. Note that since we are dividing by the chi-square value, the *higher* confidence level limit is found when we use the *lower* chi-square value, and vice versa.

- Select cell B6. Enter the Excel formula that will calculate σ^2 according to the formula above, using the lower chi-square value in E4. Notice that the formula requires the sample variance (s^2), while the worksheet contains the sample standard deviation (s). The displayed value should be "8.780285."

- Select cell B7 and enter the Excel formula to calculate the lower bound of the confidence interval on the variance by using the higher chi-square value in E3. The displayed value should be "2.766117."

- Enter formulas in cells B8 and B9 that will determine the boundaries of the confidence interval on the population standard deviation. Each boundary is simply the square root of the corresponding variance boundary. The displayed values should be "2.963155" and "1.663165."

The 95% confidence interval on the variance of the temperature for all batches of cookies is 2.8 to 8.8, while the 95% confidence interval on the standard deviation of the temperature is approximately 1.7 to 3.0.

Check your worksheet by using it to solve the following problem:

A manufacturer of light bulbs is monitoring the life of 60-watt bulbs made under a new process. A sample of 150 bulbs was chosen, and the standard deviation in the life of those bulbs was 23.5 hours. Based on this result, and assuming the life of light bulbs is normally distributed, determine a 90% confidence interval on the standard deviation of all bulbs produced by that process.

Your worksheet should show that the 90% confidence interval is from 21.47137 hours to 25.99324 hours.

▼Hypothesis Tests on a Population Variance

Prepare a worksheet for hypothesis tests on a population variance.

- Switch to the Sheet3 worksheet and rename it "Hyp Test on Var."

- Enter labels on the worksheet so that it looks like the picture below.

	A	B
1	n	
2	s^2	
3	hypothesized sigma^2	
4	sample chi square	
5	p value	
6	significance level	
7	critical chi square	

Probably the most common hypothesis test on a population variance tests whether the variance has exceeded some target level. This is the type of test that would arise in quality control since the object there is to keep the variance as low as possible. The tests for whether a population variance is below a certain value or differs from a certain value (two-tail) is similar. We will develop a worksheet for all types of tests, but the first example will be a typical quality control-type problem.

A laundry detergent company packages its product in boxes labeled as containing 64 oz. Although some variation in the amount of detergent placed in each box is unavoidable, it is desirable for that variation to be kept as low as possible. If too much detergent is placed into the box, it may spill over and be wasted. If too little is placed into the box, customers may be unhappy and the company may face regulatory difficulties. Given the characteristics of current filling technology, a standard deviation in the amount of fill in each box of 1.6 ounces is normal and unavoidable. A higher standard deviation, however, indicates a problem with the process. In order to monitor the process, the firm carefully measures the amount of detergent in a random sample of 50 boxes chosen from each batch. In a recent sample, the measured sample standard deviation was 1.9 oz. At the .05 level of significance, does the company have evidence that the standard deviation in the fill of all boxes exceeds 1.6 oz?

The Null Hypothesis for this problem is $H_0 : \sigma \leq 1.6$, and the Alternate Hypothesis is $H_A : \sigma > 1.6$. For this sample, the sample standard deviation, s, is 1.9, which is greater than 1.6. Therefore, the sample is not consistent with the Null Hypothesis, and we have to determine if this might be due to chance.

As indicated by the labels, the worksheet we are developing is designed to accept standard deviations (rather than variances) as input. This is an essentially arbitrary choice, but is consistent with the wording of this problem, which refers to standard deviations rather than variances.

- Enter the values from the problem in the appropriate places in the worksheet. The value for σ from the Null Hypothesis goes in cell B2, the sample size and sample standard deviation go in cells E2 and E3, and the significance level goes in cell H2.

- Enter an Excel formula in cell E4 that will calculate the value of the chi-square statistic for this sample, assuming that σ has the value given by the Null Hypothesis (in B2). The formula for the chi-square statistic (χ^2) can be found on page 292. The value displayed in cell E4 should be "69.09766."

If the Null Hypothesis is true (interpreted as σ = 1.6), the expected value of a sample standard deviation would also be 1.6, and the expected value of the chi-square statistic would be 49 (the degrees of freedom or $n - 1$). The probability that a sample would have a sample standard deviation of 1.9 or more is the same as the probability that a sample would have a chi-square statistic of 69.09766 or more. That probability is the *p* value and can be determined by using the CHIDIST function. The *p* value equals the shaded area of the graph of the density function (shown below) for the chi-square distribution with 49 degrees of freedom.

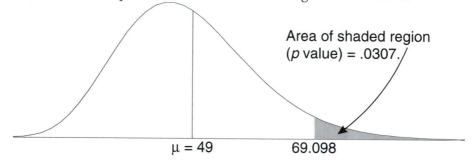

Area of shaded region
(*p* value) = .0307.

μ = 49   69.098

- Select cell B7. Click the Edit Formula button and choose "CHIDIST." Since the CHIDIST function returns the probability of a chi-square statistic *greater* than that given as the "X" argument, the cell address of the sample chi-square statistic should be put in the "X" argument field. The "Deg_freedom" field should contain an expression that will calculate $n - 1$. The value displayed as the *p* value should be "0.030749."

Since this *p* value is less than the significance level, we conclude that this sample could not have been drawn from a population described by the Null Hypothesis (with σ = 1.6). The Null Hypothesis is rejected. "Yes, there is evidence that the standard deviation in the fill of all boxes exceeds 1.6 oz." The company should investigate the package-filling process to determine what has gone wrong.

The test could also be done using a critical value. For this problem, the critical chi-square would be the value for which the probability of a greater chi-square exactly equals the significance level. To convert the significance level (a probability) to a chi-square value, use the CHIINV function.

- Select cell F7, click the Edit Formula button, and select the "CHIINV" function. The "Probability" argument field should have the address of the significance level, and the "Deg_freedom" field should contain an expression that will calculate $n-1$ as before. The critical chi-square for this problem is 66.33865, which should display in cell F7.

The rejection region lies above 66.33865. Since the sample chi-square (69.09766) is greater, and therefore is in the rejection region, the critical value approach (as it must) also leads to a rejection of the Null Hypothesis, the same conclusion found with the p value.

▼Two-Tail Test on Population Standard Deviation (or Variance)

Although this is not generally the concern of quality control, suppose the question to be determined was whether or not the sample provided evidence at the .05 level of significance that the standard deviation of detergent fill was *different* from 1.6 oz. In this case the Null Hypothesis would be $H_0: \sigma = 1.6$, and the Alternate Hypothesis would be $H_A: \sigma \neq 1.6$. This Null Hypothesis could be rejected if the sample standard deviation was less than 1.6, while the one-tail test just considered could be rejected only if the sample standard deviation exceeded 1.6.

As in other hypothesis tests, the two-tail p value is twice the one-tail p value.

- Enter the formula in cell B8 that doubles the one-tail p value in cell B7.

Since the two-tail p value is .061499, which exceeds .05, we Fail to Reject the two-tail Null Hypothesis. It may seem puzzling that at the same significance level we can find evidence that the population standard deviation *exceeds* 1.6 oz, but we can't find evidence that it *differs* from 1.6. Remember, though, that a sample with a standard deviation below 1.6 could not possibly lead to the conclusion that the population standard deviation exceeds 1.6 oz but could lead to the conclusion that the population standard deviation differs from 1.6 oz. The significance level is the probability of committing Type I error. *If* the true population standard deviation is 1.6 (the Null Hypothesis is true), the probability of incorrectly rejecting that Null will be .05 for both one- and two-tail cases.

Determining the critical chi-square values for a two-tail test is almost exactly the same as determining the chi-square values for a confidence interval. To translate a significance level to the corresponding confidence level, subtract it from 1. In this case, the significance level is 0.05. The critical chi-square values are the same as those for a $1 - 0.05 = 0.95$, or 95% confidence interval. Look at the diagram on page 297. The two values, shown there as χ_1^2 and χ_2^2, define two tails with equal areas that sum to 0.05. These are the critical chi-square values for a hypothesis test at the .05 significance level. The values can be determined by using the CHIINV function and providing that function with the area to the right of each critical value. The area to the right of χ_2^2 is half the significance level, 0.025. The area to the right of χ_1^2 is one minus half the significance level.

- Select cell F9. Use the CHIINV function to determine the upper critical value, χ_2^2, for the significance level and sample size entered on the worksheet. The value displayed in cell F9 should be "70.22236."

- Select cell F10 and use the CHIINV function to determine the value of the lower critical chi-square, χ_1^2. The displayed value should be "31.55493."

The critical chi-square values are 31.55493 and 70.22236. Since the sample chi-square, 69.09766, lies between these two values, the sample is not in the rejection region, and we would Fail to Reject the Null Hypothesis, the same result obtained with the two-tail p value.

▼Test on a Population Variance Being Below a Given Value

The remaining hypothesis test to consider is one in which we look for evidence that the population variance is below a given value. Consider the following problem:

The laundry detergent company is evaluating a new package-filling process developed by a group of its engineers. The new process promises to increase quality by reducing the standard deviation of the fill placed into each box. Under the old process, the standard deviation was 1.6 oz. The new process was put into operation and a random sample of 50 boxes filled by that process was chosen. The standard deviation in the fill of those 50 boxes was 1.35 oz. At the .05 level of significance, does the company have evidence that the standard deviation of all boxes filled by the new process is less than 1.6 oz?

The Null Hypothesis for this problem is $H_0: \sigma \geq 1.6$, and the Alternate Hypothesis is $H_A: \sigma < 1.6$. The sample standard deviation is 1.35, not consistent with the Null Hypothesis, so we have to determine if this could be due to chance.

- The only change in the values from the previous problem is the sample standard deviation. Change the appropriate cell in the worksheet to reflect this change.

The worksheet immediately updates. The correct sample chi-square value in this case is 34.88379, as is shown in the worksheet. The *p* value shown in the worksheet, "0.936075," is wrong, however. The situation is shown in the diagram below.

The *p* value for this problem is the probability that if the population variance equaled 1.6 oz (the Null Hypothesis were true), a sample of 50 boxes could be chosen whose sample variance by chance was 1.35 or less. This is identical to the probability that the sample's chi-square statistic would be 34.88379 or less. It is this probability that is illustrated in the diagram below of the density function of the chi-square statistic.

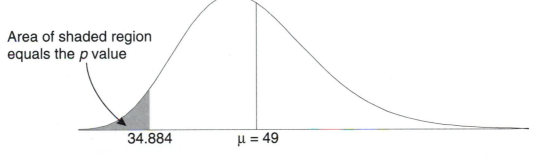

Area of shaded region equals the *p* value

34.884   μ = 49

Compare this diagram with that shown on page 300. In that case, the *p* value was equal to the area to the *right* of the sample chi-square. In this case, it is equal to the area to the *left* of the sample chi-square. The problem with the formula in cell E6 calculating the *p* value is that it is calculating the area to the right of 34.884 instead of the area to the left. The correct *p* value is not .936075 but 1 minus .936075.

In other words, the CHIDIST function returns the correct *p* value for problems like the previous one-tail problem where the *p* value is the area of a right tail. To get the *p* value for problems like this one, when a left-tail area is desired, we must calculate one minus the probability returned by CHIDIST. Is there a way we can enter a formula which will determine whether the *p* value is the value returned by CHIDIST or one minus the value returned by CHIDIST?

If we calculate both the area to the right of the sample chi-square (the value returned by CHIDIST), and the area to the left of the sample chi-square (one minus the value returned by CHIDIST), the correct value is always the smaller. As long as we remember that the *p* value given by the worksheet is only meaningful if the sample is not consistent with the Null Hypothesis, the *p* value can never exceed .5.

Excel has a built-in function, MIN ("Statistical" category), which takes two or more arguments and returns the value of the smallest. We can use this to have the correct formula for the *p* value chosen automatically.

- Select cell B7. Look at the expression in the Formula Bar. One of the arguments of MIN will be that expression, and the other will be one minus that expression. Use the mouse pointer to highlight the expression (don't include the equal sign) and click the Copy button on the Standard Toolbar.

- Erase the contents of cell B7. We are now ready to enter a new formula.

- With B7 selected, click the Edit Formula button, and select "MIN."

- The dialog box for MIN shows two arguments: "Number1" and "Number2." Click the mouse pointer in the "Number1" argument field and click the Paste button. In the value field to the right of the argument field you should see the number that used to be displayed in B7, "0.936075." This is the probability of a random chi-square variable *exceeding* the sample chi-square value.

- Click the mouse pointer in the "Number2" argument field. Notice how this causes a "Number3" argument field to appear (which we won't use). The MIN function doesn't have a fixed number of arguments, and whenever you use the last one in the dialog window, a new one will appear until the maximum of 30 arguments have been used.

In the "Number2" argument field, you should enter an expression that will calculate one minus the probability of a chi-square variable being greater than the sample chi-square.

- Begin the expression by entering "1-" (without quotes) in the "Number2" argument field. Click the Paste button. The number appearing in the value field is "0.063924595," which is 1 minus 0.936075405. This is the probability of a random chi-square variable being *less* than the sample chi-square value

- Click the OK button. Cell B7 will display the value "0.063925," which is the smaller of the values in each of MIN's arguments.

Since this p value exceeds the significance level, the Null Hypothesis is not rejected. The manufacturer does not have evidence at the .05 level of significance that the new filling process reduces the standard deviation (or variance) of the fill in all detergent boxes.

All that remains is to determine the critical chi-square value for the lower one-tail test. This is the chi-square value for which the area under the density function to the left of the value equals the significance level. Since CHIINV interprets the probability given it as the area to the right of the value it is to return, we must convert the significance level to the corresponding right area by subtracting 1.

- Select cell F8. Click the Edit Formula button and choose the "CHIINV" function. In the "Probability" field, enter an expression that calculates one minus the significance level. In the "Deg_freedom" field, enter an expression that calculates $n - 1$. Click OK. The value appearing in F8 is "33.93029."

Since the sample chi-square exceeds the critical chi-square, the sample does not lie in the rejection region.

▼Exercises

Close your current workbook. The workbook in "Exercises.xls" in the Chap_11 folder contains the data for these problems.

1. A detergent-box filling machine fills empty boxes with detergent. A sample of boxes filled by the machine was selected, and the weight of the detergent (in ounces) placed in each box was measured. The measurements are

   55.67, 47.28, 54.55, 48.19, 46.94, 52.34, 49.62, 51.48, 49.77, 49.71, 48.09, 49.78, 48.39, 49.81, 53.83, 48.41, 47.30, 46.68, 48.40, 48.85, 47.97, 49.98, 51.20, 51.57, 55.81

   Determine a 95% confidence interval for the standard deviation of the amount of detergent placed in each box in the population.

2. A bank office wished to estimate the amount of time required to approve a home equity line of credit measured from the original application. A sample of applications was selected, and the amount of time (in working days) required to approve each application was determined. The values are

   8, 16, 17, 12, 11, 16, 16, 21, 18, 11, 16, 18

Determine a 90% confidence interval for the variance of the amount of time required to approve all home equity lines of credit.

3. A ball-bearing manufacturer wants to determine the diameter of a particular ball bearing. A sample of bearings was selected, and the diameter of each bearing (in cm) was measured. Those numbers were

9.66, 8.34, 11.09, 9.53, 9.22, 10.10, 11.51, 10.13, 8.62, 9.62, 9.29, 10.66, 12.28, 10.06, 11.63, 9.42, 9.24, 9.31, 9.29, 11.75

Determine 99%, 95%, and 90% confidence intervals of the standard deviation.

4. A large university offers many sections of undergraduate statistics. A sample of sections for the past five years was chosen, and the section GPA was calculated. These data are

1.8, 1.8, 2.2, 2.4, 3.2, 1.6, 3.1, 3.0, 1.5, 2.4

Based upon these data, determine a 95% confidence interval for the variance in all sections' GPA's for the past five years.

5. A manufacturer of aircraft control cable makes a particular cable designed to have a breaking strength of 1,000 kg. A sample of cable was chosen and tested to determine breaking strength. The measured breaking strengths of the sample cables (in kg) were

996, 993, 990, 1010, 995, 989, 999, 1011, 981, 1000, 980, 994, 1003, 990, 999

Based upon these data, determine a 75% confidence interval estimate for the variance of the breaking strength of all cable.

6. A machine is designed to fill cereal boxes so that the average fill is 16 oz with a standard deviation of 1.1 oz. A sample of 15 boxes of cereal was selected and measured. The following measurements were recorded.

16.81, 11.18, 17.36, 14.55, 15.64, 17.29, 20.8, 17.26, 16.07, 14.86, 13.95, 14.51, 17.65, 14.91, 18.41

At the .01 level of significance, is there evidence that the machine is not meeting specifications with respect to variation?

7. Experience has shown that variability in the output of a bolt-making machine increases shortly before a machine failure. Amalgamated Bolts has determined that properly operating machines produce an average of 1,000 bolts per hour, with a variance of 25.0. In order to anticipate a possible breakdown, the output of each bolt-making machine is monitored. As part of this program, the output of one partic-

ular bolt-making machine was monitored this week during a random sample of 20 hours. The measurements were as follows:

1001, 1005, 997, 1000, 994, 1001, 999, 1006, 994, 1004, 998, 1000, 1001, 994, 996, 1000, 1008, 996, 994, 1002

Based on this sample, is there evidence at the .10 level of significance that this machine is about to break down?

8. A specialty light bulb used by the manufacturer of a computer projection system is supposed to have an average life of 200 hours with a standard deviation of 12 hours. A new supplier of the bulbs has promised the projection system manufacturer light bulbs that have less variation in their life. In order to test this, the projection system manufacturer selected a random sample of 12 bulbs and subjected them to testing. The lifetimes of the 12 bulbs were

180.6, 211.9, 175.1, 181.4, 196.5, 188.9, 206.3, 189.7, 223.3, 180.0, 211.3, 193.7

Based on this sample, does the projection system manufacturer have evidence (at the .05 level of significance) that supports the new supplier's claims?

The data for the following problems is found only on the Exercises.xls workbook.

9. A manufacturer of carabiners has a model whose specifications require that the average strength (gate closed) of all sold be at least 35 kilonewtons (kn) with a standard deviation of 5 kn or less. Is there evidence at the .01 level of significance that the standard deviation of the breaking strengths of all carabiners in the production batch exceeds 5 kn?

10. A bottle-filling machine is designed to fill soft-drink bottles with an average of 3.1 liters and a standard deviation of .05 liters. At the .10 level of significance, is there evidence that the standard deviation of the fill of all bottles filled by the machine exceeds .05 liters?

11. A manufacturer of climbing rope has a model whose designed strength is at least 27 kilonewtons with a variance of no more than 14. Based on the sample in the Prob 11 worksheet, is there evidence that the variance of the breaking strength of all ropes exceeds 14?

Chapter 12

Inferences on Two Population Means

All of the inferential statistics investigated so far have been *univariate*—they were concerned with only a single variable. Techniques that are concerned with more than a single statistic add an important dimension to inferential statistics—the investigation of relationships among two or more variables. The techniques explored in this chapter do not enable the investigation of as many different types of relationships as those in later chapters. The one type of relationship they do handle, however, is an important one: the relationship between the mean of an observation and which of two groups that observation is in. This is a relationship between two variables, one of which is discrete, with exactly two values, and the other of which is continuous.

All of the techniques considered here have certain features in common. There are always two samples, each drawn from a different population. A sample mean is computed from each of the two samples, and the difference between those two means is calculated. This difference is a random number, like all sample statistics considered earlier, and its distribution is used to make inferences about the difference between the two population means. These inferences can be either confidence intervals or hypothesis tests, but the Excel procedures we will examine have been created with hypothesis testing in mind. Although the hypothesized difference between the two population means can be any value, by far the most common value is 0. A Null Hypothesis with a difference of 0 between the means is appropriate for a question that asks, "Is there evidence of a difference in the two population means?" or, for the one-tail case, "Is there evidence that the mean of one of the populations exceeds the mean of the other?"

There are two different ways in which data can be collected for these tests, and they require different analysis techniques. One method is the *paired samples approach*, and the other method is the *independent samples approach*. In the paired sample approach, each observation in one sample is linked to a matching observation in the other sample. The observations are matched so that, ideally, they are identical in all characteristics that might affect the variable whose means are being compared *except* for the difference in the populations from which each is drawn. Since each observation in one sample is matched to an observation in the other sample, the two samples must be the same size. In the independent samples approach, no attempt to match characteristics between observations is made: The two samples are each randomly drawn from their respective populations. The samples may or may not be the same size.

It is always more difficult to select paired samples than independent samples, but the test for paired samples is more sensitive and, for this reason, is preferable to the independent samples approach. It frequently is the case, however, that the paired samples approach is simply impossible. The paired samples approach is most often used when the data are to be collected from a future experiment over which the investigator has some control. The issue of matching samples is part of a much larger topic called *experimental design,* which is very important in laboratory science, where the investigator has considerable control over the process generating the data. Sometimes this is the case in business and economics, but more often it is not.

▼ Inferences from Paired Samples

Consider the following problem:

A tire manufacturer wants to determine if a new rubber formulation will improve tread wear. One set of 12 tires was manufactured with the old formulation, and another set was manufactured with the new formulation. Both sets of tires were identical in all respects except for the rubber. Six test cars and drivers were chosen for the test. Each car received two tires with the old rubber formulation and two with the new. One of each was placed on the front and one of each was placed on the rear. Each car drove until a tire wore out. That tire's mileage was recorded, and the car continued driving until all of the test tires had worn out. The mileage each tire received is shown in the table on the next page.

Based on the data in that table, does the manufacturer have evidence at the .05 level of significance that the average tread life of all tires made with the new rubber formulation exceeds the average tread life of all tires made with the old rubber formulation?

The Null Hypothesis for these data is $H_0 : \mu_{new} \leq \mu_{old}$, and the Alternate Hypothesis is $H_A : \mu_{new} > \mu_{old}$. Because of the methods used with inferences on two population means, it is common to formulate the hypotheses in terms of the difference between the two population means.

Car	Tire Location	Total Tread Life in Miles	
		Old Rubber	New Rubber
1	Front	37,661	31,902
	Rear	42,342	41,203
2	Front	31,108	38,816
	Rear	41,239	43,305
3	Front	32,903	35,375
	Rear	42,658	52,353
4	Front	29,829	30,883
	Rear	39,616	49,424
5	Front	34,625	38,724
	Rear	42,650	43,234
6	Front	31,923	34,565
	Rear	39,990	43,861

If $\mu_D = \mu_{new} - \mu_{old}$, an alternative formulation for the Null Hypothesis is $H_0 : \mu_D \leq 0$, and for the Alternative Hypothesis: $H_A : \mu_D > 0$. These samples are clearly paired because each tire with the old rubber formulation has a corresponding tire with the new formulation.

The data for this problem are provided in an Excel workbook named "Tires.xls" in the subdirectory for this chapter.

- Open the workbook Tires.xls. After opening it, select "Save As…" from the File menu on the Menu Bar and give the workbook the name "chap12.xls." Alternatively, you can open a new workbook and enter the labels "Old" and "New" in cells A1 and B1 and enter the data in the two rightmost columns of the table below their respective labels. Save this workbook under the name "Chap12.xls."

- Change the name of the Sheet1 worksheet to "Paired."

- Enter the label "XD" in cell C1. We will symbolize the diffence between each pair of values as x_D. In cells C2 through C13, enter formulas that will calculate the value in each row in column B (the mileage with the new formulation) minus the value in column A (the mileage with the old formulation). The value displayed in cell C13 should be "3,871." If you used the Tires.xls workbook, you will notice that the cell formatting shows negative numbers in parentheses rather than with a minus sign. The value in C2, for example, will display as "(5,759)."

Each of these values is a random number. Think of them as being selected from a population of differences. Imagine that each tire in the population of tires made with the new rubber formulation was paired with a corresponding tire in the population of tires made with the old formulation and the difference in the mileage of the two pairs was calculated. This would be the population of differences. The formulation of the Null and Alternate Hypotheses, which use "μ_D," are referring to the mean of this population of differences. The values you have in column C are a sample from that population and can be used to test hypotheses on the population mean, μ_D. The methods described below are identical to those used in Chapter 9. You may wish to review the methods of testing a hypothesis on a population mean in that chapter.

- Enter the label "x bar D" in cell B14, "Standard Deviation" in cell B15, "n" in cell B16, "Standard Error" in cell B17, "t" in cell B18, and "p value" in cell B19. Adjust the width of column B.

- Enter formulas in cell C14 and C15 to calculate the average and standard deviation, respectively, of the numbers in C2:C13. The displayed values will be "3092" and "4471.701."

- Enter the formula in C16 to count the number of values in C2:C13. The displayed value should be "12."

Notice that since the sample mean is positive, it is not consistent with the Null Hypothesis. It will be necessary to calculate a sample t and determine from it if the positive sample mean could reasonably be due to chance. The calculation of this sample t is almost identical to the calculation of a sample t for a hypothesis test on a population mean. The only real difference is that it calculated on the value of the x_D's instead of the x's:

$$t = \frac{\overline{x}_D - \mu_D}{s_{\overline{x}_D}}$$

Where $s_{\overline{x}_D}$ is the standard error of the differences, calculcated as the standard deviation of the x_D's divided by the square root of n.

- Enter a formula in C17 to calculate the standard error. The displayed value should be "1290.87."

- Enter the formula in C18 to calculate the sample t for the Null Hypothesis that the population mean is less than or equal to zero. The displayed value should be "2.395092."

- Enter the formula in cell C19 to calculate the one-tail p value from that sample t value. The displayed value should be "0.01777."

Since this p value is less than the significance level, we would reject the Null Hypothesis and conclude that there is evidence that the average tread life of all tires made with the new rubber formulation exceeds that of all tires made with the old formulation.

Notice that the standard error and means you have calculated could also be used to calculate a confidence interval on the difference between the average tread life of the two populations of tires.

▼Using the Analysis Tool for a Paired Samples Test

Although analyzing data from paired samples is very straightforward, Excel provides an Analysis Tool for this very task. The Analysis Tool automatically does all of the calculations and produces an output. The output, however, is in the form of numbers rather than formulas. As a result, the tool must be used each time the data change. It is not possible using an Analysis Tool to develop a worksheet that will automatically recalculate when the data change.

- Open the Tools menu on the Menu Bar and click "Data Analysis...." If "Data Analysis..." is not present on your Tools menu, see Appendix B.

- When the Data Analysis dialog window opens, scroll down through the list of Analysis Tools and choose "t-Test: Paired Two Sample for Means." The dialog window for this tool will open.

- In the fields for the "Variable 1 Range" and "Variable 2 Range," enter the cell address ranges for the columns with the mileage for the "Old" and "New" rubber formulations, respectively. Include in these ranges the cells in the first row containing the labels "Old" and "New."

- In the "Hypothesized Mean Difference" field, enter the number "0."

- Click the small box beside the word "Labels" so that a check appears. By doing this you tell the Analysis tool that the first cell in the variable ranges contains a label. It is always good to do this because it enables the Analysis Tool to use your labels in the output.

- The "Alpha" field should contain the significance level, "0.05." The Excel Analysis Tools generally seem to start assuming this is the significance level you want, but you can change it to another value.

- Click the button to the left of "Output Range" and enter the address "D1." The output of the Analysis Tool will be placed immediately to the right of the data already entered in the worksheet.

- Click the OK button. The output will be written to columns D, E, and F, and the cells containing that output will be selected. As with all the output of all the Analysis Tools, the column widths are not adjusted to fit the output, which you must do next.

- Open the Format menu on the Menu Bar. Select "Column" and, from the submenu that opens, select "AutoFit Selection." This will adjust the widths of the columns so that you can see the output of the Analysis Tool.

As you examine the output of the Analysis Tool, you will notice that it provides a number of statistics, such as the means of each sample, which we did not calculate before, and omits some (such as the mean sample difference) that were calculated before. These means are useful because they help you determine how the tool made its calculations. Look, for example, at the sample *t* (labeled "t Stat") in cell E10. It has the same absolute value as the sample *t* earlier calculated in cell C17, but a different sign. The differences in column C were calculated by subtracting the values in column A from those in column B (that is, B − A). However, the Analysis Tool calculated the differences as A − B. In the case of one-tail tests, it is important to check the means of each sample to ensure that the sample data are not consistent with the Null Hypothesis. It is also wise to include labels with the data analyzed so that the output will be clearly labeled.

In addition to giving both one-tail and two-tail *p* values, the output of the Analysis Tool also includes critical *t* values. The value given in the tool's dialog window is used to determine these values. Notice that the output does not indicate if the Null Hypothesis is rejected. When you use an Analysis Tool to do a hypothesis test, you must still determine if the Null Hypothesis is rejected, including whether or not the sample is consistent with the Null Hypothesis (for one-tail tests). Notice also that the output does not include a standard error of the mean of the differences. It cannot, therefore, be used to derive confidence intervals.

▼Tests of the Difference of Means for Independent Samples

When samples drawn from two populations are not paired, they are called *independent* samples. Such samples need not be the same size. Excel provides three different Analysis Tools for hypothesis tests on independent samples. The appropriate one to use depends on the information you have on the variances of the two populations. There are three possibilities, and each requires different calculations.

1. You know the two population variances. This situation arises primarily in statistics texts since the usual situation is one in which you know nothing about the populations. In this case, a sample statistic with a z distribution can be calculated from the data in the two samples.

2. You don't know the population variances, but you believe they are equal or are willing to assume they are equal. Even if the two population variances are equal, the two sample variances will differ purely by chance. Each sample variance is an estimate of the same population variance, and the appropriate approach is to combine the two sample variances so as to get a better estimate of that common population variance. This estimate is referred to as the *pooled sample variance*. From the two sample means and the pooled sample variance, a sample statistic with a t distribution can be calculated. The degrees of freedom of the t distribution is $n_1 + n_2 - 2$, where n_1 and n_2 are the sizes of the two samples.

3. You don't know the population variances, but you believe they are unequal or do not want to assume they are equal. This situation is what statisticians refer to as the *Behrens-Fisher problem*. A sample statistic is calculated from the sample data. This statistic approximately follows the t distribution, and for this reason some texts refer to it as t', although Excel's output simply designates it as "t Stat." The degrees of freedom is calculated by a formula known as *Satterthwaite's approximation* and is rounded to the nearest integer. This is then used to determine both p values and critical values using the t distribution.

Let's consider the realistic case where you do not know the variances of the two populations. In this case you must use options 2 or 3 above. It is very likely that you may be uncertain as to whether the population variances are equal or unequal. It is reasonable, therefore, to use both procedures in all problems involving hypothesis tests on the equality of means when the data are independent samples. Although the two tests will result in different p values, in most cases the two p values will be close. Either both will be greater than the significance level or both will be less than the significance level, and they will therefore be in agreement on the rejection of the Null Hypothesis. In this case, doing both procedures establishes that the result of a hypothesis test does not depend on the equality or inequality of population variances.

What if both procedures are done and they lead to different conclusions on whether or not the Null Hypothesis should be rejected? Although rare, this *can* happen. The decision on whether the two populations have equal means in this case depends on whether they have equal variances. There is an Analysis Tool within Excel that tests for the equality of two population variances. This test may be inconclusive, however, and a final conclusion may elude the investigator, who really has no additional data on the populations. Fortunately, this is a rare situation whose primary use is to worry students of statistics.

Consider the following problem:

A firm supplying computer display projectors is considering switching to a new supplier of specialty bulbs because of that supplier's claim that its bulbs last longer. The firm has data from tests of sample bulbs of its old supplier and has recently acquired and tested a sample of bulbs from the potential new supplier. Based on these data, does the firm have evidence at the .05 level of significance that the bulbs from the new supplier have a longer average life than bulbs from the old supplier?

The Null Hypothesis for this problem is $H_0: \mu_{new} \leq \mu_{old}$, and the Alternate Hypothesis is $H_A: \mu_{new} > \mu_{old}$. A necessary condition for the rejection of the Null Hypothesis is that $\bar{x}_{new} > \bar{x}_{old}$ (the sample is not consistent with the Null Hypothesis).

- Select the Sheet2 worksheet. The data on bulb life are located there, with the sample data for bulbs from the old supplier in column A and those from the new supplier in column B. The first sample is larger than the first.

- Rename the Sheet2 worksheet to "Independent."

We will first use the tool that performs the test which assumes that the two populations have equal variances. The output from that test will enable us to check whether or not the sample data are consistent with the Null Hypothesis. If they are not, we will also use the tool for the analysis, assuming the population variances are unequal.

- Click on "Data Analysis..." on the Tools menu. In the Data Analysis dialog window, select "t-Test: Two-Sample Assuming Equal Variances."

- Enter the range address of the "Old" data in the "Variable 1" field. Include the address of the cell containing the label "Old."

- Enter the range address of the "New" data in the "Variable 2" field, also including the address of the label.

- Enter the number "0" in the "Hypothesized Mean Difference" field and click the box beside "Labels" so a checkmark appears.

- Click the radio button beside "Output Range" so it is selected and enter the address "C1" in the "Output Range" field. Click OK.

- When the tool has completed writing the output, and the range containing the output is selected, click the Format menu on the Menu Bar, and select "Column" and then "AutoFit Selection" to adjust the column width so the output can be seen.

The first row of the output, labeled "Mean," gives the value of the sample means. You should have 47.5 for the mean of the sample of bulbs from the old supplier and 52.41666667 for the mean of the sample from the new supplier. This means that $\bar{x}_{new} > \bar{x}_{old}$. Since the Null Hypothesis is $\mu_{new} \leq \mu_{old}$, the sample is *not* consistent with the Null and the reported p values are therefore valid.

Notice the output gives the estimated "Pooled Variance," and it is between the two sample variances.

The most important part of the output is the reported p values. The one-tail p value is .051746314. This is slightly greater than the significance level (.05). On that basis we would fail to reject the Null Hypothesis and conclude that there is not evidence at the .05 level of significance that bulbs from the new supplier outlast those from the old supplier.

Let's now see if the results are different if we assume the two populations have different variances.

- Recall the Data Analysis dialog window. Choose "t-Test: Two-Sample Assuming Unequal Variances" (immediately below the previous choice).

- The dialog window for this tool looks like that of the previous tool except for the title bar, which has the words "Assuming Unequal Variances." Complete the fields of this dialog window exactly as you did the one for the previous tool except direct the output to cell C16, which will put it directly below the previous tool's output. Click "OK."

The output of this tool is similar to that of the previous one. A good check to be sure you haven't made an error is to verify that the reported sample means on this output are the same as they were for the output above it. No "Pooled Variance" is reported since none is calculated if the population variances are believed unequal.

The one-tail p value on this output is .025783329, which is less than the 0.05 significance level. Although in most cases these two outputs will lead to the same conclusion, they do not for this problem. The small p value in this procedure indicates that the Null Hypothesis should be rejected, and that we should conclude at the 0.05 level of significance that there *is* evidence that bulbs from the new supplier outlast those from the old! When the two procedures come to different conclusions, how are we to choose?

▼Testing for a Difference in the Variance of Two Populations

The decision for this problem depends on whether or not the variance in the life of the population of bulbs from the old supplier equals the variance in the life of the population of bulbs from the new supplier. With our samples from each population, we do have some information on this issue. Both outputs provide the sample variances. Take a look at them. For the sample of bulbs from the old supplier, the variance is a bit less than 90.55. For the sample of bulbs from the new supplier, the variance is just under 21.54. This seems like a substantial difference. Is it possible that such a difference in sample variances could arise if the samples were drawn from populations with the same variance? It certainly is *possible,* but it would be interesting to know how likely such a result would be. If this seems to you like a hypothesis-testing question, good for you! This is exactly what we can do. Excel provides us with a method of determining whether or not these samples provide evidence that the two populations have different variances.

To look for evidence of a difference in population variances we can test the Null Hypothesis $H_{0:}$ $\sigma^2_{new} = \sigma^2_{old}$ against the Alternate Hypothesis $H_{A:}$ $\sigma^2_{new} \neq \sigma^2_{old}$. The sample statistic in this case is the ratio of the two sample variances which, under the assumption of population normality, follows the F distribution. If the Null Hypothesis is rejected, we have evidence that the population variances differ. If they differ, the second t-Test output is the correct one for testing the equality of population means.

- Recall the Data Analysis dialog window and select "F-Test Two-Sample for Variances." The dialog window for this tool is very similar to those you have filled out for the two procedures testing the equality of means. The major difference is that this tool's dialog window has no field for "Hypothesized Mean Difference." Enter the same cell addresses in the "Variable" fields here as you did for the previous tools. Select the Output Range radio button and direct the output to cell C30, placing it below both previous outputs. Click OK.

The output from this tool testing the equality of variances is similar to that of the two previous outputs testing the equality of means. Like the others, it provides the two sample means. Check to be sure the sample means in this output are identical to those of the other outputs, verifying that the correct data were used for the analysis. The sample statistic calculated in this analysis is the sample F, 4.204110346. The most important part of the output is the p value (labeled "P(F<=f) one-tail"), which in this case is slightly over .0088. Unfortunately, the Null Hypothesis we want to test ($H_0 : \sigma_{new}^2 = \sigma_{old}^2$) requires a *two-tail* test, and this output gives only a *one-tail* p value (and critical value). Fortunately, it is easy to convert a one-tail p value to its two-tail counterpart: multiply by 2. This must always be done when Excel's F test is used in the context of choosing between the two t tests on the equality of two population means.

- Select the region containing the last row of the output (C39:E39). Use the mouse to move that region down one row so that the row below the one-tail p value is blank.

- In (now blank) cell C39, enter the label "2-tail p value." In cell D39 enter a formula that will multiply the value of cell D38 by 2. The displayed value will be "0.017676129."

This is a fairly small p value. At the .05 or .02 significance level (but not .01), we would Reject the Null Hypothesis that the population variances are equal and conclude that we have evidence that they are unequal. This, in turn, implies that the proper procedure for testing the equality of the means is the second procedure, which assumes the population variances are different. The low p value from this procedure (just under .026) led to the conclusion that there is evidence that the average life of bulbs from the new supplier exceeded that of the old supplier. This would be the ultimate conclusion from our analysis of the data.

In most cases the need to test a hypothesis about two population means will not require a test of equality of the two population variances because both procedures testing the means will yield the same result. Only in cases where they differ can an F test possibly be useful in determining which means test procedure should be relied on. In the example discussed here, the small p value in the F test led to a rejection of the Null Hypothesis of equal variances—a clear indication that the assumption of unequal variances is the correct choice. But what if the p value in the F test were large and the Null Hypothesis could not be rejected? As we saw in Chapter 8, failing to reject the Null Hypothesis is not the same as *accepting* it because we cannot determine the probability of committing Type II error. A failure to reject the Null Hypothesis that the population variances are equal is therefore *not* a solid justification for choosing to assume they are equal and using that assumption to test the population means. In fact, the only reliable guidance the *F* test can give us is to choose the assumption of unequal variances. It can't tell us to assume the assumption of equal variances. If a decision on the test of population means depends on the equality of variances (and it usually doesn't), and if the *F* test results in a *p* value too large to conclude the variances are unequal, we are left in a kind of statistical limbo. Without additional information it would be difficult to draw any conclusion.

▼Exercises

1. The paired samples approach was described as being more *sensitive* than the independent samples approach. What, exactly, does this mean? In the paired samples problem on tire life, the average tread life of the tires made with the new compound was 3,091.75 miles greater than the average tread life of the tires made with the old compound (40,304 miles versus 37,212 miles). This difference was great enough to conclude the new rubber compound made a significant difference. Suppose we had the same sample data but from independent samples. Would we then have found evidence of a difference? Check this by analyzing the tire data using the two independent samples approaches. Explain why this makes the paired samples approach more *sensitive*.

The data for the problems given below can be found in an Excel workbook in the file named "Exercises.xls." The questions below indicate which worksheet has the data for each problem.

2. A manufacturing firm has plants in two different states and wants to compare the productivity of workers in one plant with workers in the other plant. The managers of each plant were asked to provide output per worker for a sample of 31 days. The resulting data are on the worksheet Plants A & B. Based on these data, is there evidence (at the .10 level of significance) of a difference between average worker productivity (measured as output per worker) in the two plants? Provide the Null and Alternate Hypotheses for this test, give your reasons for rejecting or not rejecting the Null, and provide a "yes" or "no" answer to the question of whether there is evidence of difference in average productivity.

3. A long-distance trucking firm wants to determine whether increased maintenance will increase the gas mileage of trucks. A random sample of 25 trucks and drivers who repeatedly drive the same routes was placed on the standard maintenance routine for one week and

the intensive maintenance routine for another week. The average gas mileage for each truck under each routine was collected and is presented in the worksheet named "Maintenance," in which the data for each truck are in one row. Based on these data, is there evidence (at the .01 level of significance) that the intensive maintenance increases gas mileage? Provide the Null and Alternate Hypotheses, the basis for rejecting or not rejecting the Null, and a yes or no answer to the question of whether intensive maintenance increases mileage.

4. The sales department of a firm is considering enrolling their salespeople in a program in positive sales motivation offered by a national consultant. In order to determine the effectiveness of the program, the firm sends a random sample of 30 salespersons to attend their program and measures their sales over the following month. A control group of 30 salespersons who did not attend the program is also chosen at random, and their sales are also measured during the same month. Total monthly sales for each sample are on the Motivation worksheet. Based on these data, is there evidence that attending the program would increase the average sales of all salespeople? Provide the Null and Alternate Hypotheses, the basis for rejecting or failing to reject the Null, and a "yes" or "no" answer to the question of whether there is evidence that program attendance would increase average sales.

Chapter 13

▼

Analysis of Variance

Analysis of variance (or ANOVA) is another technique for testing the equality of different population means. Its name comes from the fact that it uses variance-like measures to make inferences about population means. One of the most useful characteristics of the analysis of variance technique is that it can be extended to any number of populations. Excel's Data Analysis Tools provide three different analysis of variance techniques. These techniques are appropriate for different types of data collection—analogous to the difference between paired samples and independent samples used in the t test for differences in two population means.

All of these techniques have certain things in common, however. All of them are designed to test the Null Hypothesis that all the populations from which the samples were drawn have equal means. The Alternate Hypothesis is that at least one of the population means differs from the others. If there are n different samples (drawn from n different populations) the Null Hypothesis can be symbolized as $H_0 : \mu_1 = \mu_2 = \ldots = \mu_n$. There is no succinct way of expressing the Alternate Hypothesis (except as *not* the Null Hypothesis). The Alternate Hypothesis is true if many different conditions are met, including, among many others, none of the population means being equal or all of the population means being equal except one. Analysis of variance techniques also share assumptions about the data. In addition to assuming the samples are random, they also assume the populations are normally distributed and have equal variance.

▼Single-Factor Analysis of Variance

The (mathematically) simplest form of analysis of variance is the single-factor analysis (also frequently called *one-way* analysis of variance). It is used when the data are like those used in the independent sample approach to a test of the equality of two population means. The only difference accounted for in the sample observations is the different populations from which each observation came. Since, like all ANOVA techniques, the populations are assumed to have equal variance, this technique is an alternative to the *t* test for the equality of two population means, assuming equal population variances. It is more versatile than that test because it is not restricted to two populations. When used with two populations, it gives exactly the same (two-tail) results.

In addition to single-factor analysis of variance, Excel has tools for two other types of ANOVA. They are all conceptually similar, and we will take a close look at how single-factor ANOVA works to gain an understanding of the essentials of any ANOVA procedure.

Let's consider the following problem:

A company is considering two competing sales training courses for new salespersons. In order to compare their effectiveness, with each other and with no course, three groups of five randomly chosen new salespersons are selected. One group is sent to sales training course "A," the second is sent to sales training course "B," and the third receives no training at all. After the two groups have completed their training, sales records for each salesperson for the next two-week period are collected, and the results for each group are shown in the table below.

Course A	Course B	No Course
$2,058	$3,339	$2,228
$2,176	$2,777	$2,578
$3,449	$3,020	$1,227
$2,517	$2,437	$2,044
$944	$3,067	$1,681

Based on the data in the table, is there evidence at the .10 level of significance that there would be a difference in the means of all salespersons if they were sent to a training course?

What characteristics of these sample data would lead us to find evidence of a difference in the population means?

First, a large difference in sample means is more likely to lead to the conclusion of a difference in population means than would a small difference in sample means. Sample means are randomly distributed around their population means. The means of any set of samples might be closer together or might be further apart than the population means, but sample means are unbiased estimates of population means. Sample means that are far apart are more consistent with differing population means than with identical population means.

Second, small sample variance is also more likely to lead to the conclusion that the population means differ than is large sample variance. Small sample variance is consistent with small population variance, and if the population variance is small, the sample means are likely to be close in value to the population means. Differences in sample means are less likely to be the result of chance and more likely to be the result of a difference in population means. We can get a sense of both the difference in sample means and the sample variance by making a chart of the data.

The chart we will make will be a type of scatter plot in which the data for each sample will be displayed as points in a vertical array. The three samples will be shown side by side, with the group and grand means. This chart will make it easy to visually compare the locations and variances of the three samples and to see how each sample clusters around its sample mean and the grand mean.

- Open the Excel workbook in the file Anova.xls in the Chap_13 folder.

- The data for this problem are on the Sheet1 worksheet in the range B1:D6. Change that worksheet's name to "Sales Course." Change the name of the Sheet2 worksheet to "Calc."

- Select cells B6:D6 in the Sales Course worksheet. Click the arrow beside the Borders button on the Formatting Toolbar (▦▌) and choose the button from the set that opens, which will draw a dark underline below the selected cells.

- In cell A7 enter the label "means," and in cell A8 enter the label "grand mean."

- In cells B7:D7 enter formulas that will calculate the average of each column of five numbers. The values appearing in B7 through D7, respectively, should be "2228.8," "2928," and "1951.6."

- Enter the formula in cell D8 that will calculate the average of 15 numbers in B1:D6. The displayed value should be "2369.467."

In order to make the chart discussed above, we need a reorganized copy of the data in which all data values are placed in a column. Other columns will contain the group number for each of the values, that value's group mean, and the grand mean. This copy will be constructed so that changes in the original will automatically update the copy. One way of doing this would be to use a simple equation setting the value of each copy equal to the original. The procedure shown on the next page is equivalent, and you may find it easier.

- Switch to the Calc worksheet. Enter the labels "Sample" in cell A1, "x" in cell B1, "Sample Mean" in cell C1, and "Grand Mean" in cell D1. Adjust the column widths to hold the labels.

- Place a dark underline below the labels in A1:D1 with the Borders button. The heavy underline selection you made earlier will be the choice displayed on the button for the rest of the session until you make another choice. As long as you want heavy underline in this session, you need only click the button on the toolbar.

- Return to the Sales Course worksheet. Select cells B2:B6 (the "Course A" data) and click the Copy button ⊞ on the Standard Toolbar.

- Go to the Calc Worksheet. Select cell B2. Open the Edit menu on the Menu Bar. Select "Paste Special...." When the dialog window opens, click the Paste Link button on the right side (shown below). The numbers will appear to have been copied, but the Formula Bar will show that each cell contains an equation referring to cells in the Sales Course worksheet. Changing the values there will cause the corresponding values in the Calc worksheet also to change.

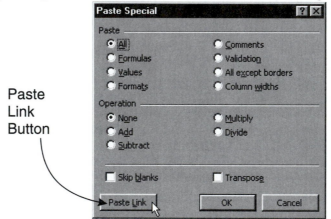

Paste
Link
Button

- Select cell B7 in Sales Course (the mean of "Course A") and click the Copy button again.

- Return to Calc and select the cell range C2:C6. Open the "Edit" menu on the Menu Bar, select "Paste Special...," and, when the dialog window opens, again click the Paste Link button. Each of the cells in C2:C6 will display the number "2228.8," but will actually contain a formula referring to cell B7 in Sales Course.

- Enter the number "1" in cell A2 and then copy it down to cells A3:A6.

We now have the beginning of a table containing each value (in column B), the sample number in column A, and the sample mean in column C.

The same data for the other two samples will appear in the same columns immediately below the data just entered.

- Go to the Sales Course worksheet and select cells C2:C6. Click the Copy button. Switch to Calc. Select cell B7, click "Paste Special..." off the Edit Menu, and click the Paste Link button in the dialog window. The data from "Course B" will now appear directly below that of "Course A."

- Return to Sales Course. Select cell B7 (the mean of "Course B"), click the Copy button, switch to Calc, select the range C7:C11, and again make a Paste Link by opening the Edit menu, clicking "Paste Special...," and then clicking the Paste Link button.

- Enter the number "2" in cells A7:A11.

The data for the second sample now appear directly below the first. The third sample will be placed below the second.

- Using the same procedures as before, create a Paste Link reference in cells B12:B16 in the Calc worksheet to cells D2:D6 (the "No Course" sample) in the Sales Course worksheet. Check the Formula Bar for a cell in the range B12:B16 to be sure it contains a formula referring to a cell in the Sales Course worksheet and not simply a number.

- Create a Paste Link in cells C12:C16 of Calc to the mean of the "No Course" sample in cell D7 of Sales Course. Each of the cells in C12:C16 should display the value "1951.6," but should show a formula in the Formula Bar.

- Enter the number "3" in cells A12:A16 of Calc.

The last step is for each of the cells in column D of the table to refer to the "Grand Mean" of all the samples.

- Select cell D8 in the Sales Course worksheet, which contains the average of all 15 numbers, and click the Copy button. Go to the Calc worksheet. Select cells D2:D16, open the Edit menu, click "Paste Special...," and then click the Paste Link button. Each of the cells in D2:D16 will display the 15-number mean but will contain an equation referring to cell D8 in Sales Course.

▼Charting the Sample Values and the Means

The next step will be to produce a scatter plot that graphically displays the sample values, the sample means, and the grand mean.

We will initially create the chart on the Calc worksheet that contains the data in a form that can be used by the Chart Wizard, and then it will be moved to the Sales Course worksheet. We will then be able to change the data on that worksheet and see how those changes affect the chart.

- Select the region A1:D16 on the Calc worksheet and click the Chart Wizard button.

- In the Step 1 Chart Wizard dialog window, select "XY (Scatter)" from the "Standard Types" and choose the chart subtype at the top that shows data points with no lines.

- Click the Next> button three times so that you are at Step 4. In that step have the chart placed in the Sales Course worksheet by selecting that worksheet, as shown below.

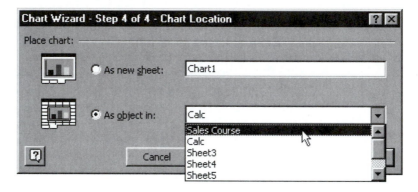

- Click the Finish Button. The chart will be placed on the Sales Course worksheet.

- Enlarge the chart and arrange the worksheet so that both the entire chart and the numbers are visible without scrolling the worksheet.

We will make a few editing changes to improve the chart. These will include connecting the sample means and grand means points with separate lines and eliminating the horizontal axis. Let's first deal with the means.

- Place the mouse pointer directly on one of the three points showing the grand mean. If you have the pointer correctly placed and leave it for a second, a marker will appear identifying the point as being in the "Series 'Grand Mean'" followed by the horizontal and vertical axis values. Click the (left) mouse button once. All three grand mean points will change color indicating that they have been selected.

- Open the Format menu on the Menu Bar and click "Selected Data Series...." When the Format Data Series dialog window appears, click the "Patterns" folder tab, unless it is already on top.

The left side of the dialog window allows you to determine if a line connects the points and, if so, the color and other characteristics of that line. The right side of the window allows you to determine the appearance of the markers that show the position of the data points. We want to connect the points with a line and have no markers at all.

- In the left side of the dialog window in the "Line" area, click the Custom radio button and select a solid line "style." You may change the color and weight of the line if you wish.

- On the right side of the dialog window in the "Marker" area, click the None radio button. Click the OK button. Click on a blank portion of the chart to remove the selection of the grand mean points. The next step will give a similar treatment to the sample means.

- Select the sample means by placing the mouse pointer on one of them and clicking the (left) mouse button. Format the series so that it has a line connecting the points that differs in style (not solid) and color from that connecting the grand mean. Eliminate the markers for the sample means as you did for the grand mean.

The last step involves eliminating the present horizontal axis and substituting character labels to identify the three samples. This is a cosmetic change.

- Select the horizontal axis by clicking the mouse pointer on one of the numbers on that axis. You should see "handles" at each end of the axis.

- Open the Format menu on the Menu Bar and click "Selected Axis...." An alternative is to click the right mouse button and select "Format Axis" on the pop-up menu.

- Click the "Patterns" folder tab. On the left side of the dialog window is the "lines" region. Click the None radio button. On the bottom right side is the "Tick mark labels" region. Click the None radio button here as well. Click OK.

- Place the labels "Course A," "Course B," and "No Course" below the horizontal axis by entering each label's text in the Formula Bar, pressing the Enter key, and then moving the label into position. For more details on this process, refer to page 51.

- Adjust the font sizes of the text on the chart to give the graphics more space, if needed.

Your completed chart should look like the picture at the top of the next page.

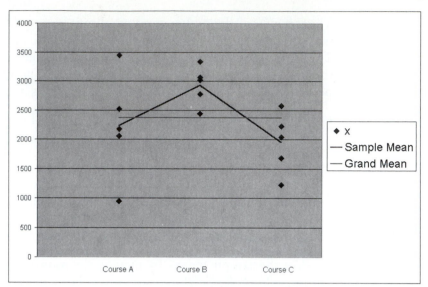

It is clear from the chart that those who took course "B" did better on average than either of the other groups, and those who took no course did the worst, on average. This suggests that the sales courses do make a difference. A statistical test will enable us to determine if this pattern could reasonably have arisen by random chance. The test, single-factor ANOVA, is discussed below.

▼Determining the Sum of Squares

A population variance is the average sum of squared deviations from the mean. A sample variance is an unbiased estimator of a population variance. To be unbiased, the sum of squared deviations must be divided by the degrees of freedom rather than by the number of observations. An analysis of variance involves calculating several variance-like measures. Each of them is a sum of squared deviations around some measure divided by the degrees of freedom. We will extend the table in the Calc worksheet to calculate these measures. Once this worksheet is finished, the results will be placed back on the Sales Course worksheet. We will then experiment with samples drawn from different populations to see how the chart and the statistical tests reflect those changes.

• Select the Calc worksheet.

Most of the calculations will be done in additional columns added to the present table. Row 1 will contain labels for these columns. In those labels we will use "s bar" to refer to the *sample* means, which differ for each sample, and "g bar" to refer to the *grand* mean, which is the same for all samples.

- Enter the following labels in row 1, columns E through J: "x-s bar" in E1, "(x-s bar)^2" in F1, "s bar-g bar" in G1, "(s bar-g bar)^2" in H1, "x-g bar" in I1, and "(x-g bar)^2" in J1. Adjust the column widths. A quick way of adjusting them all at once is to select cells F1:J1 (E1 should already have enough room), and open the Format menu on the Menu Bar. Select "Column," then select "AutoFit Selection."

- Place a heavy underline under these cells like the one under the labels entered previously.

In all of the formulas below, use *relative* addresses. First, enter the formulas for the first row. A simple copy will generate the formulas for the rest of the cells.

- In cell E2, enter a formula to calculate the difference between the x value in that row (column B) and the sample mean for that row (column C). The displayed value should be "-170.8." In the language of ANOVA, this is a *deviation* from the sample mean.

- In cell F2, enter a formula that will calculate the square of the number in cell E2. This value ("29172.64") is a *squared deviation*.

- In cell G2, enter a formula to calculate the difference between the sample mean in that row (column C) and the grand mean (column D). This value, "-140.6667," is the *deviation* of the sample mean from the grand mean.

- In cell H2, enter a formula to square the value in G2. This value, "19787.11111," is another *squared deviation*.

- In cell I2, enter a formula to calculate the deviation of the x value in that row from the grand mean. The displayed value should be "-311.5."

- In cell J2, enter a formula to calculate the squared deviation of the x value in that row from the grand mean by squaring the value in I2. The displayed value should be "97011.48."

The next step is to copy these formulas down their columns.

- Select cells E2:J2. Place the mouse pointer over the fill handle in the lower-right corner of J2. When the pointer changes to a black cross, press and hold the (left) mouse button and drag the outline border down until it includes row 16. Release the mouse button, and the rest of the table will be filled with numbers.

- Use the Borders button to put heavy underlines beneath the last cell in each of the three columns of squared deviations: F16, H16, and J16.

- Enter the label "Sums" in cell A17, "SSW" in cell E17, "SSB" in G17, and "SST" in I17. "SSW" stands for "Sum of Squares Within," "SSB" for "Sum of Squares Between," and "SST" for "Sum of Squares Total."

- In cell F17, use the AutoSum button to enter a formula to add the numbers in column F. The value is "4790788." The numbers in column F are squared deviations, and F17 is a *sum of squared deviations* or a *sum of squares*. Since it is based on the difference between each value and that value's sample mean, it is the sum of squares within each group (or sample), SSW.

- Using the AutoSum button (or other means), enter formulas in cells H17 and J17 to calculate the sum of squares for their respective columns. H17 will display "2531795.733," and J17 will display "7322584."

H17 is the sum of squares between groups (SSB), and J17 is the total sum of squares (SST). The three sums of squares will be used for calculations in the *ANOVA table*.

▼Preparing the ANOVA Table

- Switch to the Sales Course worksheet.

- The ANOVA table will be put in the region of cells A10:F13. Move the chart if necessary. Scroll your worksheet and enter labels for the table as shown in the picture below.

	A	B	C	D	E	F
10		SS	df	MS	F	p value
11	Between					
12	Within					
13	Total					

The "SS" label stands for "Sum of Squares." The first step will be to create a link between each of the three cells in that column and the corresponding sum of squares in the Calc worksheet.

- In cell B11, enter a formula that refers directly to the value of SSB in the Calc worksheet (H17). Enter an equal sign in B11 and then click the appropriate cell (F17) on the Calc worksheet.

- Using the same procedure, create links for "SS Within" and "SS Total" in the Sales Course worksheet to the corresponding values (SSW and SST) in row 17 of the Calc worksheet.

The degrees of freedom of SST is the sum of the sample sizes minus 1. If all the samples were drawn from a single population and were combined into a single sample, this would be the degrees of freedom of the variance of that single sample. In this case there are three samples each of size 5. The degrees of freedom of SST is $5 + 5 + 5 - 1 = 14$.

- Enter the number "14" in cell C13 of Sales Course.

If a separate variance were calculated from each sample, the degrees of freedom for each sample would be the sample size minus 1. The degrees of freedom of SSW is the sum of the degrees of freedom of each sample. This is the sum of the sample sizes minus the number of samples. For this problem there are three samples. The degrees of freedom of SSW is $5 + 5 + 5 - 3 = 12$.

- Enter the number "12" in cell C12.

The variance of SSB is the variance of sample means around the grand mean. There are only as many sample means as there are samples. The degrees of freedom is the number of samples minus 1. For this problem there are three samples. The degrees of freedom of SSB is $3 - 1 = 2$.

- Enter the number "2" in cell C11.

Notice in the table that the total sum of squares is the sum of the two sum of squares above it, and the degree of freedom of the total sum of squares is the sum of the two degrees of freedom above it.

Dividing a sum of squares by the appropriate degrees of freedom results in a variance-like measure. It is traditional in ANOVA to do this only for the within-groups and between-groups measures.

- Enter formulas in cells D11 and D12 to divide the sum of squares in each row by its degrees of freedom. The displayed values should be "1265898" (D11) and "399232.3" (D12).

- In cell E11 enter the formula that will take the value in cell D11 and divide it by the value in cell D12. The displayed value will be "3.17083."

This number, essentially a ratio of two variances, is a random number distributed under the F distribution. The F distribution is the ratio of two independent chi-square distributions, each of which is divided by its degrees of freedom. The assumption of equal values for σ in all populations will cause this to simplify to a ratio of sample variances in many cases. A large value for the between-groups variance compared to the within-groups variance indicates that the sample values are relatively closer to the sample means (small sample variation) than the sample means are to the grand mean (large difference in sample means). This is the kind of result that would be expected if the samples were drawn from populations with different means. A *p* value can be determined by using the *F* distribution function in Excel to determine the probability that a value as high or higher than that in cell E11 could occur by chance.

- Select cell F11. Click the Edit Formula button. In the "Statistical" function category, choose "FDIST." There are three arguments for this function.

The "X" argument field should have the cell address of the value for which we want the probability that an *F* distributed random variable will exceed E11. The two "Deg_freedom" arguments are the degrees of freedom of the numerator variance (in C11) and the denominator variance (in C12).

- Enter the appropriate cell references in the "FDIST" argument fields and click the OK button. The displayed value in F11 should be "0.078425."

Since this *p* value is less than the significance level of .10, we would reject the Null Hypothesis and conclude that there is evidence that the averages of all salespersons sent to the two courses and those sent to no course are not equal.

▼Analyzing Simulated Samples

We can use Excel's Random Number Generation tool to simulate new samples for the chart and ANOVA table. In order to meet the assumptions of analysis of variance, these random numbers will be drawn from a normal distribution.

- Open the Tools menu. Select "Data Analysis...," and choose "Random Number Generation" from the dialog window.

- On the Random Number Generation dialog window, enter "3" in the "Number of Variables" field (to overwrite the three columns of data in A1:D8) and "5" in the "Number of Random Numbers" field (for the five rows of data to be overwritten). Select "Normal" in the "Distribution" list and enter "2000" and "300" in the "Mean" and "Standard Deviation" fields, respectively. Click the Output Range radio button and enter the cell address for the upper left-hand corner of the existing data table (B2). Click the OK button. Click the OK button in the window warning you that data will be overwritten.

- Examine the new *p* value and look at the chart.

What we have done is simulate drawing three samples from a population with mean 2000 and standard deviation 300. The sample means and standard deviations will, of course, differ due to chance, but all samples were drawn from populations with the same means. The correct result of an analysis of variance of these samples would be to Fail to Reject the Null Hypothesis (that the three samples are drawn from populations with the same mean). A large p value is what would be expected.

It is easy to draw an additional set of samples from the same population because the Analysis Tool will retain the values you previously entered. Try drawing additional samples from this population.

- Open the Tools menu and click "Data Analysis." Three dialog windows will appear in sequence; simply press the Enter key as soon as each appears, and a new sample will be drawn. (You must unselect the chart—click off the chart on the worksheet—before drawing additional samples.) Do this a dozen times or so, and look for a relationship between the p value and the chart. If you get a p value greater than .80 or less than .10, print its chart. Remember that to print just the chart, click it before choosing "Print Preview." In the page header, put your name and the p value.

Even though ANOVA should always produce large p values when the samples are all drawn from the same population, if you choose enough samples you will occasionally see ANOVAs with small p values—caused by random differences in samples. These small values would cause you to Reject the Null Hypothesis. Since the samples are all drawn from the same population, it would be incorrect to reject the Null Hypothesis—an example of Type I error.

Let's next examine how ANOVA handles data when the samples are drawn from populations that don't have equal means. It is not quite as convenient in Excel to generate repeated sets of samples in this case, but we will make it as easy as possible by continuing to draw the first two samples from the same population and drawing only the third sample from a population with a different mean.

- Recall the Random Number Generation dialog window. Change the value in the "Number of Variables" field from "3" to "2" and click OK until the values are generated. This will generate new values for the "Course A" and "Course B" samples but not the "No Course" sample.

- Again recall the Random Number Generation dialog window, this time to generate new values for the "No Course" sample from a population with a different mean.

- Change the value in the "Number of Variables" field from "2" to "1." Only one column of numbers will be written.

- Change the value in the "Mean" field from "2000" to "2100." This is the new population mean for this sample.

- Change the address in the "Output Range" field from "$B$2" to "$D$2" (or "D2"). This will place the numbers in the "No Course" sample. Click OK (twice) so they will be generated.

Examine the graph and the p value. It is likely that this result is not very different from those obtained when all three samples were drawn from the same population. The p value is probably above .10, too high to conclude from the samples that the population means differ (even though we know they do). Furthermore, it's quite likely that the "No Course" sample, drawn from the population with the highest mean, doesn't even have the highest sample mean. Let's look at a few more samples drawn from these different populations. The easiest way to do this is to simply rerun the Random Number Generation tool with the last set of values and then rerun it with the changes needed for the other sample or samples.

- Recall the Random Number Generation tool. Repeatedly click OK (or press the Enter key) until a new set of numbers is generated. Since the tool was last used for the "No Course" sample, that sample will be re-generated.

- Again recall the Random Number Generation tool. Make the changes needed to have it draw new values for the two "Course" samples. Change "Number of Variables" to "2," "Mean" to "2000," and "Output Range" to "$B$2." Click OK until the new random numbers are generated. Examine the chart and ANOVA table again.

- Generate yet another set of samples by first recalling and rerunning the Random Number Generation tool without change. This will result in new numbers for the two "Course" samples. Again recall the tool and make the changes needed to generate the "No Course" sample ("Number of Variables"= 1, "Mean" = 2100, "Output Range" = $D$2). After the new values are generated, check the chart and ANOVA table.

- Repeat the process of generating the two sets of samples a few more times. Each time the Random Number Generation tool must be run twice. The first time, run it unchanged from the previous time. The second time, change the three fields ("Number of Variables," "Mean," and "Output Range") to generate the rest of the data.

You should see from this exercise that ANOVA cannot reliably detect a difference between population means when the difference is only 100 and population variances are 300. Failure to Reject the Null Hypothesis in this case is an example of Type II error. Avoiding this error requires some combination of a larger difference in population means, a smaller variance, or larger samples.

- Regenerate the two sets of samples except change the value of "Mean" for the "No Course" sample from "2100" to "3000" (and leave the others at "2000"). This time you should get a quite different result. The ANOVA *p* value should be quite small (less than .01), and the chart should clearly show the third sample as having a mean clearly greater than the other two. If you don't get this result, regenerate the two sets of samples a couple of more times.

- Regenerate the two sets of samples again. This time change the "Mean" of "No Course" back to "2100" (leaving the other two at "2000"). Change the "Standard Deviation" of *both* sets of samples from "300" to "30." Even though the difference in the means is again only 100, the reduced variance of the population makes it easy for ANOVA to detect the difference from the samples. The *p* value should be very small, and the chart should clearly show higher values for the "No Course" sample than for the other two samples.

▼ Using the One-Factor ANOVA Tool

Excel has an Analysis Tool that will automatically create an ANOVA table and will also display other statistics not shown on the ANOVA table we have created. Like all Analysis Tools, it must be rerun whenever there is a change in the data.

- Select "Data Analysis…" from the Tools menu on the Menu Bar.

- Choose "Anova: Single Factor," which is located at the top of the list. You will probably have to scroll the list of tools up to see it.

- Enter the cell addresses of the sample data in the "Input Range" field. The addresses should contain the sample labels in the first row, so the address you enter should be "B1:D6."

- Click the square beside "Labels in First Row" so that a checkmark appears.

- The "Alpha" value allows you to specify a significance level for a critical *F*, a statistic not present in the ANOVA table prepared earlier. Enter "0.1" in this field. This corresponds with the significance level given in the original problem.

- Click the radio button beside "Output Range" to choose it and enter the cell address "A15" in the field to the right. This will place the tool's ANOVA table directly below the one already on the sheet.

- Click OK. As soon as the output is written, and while it is still selected, open the Format menu on the Menu Bar, select "Column," and then select "AutoFit Selection." If part of the output is covered by the chart, click the chart once in the margin and move it out of the way by placing the mouse pointer on the chart and dragging it (with the left mouse button pressed) to the right.

The output consists of a summary table providing the sums, means, and variances of the data in each sample and an ANOVA table. Except for minor formatting differences and the presence of a critical *F* value (which should be 2.80679302), the table produced by the Analysis Tool should be identical to the table prepared earlier above it. If the two tables are not the same on your worksheet, you have made an error, probably in the dialog window of the Analysis Tool. Recall that dialog window and pay special attention to the "Input Range" field. Does it have either "B1:D6" or "$B$1:$D$6"? Is the "Labels" box checked?

▼Two-Factor Analysis of Variance

Excel provides two Analysis Tools for two-factor analysis of variance (also called *two-way* analysis of variance). In addition to controlling for which population an observation came from, two-factor analysis controls for other factors that might affect the variable being analyzed. The difference between two-factor and one-factor analysis is similar to the difference between the paired samples and independent samples in Chapter 12. One of the two-factor analysis tools is termed "Without Replication," and the other is termed "With Replication." There are several other common terms used for these analyses that you may see. The two-factor analysis without replication is often called *two-way analysis without interaction* or *randomized block* design. The two-factor analysis with replication is also known as *two-way analysis with interaction* or *factorial* design. The Excel terminology will be used here.

▼Two-Factor Analysis without Replication

Consider the following problem:

In recent years, a number of "ergonomic" computer keyboards have become available. A business office wants to determine if the keyboard de-

sign has any effect on the speed of typists. Five typists of varying ability are chosen at random. Each is given the opportunity to become familiar with each keyboard prior to taking a test with that keyboard, and each typist is tested with all three keyboards. The results of that test are shown below (the numbers represent words per minute typed).

	Keyboard		
Typist	A	B	C
1	51	57	72
2	109	112	117
3	47	43	51
4	98	98	107
5	70	69	77

Is there evidence (at the .01 level of significance) that average typing speed differs among the three keyboards?

One of the factors that strongly influences a typist's speed is that person's skill. Two-factor analysis of variance provides a technique that accounts for the fact that much of the difference in typing speed is owing to ability differences among the typists, not keyboard differences.

- The data for this problem are on Sheet3 (cells A1:D6) of the Anova.xls workbook. Select that worksheet and change its name to "Blocked." (This name will be explained below.)

The data in the worksheet are arranged the same as the data in the table. This follows a convention in statistics in which the characteristic distinguishing the data in one column from that in another is the characteristic to be analyzed. The characteristic distinguishing one row from another is controlled by the researcher and is used to permit better identification of the difference to be analyzed. It is standard terminology to refer to the column differences as *treatment* and the row differences as *blocking* or *blocks*. Think of an agricultural experiment to determine the effectiveness of different fertilizers on plant growth. Plant growth is also affected by other conditions, such as amount of water, soil characteristics, and amount of sunshine. In order to test the fertilizer, numerous small sections of land (*blocks*), which have identical soil, water, and sun, would each get plants that received each of the test fertilizers (*treatments*).

- Open the Tools menu, select "Data Analysis…," and choose "Anova: Two-Factor Without Replication."

- In the "Input Range" field, enter the cell range that contains the data and the labels for both the rows and columns. Note that with this Analysis Tool "labels" means both row labels and column labels. You cannot simply have column labels as was done with the data for one-factor ANOVA.

- Click the box beside "Labels" to place a checkmark in it indicating that the cell range includes row and column labels.

- Change the value in the "Alpha" field to "0.01." This will cause the output to have the correct critical F values. This is unnecessary if the p value is used for the decision on the Null Hypothesis.

- Click the radio button beside "Output Range" and enter the address "E1" in the field to the right. Click OK. When the tool finishes writing the output, select the following menu sequence: "Format," "Column," and "AutoFit Selection."

The organization of the output is similar to that of the one-factor ANOVA. The summary table provides summary statistics for each column *and* each row in the data. The ANOVA table also has more entries than did the one-way ANOVA table, but the structure of the calculations within the table is very similar.

Separate sums of squares are calculated and provided for the rows and columns (many statistics texts would use the terms *blocks* and *treatments* to mean the same thing). The "Rows" sum of squares is calculated from the difference between each value and the average of the three values in that row. That difference is then squared, summed for all columns, and multiplied by the number of values in each row (the number of columns). The "Columns" sum of squares is computed exactly as the "Between Groups" sum of squares was in single-factor ANOVA. The difference between each number and the average of the numbers in the same column is determined, squared, summed for all rows, and then multiplied by the number of values in each column (number of rows).

The calculation of the error sum of squares is a bit different. For each number, the sum of the average of all numbers in the row plus all numbers in the column is computed. That sum is then subtracted from the grand average of all the data. The difference between the value of that number and this result is then determined, squared, and added for all the numbers in the data. The error sum of squares is analogous to the single-factor "Within Groups" sum of squares.

The total sum of squares is calculated the same as in single-factor ANOVA: The difference between each value and the grand average of all the data is calculated, squared, and summed for all the data. The total sum of squares is also the sum of the row, column, and error sums of squares.

The degrees of freedom of the rows sum of squares is the number of rows minus 1, which is 5 for this problem. Dividing the rows sum of squares by its degree of freedom gives the rows mean squares, which is a measure similar to a variance. Similarly the degrees of freedom of the columns sum of squares is the number of columns minus 1. Dividing the columns sum of squares by its degrees of freedom gives the columns mean square error, another variance-like measure. The degrees of freedom of the error sum of squares is the product of the rows sum of squares degrees of freedom and the columns sum of squares degrees of freedom. Dividing the error sum of squares by its degrees of freedom yields the mean square error.

Two *F* values are given in the printout, along with their *p* values and corresponding critical values. The significance level for the critical values is set by the number in the "Alpha" field of the Tool's dialog window. The values in the "Rows" row of the table is appropriate for the Null Hypothesis that the means of populations from which each row was drawn are all equal. The low *p* value (5.42004E-08 or 0.0000000542) provides a strong basis for rejecting that Null Hypothesis and concluding that there is a difference in the population row means. This result, however, does not address the problem that the analysis is designed to solve. The rows correspond to the different typists. Rejecting the Null Hypothesis means that there is a real difference in the average typing speed of different typists, something we knew before analyzing the data. The only value of the "Rows" test is to help identify a situation in which we have erroneously chosen a control factor that is not strongly related to the outcome measure (typing speed) in which we are interested. This problem clearly does not suffer from that error.

The more important result is found in the "Columns" row of the ANOVA table. The low *p* value in that row (a bit less than .00343) is a strong basis for rejecting the Null Hypothesis of no difference in the population means of the three keyboards. By rejecting that hypothesis, we have evidence (at the .01 level of significance) that the keyboard *does* make a difference in average typing speed.

▼ Two-Factor Analysis with Replication

Two-factor analysis of variance with replication is a technique for examining the relationship between two different characteristics believed to affect a particular outcome. It differs from the two-factor analysis without replication in the following ways:

1. Usually the investigator is interested in both factors, unlike the typical situation with two-factor analysis without replication, where one of the factors is used as control or "blocking."

2. There is more than one observation for each set of values of the factors.

3. In addition to the effect of each factor, the analysis also looks at "interactions," the possibly different effect associated with combinations of factors.

These issues will be clearer as we look at an example:

A perfume manufacturer has test marketed a new perfume in a number of cities. In addition to the scent of the perfume, experience has shown that sales depend heavily on packaging and on advertising strategy. Three different advertising strategies (termed "Sophisticated," "Athletic," and "Popular") and three different package designs were tested along with the new perfume. Each combination was tested in two different markets, and each test market program was six months long. At the completion of the program, the level of sales per thousand women in the market was collected. The results, arranged by advertising strategy and package design, are shown below.

Package Design	Advertising Strategy		
	Sophisticated	Athletic	Popular
1	2.80	2.04	1.58
	2.73	1.33	1.26
2	3.29	1.50	1.00
	2.68	1.40	1.82
3	2.54	3.15	1.92
	2.59	2.88	1.33

These data are also present on Sheet4 of the worksheet in Anova.xls.

Based on these data, is there evidence of a difference in population means for different advertising strategies? Different package designs? Interactions between package designs and advertising strategy?

In this example, we would expect to find *interactions* if the effect of the package design depended on the advertising strategy. It is reasonable to expect interactions in this case. Suppose, for example, one of the package designs was somehow more "sophisticated" than the others. It would make sense for this design to have a different (more positive) impact if the perfume were advertised with the "Sophisticated" strategy than if it were advertised with the "Athletic" strategy.

The fact that each "cell" (that is, each combination of a specific advertising strategy and package design) has more than one observation enables us to calculate a mean of those observations and use them to form an additional sum of squares. This will result in *four* sums of squares: one for the rows, one for the columns, one for the interactions, and an error sum of squares. These sums of squares are handled in an ANOVA table in a manner very similar to the previous ANOVA tables.

In two-factor analysis of variance with replication (unlike two-factor analysis without replication), there is no conceptual difference between the columns and the rows. The factor represented by the rows and that represented by the columns are both to be analyzed. The situation is thus different from the previous approach, where the column factor was the only one to be analyzed while the row factor was designed by the researcher to account for things already known to affect the outcome to be analyzed.

Excel's Analysis Tool does impose one requirement on the structure of the data: Each value of the column factor must occupy a single column on the spreadsheet. Since there are multiple observations per cell, each value of the row factor must occupy *more than one* row. The data in the table on page 340 are organized this way, as are the data in the worksheet.

- Switch to Sheet4 of the Anova.xls worksheet. Rename that worksheet "Interactions."

- Open the Tools menu, select "Data Analysis…," and choose "Anova: Two-Factor With Replication."

- In the "Input Range" field, enter the address for the cell range containing the data table, including the labels in row 1 and column A.

Note that in this tool, unlike the two other ANOVA tools, labels *must* be present for *both* the columns and rows, and their addresses *must* be included in the "Input Range" field. There is no "Labels" check box because labels are required.

- The "Rows per Sample" field should indicate how many observations are in each cell. Since Excel requires them to be in different rows, this is equivalent to the number of rows for each value of the row factor. For this problem, the number is "2." Enter that value in the field.

- Make the entries required to have the tool place the output on the same worksheet, beginning in cell E1. Click OK. Once the output is written, use the Format menu to adjust the column widths.

The table of summary statistics is now quite long, although the same basic descriptive statistics given in the previous ANOVA tools are given here as well. For this output the statistics are arranged in a matrix, allowing you to determine the values for each cell (each combination of a particular row factor value and column factor value). A good check to be sure the dialog window was filled in correctly is to verify that Excel reads two values for each cell and that the labels given in this output include all the row and column labels in the original data. The rightmost column and bottom row are labeled "Total." These give the summary statistics for all of the observations for each value of the column factor and row factor, respectively.

The ANOVA table is quite similar to all the other ANOVA tables except for the presence of the "Interaction" row. Excel uses the term "Sample" to denote what had been termed "Rows" in the two-factor analysis without replication. "Rows" would have been clearer here since the statistic in that row accounts for differences in the row factor. The calculations of the sums of squares and degrees of freedom are similar to those of the other ANOVAs, and the mean squares (MS), a variance-like measure, is determined by dividing each sum of squares by its degrees of freedom. The three F values were calculated by dividing each of the mean square values in that row by the mean square error. The answers to the problem are given best by the three p values.

The p value of slightly over .0761 for the rows ("Sample") factor indicates that we (just) Fail to Reject the Null Hypothesis (at the .05 level of significance) that there is no difference in the population means for the different package designs. The p value of a bit over .00037 for the column factor provides a strong basis for rejecting the Null Hypothesis of no difference in the population means of the different advertising strategies. In other words, advertising strategy clearly affects sales, while it appears that package design may not. The p value for interactions of slightly over .022 is especially interesting. This low value would lead to rejecting the Null Hypothesis of no difference in the population means of the different interactions. This suggests that while we were unable to conclude that packaging had any overall effect on mean sales, it appears that it does have an effect with certain advertising strategies. It would thus be a mistake to conclude that packaging is not important. A result like this clearly calls for additional research to determine with more precision how the interaction between packaging and advertising strategy works.

▼Exercises

1. Use one-factor analysis of variance to analyze the data on the effect of keyboards on typing speed in the Blocked worksheet. Produce a printout that shows the results of both the one-factor and two-factor without replication analyses. Which technique is preferable? Why?

2. The results of the perfume data indicated the presence of significant interaction effects between advertising strategy and package design. For which advertising strategy are these effects important? Answer that question by using separate one-factor analysis of variance on the data for each advertising strategy to test for differences in the population means of different package designs. Produce a printout showing your results for each strategy. When is package design important?

3. Property taxation requires that appraisers periodically determine the market value of all the houses in a jurisdiction. Ideally this determination is completely objective, and every appraiser would come up with the same value. In practice this is impossible. The tax division of a county government wants to determine if there is evidence of a difference in the averages of appraised values among four different appraisers. In order to determine this, each appraiser is asked to determine the value of four houses. The same four houses are appraised by each appraiser with the following results:

| House | Appraiser | | | |
	Mike	Sally	Tom	Jane
1	$101,900	$101,944	$100,967	$100,175
2	$72,744	$76,893	$73,206	$74,820
3	$132,217	$136,232	$131,935	$132,889
4	$211,213	$213,941	$212,735	$213,796

Is there evidence (at the .05) level of significance of a difference in average appraised value among appraisers? Print the results of the appropriate analysis in Excel and explain why you chose that particular analysis rather than the others. Be sure to provide a "yes" or "no" answer to the question and your basis for that answer. (A copy of the data is in Sheet6 of the workbook in Anova.xls.)

4. A grocery chain wants to determine if background music affects the average daily sales of stores. A sample of similarly sized stores was chosen and each was randomly assigned to four different groups: no background music, classical, hard rock, and soft rock. The results (in

$10,000) are shown below. (These data are also on Sheet7 of the workbook in anova.xls.)

None	Classical	Hard	Soft
13	16	13	13
9	19	14	12
10	11	16	15
17	9	4	9
10	11	15	15

Based on this result, is there evidence at the .05 level of significance that music choice would affect average sales for all stores? Print the Excel analysis and explain how you determined your answer. Be sure to give a "yes" or "no" answer to the question and your basis for that answer.

▼

Chapter 14

Simple Linear Regression

Regression analysis gives us a way to investigate the relationship among a group of variables. *Simple* regression analyzes the relationship between two variables. *Multiple* regression removes this restriction and permits the analysis of the relationship among any number of variables. Although the mathematics of multiple regression is a reasonably straightforward extension of simple regression, the increased flexibility makes it a much more versatile and complex analysis tool than simple regression. By studying simple regression before multiple regression, we postpone some of the complexities of regression analysis and focus on the essentials. Another reason to study simple regression first is that the restriction to two dimensions (two variables) makes it easy to represent regression analysis graphically.

When a researcher uses simple linear regression to analyze a set of data, she must already accept certain assumptions. If these assumptions cannot be accepted, some technique other than simple regression will be required to analyze the data. In many (but not all) cases, multiple regression may offer a good technique for analyzing such data.

Data appropriate for simple linear regression consist of observations that each have two different measures. For example, we might have a sample of houses and, for each house, a measure of that house's size and its selling price. Perhaps we have a sample of families, and for each family we have annual income and annual expenditures on clothing. A classic problem in regression analysis involves data containing the height of individuals and the average height of each individual's parents (the measure of height was adjusted for gender differences).

Simple regression allows us to investigate the relationship between the two measures and answer such questions as "What sales price could be predicted for a house with 965 square feet?" or "Do taller parents tend to have taller children?" or "Of every additional $1 increase in income, how much on average goes to additional expenditures on clothes?" Implicit in these questions is the notion of *causality*. The size of a house determines, or causes, the level of the sales price, and not vice versa. Similarly, tall parents are responsible for tall children. The height of the child doesn't determine the height of the parents. A family's income determines how much that family spends on clothes; the amount it spends on clothes doesn't determine its income. Note that regression is of no use in determining the direction of causality; that determination must be made before regression analysis is used.

In a causal relationship between two factors, one factor causes changes in the other factor, not vice versa. The causing factor (house size, height of parents, and family income in the previous examples) is termed the *independent variable*. The idea here is that whatever determines the level of that measure is outside, or independent, of the relationship being analyzed between the two measures. Other names for this measure include *exogenous variable* and *x variable*.

The factor experiencing the effect of a change in the independent variable in the relationship (such as house selling price, height of children, and expenditure on clothes) is termed the *dependent variable*. Its value depends on the value of the independent variable. Other names for this measure include *endogenous variable* and *y variable*.

▼ Linear Relationships

When a set of data is analyzed by simple linear regression, the result is an equation that traditionally contains a *y* on the left-hand side of the equal sign and an *x* on the right-hand side. When a value is substituted in the equation for the symbol *x*, the equation provides the computation of a *predicted* value for *y*. The equation is called *linear* because it gives a relationship between the *y* and *x* variables that, when plotted, results in a straight line. Any equation for a line can be written in the following form:

$$y = b_0 + b_1 x$$

Both "b_0" and "b_1" would be numbers in a specific equation; when their values are determined, the equation is determined. Simple linear regression determines the values of "b_0" and "b_1" that "best" fit the data according to a specific criterion. When a linear equation is written in the form shown above, "b_0" is sometimes called the *y intercept* and "b_1" is called the *slope*. Let's use Excel to explore these meanings.

- Open the Excel workbook in the file Simpreg.xls. Go to the first worksheet, which is titled "b0 & b1."

- In cell B17, enter the number "1." This will be an intercept value.

- In cell B18, enter the number "2." This will be a slope value.

- Select cell B2. This cell will contain a y value to go with the x value of −3. Each cell below it will contain the y value to go with the x value beside it.

- Enter the Excel formula in cell B2 that will take the value in cell B17 (which is "b_0") and add to it the value in cell B18 ("b_1") times the value in cell A2 ("x"). Make the references to cells B17 and B18 *absolute* and the reference to A2 *relative*.

This formula is the Excel version of the equation of a line given above. With the values for "b_0" (1) and "b_1" (2) given above, the form of the equation is $y = 1 + 2x$. If −3 is substituted for x, the value of y is −5. This value should be displayed in B2.

- Copy the formula in B2 to B3 through B15. If error values are displayed in any of the cells, select B5 and double check it. Be sure the references to B17 and B18 are *absolute* and A5 is *relative*. If the value in A5, "0," is substituted for x in the equation $y = 1 + 2x$, the result is 1. This is the value that should be displayed in B5. Similarly, the value in B15 should be 21.

- Select the region A1:B15. Click the Chart Wizard Button (▣).

- When the Step 1 dialog window of the Chart Wizard opens, select "XY (Scatter)" from the "Standard" types. Select the subtype shown in the bottom row on the right, which will connect the points with lines without data markers. Click the Next> button twice.

- In the Step 3 dialog window, select "Titles." Make the chart title "Slope and Intercept," the "Value (X) axis title" "X," and the "Value (Y) axis title" "Y." Select "Legend" and make the legend no longer visible. Click Finish. Make the chart as large as you can so that you can view it and the data in columns A and B without scrolling.

If the data for an Excel chart change, Excel will normally rescale the axes so that all of the new data will fit. We will change the values of the slope and intercept to see how the line changes. In this case, a rescaling of an axis will make it more difficult to see exactly how the line changes. To avoid this, we can "fix" the vertical axis so that Excel will not change it.

- Place the mouse pointer on one of the the numbers along the horizontal (x) axis and click the (left) mouse button to select the axis. Either click the right mouse button and select "Format Axis..." or open the Format menu on the Menu Bar and and click "Selected Axis...."

- Click the "Scale" folder tab at the top of the window. On the left side of the window is a series of fields under the title "Value (X) Axis Scale." Change the value in the field to the right of "Maximum:" to "10." Notice that this removes the checkmark to the left of "Maximum." That checkmark indicated that Excel was to determine the value automatically. By entering a value, you have told Excel to always use the value entered rather than to determine that value from the data. The dialog window should look like the picture below. Click the OK button.

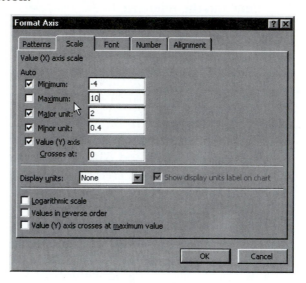

- Click a number on the vertical (*y*) axis to select that axis. Open the Format Axis dialog window, click "Scale," and remove the two checkmarks to the left of "Minimum:" and "Maximum:" by clicking them. This will prevent Excel from changing the *y* axis when the data change.

Changing the value of the intercept (in B17) and the slope (B18) will make the line change. Observe how these changes work in the steps below so that you can think of a line you see in terms of its intercept and slope. Notice also the relationship between the *x* and *y* values in columns A and B.

- Change the value of the intercept to 5. Observe where it crosses the vertical axis. Change it to 10, 15, and then 20.

- Change the intercept back to 1. Make the slope larger and note the effect it has on the line. Try values of 5, 10, 15, 20, and 22. After each change, look at the *x* and *y* values in columns A and B.

- Make the slope 0. Look at the relationship between the values of *x* and *y* in the table. Change the intercept to 12 and reexamine the table.

- Keep the intercept at 12. Make the slope increasingly negative. Try values of –2, –5, –10, –50. Study the relationship between *x* and *y* in the table after each change.

When a line has a positive slope, increasing *x* values are associated with increasing *y* values. When a line has a negative slope, increasing *x* values are associated with decreasing *y* values. A positive slope indicates a *positive* or *direct* relationship between *x* and *y*. A negative slope indicates a *negative* or *inverse* relationship between *x* and *y*.

What happens to the relationship between the values in columns A and B when the slope is 0? A horizontal line has a special significance because it represents *no relationship* between the two variables. Changes in the value of the *x* variable in column A have no effect at all on the *y* variable in column B, and knowing *x* doesn't affect our best guess of *y*. The basis of some of the goodness of fit tests for a regression line involves comparing the relationship implied by the line that "best" fits the data with a horizontal line—equivalent to comparing the "best" relationship to no relationship at all.

▼The Simple Linear Regression Model

When we use simple linear regression to analyze a data sample, we are making certain assumptions about those data. We assume, for example, that a linear relationship exists between two measures or variables in the population, which can be represented by the following equation:

$$Y = \beta_0 + \beta_1 X + \varepsilon$$

Compare this equation to the equation on page 346. The equation here shows a relationship in a population; that is why capital Y and X are used here rather than lowercase *y* and *x*. It is also why Greek letters β_0 and β_1 (*beta*) are used rather than b_0 and b_1. The meanings of β_0 and β_1 here are the same as b_0 and b_1 in that earlier equation. β_0 is the *y* axis intercept and β_1 is the slope of the line. Both of the β's are fixed numbers—population parameters. Like other population parameters (such as μ), we generally do not know their value and seek to estimate them by analyzing a sample of data drawn from the population.

The most important difference between the equation above and the one on page 346 is the "ε" (the Greek letter *epsilon*). Unlike the β's, ε is a random number. Its presence means that the relationship cannot be perfectly represented by a straight line. Even if we knew β_0 and β_1, we still couldn't perfectly predict Y. There is a difference between the actual value of Y and what the value would be if the relationship were perfectly linear. That difference is ε, and its value differs randomly for each observation. ε is usually regarded as representing the effect of a large number of individually insignificant and independent factors which affect the value of *Y other than* X. Regression analysis requires certain assumptions about the distribution of ε: It is normal with a mean of 0 and a constant variance. The values of ε are assumed independent of one another.

▼Fitting a Line to Sample Data

The values of β_0 and β_1 are estimated by selecting a sample of data and then finding the line that best "fits" the data according to a specific criterion: minimizing the sum of squared errors. This estimation line is represented by the following function:

$$\hat{y} = b_0 + b_1 x$$

The $\hat{y}$ is termed the "predicted" value of *y* given by the linear equation and is often called "*y* hat." Recall that each observation in the population has a value for ε associated with it, and these values cause the population values not to have a precise linear relationship. When a sample is chosen, the sample values will not lie precisely on a straight line. As a result, there will generally be a difference for each observation between the value of $\hat{y}$ and the value of *y*. This will be clearer if we consider a specific example.

A firm that manufactures a particular type of hardware fastener wants to determine the relationship between monthly operating costs and monthly output for its manufacturing plants. Each plant submits a report each month that includes this information, and from these reports the firm has selected a sample showing output (in thousands of pounds) and operating cost (in thousands of dollars). Based on this information, what is the relationship?

The data for this problem can be found on the Line Fit worksheet of the workbook in Simpreg.xls. We will use the procedures above to try to manually fit a line to the output and cost data and see the relationship between the visual fit between the line and data and the sum of squared errors.

• Switch to the Line Fit worksheet.

The worksheet already contains observations with *x* and *y* values in columns A and B, respectively. Column C (labeled "y hat") will contain a second set of *y* values derived from a line whose intercept and slope will be entered in C16 and C17 using the same procedure as was used on the previous worksheet.

- Enter the value "2" in cell C16 and "1.5" in cell C17. We will see how well this line fits the data and then make changes to improve the fit.

- Enter formulas in cells C2:C15 that calculate the y value associated with the corresponding x value in column A for a line whose intercept and slope are given in C16 and C17. These formulas will be very similar to the ones you entered in column B on the b0 & b1 worksheet. Be sure to multiply the value in C17 (b_1) by x (column A) and not y. Also be sure the addresses for b_0 and b_1 in the equation are *absolute*. When the correct formulas are entered, cell C2 will display the value "3.575," and cell C15 will display "6.29." These values are the *predicted y values*.

The goal of fitting a line to the data is to come up with the values for the slope and intercept that result in values in column C that are "closest" to those in column B (predicted values close to actual values). For regression, "close" is defined in terms of the sum of squared errors.

- Enter the formulas in cells D2:D15 that will, for each row, calculate the value in column B minus the value in column C. It is these differences that are to be collectively minimized. Cell D2 should display "2.06," and cell D15 should display "3.61." These values are often called the *errors* or *residuals*, and fitting a line involves a way of collectively minimizing them.

- Use the AutoSum button to enter the formula in cell D16 that will calculate the sum of the numbers in D2:D15. The displayed value should be "99.4750." This is the *sum of the errors*. The sum is positive, like most of the individual errors. On average, the actual values exceed the predicted values.

- Enter formulas in cells E2:E15 that will calculate the square of the corresponding value in column D. E2 should display "4.2230," and E15 should display "13.0321." These are the *squared errors*.

- Enter the formula in E16 that will calculate the sum of the values in E2:E15. This is the *sum of squared errors*. The value displayed in E16 should be "1004.1859."

- Enter the label "SSE" (for sum of squared errors) in cell E17. This is a commonly used abbreviation in statistics.

As stated above, regression fits a line to the data by determining the value of the intercept and slope that minimizes the sum of squared errors (in E16). You may wonder why the sum of errors (in D16) isn't minimized instead. To examine this and the relationship between fit and sum of squared errors, we will plot the data and the line given by the value of the slope and intercept in C16 and C17.

- Select the region A1:C15.

- Click the Chart Wizard button. Choose "XY (Scatter)" from the "Standard" types.

- Choose the subtype at the top that shows symbols at the data points but no connecting lines. Click Next>.

- Examine the small preview plot in the Step 2 window. You should see two sets of data plotted; the symbols used to show the points should have different shapes and different colors. Look at the legend on the preview plot and identify which points correspond to "y hat." They should appear to lie along a straight line. We will convert the representation of those points to a line, and you need to remember which they are because we will remove the legend in the final chart to give the plot area more room.

- Click Next>. In the Step 3 window, remove the chart's legend. Click Finish.

- Move the chart so that the top of the chart is in row 18. Scroll your worksheet so that row 16 is the top row visible. Make the chart larger, but be sure the entire chart and rows 16 and 17 are all visible without scrolling the worksheet.

- Place the mouse pointer over one of the "y hat" points and single click. Many (or all) of the points should change color ("light up"). Be sure you have the points that lie along a line.

- Open the Format menu on the Menu Bar and click "Selected Data Series…" (or click the right mouse button and select "Format Data Series…"). The Format Data Series dialog window will appear.

- Click the "Patterns" folder tab at the top of the dialog window. In the area titled "Line," click "Custom." In the area titled "Marker," click "None." Click the OK button.

- Place the mouse pointer on a part of your worksheet off the chart and click once to deselect the "y hat" points. The chart should show a line with no point symbols on the line.

Clearly the line does not "fit" the data points very well; it is too low. As we noted before, most of the errors are positive; the points lie above the line. We will adjust the line so that the fit improves and observe what happens to the sum of squared errors (in E16). What about the sum of errors?

- Enter the number "17.28357" for the intercept and "0" for the slope. What happens to the sum of errors (D16)? (It should be 0.) This horizontal line clearly doesn't fit the data very well. Jot down the value of the sum of squared errors (SSE).

- Enter the number "28.18786" for the intercept and "-2" for the slope. What is the sum of errors (D16) this time? (It should again be 0.)

What is going on here? It turns out that any line that goes through the point whose x value is $\bar{x}$ (5.452143 for these data) and whose y value is $\bar{y}$ (17.28357) will have a 0 sum of errors. Both of the two lines you just examined went through that point. Lines containing this point may not fit the data well! Although the horizontal line was a poor fit, it was better than the second line. The SSE reflected this, increasing from 1027.219 to 2778.444.

- To see a line that fits the data much better, try an intercept value of "1.5" and a slope of "3.2." The SSE for this line is 113.6625, much smaller than was the case before.

- Look carefully at the line and the data points. Does the line look just a bit high and perhaps a bit too steep? Adjust the intercept and slope to improve the fit. Try to reduce the sum of squared errors as low as possible. You should easily be able to find a line whose SSE is less than 100. Can you find one whose SSE is less than 70? (yes), less than 65? (good luck).

▼Determining the Regression Line

Calculating the slope and the intercept of the line which minimizes the sum of squared errors is very straightforward and similar to the calculations done in ANOVA. The formulas for the regression coefficients (intercept and slope) are

$$b_1 = \frac{\sum (x_i - \bar{x})(y_i - \bar{y})}{\sum (x_i - \bar{x})^2}$$

$$b_0 = \bar{y} - b_1 \bar{x}$$

The numerator of the expression above for b_1 is often represented by the symbol SP_{xy} (for Sum of Products). The denominator, which you should recognize as the sum of squared deviations of x from its mean, is represented by SS_x.

Since SS_x *must* always be positive, the sign of the slope of the regression line is determined by the sign of SP_{xy}. When a set of data has a positive relationship, small values of x will generally be associated with small values of y. Since these small values will be below the mean, both $(x_i - \overline{x})$ and $(y_i - \overline{y})$ will be negative, and their product will be positive. Large values of x will generally be associated with large values of y. Both $(x_i - \overline{x})$ and $(y_i - \overline{y})$ will still be positive, and their product will also be positive. When these are added up, they result in a positive value for SP_{xy}. On the other hand, if there is a negative relationship between x and y, small values of x tend to be associated with large values of y. In this case $(x_i - \overline{x})$ will be negative but $(y_i - \overline{y})$ will be positive, causing their product to be negative. When x is large and y small, the two expressions switch signs, but their product is still negative. Summing up these negative values will make SP_{xy}, and b_1 also, negative.

These formulas require a lot of arithmetic, but they are easy to set up in Excel.

- Switch to the Regression worksheet, where you will find the same output and cost data and the labels for calculating the values of b_0 and b_1. Columns D, E, and F require $\hat{y}$, which will be calculated after the regression coefficients.

- Enter formulas in B17 and C17 that will calculate the average of the data values in their respective columns. B17 should display "5.45," and C17 should display "17.28." Note that these cells have an Excel format that limits their display to two decimal places. You can use the Increase Decimal button to display more precision, but regardless of display, Excel uses full precision in calculations.

- Using either Paste Link or a simple formula with an absolute address, set the cells in the range G2:G15 so that they will refer to cell B17 and will display the same value displayed in B17.

- In the region H2:H15, enter the formula that will calculate the difference between that row's value for x in column B and the mean of the x's in column G. H2 should display "-4.40," and cell H15 should display "-2.59." Use the AutoSum button to display in cell H16 the sum of the values in the column above. The sum should be zero.

- Enter formulas in each cell of region I2:I15 that will square the value in column H of that row. I2 should display "19.3789," and I15 should display "6.7192." Use cell I16 to calculate and display the sum of the values above. This sum should be "111.1582." This is SS_x. Enter the label "SSx" in cell I17.

- Enter formulas in rows 2 through 15 of columns J, K, and L that give y the same treatment x received in columns G, H, and I. Cell L2 should display "248.4902," and cell L15 should display "54.5171."

- Enter formulas in row 16 of columns K and L that will display the column sums. K16 should display "0," and L16 should display "1027.22." This is the value of $\sum (y_i - \bar{y})^2$, also called SST. It is not needed to determine the regression coefficients, but will be used later.

- Enter the label "SST" in cell L17.

- Enter formulas in the region M2:M15 that will calculate and display the product of each row's value of $(x_i - \bar{x})$ in column H and $(y_i - \bar{y})$ in column K. The displayed value of M2 should be a little over 69.39 and that of M15 should be just under 19.14. Use M16 to determine a sum of the values in column M. That sum should be approximately 326.648. This is SP_{xy}. Enter the label "SPxy" in cell M17.

Notice that most (all but one) of the values in column M are positive. Look at how these positive values are the result of the signs of the numbers in each row in columns H and K. Both x and y tend to be associated with values on the same side of the mean.

- Select cell B19, which is to contain the regression value for b_1. Enter a formula that will divide the value of SP_{xy} in the worksheet by the value of SS_x. Cell B19 will display the value of the regression line's slope, "2.938587."

Recall that the formula for the intercept is $b_0 = \bar{y} - b_1 \bar{x}$. The value for b_1 is in B19, the value for $\bar{y}$ is in C17, and the value for $\bar{x}$ is in B17.

- Enter the formula in B18 to calculate b_0. The result should display as "1.261978."

With these results, we can now write the regression equation as

$$\hat{y} = 1.261978 + 2.938578x$$

The slope coefficient can be interpreted as estimating that a one-unit (that is, 1,000 pounds) increase in output results, on average, in a little less than a 2.94 unit (thousands of dollars) increase in monthly operating costs. This is equivalent to just under $2.94 a pound. The equation can be used to predict the average monthly cost for any level of output. We will first use it to provide predicted values for the output levels in the data.

- Using the same approach as on the previous worksheet, enter formulas in cells D2:D15 that will provide a predicted y value ($\hat{y}$) for each x value in the row, using the values for b_0 and b_1 given in cells B18 and

B19. The value displayed in cell D2 should be "4.3475," while that in D15 should be "9.6663."

- Enter formulas in E2:E15 to calculate the difference between the actual y value in column C and the value for $\hat{y}$ in column D (the *errors* or *residuals*). E2 should display "-2.827," and E15 should display "0.234." Sum the values of column E in E16. The sum should be zero.

- Enter formulas in F2:F15 to calculate the squared errors. The value in F2 should be "7.9947" and that in F15 should be "0.0546." Use F16 to calculate and display the sum of squared errors (SSE). The displayed value should be "67.3350." Enter the label "SSE" in F17.

Recall that the regression-determined intercept and slope result in the smallest possible value for SSE.

- Compare the SSE here with the value you got when you manually tried to find the slope and intercept that minimizes SSE (cell E16 on the Line Fit worksheet).

▼ Using Regression to Predict *y* Values

The process you used to develop a value for $\hat{y}$ for each of the x values in the data can also be used to provide predicted y values (that is, $\hat{y}$'s) for any x value, not just ones actually in the data.

- Enter the labels "x" and "y hat" in cells C20 and C21 of the Regression worksheet.

- Enter the number "5" in cell D20.

- Enter a formula in D21 that will use the value of b_1 in cell B19, the value of b_0 in cell B18, and the value of x in D20 to calculate the regression equation for the x value in D20. The displayed value for D21 will be "15.95491."

The regression analysis enables us to predict that a monthly output of 5,000 pounds would incur an operating cost of $15,954.91. What would be the predicted operating cost for an output of 3,000 pounds?

- Enter the number "3" in cell D20. After you press the Enter key, the value "10.07774" should immediately be displayed in cell D21. The predicted cost of a monthly output of 3,000 pounds would be $10,077.74.

Using regression to predict the y values in this way will yield the most accurate results when the x value is close to the average value of the x's used to determine the regression coefficients (5.45 in this case). Special caution must be used in predicting a y value for an x value outside the range of x values used to determine the regression coefficients (1.05 to 9.98 in this case).

▼Goodness of Fit—Descriptive Approach

For any set of data, regression analysis will always find the line that fits the data best in the sense of minimizing the sum of squared errors. Even if there is no relationship at all between the two measures, regression will provide the intercept and slope that best fits that "relationship." In this case the "best" fit will not be a "good" fit. As a result, whenever we do regression analysis we need to have, in addition to the estimated parameters (intercept and slope) that define the regression line, an indication of whether the fit between the line and data is "good." We will explore how that is done.

- Switch to the Data worksheet. You will find two columns of numbers under the heading "Bad Fit." Select the cells containing the numbers (A3:B16), click the Copy button, switch to the Line Fit worksheet, select cell A2, and click the Paste button. The previous data will be overwritten with the "Bad Fit" data.

Changing the data in the Line Fit worksheet will also change the data in columns B and C of the Regression worksheet. There is a "Paste Link" connection between those Regression worksheet cells and the ones in the Line Fit worksheet.

- Scroll the screen in the Line Fit worksheet so that row 16 is at the top and examine the chart. There is no line that will fit these data closely.

- Switch to the Regression worksheet. Copy the value for the mean of the y values ($\bar{y}$) into the clipboard by selecting cell C17 and clicking the Copy button.

Remember that cell C17 contains a formula for calculating the average of the y values in column C. If we use the Paste button to paste the clipboard, that formula would be copied to the cell we pasted to. We want to paste not the formula but the *current value* of the formula. It is this value (sometimes rounded) that is displayed in the cell.

- Switch back to the Line Fit worksheet and select cell C16 (the intercept of the line drawn on the chart). Open the Edit menu on the Menu Bar (or click the right mouse button) and select "Paste Special…." When the Paste Special dialog window appears, click "Values" under

"Paste" on the left side of the window so the radio button beside it is chosen (as shown below).

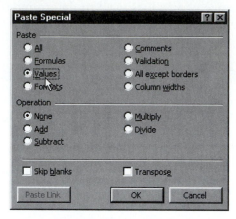

- Click the OK button in the dialog window. The value for $\bar{y}$ (about 17.35074) will appear in cell C16.

- Enter the value "0" in cell C17 (the slope of the line). Scroll your worksheet and look at the values of $\hat{y}$ in C2:C15. They should all be equal to $\bar{y}$.

- Scroll your worksheet down so that cell A16 is in the upper-left corner. Your screen should show the chart with a horizontal line.

Remember that a horizontal line represents no relationship between the x value and the y value. The horizontal line that goes through $\bar{y}$ has a lower sum of squared errors than any other horizontal line.

- Copy the value of $\bar{y}$ in cell C16 to cell F16 (use the Copy and Paste buttons). Also copy the *value* of SSE cell E16 to cell G16 (use the Copy button and "Paste Special"). Enter the label "horizontal SSE" in G17. As you make changes to the intercept and slope, compare the changing SSE in cell E16 to the SSE from the horizontal line through $\bar{y}$ in G16.

- Make small changes to the value in C16. You should see the horizontal line shift up and down depending on whether the changes increase or decrease the value in C16. Notice that any change in C16 alone will increase the value of the sum of squared errors in cell E16 (as compared to the original value in G16).

- Copy the value for $\bar{y}$ in cell F16 back to cell C16.

When you went through the process earlier in this chapter of manually fitting a line to the original set of data, you also started with a horizontal line through $\bar{y}$. With those data, it was not difficult to find a value of the slope and intercept that would reduce the sum of squared errors. For the current set of data, it will not be so easy (although it can be done).

- Adjust the values of b_0 and b_1 (in cells C16 and C17) to reduce the value of SSE in E16 below the horizontal line SSE in G16.

Not only is it more difficult to find values for b_0 and b_1 that reduce SSE, but the amount of reduction is less for this data set than it was for the original data set. By using the regression coefficients, we can determine the minimum value for SSE.

- Switch to the Regression worksheet. Copy the regression values for b_0 and b_1 (in cells B18 and B19) to the clipboard by using the Copy button. Switch back to the Line Fit worksheet. Select cell C16. Paste the *values* in the clipboard by using "Paste Special."

Despite the fact that it doesn't fit these data very well, the regression intercept and slope are identical to the regression intercept and slope of the previous data. We can't tell from the regression coefficients alone whether the fit is good or not.

Compare the values in E16 (SSE with regression line) and G16 (SSE with horizontal line). They are clearly much closer in value to each other than were the corresponding SSE's for the original data (which were 67.33504 for the regression SSE and 1027.22 for the horizontal line SSE). When a regression line fits a set of data well, its SSE is much lower than the SSE of a horizontal line through $\bar{y}$. If *no* line fits a data set very well, the regression SSE will be only a little smaller than the horizontal line SSE.

- Compare the value of the horizontal line SSE in cell G16 of the Line Fit worksheet with the value we earlier labeled "SST" in cell L16 on the Regression worksheet.

SST was calculated by summing the squared differences between $\bar{y}$ and each y. It is equivalent to the SSE derived from a horizontal line through $\bar{y}$ (if $b_1 = 0$ then SSE = SST). You should also recognize it as the numerator of the expression defining the variance of y. SST and SSE may also remind you of the sums of squared differences that constitute the building blocks of ANOVA. As with ANOVA, a simple relationship exists among the various sums of squares, one of which has not yet been introduced.

- Replace the "horizontal SSE" label currently in cell G17 on the Line Fit worksheet with the label "SST."

- Change the contents of cell G16 (either by entering a simple formula or using Paste Link) so the value displayed in that cell will always be the calculated value of SST in cell L16 of the Regression worksheet.

This will not change the currently displayed value of G16, but the value will now change when the data in columns A and B are changed.

SST measures the "Total" sum of squared differences, or variation, in a set of data. After a regression line is fit to the data, SSE measures the variation that the regression line cannot explain ("Error"). If the line fits the data well, SSE will be substantially less than SST, as we just saw. If no line fits the data well, SSE and SST will be close in value. The difference between SSE and SST is termed SSR, the sum of squares due to "Regression." It can be directly calculated as $\sum(\hat{y}_i - \bar{y})^2$ (this is left for an exercise) or from the relationship SSR = SST − SSE.

- On the Line Fit worksheet, enter the formula in cell F16 (replacing the current contents) to display the value of SSR by subtracting the SSE in cell E16 from the SST in cell G16. The displayed value is "426.24615." Enter the label "SSR" in cell F17.

As we have seen, the greater the difference between SSE and SST, the better the regression line fits the data. Since SSR is the difference between SSE and SST, an equivalent formulation would be to say that the closer SSR is to SST, the better the regression line fits the data. A common measure of goodness of fit is the r^2 (or coefficient of determination) statistic, which calculates SSR as a proportion of SST:

$$r^2 = \frac{\text{SSR}}{\text{SST}} = \frac{\text{SST} - \text{SSE}}{\text{SST}}$$

An interpretation of r^2 is that it measures the proportion of the total variation in y which is explained by the variation in x. It must have a value between 0 and 1.

- Enter the formula in cell D16 (replacing the current contents) to calculate the value of r^2. The displayed value for this data is 0.0916. Enter the label "r squared" in cell D17.

For the "bad fit" data, slightly over 9% of the variation in the y values is explained by variation in the x values. Let's compare the value of r^2 for these data with that from the original data we used.

- Select the Data worksheet. Copy the contents of the original data in D3:E16 to the clipboard. Return to the Line Fit worksheet and paste those data in A2:B15.

Notice that the value of r^2 is now over 0.93! For these data, over 93% of the variation in the values of y is explained by the variation in the values of x. Note that normally when the data changes like this, the values of the coefficients in C16 and C17 need to be changed to the regression coefficients. In this case, however, the two sets of data we have examined happen to have the same regression coefficients. Hence, we need not copy new values for the slope and intercept from the Regression worksheet.

▼Goodness of Fit—Inferential Approach

The r^2 statistic is descriptive—it tells us how well the regression line fits the particular sample on which it has been estimated. A different, although related, approach to goodness of fit is the inferential approach that looks at the issue from a different perspective. Recall that regression analysis assumes that the sample data on which a regression line is estimated have been selected from a population. In that population the X and Y variables have a relationship that can be expressed by the formula $Y = \beta_0 + \beta_1 X + \varepsilon$. When a regression line is estimated, the resulting regression equation is $\hat{y} = b_0 + b_1 x$. We can regard b_0 and b_1 as *estimates* of β_0 and β_1, respectively. Just as $\bar{x}$ is an estimate of μ, b_1 is an estimate of β_1. Both $\bar{x}$ and b_1 (and b_0, for that matter) are random numbers (*statistics*) whose values will vary from sample to sample and which will never precisely equal their corresponding fixed parameters (μ, β_1, and β_0).

If there is no relationship in the population between y and x, the value of β_1 is 0. In such a case, the value of b_1, determined by regression from a sample, will, in all probability, be nonzero just by chance. The inferential approach treats the issue of goodness of fit in a hypothesis-testing or confidence interval framework. Two different sets of calculations can be used in regression to implement the inferential approach. For simple linear regression they always yield identical results, but in multiple regression they have different interpretations and different results.

SSE, as we have seen, is similar to the numerator of a variance formula. If SSE is divided by its degrees of freedom, the result is termed *MSE* (mean square error), or *residual variance*, and is represented by the symbol s_ε^2.

$$s_\varepsilon^2 = \text{MSE} = \frac{\text{SSE}}{df}$$

where *df* is degrees of freedom of SSE.

MSE measures the variance of the y values around the regression line in the same way that an ordinary variance is measured around the mean of the y's. It is analogous to a sample variance; the corresponding population variance for which it is an estimate is the variance of the residual values ε in the population equation.

- Select the Regression worksheet. Enter the label "MSE" in cell F18. Cell G18 will be used for the formula to calculate and display the value of MSE.

For simple linear regression the value for the degrees of freedom of SSE is $n - 2$, where n is the number of observations used in the regression analysis.

- Enter the formula in cell G18 to calculate and display the value of MSE. The displayed value should be slightly over 5.611.

You may recognize this step as similar to those used in analysis of variance. One of the inferential approaches to goodness of fit is an ANOVA approach. At this point we will consider the other approach.

As noted above, b_1 is a random number. It therefore has a distribution (whose mean is β_1) and a standard deviation. As a statistic, its standard deviation is termed a *standard error* just as the standard deviation of $\bar{x}$ is called a standard error. Once we determine the standard error of b_1, we can construct a confidence interval on β_1 and perform hypothesis tests on β_1. These will provide techniques for investigating whether or not there is a relationship between y and x in the *population* from which the sample was drawn.

The standard error of b_1 is easily calculated from MSE and SS_x (the sum of squared deviations of x from its mean—already calculated in cell I16) by the following formula:

$$s_{b_1} = \sqrt{\frac{\text{MSE}}{\text{SS}_x}}$$

Notice that if the regression line fits the data well, SSE and thus MSE would be small, as would s_{b_1}. A smaller standard error will also occur if there is a high variation in the x values.

- Enter the label "standard error b1" in cell A20 (and adjust the column width). In cell B20 enter an Excel formula that will calculate s_{b_1} as shown in the equation above by referring to the cells on this spreadsheet where MSE and SS_x are calculated. The cell should display the value "0.224677."

The statistic b_1 follows the t distribution with $n - 2$ degrees of freedom, much as the statistic $\bar{x}$ follows the t distribution with $n - 1$ degrees of freedom. We can use this to examine inferential goodness of fit by asking whether this sample provides evidence that the population slope, β_1, differs from 0. This can be done by testing the Null Hypothesis $H_0: \beta_1 = 0$ against the Alternate Hypothesis $H_A: \beta_1 \neq 0$. A sample t (or t statistic) for this hypothesis can be calculated with a formula very similar to that which is used to test a hypothesis test on μ:

$$t = \frac{b_1 - \beta_1}{s_{b_1}}$$

Since the Null Hypothesis is that $\beta_0 = 0$, this expression reduces to the value of b_1 divided by its standard error. The smaller the standard error, the larger the t value.

- Enter the label "t" in cell A21. In cell B21 enter the Excel formula that will calculate the sample t value for the Null Hypothesis given above. The value displayed in B21 should be "13.07915."

The final step in the worksheet is to determine the p value for this sample t. This will involve using the TDIST function. Remember that TDIST requires that the t value you give it must be positive, and we have previously embedded the use of the ABS function to ensure a positive value. When TDIST was used for problems involving inferences on a population mean, the degrees of freedom was always $n - 1$. For this problem it is $n - 2$. Given the Null Hypothesis above, a two-tail test is appropriate.

- Enter the label "p value" in cell A22. Enter a formula in cell B22 that will calculate the two-tail p value associated with the sample t in B21 for $n - 2$ degrees of freedom. The displayed value should be "1.84226E-08" (or "0.0000000184"—a very small value).

The small p value tells us that it is highly unlikely that we could have gotten by chance a sample with a regression value for b_1 that differed from 0 as much as this one did if the sample were actually chosen from a population in which β_1 was 0. For any of the usual significance levels, we would reject the Null Hypothesis and conclude that $\beta_1 \neq 0$. There *is* evidence (strong evidence) of a relationship in the population between X and Y. Another way of saying this is to say that the regression, or the regression coefficient, is *significant*.

Finding that a regression coefficient is significant is the inferential equivalent of a good fit. The value for s_{b_1} could also be used to develop confidence intervals on the value of β_1. This could be done using almost the identical procedure used for confidence intervals on μ. The confidence interval would be $b_1 \pm ts_{b_1}$, where the t value would have $n - 2$ degrees of freedom and would have a value determined by the level of confidence. A small standard error will result in a narrow confidence interval, and a *significant* coefficient's confidence interval will not include 0.

What kind of result would we get in the case where the regression line does not fit the data well?

- Switch to the Data worksheet. Copy the "Bad Fit" data to the clipboard. Switch to the Line Fit worksheet and paste the data in the region A2:B15. Switch to the Regression worksheet.

Although the regression coefficients are the same in this case, the standard error of b_1 is much higher. This has decreased the value of the sample t and resulted in a p value of a bit more than .29. With such a high p value, we would *Fail to Reject* the Null Hypothesis that $\beta_1 = 0$. This means we don't have very good evidence that there is a relationship in the population between Y and X. We would characterize the regression coefficient (or the regression) as *insignificant*, because the estimated slope is not significantly different from 0.

▼Excel's Built-In Regression Capabilities

Excel has a number of features that will allow you to easily do a regression analysis on a set of data. These include an Analysis Tool, several built-in functions (which can be accessed through the Function Wizard), and a feature of the Chart Wizard. Although these capabilities duplicate each other, they have somewhat different advantages and disadvantages.

The Analysis Tool produces an output that is much easier to read than the functions. The functions have the advantage of being dynamic in the sense that they update their displayed value whenever a change in the worksheet affects the input data. The Analysis Tool, by contrast, must be rerun whenever the data change. Nevertheless, the tool is usually preferable for doing regression analysis. For this reason, the functions (INTERCEPT, SLOPE, TREND, FORECAST, and LINEST) will not be discussed in this chapter, although information on them can be found in Appendix D.

- Switch to the Data worksheet and copy the "Bad Fit" data (including the labels in row 2) to the clipboard. Switch to the Sheet5 worksheet and paste the data beginning in cell A1.

- Change the name of the Sheet5 worksheet to "Bad Fit."

- Using the Chart Wizard, prepare a scatter plot of the data (the same type as on the Line Fit worksheet) with the upper-left corner in cell C1. Make the chart reasonably wide, but do not let it go below row 15. Check your chart against the one on the Line Fit worksheet. Except for the lack of a regression line, they should both clearly be charts of the same data.

- Place the mouse pointer over one of the data points and click once. Most or all of the data points should change color ("light up"), indicating that they have been selected. Open the Chart menu on the Menu Bar and select "Add Trendline..." (or, with the mouse pointer on a data point, click the right mouse button and select "Add Trendline..."). In either case, the Trendline dialog window will open.

- Select the "Type" folder tab at the top. Click the picture above "Linear," which shows a straight line fitting a set of data points.

- Select the "Options" folder tab. The section labeled "Forecast" enables you to extend the line to left or right of the data points. Click the box beside "Display Equation on Chart" and the box beside "Display R-squared Value on Chart" so that each box has an "x" in it. Click the OK button.

As you may see, sometimes Excel does not place the equation and r^2 value in the best place on the graph.

- Place the mouse pointer over the equation and click once. A border will surround the equation and r^2 value. When the mouse pointer is inside the boundary, it has the insertion-point shape. Outside the boundary it is a white arrow.

- Place the mouse pointer so that the tip of the arrow is on the border. Press and hold the (left) mouse button and drag the outline containing the equation and r^2 value to the upper-left corner of the chart where there are no data points. Click the mouse pointer once off the graph to remove the border.

Excel's presentation of the regression line on a plot is nonstandard in that y is used instead of $\hat{y}$, and b_0 is put after, instead of before, b_1.

Compare the chart on this worksheet with that on the Line Fit worksheet. This is certainly an easier way of putting a regression line on a scatter plot! What happens if you change the data?

- Select cell B15 (which now contains "35.24"). Enter the value "0" in the cell. Observe what happens to the chart when you press the Enter key. Click the Undo (⟲) and Redo (⟳) buttons to switch back and forth between the original and new values of B15.

Did the regression line change? Look at the equation and r^2 value written on the chart. Did they change? The answer to both questions should be "yes."

The fact that changing a single observation caused such a drastic change in the regression line is further evidence of the lack of a good fit with these data. This is a demonstration of the result of the test we performed on the Null Hypothesis that the value of β_1 is 0 and that the nonzero value of b_1 could very well be due to chance.

- Return the value of B15 to 35.24.

▼Using the Regression Tool for Simple Linear Regression

The Regression tool can be used for either simple or multiple regression. Its use is very similar to that of the other analysis tools.

- Open the Tools menu and choose "Data Analysis...." From the Data Analysis dialog window, choose "Regression."

- Enter the cell ranges for the x and y data in the appropriate fields. As with other Analysis Tools, it is a good idea to have a label in the first row and to include the address of the label in the cell ranges entered in these fields.

- Click the small box beside "Labels" so that Excel will know the first row contains labels rather than data.

- As part of its output, Excel provides confidence intervals on the population β's. Excel always provides the 95% confidence interval for each β, and, unless you indicate otherwise, provides it twice. Let's instead ask Excel to provide us also with a 90% confidence interval by first clicking the box beside "Confidence Level" so that an "x" appears and then changing the "95" in the field to the right to "90."

- Under "Output Options" select "Output Range." Enter the address "A17" in the field to the right.

There are a number of optional outputs that can be selected from the Regression dialog window. In the section titled "Residuals," you can choose four different optional outputs:

1. **Residuals**—If this is selected, Excel will produce a table showing, for each observation, the value of predicted values ($\hat{y}$), and the value of the *residual* (or error), which is $y - \hat{y}$.

2. **Standardized Residuals**—This choice will cause Excel to produce, in addition to the table of residuals just described, a column showing standardized residuals. Residuals are standardized by dividing them by the error standard deviation (also called the *standard error of the estimate*), which is calculated as $\sqrt{\text{MSE}}$. Choosing to have Excel output standardized residuals always results in the output of predicted

values and nonstandardized residuals regardless of whether or not you also select "Residuals."

3. **Residual Plots**—Selecting this will cause Excel to produce a scatter plot with the value of each observation's residual (or error) plotted on the vertical axis and the observation's value for the x variable plotted on the horizontal axis. Choosing this also always results in getting the output described in option 1 above.

4. **Line Fit Plots**—If this choice is selected, Excel will produce a scatter plot showing both the actual data points and the predicted data points lying on the regression line. For simple (but not multiple) regression, the plot is very similar to the one already drawn on the worksheet by the Chart Wizard, except that the predicted values are shown as points rather than as a line that can, of course, be changed afterwards.

In order to see all of these outputs, check all of the boxes in the "Residuals" section.

The last output choice is for "Normal Probability Plots." A normal probability plot is a chart prepared in such a way that data values are plotted against their quartile values on the standard normal distribution. In such a plot, data that are normally distributed will appear to lie approximately along a line. Excel produces a plot of the y variable, but it is not a properly done normal probability plot. Do not choose it.

- Once these choices have been made, click the OK button on the dialog window.

- When the Regression tool has finished writing the output, the column widths will need to be adjusted. While the cell region containing the output is still selected, open the Format menu, choose "Column," and then click "AutoFit Selection."

- Click on any worksheet cell to remove the selection highlighting.

The output of the Regression tool is so large that you may only be able to see a small part on your screen at one time. To get a better view of your worksheet, use Excel's ability to "zoom."

- Click the downward-pointing arrow on the right side of the Zoom Control on the Standard Toolbar: `100%`. A list of zoom factors will open. Try 75%. If your screen still cannot display columns A through L, change the zoom factor to 50%.

One of the effects of adjusting the column widths for the regression output is that the chart at the top of the worksheet has been made excessively wide.

- Adjust the width of the chart to a size more appropriate for its height. Select it by clicking it once with the mouse. Edit "handles" will appear at each corner and in the center of each side. Place the mouse pointer on the handle that is in the center of the right side. Press and hold the mouse button and drag the handle to the left until the chart's width is correct. Then release the mouse button.

- Notice that the Regression tool has placed one of the charts it has produced on top of the other one. Single click the chart on top and move it so that it is to the right of the scatter plot you produced earlier. Move both charts to the left to keep the information on the worksheet in as compact an area as possible.

- Because of the size of the space used on this worksheet, you may find it easier to follow the discussion below from a printout. If you choose to do this, first click a worksheet cell to ensure that a chart is not selected. Next click the Print Preview button: 🔍 . When the screen previewing the output appears, click the Setup… button at the top. In the Page Setup dialog window, first click the "Page" folder tab. Under "Orientation" select "Landscape." Under "Scaling" select "Fit to 1 page(s) wide by 1 tall." Select the "Sheet" folder tab. Under "Print" select "Row and Column Headings." This will permit you to determine cell addresses on the printout. Click OK. After you return to the Print Preview screen, have Excel print the worksheet.

Let's take a tour of the output. First the charts.

1. **"x Line Fit Plot,"** as mentioned above, is similar to the scatter plot you produced earlier with the Chart Wizard. The "x" in the title refers to the label for the *x* variable (the label in cell A1). A different label would result in a different title. Notice that the Analysis Tool labels both axes in the chart and provides a title and a legend. One result is that the area actually devoted to the plot is small. This can, of course, be changed by editing the chart. The regression line (called "Predicted y" in the legend) is depicted as points rather than as a line. This, too, could be changed by activating the chart, selecting the data points, and then formatting the data series exactly as was done with the scatter plot produced by the Chart Wizard.

2. **"x Residual Plot"** shows the residuals (or errors) plotted against the value of the *x* variable. Like the line fit plot, the residual plot can be useful in finding "outliers," data points that are much further from the regression line than other points. It is often worthwhile to reex-

amine those data points. Perhaps the large value of their error (residual) might be caused by a data collection or recording error. Or perhaps an overlooked factor is responsible for the large residual. A residual plot can also be used to provide some evidence on the issue of whether the assumption that the population ε has constant variance is correct.

Next are the items under "Summary Output."

3. **Multiple R** is the square root of the r^2. When given the sign of the x coefficient b_1, this value is often termed the *coefficient of correlation* and is an alternate measure of the strength of the relationship between the x and y variables.

4. **R Square** is, of course, r^2. There is a convention, followed by many statisticians, to use a lowercase r for simple regression and an uppercase R for multiple regression. Check to be sure the value here agrees with the values you determined on the Line Fit worksheet for the same data.

5. **Adjusted R Square** is meaningful only in a multiple regression context where, as a measure of fit, it takes the number of independent variables into account. The unadjusted R^2 always increases when a new independent variable is added, even if there is no real relationship between it and the dependent variable. Adjusted R^2 is useful only to compare models with the same dependent variable; it has no meaning by itself.

6. **Standard Error** is the square root of MSE. It also is called the *standard error of the regression* or the *standard error of the estimate* and is a measure of goodness of fit, which is also used in calculating other statistics associated with regression. As mentioned above, it is used in calculating standardized residuals.

7. **Observations** is, of course, the number of observations in the data used for estimating the regression equation.

The next section is the analysis of variance section. The table is organized exactly like the ANOVA tables seen in Chapter 13. The first column (df) gives degrees of freedom, the second column (SS) gives the sum of squared deviations. The third column (MS—for Mean Square) divides the sum of squared deviations by the degrees of freedom. The fourth column has the F statistic and the last column (labeled "Significance F") gives the p value for that F statistic.

The row labeled "Regression" is calculated from differences between predicted y values for each observation and the mean of the y values

$(\hat{y} - \bar{y})$. The entry under the SS column is SSR. Compare this with the value you found on the Line Fit worksheet to be sure they are the same.

The row labeled "Residual" would, perhaps, better be labeled "Error." It is the differences between predicted y values and actual y values for each observation $(y - \hat{y})$. The value under SS is SSE, and the value under MS is MSE. Check these against the values on the Regression worksheet.

The row labeled "Total" is calculated from the differences between each y value and the mean of the y values $(y - \bar{y})$. The number under SS is SST. Check it against the values on the Regression worksheet.

The next section provides inferences about the population coefficients (β_0 and β_1). The first row is for β_0 (labeled "intercept"), and the second row is for β_1 (whose label comes from the label used in the data—"x" in this case). For most purposes for which regression is used, β_1 is of greater interest than β_0 and therefore the inferences on β_1 are more important than those on β_0.

The first column gives the values for the regression coefficients, b_0 and b_1. Verify these values with the ones on the Regression worksheet. The second column gives the standard errors for the coefficients. You have calculated the standard error of b_1 on the Regression worksheet; check that this worksheet shows the same value. The Regression tool also calculates and shows the standard error for b_0. The third column gives the value of sample t's for the Null Hypotheses $H_0 : \beta_0 = 0$ (in the first row) and $H_0 : \beta_1 = 0$ (in the second row). The fourth column gives the p values (two-tail) for the respective sample t's. Compare the t and p values in the second row with those showing on the Regression worksheet. The remaining four columns give 95% and 90% confidence intervals for the values of β_0 and β_1.

The last part of the output provides, for each observation, the predicted y value ($\hat{y}$), the residual $(y - \hat{y})$, and the standardized residual. The actual y values are not given in the table, but it would be a simple matter to copy them to an adjacent column.

It is clear from the regression output that there is little evidence of a relationship between x and y for these data. The most compelling evidence of this is the lack of significance of b_1 as shown by its high p value. We noted this previously on the Regression worksheet. The output of the Regression tool includes some additional calculations.

- Compare the p value for the F statistic in the ANOVA table (cell F28) with the p value for the t statistic for β_1 (cell E34). Enter a formula in cell E29 that will display the square of the t value in cell D34. Compare this with the F value in E28.

For simple linear regression, the regression analysis of variance always provides information identical to that provided by the test on the hypothesis $H_0 : \beta_1 = 0$. Either can be used as an inferential test of the existence of a relationship in the population between the x and y variables. The confidence intervals on β_1 include 0 (as well as both positive and negative values), another way of presenting the lack of significance in this regression. The tests on β_0 also indicate that it is not significantly different from 0, although a test on β_0 does not give us information about the relationship between the two variables.

▼Exercises

1. Select the Regression worksheet. Add two columns to calculate SSR. The first column would determine, for each observation, $\hat{y} - \bar{y}$. The second column would square each of those values. The cell just below this second column would sum all of the values. Confirm that you get the same answer here as you have on the Line Fit worksheet. Add to the Regression worksheet a calculation of r^2, using the value of SSR calculated here, and verify that it is the same as that on the Line Fit worksheet.

2. Rename the "Sheet6" worksheet "Good Fit." Copy the "Original" data from the Data worksheet to this sheet, but rename the x variable "output" and the y variable "cost." Use the Regression Tool to do a regression analysis of these data. Also prepare a scatter plot of these data. On the same worksheet, use the regression coefficients produced by the tool to give an estimate of the cost associated with these levels of output (in thousands): 3.8, 5.7, 6.3. Print the worksheet showing the output of the Regression tool, the scatter plot, the original data, and the predicted costs for the three outputs. Be sure your name is printed in the page header.

3. The State Revenue worksheet in Simpreg.xls contains 1992 data on median household income and per capita state government revenue. Produce a scatter plot with a superimposed regression line. Use regression analysis to examine the effect of household income on state government revenue. Is there a significant (.01 level of significance) relationship between these two? Based on the regression, by how much, on average, does per capita state revenue change for each $1 increase in median household income? Are any of the states "outliers"? If so, can you explain why? Remove that state and reestimate the regression. Does this change your answer to the question of how much, on average, per capita revenue changes for each $1 increase in

median household income? If so, what is the new answer? Print the worksheet showing the scatter plot and both regressions. Put your name in the page header. (Data is from U.S. Bureau of the Census, *Statistical Abstract of the United States: 1994* 114th edition, Washington, DC, 1994, pp. 395, 468.)

4. Is there a relationship between a state's median household income and its violent crime rate (incidents of murder, rape, robbery, and assault per 100,000 population)? The "Crime" worksheet provides 1992 data on state median household income and violent crime rate. Produce a scatter plot of these data with a regression line. Use the Regression tool to analyze the relationship. What proportion of the variation in state crime rates is explained by variation in household income? Is the relationship significant (at the .10 level of significance)? Explain. Print the worksheet showing the scatter plot and regression. Put your name in the page header. (Data is from U.S. Bureau of the Census, *Statistical Abstract of the United States: 1994* 114th edition, Washington, DC, 1994, pp. 199, 468.)

5. Is there a relationship between a state's household income and its death rate (deaths by all causes per 1,000 population)? The Death Rate worksheet in Simpreg.xls provides 1992 data by state for median household income and death rates. Produce a scatter plot with a regression line and regression analysis of these data. Does higher income lead to higher or lower death rates? Is the relationship significant at the .05 level of significance? What proportion of the variation of death rates is explainable by variation in household income? Print the worksheet showing the scatter plot and regression output. Put your name in the header.

Chapter 15

Multiple Regression

Multiple regression analysis is a straightforward extension of simple regression analysis which allows more than one independent variable. This extension, however, makes multiple regression analysis an incredibly versatile tool that can be used in an enormous variety of statistical problems. A reasonably complete treatment of multiple regression would require a book at least as long as this one already is. This chapter will deal with some of the issues and techniques that frequently arise with multiple regression analysis. Multiple regression analysis provides the analyst with such a variety of techniques that the primary problem is to decide exactly what form the regression equation (or regression *model*) will take, including which independent variables will be used. This typically comes after investigating different possibilities, a process known as *model building*.

Although the basic principles are straightforward, their application to any actual set of data often requires a judgment that comes with experience. There is a skill, almost an art, to regression analysis. One of the reasons for this is that for a given set of data, different objectives will likely lead to different regression equations. Regression analysis is often used for prediction, for example, and an equation developed for predictive purposes may well be different from an analytical model developed to better understand the relationship among the variables in a set of data.

For some types of analysis where multiple regression is used, Excel is probably not the best software. Although Excel provides the basic regression output, many specialized statistical packages also provide additional output. Excel, for example, does not provide an easy method to determine confidence intervals on predicted values, it lacks some of the diagnostic statistics useful for evaluating the analysis of time series data, and it does not easily permit certain types of hypothesis tests on population coefficients. On the other hand, Excel's matrix-handling capability does make it possible to construct these tests and even to create macros for them. No attempt will be made here, however, to cover these more advanced topics in this chapter.

▼ Multiple Independent Variables

Let's consider a simple case involving two independent variables. From this we will be able to see how to interpret the output of a regression involving any number of independent variables.

A music CD chain is trying to determine the effectiveness of television and radio advertising. It has collected data from stores in the chain on monthly record sales and on monthly advertising expenditures for both television and radio advertising. Based on these data, is there evidence of a relationship between expenditures on each type of advertising and sales? Which form of advertising appears to be more cost-effective?

Probably the chain would want to include other information, including market size, market type, average family income, and average age in a model explaining record sales. We're keeping it simple here.

- Open the Excel workbook in Multireg.xls and switch to the CDs worksheet.

- Summon the dialog window for the Regression tool by first opening the Tools menu on the Menu Bar and then selecting "Data Analysis...."

The dependent (or *y*) variable is in the column labeled "Sales," which gives monthly sales in thousands of dollars. The two independent variables have the labels "Radio" and "TV," which give monthly advertising expenditures on those two media.

- In the "Input Y Range" field enter the range address "A1:A21," which has the level of sales with the label.

- In the "Input X Range" field enter the range address "B1:C21." Notice that this range includes two columns containing both of the independent variables. It is a restriction of the Regression tool that independent variables have to be in adjacent columns.

- Click the square indicating that the address ranges include labels. Direct the tool to construct 90% confidence intervals on the population coefficients. Choose "Output Range" and have the output written beginning in cell D1.

- Click OK. Once the output is written, and while the cell range containing it is still selected, adjust the column widths by opening the

Format menu (on the Menu Bar), selecting "Column" then "AutoFit Selection."

You may find it easier to follow the discussion below if you print the output. If you do print the page, first choose "Print Preview" on the File menu and click the Setup button on the preview page. Click the "Page" folder tab, choose "Landscape" orientation, and "Fit to 1 page." Click the "Sheet" folder tab and select "Row and Column Headings." You will then be able to find cell addresses on your printout. Select "Header/Footer" and put your name and any other useful information in the header before you print.

For this regression, since there are two independent variables, the regression equation can be written as

$$\hat{y} = b_0 + b_1 x_1 + b_2 x_2$$

In the regression output on your worksheet, b_0 is labeled "Intercept," b_1 is labeled "Radio," and b_2 is labeled "TV."

The estimated coefficient for b_1 is 15.7151. This indicates that each additional \$1 spent on radio advertising is expected to increase sales by just under \$15.72, assuming all other factors (such as TV advertising) are unchanged. This measure is often called a *partial effect*, because it measures the impact of a change in just one of the independent variables. The partial effect is frequently referred to as the change in the dependent variable that would result from a one-unit change in one of the independent variables. It could more precisely be defined as a rate of change, but this would have the same meaning in this context. The estimated coefficient (or partial effect) for b_2 is 12.7583, indicating that an additional dollar spent on TV advertising will increase sales by just over \$12.75 (holding radio advertising constant). Based on these estimates, radio advertising looks like a better deal, but there is more to this issue, so don't regard this conclusion as final.

The value for R^2 (cell E5) of a bit over 0.36 indicates that variation in radio and TV advertising accounts for just over 36% of the variation in sales. Nearly 64% of the variation in sales is accounted for by factors other than radio and TV advertising.

Excel makes it easy to determine the significance of a coefficient or of the overall regression by providing p values. An important step in determining p values is the determination of the statistic's degrees of freedom. Consider an estimated coefficient and the t statistic calculated from that coefficient. It is desirable for the degrees of freedom to be as large as possible. A value for a t statistic can be significantly different from 0 if the degrees of freedom is large, and insignificant if the degrees of freedom is small. The degrees of freedom for an estimated coefficient's t statistic in multiple regression is $n - (k + 1)$, where n is the number of observations in the data and k is the number of independent variables. In practice the number of independent variables must be considerably fewer than the number of observations. For data with few observations, that can be a serious constraint. It is *especially* important when using regression for prediction that there not be too many independent variables.

The regression F statistic (cell H12) has a p value of approximately .021. This p value is for the the hypothesis test that *all* population coefficients of the independent variables are 0:

$$H_0 : \beta_1 = 0 \; and \; \beta_2 = 0$$
$$H_A : either \; \beta_1 \neq 0 \; or \; \beta_2 \neq 0 \; or \; both$$

If the Null Hypothesis were true, it would indicate that there is no relationship between *any* of the independent variables and the dependent variable. The p value tells us that if the Null Hypothesis were true, the probability we could draw a sample whose estimated coefficients (b_0 and b_1) differed from 0 by at least as much as the values in the regression output is about .02. This low probability provides good evidence for rejecting the Null Hypothesis and concluding that at least one of the population coefficients must be nonzero.

For simple linear regression, the p value for the F statistic always equaled the p value for the estimated coefficient of b_1's t statistic. The t statistics permit a test of whether an individual population coefficient is 0, while the F statistic can be used to test whether *all* population coefficients are zero. In simple regression these have the same meaning. In multiple regression they do not. The p value for the t statistic for spending on radio (b_1) is approximately .013 (cell H18). This is the probability that a sample with a value of b_1 as different from 0 as this sample's value (approximately 15.715) could be drawn from a population where there was no relationship between spending on radio ads and sales of CDs. This p value applies to the test $H_0 : \beta_1 = 0$ and $H_A : \beta_1 \neq 0$. We would reject the Null Hypothesis at a .05 level of significance but not at a .01 level of significance. This p value is low enough to conclude that there is good evidence of a relationship between monthly expenditures on radio advertising and sales of CDs.

The p value for spending on TV advertising is considerably higher, almost .18. Although the size of the estimated coefficient is nearly the same as that for spending on radio advertising, this high p value means we can have much less confidence about the value of the population coefficient on TV spending. If there were no relationship in the population between spending on TV advertising and sales, the probability of a sample having an estimated coefficient as different from 0 as this one (12.758) is the p value (.18). At the 10% significance level we would fail to Reject the Null Hypothesis that β_2 is 0. A common convention would label the coefficient on TV spending *not significant*, which is short for *not significantly different from 0*.

The fact that the estimated coefficient for spending on radio advertising is larger and more significant than the estimated coefficient for spending on TV advertising points to the conclusion that the music store chain should shift advertising expenditures from TV to radio. Look, however, at the two sets of confidence intervals on the population coefficients for TV and radio advertising expenditures. Notice that the upper bound of the confidence interval on TV spending is higher than the upper bound of the confidence interval of radio spending. This is true for both the 95% confidence interval (cells J18 and J19, which show the upper bound for radio to be 27.63 vs. 31.99 for TV) and the 90% confidence interval (cells L18 and L19). The fact that the estimated coefficient for TV advertising is not statistically significant does not mean that spending of TV advertising has been shown to be unimportant. As is the case in all hypothesis tests, Failure to Reject a Null Hypothesis of no relationship between TV advertising spending and sales is not equivalent to concluding that the Null Hypothesis is correct! You just can't rule it out.

One aspect of model building is the decision about which independent variables to include. As a general rule, variables that are statistically significant in a regression should be included. This does not mean, however, that variables that are not statistically significant should necessarily be excluded. A variable that *should* have a relationship with the dependent variable, in most cases, ought to be included in the regression even if its estimated coefficient is not statistically significant. In other words, the decision of what independent variables to include in a regression is never purely mechanical, particularly if the objective of regression analysis is truly analytical. It doesn't make sense that radio advertising would have a strong effect on sales while TV advertising has no effect at all. Although its significance is low, the TV advertising variable should be retained.

Sometimes the objective of regression analysis is purely predictive. In this case the question of whether or not to keep a particular independent variable can be somewhat more mechanical. The adjusted R^2 (located in cell E6) is helpful in this case. The ordinary R^2 (cell E5) discussed in the chapter on simple linear regression always increases when a new independent variable is added whether or not that variable improves the model's predictive power. The adjusted R^2 will increase only if the presence of the new independent variable improves the model's predictive power. Would elimination of the TV advertising variable improve the regression's predictive power? As a rule of thumb, if the t statistic associated with an independent variable has an absolute value less than 1.0, dropping that variable will increase adjusted R^2. In this regression the t statistic for TV advertising is just under 1.40. Eliminating this independent variable would reduce the adjusted R^2. For predictive purposes, TV advertising should be kept in the model. Although the estimated coefficient is *not* very significant, it is significant enough to contribute to the model's predictive power.

▼Nonlinear Relationships

Sometimes a relationship exists among two or more variables that cannot be represented as a straight line. In such a case a linear regression can give results that are absolutely misleading. In a case where data on more than one independent variable have been collected, nonlinearities can be present with some, but not all, of the data. For this example we will consider a case where there is only a single independent variable. This simplification will enable us to examine the relationship graphically.

A manufacturer of a precision bearings assembly produced at a number of different identical plants wants to determine the relationship between monthly output and short-run average cost. A sample of 50 monthly reports giving output and short-run average cost from several plants was collected. Based on these data, is there a relationship between level of output and average cost? (The data for this problem can be found in Multireg.xls on the Bearings worksheet.)

An obvious first step would be to use simple linear regression.

- Select the Bearings worksheet. Use the Regression Analysis tool to perform a regression analysis using monthly "Output" as the x variable and average "Cost" as the y variable. If the dialog window opens with the fields already containing values, they are left over from the last regression and must be changed. Have Excel place the output beginning in cell D1.

- In the "Residuals" section of the dialog window, select "Residual Plots."

- Click OK. Use the "Format–Column–AutoFit Selection" menu sequence to adjust the column widths for the regression output. If you have done the regression correctly, the value for r^2 (in cell E5) will be "5.19084E-06." The number of observations (in cell E8) will be 50.

- Change the value in the Zoom Control on the Standard Toolbar to 50%. Locate the residual plot (which Excel will place to the right of the regression output), and move it so that it is below the portion of the output giving the estimated coefficients and their statistics, and to the right of the residual output. Click a cell right below the chart and change the Zoom Control back to 100%.

- Excel tends to make residual plots too short. Make the plot taller by selecting it (so that there are "handles" in each corner and in the middle of each side). If you accidentally "activate" it (so that is surrounded by the activation boundary), click the mouse pointer on a location on the worksheet away from the chart. Place the mouse pointer on the handle in the center of the bottom side. The pointer will change to this shape: $\updownarrow$. Press and hold the (left) button and drag the handle down until the shape of the chart is more like a square.

It may be useful to print the worksheet. If you choose to do this, first unselect the chart by clicking the mouse pointer on a spot on the worksheet off the chart. This worksheet will print best if you first select "Print Preview" from the File menu. Click the Setup button at the top of the preview screen. Select the "Page" folder tab. Select "Portrait" orientation and scale to fit one page. Click the "Sheet" folder tab and select "Row and Column Headings" in the "Print" section. Click OK then Print.

It appears from this output that there is no evidence of a relationship between output and average cost. The R^2 is extremely low. Also, the slope (estimated coefficient for "Output" in E18) is "-8.81558E-05," a number which is very close to 0. Even more telling, the p value for the coefficient (H18) is over .98, suggesting that this result is very consistent with a population coefficient of 0—no relationship. This conclusion would, however, be *wrong*.

Economic theory tells us that the relationship between output and short-run average cost should be U-shaped, not linear. Starting with a very low level of output, average cost should decline as the production machinery and other fixed capital become more fully used. If output continues to increase, average cost would again increase since, in the short run, the machinery cannot be increased and would become overloaded. A U-shape is a curve, not a straight line. If this is the case, it is possible that no straight line can do a good job of approximating even a very strong relationship.

▼Curved Relationships and Residuals Plots

If the relationship between a particular independent variable and the dependent variable were in the form of a simple curve, this would create a U-shaped (or inverted U-shaped) pattern in the residuals. Consider the charts below.

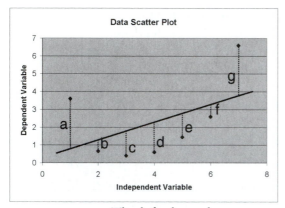

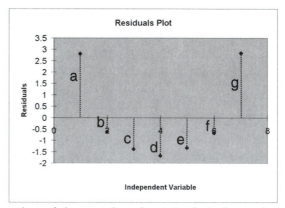

The left chart shows a scatter plot of data with only a single independent variable. The simple linear regression line is superimposed, and vertical lines are drawn between each point and the regression line. Notice that the relationship between the independent and dependent variable in that chart would be better represented by a curve than by a straight line.

The right chart shows the residuals plot for the same data. Each data point is identified by a letter with the same point in the two charts identified by the same letter. The length of the dotted line between each point and the horizontal axis measures the value of that point's residual.

Consider point *a* in the left chart. It lies above the regression line. The length of the dotted line between it and the regression line is the "error" or residual associated with that value. That length represents the same value as the length of the dotted line on the right between point *a* and the horizontal axis. Points *b*, *c*, *d*, and *e* all lie below the regression line in the chart on the left. Their residuals are negative. Exactly the same pattern is seen on the chart on the right. The point of this is that the curved relationship evident in the chart on the left is also (even more) evident in the residuals chart on the right.

If the curved relationship is apparent in the scatter plot, you may wonder why we bother to also consider a residuals plot. A residuals plot has a fundamental and important advantage when there is more than one independent variable—the usual situation in multiple regression. It is not really possible to do a meaningful scatter plot in this case. Although a scatter plot of the dependent variable against a single independent variable could be done, it would not be useful because it does not account for the values of the other independent variables. If the predicted values from a multiple regression equation were plotted on such a chart, they would not even appear to lie on a straight line. Residuals plots avoid many of these problems and are an often-effective means of detecting a curvilinear (or nonlinear) relationship between the dependent variable and one of the independent variables. When Excel is asked to provide residuals plots, it produces one plot for each independent variable in the model.

Let's consider the residuals plot for the precision bearings average-cost problem. That plot should be present on your Excel output. Click the mouse pointer once on the chart and use the "handles" to make the chart bigger and taller. Your chart should look like the one below.

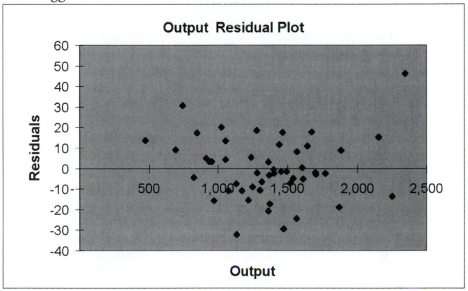

This chart does not show as clear a curved relationship as did the previous chart. Look at it carefully. The data points in the center of the chart are more likely to lie below than above the horizontal axis, while those to the left and right appear more likely to lie above the axis. This is enough of an indication to warrant exploring a curved relationship between output and short-run average cost.

▼ Polynomial Regression

One common technique for estimating a curved regression is with a quadratic regression, which is an example of a polynomial regression. If there is a single independent variable, a quadratic equation would have the following form:

$$\hat{y} = b_0 + b_1 x_1 + b_2 x_1^2$$

This equation is quadratic because it has a squared term. Excel treats it as a separate variable. It's just another x_2 to Excel; the Regression Tool doesn't know where it came from. What changes is your *interpretation* of the results.

Although there is only one independent variable, a quadratic equation can have other independent variables as well as either linear terms (not squared), quadratic terms (squared), or both. The bearings problem only has a single independent variable (output), so we will estimate the equation shown on the previous page.

▼Estimating a Quadratic Regression

The basic method for estimating a quadratic equation will be to create a new column of data in which the values in each cell are the square of the values in the "Output" column. A regression will then be run in which these data will be treated like a separate independent variable.

- Switch to the Bearings (2) worksheet. This worksheet is identical to the original Bearings worksheet.

- Select any cell in column B.

- Open the Insert menu on the Menu Bar and select "Columns." A new column B will open between the two columns of data. The "Cost" data will move to column C. Column B will be used to put the new output-squared independent variable. It has to be beside the "Output" column because Excel requires independent variables to be adjacent.

- Enter the label "Output Sq" in cell B1.

- Enter formulas in the cells in column B so that each cell will display the value that is the square of the value in the same row of column A. You will have to adjust the width of column B to see these values. Cell B2 should display "2122849," cell B3 should display "2452356," cell B4 should display "881721," etc.

- Open the Regression tool's dialog window. The entries for the input fields will have to be changed if they have the previous problem's values. Enter the address range of the "Cost" data in the field for the y variable and the address range for the columns with both the "Output" and "Output Sq" data for the x variable. Include the cells containing the labels, indicate in the dialog window that labels are included, direct the output to cell D1, and ask for residuals plots.

- Click OK. When the tool has finished writing the output, use the "Format—Column—AutoFit Selection" menu sequence to adjust the column widths containing the output.

- Use the Zoom Control to change the zoom factor to 50%. Locate the residuals plots. Since this regression has two independent variables, Excel produces two plots. Notice that Excel stacks them so that it is impossible to see the one on the bottom without moving the one on top.

- Select the top residuals plot and move it directly below the plot below it. Click on the worksheet just below and to the right of the bottom plot, change the zoom factor back to 100%, and compare the two residuals plots.

One of the residuals plots shows the residuals values plotted against output. The other shows the same residuals values plotted against output squared. Compare them carefully. Although the two plots are not identical, the pattern of residuals is the same. The plots are not exactly identical because the horizontal scaling is slightly different for the squared term, but you can recognize the common pattern. Since the two plots provide the same information, there is no reason to keep them both.

- Switch the zoom factor back to 50%. Delete the residuals plot for "Output Sq" by selecting it and then pressing the Delete key. Move the residuals plot for "Output" below the regression output (the same place used for the regression on the first Bearings worksheet). Increase the height of the residuals plot as you did with the previous worksheet.

You may again decide to print this worksheet to better follow the discussion below. Use the same procedure described for the previous regression given on page 379. Adjust the width of column B if needed to see the data values.

Although the simple linear regression showed no evidence of a relationship between *output* and average cost, the quadratic regression provides strong evidence of such a relationship. The r^2 (in cell E5) has increased to a value slightly over .20. The F test has a p value (cell I12) of .0052, versus .98 for the simple linear regression. This is sufficient to reject the Null Hypothesis of no relationship between the independent and dependent variables at all typical levels of significance.

Perhaps most striking in the quadratic regression is the significance of both *output* and *output squared*. The p values for the t tests of the significance of each variable are approximately .0015 and .0013 (cells H18 and H19), respectively. In the simple linear regression where output was the only independent variable, the estimated coefficient was insignificant. As well as having a significant coefficient itself, *output squared* causes the coefficient of *output* to become significant as well.

The estimated coefficients are in cells E18 and E19, and give the following regression equation:

$$\hat{y} = 90.24 - 0.0863x + 0.0000305x^2$$

The coefficient on *output squared* may appear to be very close to 0, but this must be evaluated in relation to the size of the numbers it is likely to be multiplied by. Look at the values of *output squared* in column B. In many cases, these numbers are in the millions. When such large numbers are multiplied by the coefficient shown above, the product will have a value between 10 and 100, a range that is reasonably large, given the *y* values.

▼Partial Effects in Polynomial Regressions

When each independent variable in a multiple regression equation is included only as a linear term, the coefficient for that variable is also a measure of its partial effect. For polynomial regressions, the measure of the partial effect is not as simple. In estimating the regression considered here, Excel treats *output* and *output squared* as if they were separate independent variables. In determining partial effects, however, they cannot be regarded as separate. There is no way of changing *output* without also changing *output squared*. The estimated partial effect must be determined by taking the derivative of the dependent variable with respect to the independent variable. For a quadratic regression of the form $\hat{y} = b_0 + b_1 x + b_2 x^2$, the partial effect is not b_1, but $b_1 + 2b_2 x$. For the regression discussed here, the partial effect of output on average cost is $-.0863 + .0000611x$. The effect of a change in output on average cost *depends on what the total level of output is*. For small levels of output, increases in output will decrease average cost because the negative term will dominate. As output gets larger, this negative effect will diminish. Eventually the partial effect's term with the *x* will dominate and increases in output will increase average cost. The partial effect of output on cost measures marginal cost. According to economic theory, marginal cost initially declines, reaches a minimum, and then increases. This is exactly the kind of behavior implied by the estimated regression equation.

▼When Should Polynomial Regression Be Used?

Determining the set of independent variables for a particular dependent variable is much easier than knowing whether the relationship is likely to be linear or curved. As a general rule, it is best to keep a regression model as simple as possible. In some cases, such as the example given here of the relationship between output and average cost, there is good reason to expect a curved relationship and even to have some idea of the general shape of the curve. Other techniques exist within multiple regression analysis for estimating more complex curved relationships. One technique, for example, is to use higher-order polynomials. This could be done by including a cubed term, or perhaps a term raised to the fourth power, among the independent variables. This should be avoided in most cases. Although it is appropriate to examine the residuals from a linear regression for evidence of a curved relationship, it is best to avoid higher-order polynomials (and other techniques) unless you have good theoretical reasons to expect the relationship to have some specific shape that can only be represented by a polynomial of order greater than two.

▼Dummy Variables and Categorical Data

The data used in the regressions we have looked at so far have been continuous. Such measures as output and household income can take on different values, and we expect changes in the values of these variables to have a consistent effect on the value of the dependent variable. Categorical data are different. These data place observations into a particular category, and there may be no obvious ranking to these categories. A fast-food chain, for example, may wish to develop a model predicting sales at individual restaurants. One of the important factors affecting sales may be differences in behavior among people living in different regions and different countries. The country or the region where a fast-food restaurant is located may have a big effect on its sales. A variable giving this information is categorical—very different from the continuous variables we have considered so far with regression.

We have considered categorical data in connection with another statistical technique—analysis of variance. We looked at the effect of keyboard design on typing speed (page 336), for example, and the effects of package design and advertising strategy on perfume sales (page 340). Keyboard design, package design, and advertising strategy are all examples of categorical variables, and analysis of variance is designed exclusively to analyze the effect such variables have on a continuous measure (such as typing speed or perfume sales). The dummy variable technique enables multiple regression analysis also to handle categorical independent variables. With this technique, multiple regression analysis can handle any problem that could be analyzed with ANOVA (and will provide the same results). Unlike ANOVA, multiple regression analysis can handle problems involving a mixture of categorical and continuous variables.

A dummy variable is one that has only two possible values—0 or 1. When a dummy variable is used to indicate a single characteristic, observations that possess the characteristics will have the dummy variable made equal to 1, while observations without the characteristic will have it equal to 0. Let's consider the following example:

A university is interested in comparing the performance in business statistics classes of students who use computers to learn business statistics with those who do not use computers. Data were collected from a sample of statistics students who took courses that either used or did not use computers. Average course grade and GPA were also collected. Is there evidence that using computers increased average course grades, controlling for GPA?

To determine whether there is evidence that students using computers receive higher grades, we would test $H_0 : \mu_{computer} \leq \mu_{no\ computer}$ vs. $H_A : \mu_{computer} > \mu_{no\ computer}$, holding constant the effect of GPA. This is a one-tail test.

• Select the Computers worksheet.

The data in this worksheet will be used to estimate a regression model in which a student's average statistics course grade is analyzed as a function of GPA and of whether or not the student used computers to learn statistics. GPA is included because it is expected to have a major impact on the statistics grade, and it may be related to whether or not the student took a course which used computers. Although the column labeled "Use Computers?" has the information for a dummy variable, it cannot be used as is because it does not have just the values 0 and 1. We will need to create a dummy variable from the values in this column. For any observation with the answer "Yes," the dummy variable will have the value "1." When the answer is "No, " the dummy variable will equal "0." Note that the yes/no information is logically exactly the same as 1/0.

The Regression tool requires that all the independent variables be adjacent. We will thus first move the current data on computer use out of column C and create a dummy variable in that column.

• Select region C2:C21 and move the data from column C to column D so that each value stays in the same row. Column C will be used to create the dummy variable, which must be adjacent to the other independent variables.

- Enter the label "Computer Dummy" in cell C1.

- Select cell C2. Since the observation represented by this row is of a student who did use computers, we want this cell to contain the value "1." Use the Function Wizard button to select the "IF" function (in the "Logical" category). In the "logical_test" field, enter an expression that will be true if the value of cell D2 equals "Yes" (you must include the double quotes). You should see the word "TRUE" in the region to the right of the "logical_test" field where Excel shows the parameter's value.

- When the expression is true, have C2 equal "1," and when it is false have C2 equal "0" (without the quotes). After you click the Finish Button, cell C2 should display the value "1."

- Copy the contents of cell C2 to cells C3 through cell C21. Check that those adjacent to a "No" in column D (like cell C6) display "0," while those adjacent to a "Yes" display "1."

You now have a completed dummy variable in column C. When running a regression, the data in column C (and *not* column D) will be used as an independent variable.

- Using the Regression Analysis tool, regress Course Average in column A (*y* variable) against GPA and Computer Dummy in columns B and C (*x* variables). Be sure not to include column D. Have Excel place the output on the same worksheet, beginning in cell E2. Residual plots will not be needed.

The estimated coefficients and significance statistics are shown below.

E	F	G	H	I
17	Coefficients	Standard Error	t Stat	P-value
18 Intercept	35.98582354	3.33531463	10.789334	5.02772E-09
19 GPA	14.34949132	1.097573966	13.07382624	2.68301E-10
20 Computer Dummy	5.86737271	2.031507889	2.888186032	0.010215054

These coefficients provide the following estimated equation:

$$\hat{y} = 35.99 + 14.35x_1 + 5.87x_2$$

where x_1 is GPA and x_2 is the "use computers" dummy variable.

The coefficients suggest that a one-point increase in GPA results in an average increase in the course grade of 14.35, holding constant computer use. Observations on those who use computers will have the value "1" for x_2, while those who do not will have the value "0." Those with the value "1" are going to have a predicted grade ($\hat{y}$) which is 5.87 higher than those with the value "0" *and the same GPA.* This coefficient (5.87) is a measure of the value of using computers *controlling for the independent effect of GPA.*

Had we simply regressed average grade against the computer dummy without including GPA, we might also have found that those students using computers scored higher grades. In that case, however, *we would not have been sure that this wasn't because better students (with higher GPAs) were more likely to take courses that used computers than were weaker students.* If this were the case, the apparent higher grades of those using computers might not have been because of the computer use. It might have been simply that better students (who would have gotten higher grades anyway) happened to be the ones using computers. By including GPA as an independent variable, we have specifically eliminated this possible interpretation. Our results indicate that *regardless of GPA,* students using computers did better than those who did not, a result which is inconsistent with the Null Hypothesis.

This result is equivalent to saying that there is one equation relating GPA and average statistics grade for those who use computers and another equation for those who do not. This situation is shown on the graph below. The dashed line shows the estimated relationship between GPA and average statistics grade for those using computers, while the lower solid line shows the estimated relationship for those not using computers. The vertical distance between the two lines is the estimated value of using computers, the coefficient on the dummy variable, 5.87.

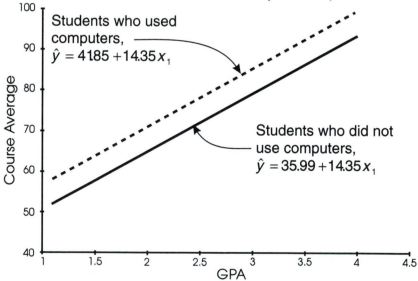

In this equation only one coefficient for GPA is estimated; it applies to both those who do and those who do not use computers. Thus the two lines are parallel, and their common slope is the estimated coefficient on

GPA, 14.35. The dummy variable has an effect like a change in the constant term (y intercept or b_0). For those not using computers, the constant term is the constant term from the printout, approximately 35.99, but for those using computers it is that *plus* the coefficient on the dummy variable, or approximately 41.85.

Is the difference statistically significant? The Null Hypothesis we are testing is $H_0 : \mu_{computer} \leq \mu_{no\ computer}$. When using dummy variables, think of the equivalent $H_0 : (\mu_{computer} - \mu_{no\ computer}) \leq 0$. The estimated coefficient on the dummy variable is an estimate of a β that measures the difference between the average grades of those using and not using computers: in other words $\mu_{computer} - \mu_{no\ computer}$. So the Null Hypothesis could also be written as $H_0 : \beta_{computer\ dummy} \leq 0$. The estimated coefficient is 5.87, clearly not consistent with H_0. The reported p value is .0102. This, however, is a two-tail p value. To convert it to a one-tail p value, it must be divided by two, giving .0051. This low p value is highly significant, leading us to Reject the Null Hypothesis and conclude that there is evidence that those using computers received higher average grades, controlling for the effect of GPA.

▼Multilevel Categorical Data

Categorical data often have only two levels or values, such as the measure in the example above of whether or not a student used a computer. Any variable giving the answer to a yes/no question has two values. A single dummy variable will, in these cases, enable us to estimate the effects of the categorical variable. Much categorical data, however, have more than two levels or values. Location is one common such variable. An observation in a data set might include a variable indicating the state in which a respondent is located. If observations come from more than two states, the location variable can have more than two values and is referred to as *multilevel*.

A multilevel categorical variable is represented in multiple regression analysis by a *set* of dummy variables. Each dummy variable measures the presence or absence of a *single value* of the multilevel categorical variable. The total number of dummy variables equals the number of different values (or levels) of the categorical variable *minus one*. If, for example, a location variable could have nine different values (referring, for example, to nine different states), there would be *eight* dummy variables, each of which would have the value of 1 or 0 for each of eight different locations. If an observation came from the ninth location, for which there is no dummy variable, the value of all eight dummy variables would be 0. When creating a set of dummy variables for a multilevel categorical variable, one of the values will not have a dummy variable; that value is said to be *omitted*. The reason for this, as well as the issue of which value to omit, will be considered in the example below.

As with most American municipalities, the primary revenue for the town of Elder Hollow comes from the property tax. To administer the tax, the value of each piece of property is estimated by a tax assessor. The town's Board of Equalization has the task of ensuring that all taxpayers are treated equally. A complaint from several residents of the Chester Court development asserts that residences in that neighborhood are assessed at a higher level than houses of the same value in the town's other neighborhoods, Armsley Hills and Blawndale. A higher assessment would cause tax bills in Chester Court to be higher than those of identically valued houses in other neighborhoods. In order to test the assertion, you have selected a random sample of residential properties from each neighborhood that have recently sold. Data on the sales price and the assessed value, together with the property's neighborhood, have been collected. Based on these data, is there evidence that properties in Chester Court are overassessed compared to properties in the other two neighborhoods?

The Null Hypotheses for this problem would be $H_0 : \mu_C \leq \mu_B$ and $H_0 : \mu_C \leq \mu_A$, while the Alternate Hypotheses would be $H_A : \mu_C > \mu_B$ and $H_A : \mu_C > \mu_A$. These require one-tail tests, which means that we will have to modify the two-tail test provided by Excel.

Ideally, each property's tax assessment would exactly equal the sales price, but this ideal can never be achieved in practice. Equity is achieved if there is no consistent difference among neighborhoods of the relationship between sales price and assessed value.

- Select the Assessment worksheet. The data for this problem are located there. We will estimate a regression with assessed value as the dependent variable and sales price and neighborhood dummies as independent variables.

There are three values for the "neighborhood" variable. Two dummy variables must be created. Since we are interested in a comparison between Chester Court and the other neighborhoods, Chester Court will be the omitted value. One dummy variable will therefore indicate if an observation is in Armsley Hills and the other will indicate if it is in Blawndale.

- Select the neighborhood data in column C and move it to column E, keeping each value in the same row. The now-empty columns C and D will be used for the dummy variables.

- Enter the label "A Dummy" in cell C1. The Armsley Hills dummy will be placed in column C.

- Select cell C2. Use the Formual Bar or Paste Function button to enter values for the arguments of the IF function to test whether the contents of cell E2 equals "Armsley Hills." If it does, have the IF function set the value of C2 to 1. If it does not, have the IF function set the value of C2 to 0. C2 should display the value "1." If C2 does not display "1," you may have forgotten to put quotation marks around "Armsley Hills" in the IF function's "logical_test" argument field.

- Enter the label "B Dummy" in cell D1. Select cell D2 and use the IF function to set the value of D2 to 1 if E2 equals "Blawndale" and 0 otherwise.

- Copy the formulas in cells C1 and D1 down the column of cells to row 31. Carefully check the values of the two dummy variables. Rows 2 through 10 should have "1" in column C and "0" in column D. Rows 11 through 20 should have "0" in column C and "1" in column D. Rows 21 through 31 should have "0" in both column C and column D.

The next step is to use the Regression tool on these data. Note that the set of dependent variables will include the dummy variables in columns C and D, but not the original neighborhood information in column E.

- Open the Regression Tool dialog window by selecting "Regression" from the "Analysis Tools."

- Enter the cell region address for "Assessed Value" (including label) in the field for the Y range and the cell region address for "Sales Price" and the two dummy variables (including labels) in the field for X range.

- Click the box to indicate to Excel that your data regions include labels and indicate that you want the output to start in cell F2. Residual plots are not needed. Click OK.

- Once the regression output is complete, adjust the column widths of the region containing the output. Be sure to save the worksheet. Compare your output with the one shown at the top of the next page to be sure you have done this correctly.

We will refer to this regression as "Model 1" in the following discussion.

Model 1 indicates that, in any neighborhood, for each $1 increase in the market (sales) price, the average assessed value increases by slightly more than 94¢. The estimated coefficient is highly significant. The p value is

	F	G	H	I	J	K
2	SUMMARY OUTPUT					
3						
4	*Regression Statistics*					
5	Multiple R	0.991309388				
6	R Square	0.982694302				
7	Adjusted R Square	0.980697491				
8	Standard Error	3180.036929				
9	Observations	30				
10						
11	ANOVA					
12		*df*	*SS*	*MS*	*F*	*Significance F*
13	Regression	3	14930247205	4976749068	492.1317868	5.18302E-23
14	Residual	26	262928506.7	10112634.87		
15	Total	29	15193175711			
16						
17		*Coefficients*	*Standard Error*	*t Stat*	*P-value*	*Lower 95%*
18	Intercept	-2133.13776	4324.756946	-0.49323876	0.625984356	-11022.8088
19	Sales Price	0.944474339	0.034134647	27.66908195	8.15154E-21	0.874309522
20	A Dummy	2279.492293	2026.167539	1.125026558	0.270856698	-1885.35746
21	B Dummy	-1305.06578	1431.303948	-0.91180198	0.37025011	-4247.155104

slightly more than 8.15×10^{-21}, an extremely small value. The entire regression is highly significant, as indicated by the p value for the F test (5.18×10^{-23}). The R^2 is over 0.98.

The coefficients of primary interest in this problem are those on the dummy variables. Each coefficient represents a shift in the value of the constant (or y intercept) for observations in that dummy variables group *compared to the omitted group*. For example, the coefficient for the B Dummy is about −1305. This indicates that observations for which the value of the B Dummy is 1 (residences in Blawndale) have an assessed value about $1,305 less than otherwise identical observations in the omitted group (Chester Court). If we were to calculate, for example, the predicted assessed value for a residence in Chester Court that sold for $100,000, the value of both the A Dummy and the B Dummy would be 0. The predicted assessed value would therefore be

$$\hat{y} = -2{,}133 + (0.9445 \times 100{,}000) = \$92{,}317$$

Since a $100,000 residence in Blawndale would have the value "1" for the B Dummy, its estimated value would be

$$\hat{y} = -2{,}133 + (0.9445 \times 100{,}000) + (1 \times (-1{,}305))$$
$$= 92{,}317 - 1{,}305 = \$91{,}012$$

This result appears consistent with the complaint of the residents in Chester Court. The lower assessed value for residences in Blawndale would result in lower average taxes on identically valued houses. The estimated coefficient, however, is not significant since its p value is over .185. (The p value shown on the output is slightly over .37, but this is a two-tail p value and must be divided by 2 to be converted to a one-tail p value.) Although this sample indicates that residences in Chester Court are overassessed compared to those in Blawndale, this result might well be due to chance. Thus, despite the estimated coefficient, this regression *does not* support the contention of the residents of Chester Court.

The contention of Chester Court residents that their houses are overvalued is also contradicted by the positive coefficient on the A Dummy. This dummy indicates that residences in Armsley Hills are assessed even more than identically valued residences in Chester Court, by an average of about $2,279. This estimated coefficient, however, is also not significant since its p value is about .135 (one tail). The final conclusion is that this regression does not provide good evidence that Chester Court residences are assessed any differently from residences in the other neighborhoods. This, of course, does not mean that we have evidence that residences in all neighborhoods are assessed identically. A stronger conclusion *might* result from a regression on a larger sample.

The regression provides (weak) evidence that residences in Blawndale have lower assessments while residences in Armsley Hills have higher assessments than identical houses in Chester Court. Suppose we wanted a direct comparison between Armsley Hills and Blawndale? Such a comparison would most easily be made by creating and including a dummy variable ("C Dummy") for Chester Court and omitting either the A Dummy or the B Dummy. Let's consider a regression with the A Dummy omitted and refer to it as "Model 2." It turns out that a simple pattern exists between the estimated coefficients of Model 1 and Model 2, or any pair of regressions estimated on the same data that differ only in which dummy variable in the set is omitted. All independent variables other than the set of dummy variables (only Sales Price in this case) are the same. The intercept of Model 2 will be the sum of the intercept of Model 1 and the coefficient in Model 1 of the omitted dummy variable in Model 2. The estimated coefficients for the dummy variables in Model 2 will be their Model 1 value minus the estimated coefficient in Model 1 of the dummy variable omitted in Model 2. This pattern for the regressions discussed here is summarized in the table at the top of the next page.

Although the values of the coefficients for Model 2 are easy to determine from Model 1, their significance is not as easily determined. For this reason, if we want to test whether or not there is evidence that residences in Armsley Hills are assessed more than identically valued residences in Blawndale, the Model 2 regression should be estimated. This is left as an exercise.

Coefficient	Model 1	Model 2
Intercept	–2,133	–2,133 + 2,279 = 146
Sales Price	0.9445	0.9445 (unchanged)
A Dummy	2,279	2,279 – 2,279 = 0
B Dummy	–1,305	–1,305 – 2,279 = –3,584
C Dummy	0 (omitted)	0 – 2,279 = –2,279

▼ Multicollinearity

Although we refer to the explanatory variables in multiple regression analysis as *independent*, it is very rare for them to be independent of each other in the statistical sense. In other words, independent variables tend to be correlated with each other. One of the reasons for this correlation is that two or more independent variables may contain similar information.

Consider the following problem:

A lawn service company is interested in predicting the average monthly amount households in a neighborhood will spend on lawn and garden care. A sample of neighborhoods is chosen, and the average amount spent is collected, along with average lot size, average household income, and average value of home. Use multiple regression to estimate the determinants of average household expenditures on lawn and garden care.

- Select the Lawn Care worksheet in the workbook in Multireg.xls.

The primary problem with these data is that household income and home value may be highly correlated. Those with valuable homes tend to have high incomes, and vice versa. Both variables are measures of economic well-being, which most directly affects the willingness to spend money for lawn and garden care. We would expect, however, the two factors to have positive, but somewhat different, effects. Multiple regression, however, may have difficulty distinguishing between those effects. This is the problem of multicollinearity.

- Use the Regression Analysis tool on the Lawn Care data. Lawn Care Expenditure in column A should be the *y* variable, and the three variables in columns B, C, and D should be *x* variables. Use labels. Have Excel place the output beginning in cell E2. Residual plots are not needed. When the Regression tool has finished, adjust the column widths where the output was placed. The estimated coefficients and measures of significance are shown at the top of the next page.

	E	F	G	H	I
17		*Coefficients*	*Standard Error*	*t Stat*	*P-value*
18	Intercept	-9.73670975	18.10704706	-0.53773041	0.593355346
19	Lot Size	21.21401018	3.076925279	6.894548374	1.31177E-08
20	Avg HH Income	0.000680953	0.001286404	0.529346471	0.599110592
21	Avg Home Value	-0.00018334	0.00060725	-0.30191837	0.76407513

Although lot size has the expected highly significant positive relationship with lawn care expenditures, the results for the other two independent variables are puzzling. The *p* values of approximately .60 and .76 indicate that neither variable is significantly different from 0. Average house value has a negative estimated coefficient, suggesting that as house values go up, lawn care expenditures go down. This certainly runs counter to intuition. The problem here is multicollinearity arising from the strong relationship between average household income and average house value.

When two independent variables are highly correlated, including both variables in the regression will raise the problem of multicollinearity. In multiple regression analysis, measures of the significance of a single independent variable (including the variable's standard error, *t* statistic, and associated *p* value) should be thought of as measures evaluating that variable's contribution to a model containing all other independent variables. Suppose that we have a model estimating the demand for lawn and garden service in which home value is included as an independent variable. How much *additional* explanatory power will be added by also including family income? Not much, since home value already has the information about economic well-being. As a result, the estimated coefficient on family income will be insignificant. What about the coefficient on home value? In a model that already contains family income, the additional explanatory power of home value will be small. It, too, will be insignificant. Although economic well-being is unquestionably an important determinant of the demand for lawn and garden service, including two highly correlated measures may well result in both of them being insignificant! What if one of them is removed?

- Recall the Regression tool. Change the *x* variables to include only lot size and average household income. Put the output in the range beginning with cell E23.

The coefficients should now be as shown in the picture below.

	E	F	G	H	I
38		*Coefficients*	*Standard Error*	*t Stat*	*P-value*
39	Intercept	-14.1358829	10.64538406	-1.32788848	0.190628119
40	Lot Size	21.18292929	3.045324741	6.9558852	9.53499E-09
41	Avg HH Income	0.000293061	6.43727E-05	4.552558973	3.75003E-05

Although the estimated coefficient for average household income has declined from about 0.0007 to about 0.0003, the coefficient is now highly significant, with a *p* value of 3.75×10^{-5}.

Let's try excluding household income and including average home value.

- Swap columns C and D. One way of doing this is to first select column C by clicking the column heading. Then select "Columns" from the Insert menu on the Menu Bar (or click the right mouse button while the pointer is on the column and select "Insert" from the pop-up menu). This will open a new column C and shift the worksheet contents of the previous C and above one column to the right. Move the contents of column E (Average Home Value) to the empty column C. Delete the now-empty column E by clicking on the column heading and then selecting "Delete" from the Edit menu on the Menu Bar (or from the pop-up menu, which appears when you click the right mouse button).

- Use the Regression tool to run a new regression. The fields in the tool's dialog window will be the same as for the previous regression (*x* variables in columns B and C) except for "Output Range," which should be set to cell E43.

The estimated coefficients and their significance measures for this model are shown in the picture below.

E		Coefficients	Standard Error	t Stat	P-value
58		Coefficients	Standard Error	t Stat	P-value
59	Intercept	-17.2155571	11.23778421	-1.53193519	0.132242437
60	Lot Size	21.15324399	3.051147558	6.932881347	1.03329E-08
61	Avg Home Value	0.000137695	3.04495E-05	4.522072066	4.14586E-05

Rather than being negative and insignificant as in the first regression, the estimated coefficient for average home value is positive and highly significant.

The multicollinearity between average household income and average home value caused both variables to have insignificant estimated coefficients when both were included as independent variables. Yet when either variable was included as an independent variable without the other, it was highly significant. There is clearly a relationship between economic well-being and expenditures on lawn and garden care (which both variables measure), but it is impossible to get a good estimate on the unique effect of each variable.

One question that multicollinear data poses is exactly which variables should be included in the set of independent variables. Of the three models presented here, which is correct? There is, unfortunately, no clear answer. If the object of the regression analysis is simply prediction, then the model with the highest value for the adjusted R^2 is probably the best. If the object is to understand the relationship among the variables, then the model with both independent variables may be best. The coefficients of variables that suffer from multicollinearity are unbiased, although they have large standard errors.

There are techniques that can be used to verify multicollinearity, but they are beyond the scope of this book. Excel has a Correlation Analysis tool that could be helpful in finding pairs of potential independent variables that are highly correlated. One method sometimes used involves regressing independent variables on each other. As a general rule, multicollinearity should be suspected whenever including or excluding an independent variable has large effects on the significance of the estimated coefficients of one or more other variables. In the example given here, the collinear relationship existed between only two variables. It is possible, however, for a multicollinear relationship to involve more than two variables. Detecting the exact nature of the multicollinearity can be difficult in that case.

Even when severe multicollinearity is not a problem, real independent variables are never statistically independent. There always is some degree of correlation. We call it "multicollinearity" only when the problem is severe, but it always affects regression analysis. Much of the challenge of determining exactly which set of independent variables to use in regression analysis occurs because the decision to include or exclude one variable very frequently changes the sign and significance of other variables. We will encounter this problem again when we look at model building.

▼ Heteroscedasticity and Autocorrelation

One of the assumptions of ordinary least-squares regression is that the population error terms are random, independent, and have constant variance. If the assumption of constant variance of the error term is violated, the data are said be *heteroscedastic* (or *heteroskedastic*). If the assumption of independence is violated, the data are said to be *autocorrelated*. Sometimes these problems can be handled by adding additional variables to a model or by altering the functional form of the estimated relationship. These problems can also be dealt with by using the technique called *generalized least squares*, a technique beyond the scope of this book, which uses information from the residuals to estimate the relationship between the independent and dependent variables.

The most common type of heteroscedasticity arises when the variance of the error term increases (or decreases) as the value of an independent variable increases. The most common type of autocorrelation occurs when the error term has a pattern associated with the observation over time.

Heteroscedasticity occurs most often with cross-sectional data, which are data collected from different observation units at the same point in time. It is likely to occur, for example, if the observations are very different in size. This might be the case if our unit of observation were the firm, and the data mixes small businesses with giant corporations. Heteroscedasticity can also occur in time series data (data collected from the same unit of observation at different points in time). Heteroscedasticity with such data is sometimes seen as an increase or decrease in the error term over time.

Heteroscedasticity can be detected by examining the estimated residuals $(y - \hat{y})$ to see if their variance seems to vary with the value of an independent variable, the observation number, or some other measure. Although there are formal tests that can be performed on the estimated residuals, they are not calculated by Excel's Regression Analysis Tool. Hetereoscedasticity can often, however, be detected by examining residual plots, which the Regression tool can prepare.

Consider the following problem.

It has long been known that there is an important relationship between economic development and energy consumption. To investigate this relationship, international data on per capita energy consumption (in kilograms of coal equivalent) and per capita gross national product (in dollars) were collected for 1990 (Data is from U.S. Bureau of the Census, Statistical Abstract of the United States: 1994, CD-ROM version, Washington, DC, 1994, Tables 1366 and 1393). Use these data to estimate the effect of per capita GNP on per capita energy consumption.

- Switch to the Energy worksheet. Call up the Regression tool dialog window.

- In the "Y Range" field, enter the range address of the per capita energy consumption in column B, and in the "X Range" field enter the range address of the per capita GNP in column C. Have the output placed in the range beginning with cell D2.

- In the section of the dialog window labeled "Residuals," select "Residual Plots" by clicking it so that an "x" appears in the small box to the left of the words. This will cause Excel to produce a chart showing the value of residuals plotted against each of the independent variables. Since there is only one independent variable in this case, there will be only one plot.

- Click the OK button. Adjust the column widths.

The chart showing a plot of residuals against the independent variable (Per Capita GNP) will be located on the worksheet to the right of the regression output.

- Click the residuals plot once so that sizing "handles" appear in the four corners and the middle of each side.

- Use the sizing handles to make the chart larger.

The chart should look similar to the one below.

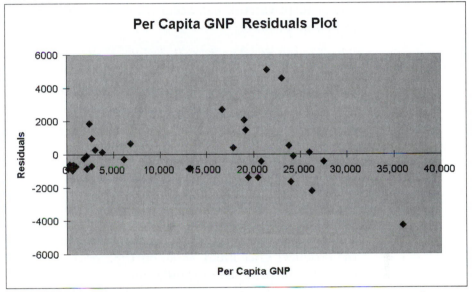

Heteroscedasticity is indicated by the change in the *vertical spread* in the residual values associated with different values of per capita GNP. For those observations with low values of per capita GNP (less than about $5,000), the points are relatively close together. As per capita GNP increases to about $25,000, the points become more separated. Although heteroscedasticity is fairly evident in this residuals plot, it is easy to mistakenly find heteroscedasticity when there are big variations in the number of observations associated with different values of an independent variable. Spread in the residuals would not be apparent for some value of an independent variable if there were few observations in the sample close to that value. In this case, by contrast, there are roughly the same number of observations with low per capita GNP as with high per capita GNP (up to a bit over $25,000). The relative lack of spread for the residuals for observations with low per capita GNP is *not* an artifact of few observations with low per capita GNP.

If you noticed that these residuals also suggest a nonlinearity, good for you! Note how the residuals at both the low and high ends of the horizontal axis tend to fall below the axis, while most of the residuals in the middle are above the axis. This model should include a squared term for per capita GNP. Would that correct the heteroscedasticity? This issue is left as an exercise.

Autocorrelation is similar to heteroscedasticity in that it is caused by a pattern in the residuals. In the case of autocorrelation, the pattern is not in the spread of the residuals but in their lack of randomness, their tendency to form a pattern. The most typical autocorrelation occurs in time series data and is caused by the fact that the effect of a change in an independent variable (which may or may not be included in the model) on a dependent variable can occur over several time periods. Consider the following problem:

The number of oil wells drilled in the United States is known to be affected by the price of oil. Higher prices should lead to more wells drilled. An oil industry trade group wants to determine that relationship more precisely. Data on the number of wells drilled in the United States each year since 1930 were collected, along with the average price of a barrel (bbl) of oil that year. Based on these data, what is the relationship? (These data are from Twentieth Century Petroleum Statistics, Dallas, Texas: Degolyer and McNaughton, 1992, pp. 34, 98.)

The data are on the Oil worksheet in the workbook in multireg.xls. In determining a response to price, it is usually necessary to correct a price series to account for inflation. That worksheet also contains the value of the Producer Price Index based on 1982 prices. This index will be used to adjust the price data for inflation.

- Switch to the Oil worksheet. Insert a blank column in front of the current column C by first clicking the column heading for column C and then either selecting "Columns" from the Insert menu on the Menu Bar or pressing the right mouse button and selecting "Insert" from the pop-up menu. The new column C will be used for the inflation-adjusted price of oil.

- Enter the label "Real Price per bbl" in cell C1.

- Enter a formula in cell C2 that will take the nominal (in 1930 dollars) price of oil in cell D2, multiply it by 100, and divide it by the price index in cell E2. Use relative addresses. The value displayed in cell C2 should be a little over 7.9865.

- Copy the formula in C2 to cells C3:C63. The value displayed in cell C63 should be slightly less than 14.1631.

- Use the Regression tool to estimate a regression equation in which Total Wells Drilled is the *y* variable and Real Price per bbl is the *x* variable. Use labels. Request residuals plots. Have the output placed in the region beginning in cell F2.

- After the Regression tool has finished, adjust the column widths of the region containing the output to fit the cell contents.

The regression output appears to confirm the relationship between price and number of wells drilled. The coefficient on the real price of oil is positive and has a *p* value of 2.55×10^{-15}, an indication of very high significance. Analysis of the residuals, however, will reveal a problem.

- Scroll your worksheet so that H25 is in the upper-left corner of your screen. That cell should contain the label "Residuals" and is the last column of a table giving predicted *y* values and residuals for each observation in the data.

- Select the entire column of residuals (H25:H87). Click the Chart Wizard button.

- Choose a scatter plot in which only the points are plotted with no connection lines. Your plot should be similar to the one below.

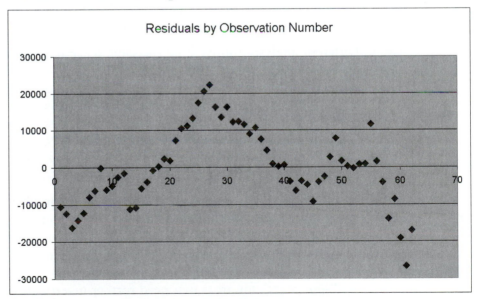

These residuals show a clear up-and-down wavelike pattern. Positive residuals tend to be adjacent to positive residuals. There is a strong indication of autocorrelation. It may be possible to correct for this by respecifying the model to include additional independent variables. These might include "lagged" values from earlier time periods. A technique other than ordinary least-squares regression may also be needed.

▼Model Building

The process of model building involves a search for the best way to specify a relationship between a dependent variable and a set of independent variables. A dependent variable is first regressed against an initial set of independent variables based upon a theoretical expectation of the relationship. The results of that regression are used to modify the set of independent variables or even the dependent variable. A second regression is estimated, and the results of that regression are used to make further modifications. Since each change in the set of independent variables may change the estimated coefficients and significances of the other independent variables, only a few modifications should be made after each regression. This iterative process continues until the analyst is satisfied that the regression best captures the relationship among the variables. Each step may involve creating new variables, as we did in the oil drilling example to create a measure of the price of oil adjusted for inflation. Dummy variables may have to be created and decisions made about which levels to omit. Squared values of independent variables may be added to correct for nonlinearities. Independent variables may have to be checked for multicollinearity and a decision made of whether to include only some or all such variables. Variables that do not contribute to the model in a logical or statistical sense need to be omitted.

Different analysts approaching the same set of data are not likely to end up with identical regression models. If there are strong relationships among the variables, they should be apparent in differently constructed models. Becoming proficient with multiple regression analysis takes practice. It is not possible to provide a set of step-by-step rules that will inevitably lead to the "best" regression models. Nevertheless, here are some tentative considerations that a beginner might find useful in the process of model building.

1. Start with the strongest possible regression equation by thinking in advance what types of relationships you expect to find. Is the set of independent variables reasonably complete? If not, can you fill the gaps by gathering additional data? Try to determine in advance what signs you expect for the estimated coefficients. Unexpected signs are "sign posts" for areas that need further investigation. Try to determine which variables you expect might have multicollinearity. Don't, however, infer multicollinearity whenever the results look a little "funny" unless you have solid evidence of multicollinearity.

2. Keep in mind that the number of independent variables you can have is constrained by the number of observations (the *degreees of freedom* problem). If you have only a few observations, you may not be

able to have as many independent variables as you might want. This can be a particular problem if you want to use categorical variables with multiple values since this may require the construction of many dummy variables, only a few of which can be included.

3. Have Excel produce residuals plots. Examine the residuals plots for nonlinearities and heteroscedasticity. For time series data, look for autocorrelation by constructing a plot of the table of residuals Excel produces by observation number. Add squared values of independent variables where nonlinearities are expected.

4. Test for multicollinearity by dropping individual variables and observing whether this increases the significance of other variables that you suspect might be measuring the same or similar factors. Then put the omitted variable back in the regression and drop one of the other variables you suspect of being in a multicollinear relationship. If you confirm multicollinearity, decide exactly which variables to keep. Remember that this decision depends partly on the objectives of the regression analysis.

5. Follow a multiple-step approach. Try to deal with only one problem in each step. Expect to estimate several regressions before you come up with a final model.

▼ A Comprehensive Example

The following problem, although still simpler than most real-world regression problems, will illustrate the step-by-step approach to model building.

A bank wants to determine the factors affecting withdrawals from automatic teller machines (ATMs) located in residential neighborhoods. A sample of daily withdrawals from such machines has been collected, together with information thought to affect total withdrawals. This information includes the median value of homes in the neighborhood, the median family income in the neighborhood, the average checking balance of customers living in the neighborhood, the distance to the next nearest ATM, and whether or not the withdrawals occurred on a weekend. Use these data to determine the factors affecting daily withdrawals from this class of ATMs.

What signs would you expect the coefficients for these independent variables to have on total daily withdrawals? Income, home value, and checking account balance should have positive coefficients but may have problems with multicollinearity. Distance to the next ATM should also

have a positive sign since the further the distance, the more likely customers are to use the one in their neighborhood. Weekend days might be
expected to have higher withdrawals because more recreational spending
and more shopping occurs on weekends, and bank offices are closed so
customers cannot cash checks there.

- Switch to the ATM worksheet in the workbook in Multireg.xls. Notice that the data on whether or not withdrawals occurred on a
  weekend is not in the form of a dummy variable that can be used in
  regression analysis.

- Construct a dummy variable whose value is "1" for weekend withdrawals and "0" for withdrawals on other days.

- Estimate a regression in which total withdrawals is the *y* variable, and
  median home value, median income, average checking balance, distance to next ATM, and the weekend dummy are the *x* variables.
  Direct the output to a new worksheet with the name "Run 1." Have
  Excel produce residual plots.

The estimated coefficients from this regression are shown below. Notice
that distance to next ATM has a negative sign, contrary to what is expected. The other coefficients have the correct sign, but median income
and median home value are not significant. Possible multicollinearity?

	A	B	C	D	E
16		*Coefficients*	*Standard Error*	*t Stat*	*P-value*
17	Intercept	99.55774256	13.99640204	7.11309537	6.9276E-09
18	Median Home Value	-0.183991147	0.145977366	-1.26040874	0.21401863
19	Median Income	0.307916152	0.13887352	2.21724165	0.03170085
20	Average Checking Balance	0.045943791	0.010212369	4.49883779	4.778E-05
21	Distance to Next ATM	-12.53377621	2.102219373	-5.96216378	3.5534E-07

- Examine the residuals plots. You will note that Excel stacks them on
  top of each other. They will have to be separated. This may be most
  easily done by first zooming to 50%. Once the plots are separated,
  make each a bit taller. Do any show signs of nonlinearities or
  heteroscedasticity? Pay particular attention to the plot of residuals on
  distance. This clearly shows evidence of a nonlinearity. None of the
  plots show evidence of heteroscedasticity.

- Return to the ATM worksheet. Create a new variable that equals distance squared. Run a new regression with all the independent
  variables previously used plus distance squared. Put the output on a
  new worksheet titled "Run 2." The estimated coefficients are shown
  at the top of the next page.

Notice that the coefficient on distance is positive while that on distance
squared is negative. If the next closest ATM is very close and is moved
away, initially withdrawals from this ATM will go up. If the nearest

	A	B	C	D	E
16		Coefficients	Standard Error	t Stat	P-value
17	Intercept	34.92043427	10.28778334	3.39435942	0.00148877
18	Median Home Value	0.018993715	0.078872682	0.24081488	0.81084313
19	Median Income	0.17476765	0.076802314	2.27555188	0.02791444
20	Average Checking Balance	0.046812573	0.005354302	8.7429836	4.3171E-11
21	Distance to Next ATM	7.362837349	3.825243965	1.92480203	0.06088635
22	Distance Squared	-2.492490449	0.469723674	-5.30629088	3.6917E-06
23	Weekend Dummy	32.39924027	3.679050953	8.80641249	3.5279E-11

ATM is very far away, withdrawals go down. This result seems surprising. Perhaps a very distant ATM means that the residents of the neighborhood are less likely to be ATM users at all. The coefficient of distance squared is highly significant; the coefficient of distance has a p value of .06. It would thus be judged significant at the .10 level of significance but not at a level of significance of .05 or below. The theoretical basis for keeping it in the model is strong, however.

The signs of the coefficients on income, home value, and checking account balance are still positive. The coefficient on income, however, has become significant. The reasons for this are not clear.

- Examine the residuals plots. You should see no evidence of heteroscedasticity or additional nonlinearities.

- Return to the ATM worksheet. Move the column of data for median income from column C to a location to the right of the other independent variables. This will allow you to estimate a regression without this variable and be able to replace it in a future regression. Estimate a new regression with all variables used in the previous model except median income. Have the output placed on a new worksheet titled "Run 3." There should be five independent variables (including the intercept). The estimated coefficients are shown below.

	A	B	C	D	E
16		Coefficients	Standard Error	t Stat	P-value
17	Intercept	36.74029379	10.73258284	3.4232481	0.00134886
18	Median Home Value	0.013803615	0.082498035	0.16732053	0.8678845
19	Average Checking Balance	0.053070573	0.004807246	11.0397042	2.8981E-14
20	Distance to Next ATM	7.051920164	4.000189594	1.76289648	0.08486258
21	Distance Squared	-2.308307963	0.484167834	-4.7675781	2.0692E-05
22	Weekend Dummy	34.87644918	3.677374393	9.48406266	3.3351E-12

The primary reason for dropping median income was to see if there was multicollinearity with median home value. If there was multicollinearity, the significance of the estimated coefficient for median home value should be higher. Is it? The p value for that coefficient on this regression is about .87. This suggests that the low level of significance for median home value is *not* the result of multicollinearity with median income. Instead, median home value seems not to be a factor determining ATM withdrawals.

- Return to the ATM worksheet. Replace the median income variable and remove the median home value variable. Estimate a new regression with the same set of independent variables as the previous regression except use median income and don't use median home value. Place the output on a worksheet titled "Run 4." The coefficients and significance statistics for this analysis are shown below.

An examination of the residuals plots reveals no evidence of nonlinearities or of heteroscedasticity. No irrelevant variables are in the set of independent variables. This, then, is the final model.

	A	B	C	D	E
16		Coefficients	Standard Error	t Stat	P-value
17	Intercept	36.21085062	8.687539719	4.16813641	0.00014152
18	Median Income	0.174232815	0.075943952	2.29422898	0.0266079
19	Average Checking Balance	0.047755477	0.003612767	13.218532	6.3411E-17
20	Distance to Next ATM	7.367160396	3.784032896	1.94690707	0.05794687
21	Distance Squared	-2.488443974	0.464370838	-5.35874299	2.9249E-06
22	Weekend Dummy	32.18719071	3.533675725	9.10869962	1.0963E-11

▼Exercises

1. Refer to the problem on page 390. Is there evidence (at the .05 level of significance) that homes in Armsley Hills are assessed at a significantly higher rate than homes in Blawndale that sell for the same price? Use the Assessment (2) worksheet, which is a copy of the one used earlier. Verify that the coefficients in your analysis agree with those in the table on page 392. Print your regression with the title "Assessment - Model 2" and your name at the top of the page.

2. In the problem on page 398, we found evidence both of nonlinearity and heteroscedasticity between per capita GNP and per capita energy consumption. Correct the model to account for the nonlinearity. Use the Energy (2) worksheet. Does this correction eliminate the heteroscedasticity? Print out the basis for your conclusion and explain your reasoning.

3. An electric utility is interested in determining whether or not it can develop a model that would be useful in predicting the electricity consumption of a residential user during the month of November. A sample of houses was selected. For each house, total electricity usage (in kWh) was measured. In addition, the size of the house (in square feet), whether or not the house meets the utility's requirement for energy efficiency, the family income of the residents, and the type of heating fuel used was also collected. The data are available in the Electricity worksheet. Use these data to develop a model that can be used to predict electricity usage for November.

4. As part of the staff of an electronics industry consortium, you have been asked to investigate the issues surrounding the manufacturing costs of integrated circuits. You have chosen a commonly used memory circuit that is currently manufactured at a large number of "foundries," as chip manufacturing plants like to style themselves. One issue of concern is whether foundries in the Pacific Rim countries have a cost advantage over those in this country.

Use the data in the IC's worksheet to investigate this issue. These data include the following:

(a) The average manufacturing cost of a lot of 1,000 chips.

(b) The foundry's daily output in millions of chips.

(c) The location of the foundry (PAC=Pacific Rim, SA=South America).

(d) The thickness of the silicon "wafer" used by the foundry for manufacturing the chip (millimeters).

(e) Whether or not the firm is vertically integrated; that is, does the firm also make products that use the chip? For example, a firm that manufactured computers as well as manufacturing the memory chip would be vertically integrated.

(f) The amount of silicon used per chip (micrograms).

Obtaining the Data

In order to make full use of this book, you must have and use the data diskette that can be easily obtained from the Internet. The first step is to download the program file LrnBStat.EXE. Execute this program once it has been downloaded, and it will write all of the data diskette files to your blank diskette (or other location).

To obtain the file from the Prentice Hall web site:

- Point your web browser to www.prenhall.com/neufeld. You will find links to this edition and one or more previous editions of this book.

- Click on the link for this book. Scroll to the bottom of the next page and click "Software Download." You will see a list of files. The file readme.txt contains a brief description of the other files.

- Click on LrnBStat.EXE. Your web browser may ask you if and where you want to save the file. Save it to the C:\Windows\Desktop folder. Close or minimize your web browser and all other applications so you can see your desktop. The icon for the downloaded file will appear on your desktop.

- Double click the icon for LrnBStat.EXE on your desktop. A dialog window will open. Click the Unzip button. By default, the data files will be written to your machines's hard disk in a folder named C:\BusStat. You can change this to any other location. If you want the files written to a diskette, change it to "A:\." Once the program has finished writing the files, click the Close button. You may then erase the file you downloaded, LrnBStat.EXE

You can also obtain the data from the author's web site (www.uncg.edu/bus_stat). This web site will also contain an updated errata list. It is strongly recommended that you obtain that list. If you find what you think is an error in this book, please send me e-mail. More information about this is in the Preface.

Appendix B

Setting Up the Analysis Tools

Excel regards the Analysis Tools as *add-ins* and does not make them accessible until you take certain steps. If "Analysis Tools…" is not one of the choices on the Tools menu, it is likely that it has not been installed. To install it, you probably will need the original installation CD. This will be the case if you did a default installation of Office 2000 Standard.

Installing the Data Analysis Tools

Open the Tools menu. Office 2000's menus only partially open at first, and the initial menu is likely to look like that shown on the left.

- Place the mouse pointer on the downward-pointing arows (⚆) and click. The entire Tools menu will open as shown on the left.

- Click "Add-ins."

A dialog window will open (shown below). Two add-ins are needed to use all of Excel's statistical capabilities, "Analysis ToolPak" and "Analysis ToolPak - VBA." They will be the first two choices at the top of the list. Click the box beside these choices, and checkmarks will appear in the boxes. Click the OK button. You may receive a message from Excel that that this feature has not been installed. If so, place the original installation CD in your machine and click OK again.

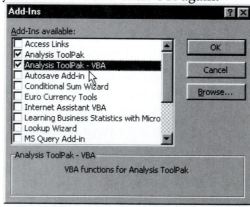

Installing the Learning Business Statistics Add-In

Several of the chapters require using tools that are provided by the Learning Business Statistics Excel add-in. This add-in is contained in the file named LearnBusStats.xla located on the data diskette. This appendix explains the procedure to install that add-in.

- Copy LearnBusStats.xla to your hard disk, unless the data files for this book are already on your hard disk.

The file can be located anywhere on your hard disk, but you must know where it is. If you accepted the default when you wrote the data files to your hard disk, it will be in C:\BusStat.

If you think the file is on your hard disk, but you don't know where or you are not sure, use the Find tool (click the Start button) and search for *.xla. This will show you the locations of all the Excel add-ins on your machine.

- Start Excel. Open the Tools menu on the Menu Bar. Click "Add-Ins." A dialog window will open showing a menu of add-ins. This menu will not, however, include the Learning Business Statistics add-in.

- Click the Browse… button. In the dialog windows that follow, show Excel the location of the LearnBusStats.xla file. Once you have located the file, double click its name in the dialog window, or click it once to highlight it and then click the OK button.

The menu of add-ins will return with the Learning Business Statistics add-in included and selected. The add-in will be loaded every time you start Excel. If you want to stop it from being loaded, retrieve this menu and click on the name so that the checkmark beside the add-in name is cleared.

Statistical Functions and Analysis Tools

This appendix provides brief information about each of the statistical functions and Analysis Tools. The goal here is to provide information that is not duplicative of that in the on-line help. In some cases, errors or possible errors have been discovered in some of the functions and tools, and these are noted. These errors may have been corrected in your version of Excel. Examples of a few of the functions can be found in the workbook Statfunc.xls.

Statistical Functions

Each of the functions in the "Statistical" category is discussed below. The argument names are the ones used in the Function Wizard. The discussion usually refers to the values of the arguments as cell or range addresses. Actual values, of course, can also be used as arguments. Note that some arguments are required; their names appear in the Function Wizard in bold type. Some arguments are optional. Some optional arguments appear in the Function Wizard dialog windows only if they might be needed. The AVERAGE function, for example, can accept multiple range addresses. Only two appear initially; if both are used, a third will appear.

AVEDEV—Calculates the Mean Absolute Deviation, sometimes used as an alternative to the standard deviation of the values in the cells within the range addresses given in the arguments "Number1," "Number2," etc. The mean of the values is calculated, the difference between each argument and the mean (the deviation) is calculated, the absolute value of each deviation is determined, and the mean of these absolute values is returned by the function. See the example in the workbook in Statfunc.xls.

AVERAGE—Calculates the arithmetic mean or average of the values in the cells within the range addresses given in the arguments "Number1," "Number2," etc. AVERAGE ignores logical values.

AVERAGEA—Same as AVERAGE except AVERAGEA also includes logical values, counting "false" as 0 and "true" as 1.

BETADIST—The cumulative probability distribution for the beta distribution, also called the standard beta. The range of values for the random numbers are between 0 and 1. The function returns the probability of a random variable whose distribution is the beta distribution with parameters given by the arguments "Alpha" and "Beta" having a value less than the value given by the value of the "X" argument. The beta distribution can be generalized to a variety of shapes including U-shaped, bell-shaped, symmetric, and skewed. When both "Alpha" and "Beta" are set to 1, the distribution becomes a continuous uniform distribution. This distribution is not used often in business statistics.

BETAINV—Inverse of the cumulative beta distribution. The function returns the value of the beta distribution such that the probability of a random variable whose distribution is the beta distribution with parameters given by the arguments "Alpha" and "Beta" is given by the argument "Probability." To generate random values from the beta distribution, enter "rand()" (without quotes) in the "Probability" argument.

BINOMDIST—Provides either the probability or the cumulative probability associated with the value of a binomial random variable given by the argument "Number_s" (number of successes). The "Trials" argument is set equal to the number of trials, and the "Probability_s" argument is set to the probability of success on each trial. The "Cumulative" argument should be set equal either to "true" or "false" (no quotation marks). "True" causes BINOMDIST to return the cumulative probability of obtaining the exact or fewer number of successes given by "Number_s." "False" causes BINOMDIST to return the probability of obtaining exactly the number of successes given by "Number_s." The use of BINOMDIST and the binomial distribution is covered in Chapter 4.

CHIDIST—Chi-square distribution. The function returns the probability that a χ^2 random variable will have a value greater than the value given by the "X" argument. The degrees of freedom of the χ^2 distribution is given by the "Deg_freedom" argument. Examples of the use of this function are given in Chapter 11.

CHIINV—The inverse chi-square distribution. The function returns the value of a χ^2 random variable such that the probability of another random value exceeding the returned value is given by the "Probability" argument. The degrees of freedom is given by the

"Deg_freedom" argument. Examples of the use of this function are given in Chapter 11. To generate random numbers from the chi-square distribution, use "rand()" (without quotes) for the "Probability" argument.

CHITEST—Implements the chi-square test for independence which also is used to test for differences in the proportion of successes between different populations. The function determines the p value for the Null Hypothesis that all populations have the same proportions. The "Actual_range" argument is the cell range address of a contingency table of values. The "Expected_range" argument is the cell range address of a contingency table of expected values assuming the proportions are the same for all populations. This last contingency table must usually be calculated. See the Statfunc.xls workbook for an example.

CONFIDENCE—Returns half the sampling error (half the width of the confidence interval) for a population mean. The arguments are "Alpha" (one minus the confidence level), "Standard_dev" (the standard deviation of the population), and "Size" (the sample size). CONFIDENCE uses the normal distribution rather than the t distribution in calculating the sampling error because the standard error is assumed to be the *population* standard error. This limits the usefulness of this function to the rare case when the population standard deviation is known. If the sample standard deviation is used and the sample is large, CONFIDENCE will return a value that is approximately correct.

CORREL—Calculates the correlation coefficient (also called the Pearson product moment correlation coefficient) for two arrays of data. The range addresses of the arrays are provided in the two arguments "Array1" and "Array2." These arrays need to have the same number of cells and the same number of cells that display numeric values. This function is identical to the PEARSON function.

COUNT—Counts the number of cells in one or more ranges that display numeric values (including dates and text that can be converted into numbers). Cells which are blank or that display nonnumeric text or error values are not counted. Range or cell addresses are provided in the "Value1" and optional "Value2"… arguments.

COUNTA—Counts the number of cells in one or more ranges that are not empty, including cells that appear empty (e.g., contain blanks) but are not empty. Range or cell addresses are provided in the "Value1" and optional "Value2"… arguments.

COUNTBLANK—Counts the number of cells in a range that are blank or empty.

COUNTIF—Counts the number of cells in a range whose values meet a specified logical criteria. COUNTIF is used in a number of chapters beginning with Chapter 3.

COVAR—Calculates the *population* covariance of two arrays of data. This can be converted to a *sample* covariance by multiplying by $\frac{n}{n-1}$. The range addresses of the two arrays are given in the "Array1" and "Array2" arguments, which must have the same number of cells and the same number of cells displaying numeric values.

CRITBINOM—This function is related to the cumulative binomial distribution that provides the probability of a given number of successes (or fewer) for a given number of trials and a given probability of success on each trial. CRITBINOM returns the number of successes given the cumulative binomial probability ("Alpha"), the number of trials ("Trials"), and the probability of success on a single trial ("Probability_s"). If the value given for "Alpha" is not exactly equal to a binomial cumulative probability, the smallest number of successes for which the cumulative binomial probability exceeds "Alpha" is returned.

DEVSQ—Calculates the sum of squared deviations from the mean for the values in one or more ranges. This is most useful as an input to other calculations. The sample standard deviation, for example, is the sum of squared deviations divided by $n - 1$. The sum of squared deviations of the y variable in a regression is also called the total sum of squares, or SST. The range addresses are provided in the "Number1" and optional "Number2"… arguments.

EXPONDIST—The exponential distribution. EXPONDIST determines the probability for the cumulative distribution function if "Cumulative" is true or the value of the probability density function (which is *not* a probability) if "Cumulative" is false. This continuous distribution is related to the discrete Poisson distribution. The Poisson distribution can be thought of as modeling the number of occurrences during a fixed time period. The exponential distribution can be thought of as modeling the period of time between occurrences. The "Lambda" argument is the reciprocal of the mean time between occurrences ($\frac{1}{\mu}$). The argument "X" is the value of the time for which a cumulative probability is desired. Suppose the average time required to complete registration at a public university is 3 hours. The probability that registration could be completed in 2.5 hours or less could be determined by EXPONDIST with "X" equal to 2.5, "Lambda" equal to $\frac{1}{3}$, and "Cumulative" equal to "true."

FDIST—Returns the probability that a random variable drawn from the *F* distribution will have a value *greater* than the value given by the "X" argument. The *F* distribution has two degrees of freedom. The numerator degrees of freedom is given in the argument "Deg_freedom1" and the denominator degrees of freedom is given in "Deg_freedom2."

FINV—The inverse *F* distribution returns the value of a random variable drawn from the *F* distribution such that the probability of a *greater* value equals the "Probability" argument. The two degrees of freedom are given as in the FDIST function. To generate a random number from the *F* distribution, enter "rand()" (without quotes) for the "Probability" argument.

FISHER—Calculates Fisher's *z* transformation. This is very seldom encountered in business statistics. It is primarily used in hypotheses tests on the correlation coefficient between two sets of data when the Null Hypothesis is that the coefficient has a value other than 0. Suppose the correlation coefficient between two sets of data is *r* and we wish to test the Null Hypothesis that the correlation coefficient equals ρ_0. The test statistic would be: $z = \dfrac{\phi(r) - \phi(\rho_0)}{1/\sqrt{n-3}}$, where $\phi(r)$ and $\phi(\rho_0)$ are the Fisher transformation of the calculated and hypothesized correlation coefficients.

FISHERINV—Calculates the inverse of the Fisher transformation.

FORECAST—This function returns a predicted *y* value for a single *x* value whose address is given in the "X" argument. The prediction is based on a simple regression calculated on a set of *y* values whose range address is given in the "Known_y's" argument and a set of *x* values whose range address is given in the "Known_x's" argument. This function is similar to TREND except that TREND can return an array of multiple predicted *y* values.

FREQUENCY—Provides a count of the number of values in a range of cells that fall within several specified numeric ranges. The output of this function is a vertical array of values. The address of the cell range containing the values to be counted is given in the "Data_array" argument. The numeric ranges are defined by a set of "bin" values, each of which is an upper bound of a numeric range (which includes the upper bound if positive but excludes it if negative). The number of values in the output array equals the number of bins. Like all functions that output arrays in Excel, entering the function is tricky. First, select the range of cells into which the output array is to be written (as many cells as "bin" values). Click the Function Wizard button, enter the argument values, and click the OK button. At this point, only a single value will be displayed in the output range. Click the mouse pointer in the Formula Bar as if you were going to edit the formula. Hold down the Shift and Ctrl keys and, while holding them down, press the Enter key. Values will appear in all of the cells of the output array. An example of the use of the FREQUENCY function is given in the workbook in the file Statfunc.xls.

FTEST—This tool calculates and returns the *p* value from an *F* test on the Null Hypothesis that two arrays have the same variance. The arguments of the function, "Array1" and "Array2," are the addresses of the two arrays of values whose variances are tested. The dialog window (and Help) asserts that the probability returned by FTEST is one-tail. It is two-tail.

GAMMADIST—Returns a cumulative probability if "Cumulative" is equal to "true" or the value of the density (which is not a probability) if it is equal to "false." The value of the variable drawn from the gamma distribution to be evaluated is given by the "X" argument. The distribution has two parameters given by the "Alpha" and "Beta" arguments. The gamma distribution is right-skewed. Small values for alpha result in greater skew. Both the exponential and chi-square distributions are special cases of the gamma distribution. The sample variance, s^2, follows the gamma distribution in which $\alpha = \dfrac{n-1}{2}$ and $\beta = \dfrac{2\sigma^2}{n-1}$. The distribution can thus be used for hypothesis tests and confidence intervals on population variances and standard deviations. It has become traditional, however, to calculate the chi-square statistic and use the chi-square distribution for these problems, doubtless because of the difficulty of constructing a table for the gamma distribution.

GAMMAINV—Inverse of the cumulative gamma distribution. GAMMAINV returns the value of a random variable drawn from the gamma distribution whose cumulative probability is given by the "Probability" argument. The parameters of the gamma distribution are given by the "Alpha" and "Beta" arguments. To generate a random number from the gamma distribution, enter "rand()" without quotes in the "Probability" argument field.

GAMMALN—Returns the natural logarithm of the gamma function (*not* the gamma distribution).

GEOMEAN—Returns the geometric mean, a descriptive measure of location favored in certain circumstances over the arithmetic mean when the data consist of ratios, percentages, rates of change, or rates of return.

GROWTH—Calculates predicted values for an exponential growth model. An exponential growth model has the form $\hat{y} = b_0 b_1^{x_1} \ldots b_n^{x_n}$, and is used when data are increasing at an increasing rate, such as biological population growth. The GROWTH function returns an array of any length. Simple versions of this model are sometimes used to predict growth against time; in this case there would be only a single x variable measuring time. To see the display of an output array containing more than one value, first select a region of cells for the output array. Click the Function Wizard button, select the "GROWTH" function, and enter the values in the argument fields. Click the OK button. Only a single value will be displayed in the selected region. Click the mouse pointer in the Formula Bar as if you were going to edit the formula. Press and hold both the Shift and Ctrl keys and, while holding those keys, press and release the Enter key. All of the cells in the selected region will now display values. The TREND function performs a similar role for the linear model.

HARMEAN—A measure of central tendency rarely used with business data.

HYPERGEOMDIST—Returns the hypergeometric probability of drawing the number of successes given by the argument "Sample_s" from a sample of size "Number_sample" if the sample is drawn without replacement from a population whose size is given by the argument "Number_population" in which there are "Population_s" total successes. For example, if you wanted to determine the probability of selecting three aces in five cards from a poker deck, the value of "Sample_s" would be 3, the value of "Number_sample" would be 5, the value of "Population_s" would be 4, and the value of "Number_population" would be 52. Note that the probability returned by this function is *not* cumulative, which reduces its usefulness for problems involving large ranges of number of successes.

INTERCEPT—Calculates a simple regression on a set of y and x values and returns the value of the intercept (b_0). Note that this (and more) is also available in the LINEST function, which is capable of multiple regression.

KURT—Returns the measure of kurtosis of a set of data. Kurtosis is a descriptive statistic that adds information about a set of numbers not captured by mean, variance, or skewness. Data with relatively high kurtosis tend to be more "peaked" than data with low kurtosis. The measure is infrequently used but does have application in the analysis of investment returns.

LARGE—Returns the largest ("k" equals 1), second largest ("k" equals 2), to the smallest ("k" equals n) value in a range of cells containing n numbers.

LINEST—Performs a multiple (or simple) regression analysis on a set of data and returns an array containing the estimated coefficients and (optionally) a number of statistics including r^2, standard errors, SSR, and SSE. An example of the use of this function can be found in the workbook in Statfunc.xls. The output of the function is an array. To use the function, select a region of cells in which the number of columns equals the number of independent variables plus one (for the intercept), and the number of rows is 5. If only coefficients are desired, set the "stats" argument to zero and select only one row in the output range. After the region is selected, click the Function Wizard button, select "LINEST," and enter the appropriate values in the argument fields. Click the OK button. Only one value will appear in the selected region. With the region still selected, click the mouse pointer in the Formula Bar as if you were going to edit the formula. Press and hold the Shift and Ctrl keys. While holding those keys, press and release the Enter key. All the cells in the selected region will now display values. If you have more than a single independent variable, some of the cells will display the #N/A error code. This is normal.

LOGEST—Returns estimated coefficients and statistics for an exponential growth model. The output of this function is an array identical to that produced by LINEST except that instead of estimating a linear model it estimates an exponential growth model of the form $\hat{y} = b_0 b_1^{x_1} \dots b_n^{x_n}$. This is the same model estimated by the GROWTH function. GROWTH returns predicted values while LOGEST returns estimated coefficients and statistics. The statistics (standard errors, r^2, etc., the same as LINEST) must be interpreted with caution. The exponential growth model is estimated by using linear regression in which the dependent variable is the natural log of the y variable in the exponential growth model. This linear regression results in estimated coefficients. The b's in the exponential growth model are the antilogs (Excel's EXP function) of the linear regression's estimated coefficients. The statistics reported by LOGEST come from the linear regression. Thus we cannot, for example, calculate a t statistic on an estimated coefficient by dividing an estimated coefficient reported by LOGEST by its standard error reported by LOGEST. That standard error was calculated from the linear regression's coefficient, the log of the value reported by LOGEST.

LOGINV—The inverse of the lognormal distribution. See LOGNORMDIST for more on this distribution. To generate a random number drawn from the lognormal distribution, enter "rand()" (without quotes) in the argument field for "Probability."

LOGNORMDIST—Returns the probability that a lognormally distributed variable will have a value less than the "X" argument. If x is a variable that is lognormally distributed, then $\ln(x)$ will be normally distributed. The error terms of exponential growth models are typically assumed to be lognormal. Lognormal variables are nonnegative and right-skewed. The extent of skew depends on the size of the variance compared to the mean. A large variance and small mean causes a greater skew. The lognormal distribution is sometimes used to model variables that are known to be skewed and nonnegative, such as family income.

MAX—Returns the largest number in one or more cell ranges. MAX ignores logical and character values.

MAXA— Same as MAX except includes logical values counting "false" as 0 and "true" as 1.

MEDIAN—Returns the median value of a set of numbers in one or more cell ranges.

MIN—Returns the smallest value in one or more cell ranges. Logical and character values are ignored.

MINA—Same as Min except that it also looks at logical values, counting "true" as 1 and "false" as 0.

MODE—Returns the modal (most frequently occurring) value in one or more ranges. If there is no modal value (e.g., each value occurs once), the function displays the #N/A error code.

NEGBINOMDIST—Returns the probability that a random variable from the negative binomial distribution will equal the "Number_f" argument. The probability is not cumulative. This distribution is useful for problems in which you want to know the probability of obtaining "Number_f" failures before you obtain "Number_s" successes, given that the probability of success in each trial is value of the "Probability_s" argument.

NORMDIST—Returns the cumulative probability (or density) of a random variable drawn from the normal distribution with mean given by the "Mean" argument and standard deviation given by the "Standard_dev" argument having a value less than the "X" argument. If the "Cumulative" argument is "true," the function returns the cumulative probability. If it is "false," density—not a probability—is returned. There is little or no practical use for density values.

NORMINV—Returns the value of a normally distributed random variable for which the probability of a smaller random variable equals the value of the "Probability" argument. The values of the "Mean" and "Standard_dev" arguments set the parameters of the normal distribution. To generate a normally distributed random variable, enter "rand()" (without quotes) in the "Probability" argument field.

NORMSDIST—Returns the probability of a standard normal (mean equal to 0, standard deviation equal to 1) having a value less than the "Z" argument.

NORMSINV—Returns the value of a standard normal random variable such that the probability of another standard normal random variable having a smaller value equals the "Probability" argument. To generate a standard normal random variable, enter "rand()" (no quotes) in the "Probability" argument field.

PEARSON—This function is identical to the CORREL function.

PERCENTILE—Determines a given percentile value in a set of numbers whose range address is given in the "Array" argument. Two aspects of this function are unusual. The percentile value is given in the "K" argument and must be a number between 0 and 1 inclusive, rather than an integer between 1 and 99, which is more common. Excel's method for determining the percentile value differs from that most widely used in business statistics. Let p represent a percentile value expressed as an integer between 1 and 99 and assume the data have been ordered from smallest to largest. The value of the pth percentile is usually defined as the $\frac{p(n+1)}{100}$th value. Excel instead selects the $\frac{pn+(100-p)}{100}$th value. These two methods give the same value for the 50th percentile, but differ for all other percentiles. If the formula does not yield an integer, Excel interpolates.

PERCENTRANK—The inverse of the PERCENTILE function. When given a range address in the "Array" argument and a value in the "X" argument, PERCENTRANK returns the percentile score of that value in the array. See the discussion under PERCENTILE for the method Excel uses to determine percentiles.

PERMUT—Calculates the permutations of "Number_chosen" objects drawn from "Number" objects. Permutations differ from combinations in that order matters for permutations. Excel also has a combinations function, COMBIN, with the same arguments as PERMUT, in the "Math & Trig" functions.

POISSON—Returns the probability or cumulative probability of drawing the value "X" from the discrete Poisson distribution in which the mean is given by the argument "Mean." If the "Cumulative" argument is "true," POISSON will return the probability of drawing a value less than or equal to "X." If "Cumulative" is "false," the probability of drawing a value exactly equal to "X" is returned.

PROB—Returns the probability of a discrete random variable equaling a specific value or falling within a given interval. The probability distribution is given in the "X_range" and "Prob_range" arguments. If the probability of a variable falling within an interval is desired, the boundaries are given in the "Lower_limit" and "Upper_limit" arguments. Those boundaries are included in the interval. If the "Upper_limit" argument is omitted, PROP returns the probability of a random variable's value being equal to the value given in the "Lower_limit" argument.

QUARTILE—Returns either the minimum, maximum, or one of the three quartile values of a set of data. The range address of the data is provided in the "Array" argument, and the value to be returned is provided by the "Quart" argument. If "Quart" is set to 0 or 4, QUARTILE returns the minimum or maximum values in the data, respectively. If "Quart" is set to 1, 2, or 3, QUARTILE returns the corresponding quartile value. As in the case of PERCENTILE, Excel uses a nonstandard definition for quartiles. Assume the data are sorted from the smallest to largest value. The first quartile is usually defined as the $\frac{n+1}{4}$th value. Excel instead uses the $\frac{n+3}{4}$th value. Similarly, the third quartile is usually defined as the $\frac{3(n+1)}{4}$th value. Excel uses the $\frac{3n+1}{4}$th value. Excel's definition of the second quartile (the median) is the same as that usually used.

RANK—Returns the position an individual number would have in a list of values if the list were ordered. The individual number's cell address or value is given in the "Number" argument and the address of the range of cells is given in the "Ref" argument. If the "Order" argument is "true," the position is given as if the list were ordered from smallest to largest. If "Order" is "false" or omitted, the position is given as if the list were ordered from largest to smallest. The #N/A error code is displayed if the number is not in the list.

RSQ—Returns the r^2 value of a simple regression of the set of values whose range address is given in the "Known_y's" argument against the set of values whose range address is given in the "Known_x's" argument. This information (along with other regression-derived information) is also provided by the LINEST function, which is also capable of multiple regression.

SKEW—Calculates and returns the coefficient of skewness of a set of numbers in one or more cell ranges.

SLOPE—Returns the slope (b_1) value from a simple regression of the set of values whose range address is given in the "Known_y's" argument against the set of values whose range address is given in the "Known_x's" argument. This information (along with other regression-derived information) is also provided by the LINEST function, which is also capable of multiple regression.

SMALL—Returns the smallest ("K" equals 1), second smallest ("K" equals 2), to the largest ("K" equals n) value in a range of cells containing n numbers.

STANDARDIZE—Takes the value given by the "X" argument, subtracts the value given by the "Mean" argument, divides the difference by the value given by the "Standard_dev" argument, and returns the result.

STDEV—Returns the *sample* standard deviation (divides by $n - 1$) of the values in one or more cell ranges. STDEV ignores logical and character values.

STDEVA— Same as STDEV except also considers logical values, counting "false" as 0 and "true" as 1.

STDEVP—Returns the *population* standard deviation (divides by N) of the values in one or more cell ranges. Ignores logical and character values.

STDEVPA— Same as STDEVP except that logical values are included, counting "true" as 1 and "false" as 0.

STEYX—Returns the standard error of the regression for a simple regression of the set of values whose range address is given in the "Known_y's" argument regressed against the set of values whose range address is given in the "Known_x's" argument. This information (along with other regression-derived information) is also provided by the LINEST function, which is also capable of multiple regression.

TDIST—If the "Tails" argument is 1, TDIST returns the probability that a random variable drawn from the t distribution with degrees of freedom given by the "Deg_freedom" argument will exceed the value of the "X" argument. If the "Tails" argument is 2, the probability is doubled. An unfortunate characteristic of TDIST is that a negative value for the "X" argument results in an error code. For this reason, it is wise to embed the absolute value function, ABS, in the "X" argument field whenever the t value to be evaluated is calculated on a worksheet. The TDIST and TINV functions were discussed and used starting on page 193.

TINV—The inverse of the t distribution. TINV interprets the value of the "Probability" argument as the equally divided area of both tails. The positive t value (upper tail boundary) drawn from a distribution with degrees of freedom equal to the "Deg_freedom" argument is returned. If the t value corresponding to a one-tail probability is desired, the "Probability" argument of TINV should be twice the one-tail probability. The TDIST and TINV functions were discussed and used starting on page 193.

TREND—Estimates a simple or multiple regression of the dependent variables whose range address is given by the "Known_y's" argument on the independent variables whose range address is given by the "Known_x's" argument. The regression is then used to provide estimated y values for another set of x values whose range addresses are given by the "New_x's" argument. The output of TREND is an array consisting of the predicted values. The number of values in this array equals the number of observations for which there are new x values. To see the display of an output array containing more than one value, first select a region of cells for the output array. Click the Function Wizard button, select the "TREND" function, and enter the values in the argument fields. Click the OK button. Only a single value will be displayed in the selected region. Click the mouse pointer in the Formula Bar as if you were going to edit the formula. Press and hold both the Shift and Ctrl keys and, while holding those keys, press and release the Enter key. All of the cells in the selected region will now display values. The GROWTH function performs a similar role for the exponential growth model.

TRIMMEAN—Estimates the mean of a set of data after eliminating a proportion of the extreme (highest and lowest) values set by the "Percent" argument. Despite its name, the value used in the "Percent" argument should be a proportion (between 0 and 1).

TTEST—Calculates a *t* test on the Null Hypothesis that two populations have the same mean. The range address of the sample from the first population is given in the "Array1" argument and that from the second population is given in the "Array2" argument. The "Tails" argument can have the value 1 or 2 and determines whether the test will be one-tail or two-tail. The "Type" argument determines which test will be used. If "Type" equals 1, the samples are assumed to be paired samples. If "Type" equals 2, the two samples are assumed to have been drawn from populations with equal variance. If "Type" equals 3, the two samples are assumed to have been drawn from populations with unequal variance. The function returns the *p* value from this test.

VAR—Estimates the variance of a *sample* of numbers in one or more ranges. VAR ignores logical and character values.

VARA— Same as VAR except it includes logical values with 0 for "false" and 1 for "true".

VARP—Estimates the variance of a *population* of numbers in one or more ranges. VARP ignores logical and character values.

VARPA— Same as VARP except it also uses logical values, interpreting "false" as 0 and "true" as 1.

WEIBULL—Returns the probability of a random variable drawn from the Weibull distribution with parameters given by the "Alpha" and "Beta" arguments having a value less than that given by the "X" argument (if the "Cumulative" argument is "true"). The Weibull distribution is not often used in business statistics. It is typically used for the distribution of time intervals such as time before failure of a mechanical component.

ZTEST—The purpose of this function is not obvious. If the value of the "X" argument is interpreted as a hypothesized population mean (Null Hypothesis H_0: $\mu \le x$), and the numbers whose range address is given in the "Array" argument are interpreted as a sample drawn from that population, the function returns the *p* value for the test. An optional argument, "Sigma" permits you to give the function the population standard deviation. Only if that argument is given would it be appropriate to use the normal distribution to calculate the *p* value, as this function does. Without the population standard deviation, the *t* distribution, not the *z* distribution, is appropriate. The on-line help description of ZTEST as a two-tail *p* value that can be used to "assess the likelihood that a particular observation is drawn from a particular population" is inaccurate.

Data Analysis Tools

The Data Analysis Tools are accessed through the Tools menu on the Menu Bar. Appendix A provides instructions for adding "Data Analysis" to the Tools menu if it is not present.

The Data Analysis Tools often duplicate procedures provided by the statistical functions. There are important differences between the tools and the functions, however. The output of a single tool generally provides more information than that of a single function. The output of most tools is formatted and labeled. The functions provide no formatting. The values written by most of the tools are numbers, not functions. An important consequence of this is that a change in the input data analyzed by a tool will not change the already written output of a tool. The tool would have to be explicitly run on the new data. The displayed value of a cell containing a function, by contrast, automatically reflects any changes in its arguments. Functions can be used directly in Excel formulas; tools cannot.

The use of most of the Analysis Tools is covered in one or more chapters of this book. The discussion below will primarily cover those tools *not* otherwise discussed in this book. The objective again is to provide useful information not available through Excel's on-line help.

Anova: Single-Factor—The use of this tool is covered in Chapter 13.

Anova:Two-Factor with Replication—The use of this tool is covered in Chapter 13.

Anova: Two-Factor without Replication—The use of this tool is covered in Chapter 13.

Correlation—Calculates the correlation (or Pearson moment correlation coefficient) between all pairs of any number of variables. The PEARSON and CORREL functions, by contrast, do the calculation for only a single pair of variables. The output of the tool is a semirectangular array in which each variable has a column and a row. If the input data have labels, the rows and columns of the output will also be labeled. The entries give the correlation coefficient for the pair of variables in whose row and column the entry lies.

Covariance—Calculates the covariance between all pairs of any number of variables. The difference between the Covariance tool and the COVAR function is like the difference between the Correlation tool and the CORREL function. Like the COVAR function, the Covariance tool provides *population* covariances rather than *sample* covariances.

Descriptive Statistics—The use of this tool is covered in Chapter 2 starting on page 66. Each of the outputs produced by this tool can be produced by a single function except the range and the "confidence." The latter is the sampling error and, if subtracted and added to the sample mean, provides a confidence interval on the population mean. If "Summary Statistics" is not selected in the dialog window, the "confidence" value is the only number the tool outputs.

Exponential Smoothing—Excel uses exponential smoothing as a form of forecasting. The formula used is $P_{t+1} = \omega A_t + (1 - \omega)P_t$, where P_{t+1} is the predicted value in time $t + 1$ and A_t and P_t are the actual and predicted values for time t, respectively. The predicted value for time 2 is set to the actual value for time 1. The "damping factor," ω, must be between 0 and 1. If "Standard Errors" is requested, Excel provides for each observation (beginning with number 4) the square root of the mean square error of the three previous observations. Unlike most tools, the output of this tool is formulas, not numbers. If the input values change, so will the output of the tool.

F-Test Two-Sample for Variances—The use of this tool is discussed in Chapter 12 starting on page 317. It has two problems. First, the p value and critical F it computes are one-tail when the proper test for the equality of two population variances is usually two-tail. This can be corrected for the p value by simply doubling it. Note that the FTEST function returns the correct two-tail p value for the same data (although it calls it one-tail). To convert the critical F in the tools output to two-tail, the value for alpha entered in the tool's dialog window should be half the desired two-tail value.

Fourier Analysis—Fourier analysis is a technique that represents a set of data as a sum of periodic (trigonometric) functions. Widely used for certain engineering problems, the technique is seldom used in business statistics, although it does have some application in sophisticated analysis of time series data.

Histogram—The use of this tool is discussed in Chapter 2 starting on page 70.

Moving Average—This is a forecasting (or smoothing) technique in which the predicted value is the average of a specified (by the "Interval" field of the dialog window) number of previous values. Excel in fact includes the current period's value in that average. Thus the values provided by Excel must be interpreted as predictions for the *next* period rather than the current period. The standard error, if requested, calculates, for each value, the square root of the mean square error of previous predictions. The number of predictions used for that calculation is the same as the number of data values used in the calculation of the moving average. Unlike most tools, the output of this tool is formulas, not numbers. The output will thus automatically change if the input data change.

Random Number Generation—This tool has been used in several places in this book to explore statistical concepts. Its use to generate discrete random numbers appears in Chapter 3 (page 91) and in Chapter 4 (page 109). Its use to generate normally distributed random variables appears in Chapter 13 (page 332). The tool will also generate random numbers from other distributions as well as nonrandom sequences ("Patterned"). It is possible to generate random numbers from any of Excel's inverse probability functions by using RAND() as the "probability" argument. This approach, however, would result in cell values that changed every time the worksheet is recalculated, which may, or may not, be undesirable. The functions can be converted to numbers by, for example, selecting their cells, clicking the Copy button, selecting "Paste Special" from the Edit menu, and selecting "Values" to be pasted. The Random Number Generation tool avoids this problem since its output is numbers.

Rank and Percentile—One or more variables are sorted from highest to lowest, and the rank and percentile of each value are shown. Rank is the position of each value within the sorted order with the largest value assigned rank 1. Excel's method of determining the percentile of each value is based on the same nonstandard method of determining percentiles discussed in the description of the PERCENTILE function.

Regression—The use of this tool is covered in Chapters 14 and 15. Variables for this tool must be arrayed in columns (not rows). All independent variables must be in adjacent columns. The "Normal Probability Plots" option does not work correctly and should not be used.

Sampling—Draws a sample from a population. The sample can be random, in which case it is drawn with replacement, or periodic. A periodic sample simply chooses elements from the population that are a fixed number of positions (determined by "period") apart.

t-Test: Paired Two-Sample for Means—The use of this tool is covered in Chapter 12.

t-Test: Two-Sample Assuming Equal Variances—The use of this tool is covered in Chapter 12.

t-Test: Two-Sample Assuming Unequal Variances—The use of this tool is covered in Chapter 12.

z-Test: Two Sample for Means—This performs a z test on the equality of two population means when the population variances are known, but the population means are unknown. This is an unlikely situation to occur in real data, but is often discussed for pedagogic reasons by statistics texts.

Answers to Selected Exercises

Chapter 2

2. In ascending order of per capita GDP: Turkey, Greece, Portugal, Ireland, Spain,..., Luxembourg, Switzerland, United States

Range	Frequency
$ 0-$ 4,000	1
$ 4,001-$ 8,000	1
$ 8,001-$12,000	2
$12,001-$16,000	4
$16,001-$20,000	13
$20,001-$24,000	3 The data are left-skewed.

Descriptive Statistics: mean =16,014.75, standard deviation = 4,441.326, etc. Left skew is indicated by fact that median (16,900) exceeds mean, and coefficient of skewness (−1.230130) is negative.

3. There is an abrupt change in the mean bolt length beginning at sample number 65 (while variance appears to remain constant). This sudden upward shift suggests an assignable cause such as equipment problems.

Chapter 3

2. Product A: expected value = $1,020, variance = 2,161,600; Product B: expected value = $1,020, variance = 3,957,100; Product C: expected value = $1,150, variance = 2,032,500. Products A and B have the same expected value, but A has a lower variance and is therefore less risky. Product C has a higher expected value and lower variance than either products A or B. Product C would be ranked highest with product A second and product B last.

3. As n increases, the proportion of stock providing each level of profit should become closer to the probability given in the distribution. For all portfolios, $E(x) = 8.00$ and $VAR(x) = 4,086$. As n increases, there should also be a tendency for the portfolio mean and variances to converge on these values, although the same kind of deviation is possible here as in the table printed for problem 1.

4. For soda, the expected value and standard deviation are 46 and 7.3485, respectively. For ice cream they are 44 and 17.1464, respectively. Since soda has a higher expected value, the vendor is likely to make more money with soda. Since it has a lower standard deviation, it is less risky. The vendor should sell soda.

Chapter 4

1. (a) 0.5832, (b) 0.023711, (c) .00002656, (d) =0.4168

2. (a) 75, (b) 7.9844, (c) 0.0499, (d) Since the number of cars requiring repair must be an integer, $P(60 \leq x \leq 90) = 0.9481$

3. (a) 0.01435, (b) $E(x) = 0.405$, $\sigma(x) = 0.19198$

4. (a) $E(x) = 98.4$, $\sigma(x) = 9.29$, (b) .0132

5. (a) .9818, (b) $E(x) = 4$, $\sigma(x) = 19960$

6. (a) $E(x) = 6.3$, $\sigma(x) = .24657$, (b) Within one standard deviation means $6.3 \pm .24657$: $38343 < x < 87657$. Since x must be an integer within this range: $4 < x < 8$. The probability of x being in this range is .6963, (c) .0016, d) $P(x \geq 10)$ with unchanged n and $\pi = .1023$

7. .4186

8. .0072

9. .00275

10. $E(x) = .96$, $\sigma(x) = .09398$

11. .1451

Chapter 5

1. $z = 1.2816$, $x = 75 + (1.2816)(10) = 87.8155$

2. $P(x < 16) = P(z < -2.2222) = 0.0131$

3. (25.7264, 30.2736)

4. $P(x > 55) = P(z > -1.4583) = 0.9276$

5. The use of the correction for continuity substantially improves the normal approximation for the binomial.

Chapter 6

1. $P(\bar{x} \leq 1.99) = P(t \leq -1.49071) = 0.0762$

2. (1.9852, 2.0548)

3. $P(\bar{x} \le 50.2) = P(t \le -2.75862) = 0.0055$

4. $P(\bar{x} \ge 2.05) = P(z \ge 1.581139) = 0.0569$

5. $z = -1.64485$, $\bar{x} = 1.9632$

6. Use the z distribution because σ is given. $\$42{,}157.64 < \bar{x} < \$45{,}842.36$.

7. The t distribution must be used because s must be determined from the sample. $t = -2.3196$. The probability of a smaller t is 0.0123.

8. The two t values are -2.0096 and 2.0096. Converted to $\bar{x}$ values, these become 3.0359 and 3.1641.

Chapter 7

1. (6.893, 8.149)

2. $n = 52$

3. Sample size is inversely proportional to the square of sampling error. As sampling error increases, required sample size decreases exponentially (that is, at a decreasing rate). Another way of looking at this is that as sampling error *decreases*, sample size must be increased at an *increasing* rate. It becomes very difficult to continue reducing the sampling error.

6. $48.97194 < \mu < 51.15766$, $n = 48$

7. $13.07286 < \mu < 16.92714$ (or $13 < \mu < 17$), $n = 38$

8. 99%-0.703417, 95%-0.51461, 90%-0.42514. $n = 33$

9. $1.847568 < \mu < 2.752432$, $n = 154$

10. $991.2779 < \mu < 999.3888$, $n = 54$

Chapter 8

1. $P(x = 0) = 0.7318$, $P(x = 1) = 0.2286$, $P(x = 2) = 0.0357$, $P(x \ge 3) = 0.0040$

2. $\bar{x} = 15.5927255$ results in $p = .0100000$. $z = -2.575830106$. p value less than .01 would result from problems asking for sample means less than 15.5927255 or greater than 16.4072745.

3. The z value is ± 2.57583. The other critical value is 16.40728.

5. For Population 2, the probability of Type II error is .00539. For Population 3, the probability of Type II error is .745553.

Chapter 9

1. $H_0: \mu = 1, H_A: \mu \neq 1$. Reject the Null. The p value is .000407. Yes, there is evidence the machine is not working properly.

2. $H_0: \mu \geq 50, H_A: \mu < 50$. Reject the Null. The p value is .001116. Yes, there is evidence that average stopping distance is less than 50 feet.

3. $H_0: \mu \geq 120, H_A: \mu < 120$. Fail to Reject the Null. $\bar{x} = 122.1778$, which is consistent with the Null Hypothesis. No, there is not evidence that the average amount of time spent by all customers in line is less than 120 seconds.

4. $H_0: \mu \geq 68, H_A: \mu < 68$. Reject the Null. The p value is .02657. Yes, there is evidence that the average height of all students is less than 68 inches.

5. $H_0: \mu = 6.10, H_A: \mu \neq 6.10$. Fail to Reject the Null. The p value is .110354. No, there is not evidence that the average pH of all bottles differs from 6.10.

6. $H_0: \mu \leq 68, H_A: \mu > 68$. Fail to Reject the Null. $\bar{x} = 62.9$, which is consistent with the Null Hypothesis. No, there is no evidence that the average height of all students is more than 68 inches.

7. $H_0: \mu = 68, H_A: \mu \neq 68$. Fail to Reject the Null. The p value is .053139. No, there is no evidence that the average height of all students differs from 68 inches.

8. $H_0: \mu \geq 20, H_A: \mu < 20$. The sample mean is 18.7143, which is not consistent with the Null Hypothesis. Other sample statistics: $n = 35, s = 3.8380, s_{\bar{x}} = 0.6487$. The sample t is -1.9819. The (one tail) p value is 0.0278. Reject the Null Hypothesis because the p value is less than the significance level. Yes, there is evidence at the .05 level of significance that the average strength of all rope is below specification.

9. Type I error would occur if the firm rejected the Null Hypothesis that nothing was wrong, concluded that something was, in fact wrong. The consequence is that the firm would needlessly bear the costs of determining what the problem was when, in fact, there was no problem. This might include ceasing production for a while, investigating the equipment, etc. Type II error would occur if the firm Failed to Reject the Null Hypotheses, thus concluding that nothing was wrong, when, in fact, the rope was weaker, on average, than specification. Since the Null Hypothesis was rejected, only Type I error could have been made.

10 $H_0: \mu = 32, H_A: \mu \neq 32$. The sample data are: $\bar{x} = 30.9914, s = 3.8465, n = 35, s_{\bar{x}} = 0.6502$. The sample t is -1.5512. The (two-tail) p value is .1301. Fail to Reject the Null Hypothesis because the p value exceeds the significance level. No, there is no evidence

at the .05 level of significance that the average fill of all bottles differs from 32 ounces.

11. $H_0 : \mu = 6.7$, $H_A : \mu \neq 6.7$. The relevant sample data are: $\bar{x} = 6.6663$, $s = 0.1124$, $n = 40$. The standard error, $s_{\bar{x}} = 0.0178$. The sample $t = -1.8994$. The (two-tail) p value is .0649. Fail to Reject the Null Hypothesis because the p value is greater than the significance level. No, there is not evidence at the .05 level of significance that the average pH of all wine newly produced from grapes from the new vineyard differs from 6.7.

12. $H_0 : \mu \geq 35$, $H_A : \mu < 35$, The sample mean, $\bar{x}$, is 35.3340, which is greater than 35. Fail to Reject the Null Hypothesis because the sample is consistent with the Null Hypothesis. No, there is no evidence that the average breaking strength of all the newly produced carabiners is less than 35 kn.

13. $H_0 : \mu \geq 15$, $H_A : \mu < 15$. The sample mean is 17.2, which is consistent with the Null Hypothesis. No p value is calculated because the sample is consistent with the Null Hypothesis. Fail to Reject the Null because the sample is consistent with the Null. No, there is no evidence that the average time required for all students would be less than 15 minutes.

14. Type I error: the firm thinks something is wrong with the production batch (the test results in a rejection of the Null Hypothesis), but nothing is wrong (the Null is correct). The consequences include possible loss of production and the cost of looking for a problem when none existed. Type II error: the firm thinks nothing is wrong with the production batch (the test results in a failure to reject the Null Hypothesis) when something is wrong (the Null Hypothesis is wrong). The consequences involve those arising from selling defective saline solution; these could involve loss of reputation, possible harm to patients, and possible liability arising from that harm. The firm can determine the relative levels of Type I and II errors by the selection of the significance level. A higher significance level reduces Type II error and increases Type I error. By increasing the sample size and lowering the significance level the firm can reduce both errors.

Chapter 10

1. 9604

2. $0.286333 < \quad < 0.430334$

3. $0.422863 < \pi < 0.478182$; 4,227

4. Weekday: $0.730958 < \quad < 0.815708$; Weekend: $0.780399 < \quad < 0.861219$. Although the sample proportion of shoppers who accepted free samples was higher on the weekend, there is consider-

able overlap in the confidence intervals. This does not provide good evidence of a difference between the proportion of the two groups of shoppers who accept free samples.

5. $0.107093 <$ < 0.228907; 371

6. $0.783282 <$ < 0.883385

7. $H_0: \pi \leq 0.20, H_A: \pi > 0.20$. $p_s = {}^{33}\!/_{200} = 0.165$. The sample is consistent with the Null Hypothesis; therefore the Null is not rejected. No, there is not evidence that the ad campaign was successful.

8. If $\pi = 0.4$, $n = 4,098$. If $\pi = 0.5$, $n = 4,269$. If $\pi = 0.6$, $n = 4,098$. If $\pi = 0.7$, $n = 3,586$. By using $\pi = .5$, the largest sample size is chosen. This assures that the sample will be large enough to achieve the desired sampling error regardless of the true value of π.

9. $H_0: \pi \geq .50, H_A: \pi < .50$. Approximate $p = .07865$. Precise $p = .089482$. No, there is not evidence that the claim is invalid.

10. $(.088287, .245047)$

11. $H_0: \pi \leq .005, H_A: \pi > .005$. Approximate $p = .170786$. Precise $p = .242155$. No, the firm should not stop the line and inspect its equipment.

12. $H_0: \pi = .29, H_A: \pi \neq .29$. Approximate $p = 0.029801$. Precise $p = .033265$. Yes, there is evidence that the proportion has changed from the value found 20 years ago.

13. $H_0: \pi \leq .20, H_A: \pi > .20$. Approximate $p = .055806$. Precise $p = .069031$. No, there is not evidence that the ad campaign was successful.

14. $H_0: \pi = .40, H_A: \pi \neq .40$. $n = 185$, $x = 61$, $p_s = .03297$. The value of x is smaller than would be expected if the Null Hypothesis were true. The exact two-tail p value is $.0586$. The approximate two-tail p value is $.05106$. Fail to Reject the Null Hypothesis because the p value exceeds the significance level. No, there is not evidence at the $.05$ level of significance that the proportion of all new-car customers willing to spend $500 for side impact air bags differs from $.40$.

15. $H_0: \pi \leq .01, H_A: \pi > .01$, $n = 300$, $x = 6$, $p_s = .02$. Sample is not consistent with the Null Hypothesis. The exact p value is $.08290$. Fail to Reject the Null Hypothesis because the p value is greater than the significance level. No, there is not evidence at the $.05$ level of significance that more than 1% of all the manufacturer's bulbs are defective. If the approximate p value were determined using the z distribution, it would be $.04086$ and the opposite conclusion would be reached.

Chapter 11

1. $2.067297 < \sigma < 3.683171$

2. $7.72548 < \sigma^2 < 33.22543$

3. 99%: $0.771618 < \sigma < 1.832073$, 95%: $0.836204 < \sigma < 1.605985$, 90%: $0.872968 < \sigma < 1.506848$

4. $0.189247 < \sigma^2 < 1.333141$

5. $55.2089731 < \sigma^2 < 134.684607$

6. $H_0 : \sigma \leq 1.1, H_A : \sigma > 1.1$. p value $= 1.64 \times 10^{-7}$. Reject the Null Hypothesis. Yes, there is evidence that the machine is not meeting specification with respect to variation.

7. $H_0 : \sigma^2 \leq 25, H_A : \sigma^2 > 25$. $s^2 = 17.5263$, consistent with the Null Hypothesis. Fail to Reject the Null Hypothesis. No, there is not evidence that the machine is about to break down.

8. $H_0 : \sigma \geq 12, H_A : \sigma < 12$. Since $s = 15.26228$, the sample is consistent with the Null Hypothesis. Fail to Reject the Null Hypothesis. No, the evidence does not support the new supplier's claim.

9. $H_0 : \sigma \leq 5, H_A : \sigma > 5$. The sample is *not* consistent with the Null; a p value must be determined. $\chi^2 = 82.1492$. The p value is .0021. Reject the Null Hypothesis because the p value is less than the significance level. Yes, there is evidence at the .01 level of significance that the standard deviation of the breaking strengths of all carabiners in the production batch exceeds 5 kn.

10. $H_0 : \sigma \leq .05, H_A : \sigma > .05$. The sample s = 0.072697, which is *not* consistent with the Null; a p value must be determined. $\chi^2 = 109.9237$. The p value is 4.94×10^{-6} or .00000494. Reject the Null Hypothesis because the p value is less than the significance level. Yes, there is evidence at the .10 level of significance that the standard deviation of the fill of all bottles exceeds .05.

11. $H_0 : \sigma^2 \leq 14, H_A : \sigma^2 > 14$. The sample variance is 13.3444, which is consistent with the Null Hypothesis. Fail to Reject the Null because the sample is consistent with the Null. No, there is no evidence the variance of the breaking strength of all rope exceeds 14.

Chapter 12

1. Using independent samples, we would not have found evidence of a difference even though the difference in the sample means was the same as in the paired sample approach. The independent sample approach would

require a greater difference in the sample means before we could conclude that there was a difference in the population means. Remember that failing to conclude that there is a difference does not mean that we conclude that there is not a difference. We are left unsure. The paired sample approach is more sensitive because it can lead us to a clear conclusion with a smaller difference in sample means.

2. $H_0: \mu_A = \mu_B$, $H_A: \mu_A \neq \mu_B$. Independent samples. For these data, the procedures assuming equal and unequal population variances yield the same two-tail p value, .3283. Fail to Reject the Null Hypothesis. No, there is not evidence of a difference in average productivity.

3. $H_0: \mu_{Std} \geq \mu_{Int}$, $H_A: \mu_{Std} < \mu_{Int}$. Paired samples approach. $\bar{x}_{Std} = 6.836$ $\bar{x}_{Int} = 6.76$. The sample data are consistent with the Null Hypothesis. No, there is not evidence that intensive maintenance increases mileage.

4. $H_0: \mu_{Prgm} \leq \mu_{Ctrl}$, $H_A: \mu_{Prgm} > \mu_{Ctrl}$ Independent samples approach. $\bar{x}_{Prgm} = 576.69$ $\bar{x}_{Ctrl} = 670.20$ The sample data are consistent with the Null Hypothesis. No, there is not evidence that program attendance would increase average sales.

Chapter 13

1. Using one-factor analysis, the p value is .8276. This would lead to a Failure to Reject the Null Hypothesis, and there was not evidence of a difference of keyboards on typing speeds. The two-factor approach is preferable because it is more sensitive and showed a difference where the one-factor approach could not.

2. The p values for each strategy are Sophisticated, .3729; Athletic, .0285; Popular, .8610. Package design is only clearly important with the Athletic strategy.

3. Use two-factor ANOVA without replication because it controls for other factors affecting house value. The p value for the Null Hypothesis that the population average of all appraisers is the same is .0226. Reject the Null. There is evidence of a difference in the average appraisals of different appraisers.

4. One-factor analysis. The p value for the Null Hypothesis that all stores have the same average is .9444. Fail to Reject the Null Hypothesis. There is no evidence of a difference in the population average sales for the different types of music.

Chapter 14

2. If $x = 3.8$, $\hat{y} = 12.4286067$. If $x = 5.7$, $\hat{y} = 18.011921$. If $x = 6.3$, $\hat{y} = 19.775073$.

3. Regression with all states: $\hat{y} = -313.47 + 0.0940x$. By this equation, state revenue increases about 9.4¢ for each dollar increase in median household income. One outlier, Alaska, probably because of the effect of oil revenue. Regression with Alaska omitted: $\hat{y} = 0.1624 + 0.0409x$. This regression suggests an effect half as great: each dollar increase in median income increases state revenue about 4.1¢. Both regressions are significant.

4. Regression equation: $\hat{y} = 617.43 - 0.001793x$. Only 0.1009% of the variation in state violent crime rates is explained by variation in median household income. The relationship is not significant ($p = .82$).

5. Regression equation: $\hat{y} = 13.25 - 0.0001556x$. Higher state household incomes appear to lead to lower death rates. About 38% of the variation in death rates can be explained by variations in household income. The relationship is highly significant.

Chapter 15

1. The Null Hypothesis in this case would be $\mu_A \leq \mu_B$, and the Alternate Hypothesis would be $\mu_A > \mu_B$. With Armsley Hills as the omitted dummy variable, the p value for the Blawndale dummy is .060213144. This is, however, a *two-tail* p value. Since the test requires a *one-tail* test, the appropriate p value is half the reported value, or .0301. Since this is less than the significance level, the Null Hypothesis would be rejected. Yes, there is evidence that homes in Armsley Hills are assessed at a higher rate than homes in Blawndale.

2. With per capita GNP squared added as an independent variable, the regression equation is $\hat{y} = 89.6060 + 0.5024 \times x_{GNP} - 0.000009952 \times x_{GNP}^2$. An examination of residuals plotted against GNP still shows that for low values of per capita GNP the vertical spread is small, while for larger values (between 20,000 and 30,000) the vertical spread is large. There is thus still evidence of heteroscedasticity.

3. Since the objective here is *prediction*, the value of the adjusted R^2 is key. Since adjusted R^2 is sensitive to the number of independent variables, it is important to eliminate independent variables that do not add sufficient explanatory power. Two dummy variables are required to account for all fuel types, but the real importance lies in whether or not electricity is used as a fuel, and this can be done in a single dummy equal to "1" if electricity is used for heat and "0" otherwise (or vice versa, of course). The resulting equation is:

$$\hat{y} = 136.23 - 42.69d_{\text{Enrgy Eff}} + 62.12d_{\text{Elec Heat}} + 0.083x_{\text{House Size}}$$
$$+ 0.0023x_{\text{Fam Income}}$$

Dummy variables are represented by d, and continuous independent variables by x. The adjusted R^2 for this is 0.5954.

4. The relationship between output and average cost is clearly nonlinear and should be handled by adding an output squared term. There is multicollinearity between the amount of silicon and the thickness of the wafer. Omitting either of these causes the coefficient on the other to become significant. Foundaries which use less silicon, or thinner wafers, have significantly lower costs. The "integrated" dummy has low significance. It's inclusion is optional. It certainly would not be wrong to drop it from the model. Several models can conclusively demonstrate that foundries in the United States have a significant cost advantage over Pacific Rim foundries. They also appear to have an advantage over South American foundries, although the significance is not as high. The following regression equation has an R^2 of almost 0.99:

$$\hat{y} = 480.48 - 9.72x_{Output} + 0.0987x_{Output}^2 + 57.62d_{PAC} + 54.30d_{SA}$$

$$+ 9.25x_{Thickness} + 3.75d_{Integ} - 5.64x_{Silicon}$$

Storing a Large File on a Diskette

In some of the chapters, including 6 and 8, the Excel workbook you create will be too large to fit on a diskette. If you are using a machine in a computer lab, you may not be able to leave files on the machine's hard disk or on a network after you finish your session with the computer. This appendix explains a method that will enable you to shrink the Excel workbook so that it can fit on a diskette and later reexpand the workbook so that you can write it temporarily to a hard disk or network disk in a later computer session.

File Compression

File compression is often used to speed the downloading of files by modem. Because of its importance, a number of programs are available to compress files. Typically these programs will not only compress files; they also have the capability of storing any number of compressed files in a single file (usually called an *archive*). This is done to allow the downloading of a group of related files in a single step. The data diskette for this book is an example of an archive file although it is *self-extracting*, which means it does not require a separate program to restore the stored and compressed files. We don't need the archiving capability, but it is a part of the compression programs we will be using.

The method we will use will involve converting a file containing a large workbook to a *Zip* file. A Zip file can contain one or more compressed files. There are a number of programs available that are capable of creating Zip files and of restoring the files in a Zip file to their original form. Included on the data diskette are two programs, zip.exe and unzip.exe, which can perform these operations. These programs are DOS programs, rather than Windows programs, but they can be freely distributed. More information about these programs can be found in the file readzip.txt, located on the data diskette. This appendix contains instructions for using these programs to compress and restore large datasets.

The most popular program for manipulating Zip files in Windows 95 is WinZip. WinZip cannot be freely distributed and is not included on the data diskette. You can, however, download an evaluation copy from http://www.winzip.com, and it may already be installed on your network or machine. Although it is not included, it is widely available and instructions for its use are also included.

Compressing a Workbook—First Things First

Before you can compress a workbook, two things are necessary. First, you need to know what folder the workbook file is located in. If you did not specify a folder when you first saved the workbook (using "Save As..." on the File menu), it probably is located in the folder My Documents on the C:\ drive. In order to locate the file, do the following:

- Click the Start button, then click "Find." Select "Files or Folders." The Find: All Files dialog window will open.

- In the "Named" field enter the file name you are looking for (such as "Chap6.xls"). If you know which disk the file is on, enter it in the "Look in:" field. If you are not sure, start with C:. Click Find Now.

All files with that name on the searched drive will be listed with the location given under the heading "In Folder." It is likely the column will not be wide enough to fully show the folder name. If so, place the mouse pointer in the header row between "In Folder" and "Size," click the (left) button and move the pointer to the right, exactly as if you were increasing the width of an Excel column. Write down the folder containing the file.

Second, the file containing the workbook must not be open—in other words, you have to get it out of Excel. Do this either by clicking "Close" on the File menu or by closing Excel completely.

Using Zip.exe to Compress a File

The instructions below will describe how to create a compressed version on a blank diskette of Chap6.xls in the My Documents folder using the zip.exe program included on the data diskette.

- Click the Start button and select "Programs" on the menu that opens. Click the "MSDOS Prompt" icon: . A DOS window will open.

- Place the data diskette (which contains the file zip.exe) in the A drive.

- Enter the following commands in the DOS window. The symbol ↵ shows where you should press the Enter key. Please note that where quotation marks are shown in the commands, they should be entered as they are shown.

```
c:\ ↵
cd "\My Documents" ↵
copy a:\zip.exe ↵
```

- After the diskette drive light goes out, remove the data diskette and insert a new diskette, preferably a blank, formatted diskette and enter

```
zip a:\chap6 chap6.xls ↵
del zip.exe ↵
dir a: ↵
```

The "a:\chap6" on the first command above gives the name of the *compressed* file that will be created on your diskette. The extention ".zip" will be automatically added. The "dir" command will cause the DOS window to show a list of files on the diskette. Be sure that "chap6.zip" is on that list.

- Enter the command:

```
exit ↵
```

The DOS window will close.

Using WinZip to Compress a File

- Place a diskette (preferably blank and formatted) in drive A.

- Click the WinZip icon: 📚 if it is on the desktop. If not, click Start then "Programs." Look for a WinZip folder and click it. The WinZip icon will be in that folder.

- If you are using the evaluation version of WinZip, a window will open explaining the conditions of use for that version. To proceed you must click the I Agree button. If you are using a registered version, this window will not appear

- WinZip has two interfaces "Wizard" and "Classic." You want the "Classic" interface. If the window before you has the title "Welcome to the WinZip Wizard," click the "Winzip Classic" button in the lower-left corner of the window.

- Click the New button. A window titled "New Archive" will open allowing you to specify the location of the compressed file. Click the downward-pointing arrow to the right of the "Create In:" field and select "3½ Floppy (A:)." In the "File name:" field you are to provide the name of the *compressed* file to be created on your diskette. Give it the same name as the workbook to be compressed, without the ".xls." If you are compressing chap6.xls, simply enter "chap6." Click OK. The Add dialog window will open.

- Use the Add dialog window to navigate to the folder containing the file to be compressed (chap6.xls) or enter the full name preceeded by the location in the "File name:" field (e.g., c:\My Documents\chap6.xls). Click the Add button. The main WinZip window will show that the workbook has been added to the archive on the diskette and will show both its original and compressed sizes.

Restoring a Workbook

In the following discussion, it is assumed that you have the compressed version of the workbook (chap6.zip) on a diskette and that you want to restore it to a machine's hard disk in the My Documents folder on drive C.

- To restore a workbook using the DOS unzip.exe program on the data diskette, place the data diskette in drive A and open a DOS window by clicking the "MSDOS Prompt" icon.

- Enter the following DOS commands in the window (be sure to enter the quotation marks as shown):

```
c:\ ↵
cd "\my documents" ↵
copy a:\unzip.exe ↵
```

Remove the data diskette and replace it with the diskette containing the compressed workbook. Enter the command unzip a:\chap6 ↵. A copy of the original file, chap6.xls, will be written. Close the DOS window.

- To restore a workbook using WinZip, insert the diskette containing the compressed workbook in drive A: and start WinZip with the "Classic" interface.

- Click the Open button. The Open Archive dialog window will open. Select "3½ Floppy (A:)" for the "Look In:" field. The file name chap6.ZIP should appear in the window with a WinZip icon. Click that name and "chap6.ZIP" will appear in the "File name:" field.

Click the Open button. The main WinZip window will appear and the original workbook name (chap6.xls) should appear with an Excel icon.

- Click the Extract button. The Extract dialog window will open. Use the "Folders/Drives" field to navigate to the location you want the restored file placed or simply enter it in the "Extract to:" field (c:\my documents). After the file has been extracted, close WinZip.

General Index

A

absolute cell addresses 36

active cell 11

active mode boundary 80

analysis of variance (ANOVA)
  regression 369
  single-factor 321-326,
    328-336
  two-factor with replace-
    ment 339-342
  two-factor without replica-
    tion 336-339

Analysis Tools
  Anova: single-factor
    335-336
  Anova: two-factor with
    replication 339-342
  Anova: two-factor without
    replication 336-339
  correlation 426
  covariance 426
  descriptive statistics 66-70,
    427
  exponential smoothing
    427
  F test: two-sample for vari-
    ances 317-318, 427
  Fourier analysis 427
  histogram 70-72, 78,
    80-81
  installing 410
  moving average 427-428
  random number genera-
    tion 91-93, 100,
    109-110, 118, 190, 227,
    332-334, 428
  rank and percentile 428
  regression 366-368,
    382-383, 387, 391, 401,
    428
  sampling 428
  t test: paired two sample
    for means 312-313
  t test: two-sample assum-
    ing equal variances
    315-316

t test: two-sample assuming unequal variance
  316-317

z test: two-sample for
  means 429

autocorrelation 397-398,
  400-401

automatic vs. manual calculation 100

AVEDEV
  See Excel functions

AVERAGE
  See Excel functions

AVERAGEA
  See Excel functions

B

Babe Ruth 117-119

BETADIST
  See Excel functions

BETAINV
  See Excel functions

BINOMDIST
  See Excel functions

binomial distribution
  107-134, 274
  normal approximation
    161-167, 274, 285
  use in tests on π 283-285

binomial word problems
  120-121, 126-128, 131

bins 71, 175

blocking, in ANOVA 337-338

C

categorical data 321-344,
  385-393

causality 345

Central Limit Theorem 171,
  182

chart, add regression line 365

chart, add regression line
  364-365

chart, editing 80, 352,
  364-365

chart axis, changing 295,
  347-348

chart color, changing 48-49

chart size, changing 73, 368

chart title font, changing 50

chart type, changing 46-48

Chart Wizard 42, 45, 347,
  352, 364, 401

chi-square distribution
  292-295, 297

chi-square statistic 292, 298,
  300

CHIDIST
  See Excel functions

CHIINV
  See Excel functions

CHITEST
  See Excel functions

Close button 5

column heading 12, 375

column width 16-17
  adjusting 367, 383, 391

CONFIDENCE
  See Excel functions

confidence interval
  diff. between two means
    312-313
  mean 206-223
  proportion 273-277
  variance 296-298

continuous vs. discrete distributions 135

copying cell ranges 32-33,
  65-66

correction for continuity 168

CORREL
  See Excel functions

COUNT
  See Excel functions

COUNTA
  See Excel functions

COUNTBLANK
  See Excel functions

COUNTIF
  See Excel functions

446

COVAR
   See Excel functions
Create New Folder button 87
CRITBINOM
   See Excel functions
critical value 246, 252, 254, 259, 301-302, 305
cross-sectional data 398
cumulative probability 114

D

Data Analysis Tools
   See Analysis Tools
data diskette 409
degrees of freedom 192, 195, 203, 205, 331, 339, 361-362, 375, 402-403
dependent variable 346
DEVSQ
   See Excel functions
dialog window 6
dummy variables 385-393, 404
Dynamic Histogram tool 175, 181

E

Edit menu
   Fill 139, 141
editing a cell 14-15
editing text 18
endogenous variable 346
entering formulas 20-21
entering fractions 118
entering text 15-16
error codes 24
errors
   See residuals
Excel functions
   AVEDEV 412
   AVERAGE 57, 412
   AVERAGEA 413
   BETADIST 413
   BETAINV 413
   BINOMDIST 114-115, 127, 163, 413

CHIDIST 292-294, 300, 303-304, 413
CHIINV 292, 297, 301-302, 413
CHITEST 414
CONFIDENCE 414
CORREL 414
COUNT 414
COUNTA 414
COUNTBLANK 415
COUNTIF 94-96, 415
COVAR 415
CRITBINOM 415
DEVSQ 415
EXPONDIST 415
FDIST 332, 416
FINV 416
FISHER 416
FISHERINV 416
FORECAST 416
FREQUENCY 416
FTEST 417
GAMMADIST 417
GAMMAINV 417
GAMMALN 417
GEOMEAN 418
GROWTH 418
HARMEAN 418
HYPERGEOMDIST 418
IF 391
INTERCEPT 418
KURT 418
LARGE 419
LINEST 419
LOGEST 419
LOGINV 420
LOGNORMDIST 420
MAX 420
MAXA 420
MEDIAN 59, 420
MIN 304, 420
MINA 420
MODE 420
NEGBINOMDIST 420
NORMDIST 139-140, 164-165, 182-184, 420
NORMINV 421
NORMSDIST 253, 282, 421
NORMSINV 211, 255, 276, 421
PEARSON 421
PERCENTILE 421

PERCENTRANK 421
PERMUT 422
POISSON 422
PROB 422
QUARTILE 422
RANK 422
ROUNDUP 212
RSQ 423
SKEW 423
SLOPE 423
SMALL 423
SQRT 64
STANDARDIZE 423
STDEV 423
STDEVA 423
STDEVP 423
STDEVPA 423
STEYX 423
TDIST 193, 198, 424
TINV 193-194, 200, 209, 424
TREND 424
TRIMMEAN 424
TTEST 425
VAR 425
VARA 425
VARP 425
VARPA 425
WEIBULL 425
ZTEST 425
exogenous variable 346
EXPONDIST
   See Excel functions

F

F statistic 318, 331, 339, 342, 376
FDIST
   See Excel functions
fill handle 29
filling cells 30-32
FINV
   See Excel functions
FISHER
   See Excel functions
FISHERINV
   See Excel functions
FORECAST
   See Excel functions
Formula Palette 56

FREQUENCY
See Excel functions
frequency polygon 70, 81, 84
FTEST
See Excel functions
Function Box 56
Functions
See Excel functions

G

GAMMADIST
See Excel functions
GAMMAINV
See Excel functions
GAMMALN
See Excel functions
GEOMEAN
See Excel functions
GROWTH
See Excel functions

H

HARMEAN
See Excel functions
headers and footers 53-54
heteroscedasticity 397-400
histogram 70-71, 175-176
HYPERGEOMDIST
See Excel functions
hypothesis testing 224-247
See also analysis of variance
mean 248-272
proportion 273, 280-282
regression coefficient 377
two means—independent
samples 308-309,
313-318
two means—paired sam-
ples 308-313
two variances 317-318
variance 299-300,
302-303

I

independent variable 346, 397
Insert Rows 262
Insert Worksheet 28

interactions in Anova
340-341
intercept 346, 348-349, 351,
355
INTERCEPT
See Excel functions

K

KURT
See Excel functions

L

landscape orientation 75
LARGE
See Excel functions
linear equation 346
LINEST
See Excel functions
LOGEST
See Excel functions
LOGINV
See Excel functions
LOGNORMDIST
See Excel functions

M

MAX
See Excel functions
MAXA
See Excel functions
mean 59-61, 79, 99
mean of a distribution 88-89,
94, 99
median 59-61, 79
MEDIAN
See Excel functions
Menu Bar 5
MIN
See Excel functions
MINA
See Excel functions
MODE
See Excel functions
model building 373, 377-378,
396, 402-406
mouse pointer 4

moving cell regions 32-33
moving worksheets 28
MSE 361-362
multicollinearity 394-397,
402-405
Multiple Random Samples
tool 173-174, 177, 216,
228, 237, 241

N

Name Box 12, 111, 139, 141,
163, 165, 174
NEGBINOMDIST
See Excel functions
new folder, creating 87
nonlinear regression 378-385
normal density function
136-137, 140-141,
144-146
normal distribution 135-169,
195
as approximation to bino-
mial 161-167
normal distribution, inverse
153-158
normal word problem 150,
153, 158
NORMDIST
See Excel functions
NORMINV
See Excel functions
NORMSDIST
See Excel functions
NORMSINV
See Excel functions
Null vs. Alternate Hypothesis
225-227, 229, 232-233,
321

O

one-tail test 257-261, 281,
284
order of precedence 20-21

P

p value 230-233, 237,
252-253, 282-285,

300-301, 303-305,
331-335, 339, 342, 363,
370, 375-377

partial effect 375, 384, 387,
391-393

Paste Special 324-325, 357

PEARSON
See Excel functions

PERCENTILE
See Excel functions

PERCENTRANK
See Excel functions

PERMUT
See Excel functions

POISSON
See Excel functions

polynomial regression
381-385, 404

portrait orientation 75

predicted value 350-351,
355-356, 370

previewing a printout 52-53,
74

price inflation, adjusting for
400

print part of worksheet 103

printing worksheet 74-76,
368, 375, 379

PROB
See Excel functions

probability density functions
(PDFs) 136

probability distributions 86

Q

quadratic regression
See polynomial regression

QUARTILE
See Excel functions

R

r^2 360-361, 365, 369

R^2 369, 375, 377, 379
adjusted 369, 377

RANK
See Excel functions

reading a workbook 40-41

reading text data 219,
267-268

recalculation, switch Excel to
manual 116

Redo button 18

regression
multiple 345, 373-407
simple 345-372

relative cell addresses 33-36,
63

renaming worksheet 55

residuals 351, 356, 366-369,
379-381, 383, 398-401,
403-404

row heading 12, 375

RSQ
See Excel functions

run chart 81-84

S

sample size for sampling error
210-212, 277-280

sampling 171-172, 177

sampling distribution 170
mean 170-206
proportion 274

sampling error 209, 212,
277-280

scientific notation 23-24

Scroll Bars 26-27

selecting a chart 74

selecting cells 12-13, 71-72

significance level 233-234,
238

skew 73, 79

SKEW
See Excel functions

slope 346, 348-349, 351, 355,
379

SLOPE
See Excel functions

SMALL
See Excel functions

sorting data 76-77

speed button
AutoSum 35, 63

Chart Wizard 42, 45, 347,
352, 364, 401
Comma Style 23
Copy 65
Create New Folder 87
Cut 66
Edit Formula 56
Help 8-9
Increase Decimal 24, 36,
99
Open 40
Paste 66
Paste Function 139
Percent Style 36, 209
Save 46
Sort 60

SP_{xy} 353-355, 362

SQRT
See Excel functions

SSE 351, 353, 356, 358-362,
370

SSR 360, 369-370

SST 355, 359-360, 370

SS_x 353-354, 362

standard deviation 61

standard error 180, 196-197,
202-203, 208, 311, 362,
369

STANDARDIZE
See Excel functions

STDEV
See Excel functions

STDEVA
See Excel functions

STDEVP
See Excel functions

STDEVPA
See Excel functions

stem-and-leaf chart 70

STEYX
See Excel functions

T

t distribution 192-193, 195,
197, 249, 362

t statistic 362-364, 370, 376

TDIST
See Excel functions

text highlighting 18-19
time series data 398, 400-401
TINV
    See Excel functions
Title Bar 5
Toolbars 6-7
treatment, in ANOVA
    337-338
TREND
    See Excel functions
TRIMMEAN
    See Excel functions
TTEST
    See Excel functions
two-tail test 256, 301-302
Type I and Type II error
    233-235, 237-238, 318

U

Undo button 17-18

V

VAR
    See Excel functions
VARA
    See Excel functions
variance 61, 99
variance of a distribution
    88-90, 94, 99
VARP
    See Excel functions
VARPA
    See Excel functions

W

WEIBULL
    See Excel functions
Windows clipboard 65-66
worksheet
    insert 28
    move 28
worksheet tabs 27

X

x variable 346

Y

y intercept 346
    See also intercept
y variable 346

Z

Zoom Control 367, 383
ZTEST
    See Excel functions